Introduction to Comparative Public Administration

For Frauke and Pauline

Introduction to Comparative Public Administration

Administrative Systems and Reforms in Europe

Sabine Kuhlmann

Professor of Political Sciences, Administration and Organization, University of Potsdam, Germany

Hellmut Wollmann

Professor Emeritus of Public Administration, Social Science Institute, Humboldt University of Berlin, Germany

Edward Elgar
Cheltenham, UK • Northampton, MA, USA

Published by
Edward Elgar Publishing Limited
The Lypiatts
15 Lansdown Road
Cheltenham
Glos GL50 2JA
UK

Edward Elgar Publishing, Inc.
William Pratt House
9 Dewey Court
Northampton
Massachusetts 01060
USA

A catalogue record for this book
is available from the British Library

Library of Congress Control Number: 2014932608

Printed on elemental chlorine free (ECF)
recycled paper containing 30% Post-Consumer Waste

ISBN 978 1 78347 358 8 (cased)
ISBN 978 1 78347 359 5 (paperback)
ISBN 978 1 78347 360 1 (eBook)

Typeset by Servis Filmsetting Ltd, Stockport, Cheshire
Printed and bound in the USA

Contents in brief

Full contents

About the authors

Sabine Kuhlmann was born in 1970. She obtained her degree in Social Sciences at the Humboldt University of Berlin in 1995. Until 2007 she was researcher at the Universities of Potsdam, Bochum, Konstanz and Berlin. She finished her PhD in 2002 (HU Berlin), and was awarded a research grant by the Maison des Sciences de l'Homme Paris. Her Post-Doctoral thesis (Habilitation) was presented in 2007 (Potsdam). From 2007 to 2009 she was Visiting Professor of Public Administration at the Humboldt University of Berlin and in 2009 at the University of Konstanz; from 2009 to 2013 she was Full Professor of Comparative Public Administration at the German University of Administrative Sciences in Speyer. Since 2013 she has been Full Professor of Political Sciences, Administration and Organization at the University of Potsdam; since 2009, chair of the Section on Policy Analysis and Administrative Sciences of the German Association for Political Science; since 2011, member of the National Regulatory Control Council of the German Federal Government; from 2012, Vice-President of the European Group for Public Administration (EGPA); editorial board member of *Public Administration Review* (PAR); deputy editor of *International Review of Administrative Sciences* (IRAS); and co-editor of the Public Policy, Law and Management journal, *der moderne staat* (dms).

Her work and research focus on comparative public administration; administration modernization/international public sector reforms; comparative local and regional government; evaluation, better regulation, regulatory impact assessment; multi-level governance and decentralization.

Her recent publications include: 'Evaluating administrative modernization in German local governments: success or failure of the "new steering model"?', *Public Administration Review*, **68**(5) (2008 with Jörg Bogumil and Stephan Grohs); 'Politik- und Verwaltungsreform in Kontinentaleuropa. Subnationaler Institutionenwandel im deutsch-französischen Vergleich' [Politics and public administration reform in Continental Europe. Subnational institutional change in Franco-German comparison] (2009, Nomos); 'New public management for the "classical Continental European administration": modernization at the local level in Germany, France, and Italy', *Public Administration*, **88**(4) (2010); 'Performance measurement in European local governments: a comparative analysis of reform experiences in Great Britain, France, Sweden and Germany', *International Review of Administrative Sciences*, **76**(2) (2010); 'Impacts of decentralization: the French experience in a comparative perspective', *French Politics*, **8**(2) (2010 with Renate Reiter, Stephan Grohs, Falk Ebinger and Jörg Bogumil); an article co-authored in 2011 with Hellmut Wollmann in the *Local Government Studies* Special Issue on Evaluating Functional and Territorial Reforms in European Countries: 'The evaluation of institutional reforms at sub-national government levels', **37**(5); and 'Competing, collaborating or controlling? Benchmarking-regimes in European local governments from a comparative perspective', *Public Money and Management*, **33**(4) (2013 with Tim Jäkel).

Hellmut Wollmann was born in 1936 and obtained his degree in Law and Political Science at the University of Heidelberg and the Free University Berlin as well as being a Fulbright student at the Wesleyan University, Connecticut, USA (1957–58). He obtained a scholarship from the Studienstiftung des Deutschen Volkes (German National Academic Foundation); completed the First and Second State Examinations in Law (1962–67); and became Dr. jur. (Doctor of Law) (1967). From 1968–74 he was a research assistant to Carl Joachim Friedrich at the University of Heidelberg and 1970–71 a Kennedy Memorial Fellow at Harvard University. From 1974–93 he was Professor of Administrative Sciences at the FU Berlin, and at the Humboldt University of Berlin (1993–2001). He was co-founder and associate of the Institute for City Research and Structural Policy Berlin (from 1974 onwards); co-founder (1972) and chairman (1975–85) of the Working Group for Local Policy Research in the German Association for Political Science (Deutsche Vereinigung für Politische Wissenschaft, DVPW); co-founder and President (1998–99) of the European Evaluation Society; Chairman of the Research Committee on the Comparative Study of Local Politics and Government in the International Political Science Association (1975–96); member of the Conseil Scientifique du Groupement de Recherche sur l'Administration Locale en Europe (GRALE), Paris (since 2003). Hellmut Wollmann has held guest professorships at numerous universities (among others in Moscow, Bejing, Tokyo, Paris, Bordeaux, Florence, Gothenburg). He is series editor of *Stadtforschung aktuell* (120 volumes since 1983) and co-editor of *Urban and Regional Research International* (14 volumes since 2002).

Hellmut Wollmann's work and research focus on comparative policy and administration research (emphasis on subnational/local level); and evaluation research.

A selection of his most recent publications includes: *Governing after Communism. Institutions and Policymaking* (Rowman & Littlefield, 2003, with Vesselin Dimitrov and Klaus H. Goetz); *Evaluation in Public-Sector Reform* (Edward Elgar Publishing, 2003, editor); *Comparing Public Sector Reform in Britain and Germany* (Ashgate, 2000, co-editor with Eckhard Schröter); *State and Local Government Reforms in France and Germany* (VERSUS Verlag, 2006, co-editor with Vincent Hoffmann-Martinot); *The Comparative Study of Local Government and Politics: Overview and Synthesis* (Barbara Budrich Publishers, 2006, co-editor with Harald Baldersheim); *Local Governance in Central and Eastern Europe. Comparing Performance in the Czech Republic, Hungary, Poland and Russia* (Palgrave Macmillan, 2008, with Tomila Lankina and Anneke Hudalla); *Local Governance Reform in Global Perspective* (VERSUS Verlag für Sozialwissenschaften, 2009, with Norbert Kersting, Janice Caulfield, R. Andrew Nickson and Dele Olowu); *The Provision of Public Services in Europe* (Edward Elgar Publishing, 2010, co-editor with Gérard Marcou).

Preface

This book is intended as an introduction to comparative public administration, which in recent times has seen an increase in relevance and even urgency that parallels the progression with European integration and the internationalization of public administration. The question thus arises of whether and to what extent national administrative systems have adapted in the meantime, or whether their historic traditions and institutional particularities even continue to exist. In view of international reform discourses and modernization concepts, new country groupings have also been developing, displaying specific common features of their public administration and thereby providing new conceptual and empirical challenges for administrative science.

This introduction to comparative public administration is meant to reach a wide range of readers and users. First, it is expected to serve as a textbook at universities for lecturers and students. Second, the book is intended to address a readership that includes politicians, administrative practitioners and journalists as well as readers generally interested in comparative issues of public administration, administrative reform policy and reform. The book draws on many years of research, partly in joint projects, conducted in comparative government and public administration. The text also builds on an earlier edition that was put to the 'practical test' as part of lectures at the Fern University, Hagen and the German University of Administrative Sciences, Speyer (Deutsche Universität für Verwaltungswissenschaften Speyer). We are grateful for the stimulating comments provided by the students. During the revision of the text as presented here, the numerous suggestions and critical comments we received from our colleagues on the first draft were extremely helpful. To them we would like to express our thanks – without singling out individual names. We also owe many thanks to the research staff in Speyer and Potsdam, particularly to Philipp Richter, Tobias Ritter, Christina Rostek, Tilman Graf, Ina Radtke and Grace Klass for additional research and for the preparation of indexes as well as other technical and formal support. Any remaining weaknesses of the text fall, of course, on the responsibility of the authors.

Sabine Kuhlmann and Hellmut Wollmann
Potsdam/Berlin, March 2014

1

Introduction

 LEARNING OBJECTIVES

At the end of this introductory chapter, you should:

- know the subject matter and the intention of the book;

- have gained an impression of the diversity of comparisons in public administration;

- have obtained an initial overview regarding the development of comparative public administration;

- be able to reflect on the conceptual and methodological difficulties in comparing public administrations;

- understand the layout and structure of the book.

> Comparing is the end of happiness and the beginning of discontent.
> (Kierkegaard)

This book is intended to provide an introduction to the study of public administration from a comparative perspective and to give an overview of administrative systems and reforms in Europe. It pursues three objectives. First, the reader should become familiar with the subject matter and the analysis concepts of comparative administrative science. Second, the book introduces key features of public administration in six countries (Germany, France, Italy, the United Kingdom, Sweden and Hungary), which represent typical administrative profiles in Europe. Third, current administrative reforms are compared, highlighting the extent to which the different administrative systems have converged or continue to persist in their respective national traditions.

Comparative studies in administrative science deal with very different aspects of public administration. Some research areas are aimed at the comparison of bureaucracy, ministerial and civil servant elites. Others focus on organizational structures, formal and informal administration rules, while still others aim at the comparison of administrative decision processes, their results and effects. A comparison of administrations can thus be targeted at the national/centralized or the subnational/local levels of administration and therefore arrive at different conclusions. Of course, the comparison of public administration may – and this generally holds true for most comparisons – be pursued over time (diachronically) or across system borders (synchronously).

From a narrower understanding, comparative public administration (CPA) relates to the latter comparative dimension, that is, comparisons between at least two institutional units (Fitzpatrick et al., 2011, p. 823). Most frequently, however, the scope of CPA is more narrowly defined, namely as comparisons between nations (Pollitt, 2011, p. 115). Administrative comparisons can refer to specific tasks and functional areas of administration (e.g., public-order–related administration, service-delivery–related administration), thus taking a policy-specific perspective, and leading to large areas of overlap with policy research. Methodologically, research may be based on many or few cases of comparison, on aggregated data, or on case studies. This has led to the well-known controversy (typical also for other areas of political science) between 'thick description' and 'large-n studies' (Raadschelders, 2011, p. 831 et seq.). Thus, it can be noted at this early stage that we are dealing with a diverse and dynamic subject matter with regard to CPA. The intention of this book is to outline this subject matter so as to make it accessible to a larger readership.

As part of this, the above-mentioned discontent caused by comparisons in general according to Kierkegaard – and hence also by comparisons in administrative science – may well be understood as productive. 'Comparing is human' (Raadschelders, ibid.), because comparing not only calls into question limits of knowledge and casts doubt on experience, it also helps to understand one's own (national) administrative system by contrasting it with others and to recognize its particularities, advantages and disadvantages, strengths and weaknesses. This can represent a prerequisite for acquiring a broad and realistic understanding of what public administration is all about, and what explanations there are for its way of functioning, its change and its continued existence. As such, the introductory quote 'The end of happiness' can be turned into a positive message in terms of a curiosity that goes beyond national administrative borders and of a critical examination of the public administration in one's own country and during one's own time.

To begin with, we will briefly recap the development of this line of research. After the end of World War II, important milestones were initially set in the US-American context for defining the research agenda and the general conceptual approach of CPA (Riggs, 1954; Heady, 1960). Subsequently, it experienced its first climax as an empirical discipline in the 1960s and 1970s. Indeed, it was conjectured that CPA was on the point of advancing to a 'Master of Science in Public Administration' (Riggs, 1976). However, the presented studies were initially not strictly comparative, but rather compilations of country reports or other individual country analyses, albeit paving the way for the later, more comparative focus of the line of research. In terms of content, the emphasis was largely on the relationship between policy and bureaucracy, the bureaucratic influence on political decision processes and the functional problems of 'modern' bureaucracies.

In order to examine these, the classic bureaucracy theory of Weber (1921) and Wilson (1941) as well as institutional economics (Downs, 1957; Tullock, 1965; Niskanen, 1971) provided a theoretical framework. On the one hand, the US-American administration provided empirical illustration, for example for Robert K. Merton (1957), who accordingly developed his concept of 'rigidity', that is, the inability of bureaucracies to learn and adapt. On the other hand, the Continental European administration provided a particularly good example for Michel Crozier (1964), for instance, to put forward the hypothesis of the 'bureaucratic vicious circle'. According to this, administrations only adapt to new social circumstances in the light of organizational crises. In a German context, the work by Fritz Morstein-Marx in particular should be mentioned as a forerunner of CPA.[1] His comparative studies on the public service (Morstein-Marx, 1959, 1962), budgeting, control and responsibility in public administration (Morstein-Marx, 1962, 1965) are noteworthy, but the contributions he made are of particular importance with regard to the stronger networking of CPA within Europe and the exchange of knowledge on different administrative systems. In this respect, a conference held in Speyer in 1968 provided an impetus on which the idea for the founding of the European Group for Public Administration (EGPA) in 1975 was based (Fisch, 2010).

Further significant milestones in the establishment of CPA were marked by research on civil service elites (Morstein-Marx, 1962; Steinkämper, 1974; Aberbach et al., 1981; Derlien, 1988) and country studies on the structure and functioning of administrations.[2] In addition to single country studies, an increasing number of comparative studies have been presented (e.g., Campbell, 1983) and country analyses have been summarized in anthologies (e.g., Suleiman, 1984). The line of research was given a further boost through the growing scholarly interest in 'the state at work'. With the establishment of implementation and evaluation research, the implementation and effects of national policies became of burgeoning interest to CPA. Following some stagnation in the 1980s, a renewed upswing of CPA took place as a result of the system transitions after 1990. Subsequent to this, comparative studies were published regarding administrative transformation processes and the results of the administrative development and reconstruction (Dwivedi and Henderson, 1990; Goetz, 1995; Goetz and Wollmann, 2001; Wollmann and Lankina, 2003).

Despite this spike experienced by the interest in CPA, in the early 1990s criticism arose that it was 'rather comparable than comparative' (Derlien, 1992). A lack of 'genuine' comparisons and the focus of research on comparable rather than comparative studies came to be criticized. The dearth of over-reaching theory and concept formation was as much a target for critics as the primarily descriptive focus on single country studies, which did not in itself provide an actual comparison of administrations (Peters, 1996; Schnapp, 2006). How can this situation, which continues to be unsatisfactory, be explained? Administrative comparisons go hand in hand with particular difficulties, methodological pitfalls, concept and transfer problems, to say nothing of a frequent shortage of empirical evidence and data. To begin with, the different conceptual roots must be taken into consideration (Ellwein, 1982, 1997). Here, the tension between the predominantly law-related state sciences, constitutional law and policy science on the one hand, and the more social-science–oriented administrative sciences on the other should be mentioned (cf. König, 2008; Bogumil and Jann, 2009, p. 28 et seq.). While the former is characterized primarily by a national focus and a 'distance to empiricism', which is problematic for comparative studies, the latter proves to be generally more open and accessible to a comparative approach due to its empirical orientation. Within the social-science–oriented administrative sciences, however, there is a rivalry in turn between the influence of the Anglo-American discipline of public administration (PA) and the discipline of comparative politics (Peters, 1996). The classic Anglo-American PA is characterized by the normative claim (and illusion) of a politics–administration dichotomy (Wilson, 1941)[3] but also by the change-oriented perspective of research on administrative reforms that primarily works qualitatively (small-n). Comparative politics by contrast, is traditionally focused on a descriptive approach (cf. Lijphart, 1971). It deals more with the comparison between formal-institutional decision-making institutions, often for large case numbers (large-n) rather than with processes and effects. The reform and action orientation typical of public administration (analysis for policy), in which particular emphasis is placed on the identification of successful or less successful administrative solutions and the development of suggestions for improvement (Jreisat, 2011, p. 834), is largely unknown in comparative politics.

As it applies in general to administrative sciences, a comparative orientation is also faced with the methodological and conceptual challenges posed by a transdisciplinary approach. The study of public administration demands recourse to several sub-disciplines of the social sciences (political science, law, economics, history, sociology and psychology) and thus requires the incorporation of different disciplinary approaches and methods. This, in turn, can negatively affect the formation of concept and theory (Ziekow, 2003; König, 2008; Jann, 2009). For comparative studies of administration, another factor is the so-called 'travelling problem', that is, the limited transferability of concepts and terms between different language-related and cultural contexts (see Peters, 1996). In light of this, researchers working in the area of comparative administration are often faced with the dilemma of generalizing from empirical peculiarities and particularities of the cases under investigation for the purposes of comparison, even though these cases appear indispensable according to the logic of individual cases. This is exacerbated by the often unsatisfactory empirical situation and limited availability of information with which to make 'real' administrative comparisons. Despite these difficulties, CPA has made considerable progress in the past few years. Although there was some interim progress in the 1960s, CPA was a rather marginal sector of administrative science that was represented by only a few specialists. Now, however, it has penetrated into the mainstream of administrative science research. This becomes pointedly apparent in the following statements: 'Comparative PA has become quite competitive. . . It has become more prominent and mainstream' (Pollitt, 2010, p. 763); 'Comparative public administration research. . .today, has considerable vitality' (Fitzpatrick et al., 2011, p. 822). These statements not only insinuate the increasing competition within the discipline, which has resulted from the rise in the number of corresponding research locations, specialization opportunities, academic journals, conferences, networks and so on, they also reflect the growing institutionalization of CPA as a sub-discipline within its own international community.[4] Progress has also been made in terms of content and analysis. This includes 'comparable' studies that deal with the more ideographic description and analysis of administrative systems of different countries. In addition, analytically more sophisticated 'comparative' studies with a somewhat nomothetic focus have since been published. These studies have attempted to categorize and generalize on a stronger theoretical and conceptual basis (Riggs, 2010, p. 752 et seq.).

Table 1.1 Types and examples of comparative public administration studies

Type of Comparative Study	Examples
Comprehensive analytical country comparisons of administrative systems/ reforms taking into account the reform process, administrative culture, institutions	Jann (1983); Lynn (2006); Wollmann (2008); Kuhlmann (2009a); Ongaro (2009); Pollitt and Bouckaert (2011); Kuhlmann et al. (2011)
Anthologies/edited books with country chapters on national administrative systems/reforms by different (teams of) authors	Kogan (1989); Gray et al. (1993); Kickert (1997, 2008); Chandler (2000); Wollmann (2003d); Kersting and Vetter (2003); Bäck et al. (2006); Döhler and Jann (2007); Wollmann and Marcou (2010)
Hypothesis-testing studies on the basis of statistical data for several countries	Davis et al. (1999); Schnapp (2004); Bastida and Benito (2007); Vandenabeele and van de Walle (2008)
Studies on the modes of operation of large reform models/ideologies (e.g., NPM) in different countries	Christensen and Laegreid (2001); Dunleavy et al. (2006); Verscheure and Barbieri (2009); Bouckaert et al. (2010)
Studies on the modes of operation of individual, specific reform instruments (e.g., agencies, benchmarking etc.) in different countries	Löffler and Vintar (2004); Pollitt et al. (2004); Wegener (2004); Hood and Lodge (2006); Andrews and De Vries (2007); Bouckaert and Halligan (2008); Bach et al. (2010)
Comparative studies of concepts (e.g., 'trust', 'public value') and language/ cognitive interpretations, and so on, on PA in different countries	Schultz and Harrison (1986); van de Walle et al. (2008); Rhodes and Wanna (2009); Rhodes et al. (2010); Smullen (2010)
Policy-/sector-specific administrative comparisons between countries (e.g., educational, environmental, etc. administration)	Kogan (1989); Woods (1993); Knill (2001); Moran and Pollitt; Arndt (2008); Bouckaert (2009)

Source: Adapted from Pollitt (2011, p. 120) with additions by the authors.

Even if to date a grand theory has not yet been presented or a general rule been put forward, the various studies do generate a number of middle-range generalizations (Pollitt, 2010, p. 762) that contain relevant statements as to the modes of operation of different administrative systems from a comparative perspective. An approximate classification of these comparative studies according to their analytic approaches is presented in Table 1.1).

This book takes up the current state of CPA and provides basic knowledge for an understanding of public administration in Europe. It is guided by the assumption that a national administrative system can only be adequately understood if it is contrasted with – that is, compared to – other administrative models. Furthermore, the authors are of the opinion that merely assuming a national perspective on public administration, albeit certainly an important and indispensable perspective, no longer does justice to today's socio-economic development characterized by internationalization and globalization. In order to capture and explain the dynamics of administration and its variability, one needs to look at the broader picture. This is what the present book is attempting to do.

The book is divided into six main chapters. Chapter 2 provides first an overview of the theories and analysis approaches of CPA. This includes an introduction of different subject areas and research foci ('law families', administrative cultures; local government systems; politicizing of administration, civil service systems; Europeanization of administrative systems) and an outline of the key administrative profiles in Europe. In addition, Chapter 2 is devoted to the presentation of administrative reform policy and the neo-institutionalist explanations of the administrative reforms that are discussed in the subsequent chapters.

In Chapter 3, administrative systems and traditions in six European countries are presented using a uniform scheme that addresses the following aspects: basic features of the government system, fundamental structures of national/central as well as subnational/local administration, and characteristics of public service. The six selected countries represent distinctive variants of public administration traditions across Europe whose spectrum is thus approximately mapped. The chapter concludes with a comparative overview of the basic features of public administration on the basis of relevant statistical data and by embedding these six countries in a broader OECD context.

Chapter 4 of the book deals with administrative reforms from a comparative perspective. After an introduction to the administrative reform policy-related discourses of the previous three decades, four areas of reform are considered more closely:

- the decentralization of state and administration, whereby a distinction is made between political and administrative decentralization, regionalization and (quasi-) federalization as well as administrative deconcentration;
- territorial reforms that have occurred in particular on a subnational administrative level;
- the privatization of public functions that has been embarked upon in many countries, in particular as part of the New Public Management

(NPM) debate, but has recently been, in part, modified by a trend towards 'remunicipalization';

- the modernization of internal structures and procedures of public administration as well as public service/public personnel that have also been strongly shaped by the NPM concept (performance management, performance measurement and comparison, agencification, customer orientation, and civil service reform).

Chapter 5 contains an evaluation of the findings guided by the questions of whether and why a convergence of administrative systems in Europe has occurred (or not). The neo-institutionalist theory approaches introduced in Chapter 2 are drawn on for explanation.

Finally, Chapter 6 provides an outlook and some thoughts and recommendations on future research in comparative public administration.

NOTES

1 Morstein-Marx was the first professor of 'comparative public administration' in Europe in 1962 at the German University of Administrative Sciences, Speyer.

2 Heclo and Wildawsky (1974) (regarding British financial bureaucracy); Mayntz and Scharpf (1975) (regarding federal German ministerial bureaucracy); Suleiman (1974) (regarding French ministerial bureaucracy); summarized by Schnapp (2006).

3 The background to this is the criticism of the so-called 'spoils system' of the US-American administration, that is, the *political* appointment of administrative and management positions and their personnel exchange following a change in government; thus, the empirically observed 'coupling' of executive politics and administrative positions.

4 To exemplify this point, we cite the (re)establishment of professional associations, international networks of scholars and institutions throughout the world focusing on public administration (PA): among others: NISPACee (Network of Institutes and Schools of Public Administration in Central and Eastern Europe, founded in 1994); IPMN (International Public Management Network, founded in 1996); IRSPM (International Research Society for Public Management, founded in 2005); and the AAPA (Asian Association for Public Administration, founded in 2010). The increase in institutionalization and internationalization of the discipline is also evidenced by various administration-related 'forms of dialogue' between regions/continents (e.g., Transatlantic Dialogue – TAD; Trans-European Dialogue – TED) and by multinational Master's programmes in the area of PA.

2

Theories and analytical approaches

 LEARNING OBJECTIVES

At the end of this chapter, you should:

- know which key typologies are used for administrative comparisons;

- be able to differentiate among five European administrative profiles with regard to their basic features;

- have obtained an overview of different types of local self-government and public personnel systems in Europe;

- know the prominent theses regarding the influence of EU integration on national administrative systems;

- understand how administrative reforms can be analysed and theoretically explained from a comparative perspective.

2.1 Comparative public administration

2.1.1 Typologies of comparison in public administration

In order to compare administrative systems beyond national borders, different typologies and analytical concepts have been proposed. As administrative traditions are multi-dimensional (cf. Painter and Peters, 2010), comparisons always require a selection of comparison criteria, the combination of which allows the formation of types. The selection of these criteria relies on the cognitive interest of the observer, so that, depending on the focus of analysis, different comparison-related typologies can be made meaningful. The classification used in this textbook incorporates institutional, administrative and legal culture-related features of comparison. Accordingly, five families or groups of countries are distinguished, each of which is characterized by typical feature combinations of their respective administrative systems and traditions (for details see Chapter 3, Sections 3.1 to 3.5). This approximate grouping should not, however, conceal the range of differences within the groups of countries:

- the Continental European Napoleonic country group (with a Southern European subgroup);
- the Continental European federal country group;
- the Scandinavian country group;
- the Anglo-Saxon country group;
- the Central Eastern and South Eastern European country group.

This typology is based on two comparison-related dimensions: (1) on a key aspect of administrative tradition and culture that links the countries of a particular 'family'; (2) on political-institutional features of the state structure and administrative organization.

With regard to administrative traditions and cultures in Western Europe, two clusters must first be distinguished: the classic Continental European rule-of-law (*Rechtsstaat*) culture on the one hand and the Anglo-Saxon public interest culture on the other (cf. Heady, 1996; Raadschelders and Rutgers, 1996; Wollmann, 2000b; König, 2002, 2006; Pollitt and Bouckaert, 2004; Kuhlmann, 2009a). This dichotomy results from a broad understanding of administrative culture that attempts to capture the 'system rationality of public administration' by means of demarcation and differentiation (Jann, 1983, p. 20; König, 2007, p. 5), and must thus remain relatively approximate.[1] The affiliation with one of these administrative culture groups is significantly shaped by the legal tradition and allocation of the respective country to a particular family of legal systems. Four such families are differentiated for Western Europe (cf. La Porta et al., 1999; Schnapp, 2004, p. 44 et seq.; König, 2008):

- Common Law;
- Roman-French;
- Roman-German;
- Roman-Scandinavian.

A central assumption is that the handed-down legal tradition of a country has a significant influence on the dominant values in administrative action and the way in which administration is implemented, as well as the relationship between politics, citizens and administration. Using specific country examples, the following will elucidate this in more detail. A summary of the

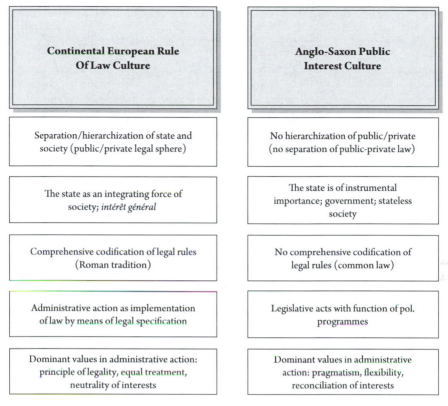

Continental European Rule Of Law Culture	Anglo-Saxon Public Interest Culture
Separation/hierarchization of state and society (public/private legal sphere)	No hierarchization of public/private (no separation of public-private law)
The state as an integrating force of society; *intérêt général*	The state is of instrumental importance; government; stateless society
Comprehensive codification of legal rules (Roman tradition)	No comprehensive codification of legal rules (common law)
Administrative action as implementation of law by means of legal specification	Legislative acts with function of pol. programmes
Dominant values in administrative action: principle of legality, equal treatment, neutrality of interests	Dominant values in administrative action: pragmatism, flexibility, reconciliation of interests

Source: Authors' own diagram.

Figure 2.1 Traditional Continental European rule-of-law (*Rechtsstaat*) culture versus Anglo-Saxon public interest culture

most important distinguishing features of traditional Continental European rule-of-law culture and Anglo-Saxon public interest culture results is shown in Figure 2.1.

Concerning the second comparison-related dimension, the structure of state and administration, the degree of centralization or decentralization of public administration and the relationship between central/centralized and subnational-decentralized/local government are crucial.

Three variants can be roughly distinguished:

- federal (separation versus integrationist model);
- unitary-centralized;
- unitary-decentralized.

In the literature, a range of further classifications for the comparison of partial aspects of public administration or whole administrative systems has been proposed. Painter and Peters (2010) distinguish among four Western administrative traditions: Anglo-American, Napoleonic, Germanic and Scandinavian (cf. Painter and Peters, 2010, p. 20). Their typologies are based on the features of (1) legal tradition, (2) relationship between state and society, (3) governmental or administrative organization and (4) public service. In contrast, Kickert (2011) assigns the Continental European countries to four administrative traditions: Napoleonic, Germanic, small European states and Southern European states. Here his cognitive interest lies in particular in explaining public management reforms in Continental Europe, thus resulting in the specific country groupings (particularly small and Southern European states). In comparative administrative reform research, the standard classification of countries as either majority or consensual democracies (Lijphart, 1984, 1999) is granted special explanatory power with regard to public management reforms (Kickert, 2011, p. 104 et seq.; Pollitt and Bouckaert, 2011, p. 48 et seq.). This has proven to be an important starting condition of New Public Management (NPM) reforms in the different countries and holds significant explanatory power as to why the reform trajectories have been fragmented or comprehensive, conflict-ridden or consensual and whether their effects have been lasting (sustainable) or unstable (see also Chapter 4, Sections 4.4 and 4.5).

In cases where the cognitive interest lies in selected partial aspects of public administration, still other country classifications come into play. Thus, for the comparison of the public service systems in Europe, the distinction between five country groups has been proposed: Anglo-Saxon, Continental European, Mediterranean/South European, Scandinavian, Eastern European (Demmke et al., 2007, p. 12; Demmke and Moilanen, 2013). These are each characterized by peculiarities in the legal structure, the mechanisms for recruitment and promotion, and for access into the public service (see also Section 2.1.4 below). However, the authors focus in particular on the national/centralized level to the extent that the vertical administrative structure and the structure of the subnational level(s) are of less interest to them.

A further frequently used classification in administrative comparisons is based on the relationship between state/administration on the one hand and society/citizens on the other. This comparative perspective can be found in administrative culture research (cf. Jann, 1983, 2002) and in the new debate surrounding 'regulation cultures' (Wegrich, 2009, p. 59 et seq.). Here, administrative traditions and systems are less in the focus than the real administrative action as a problem-solving and interaction process with the citizen at its centre (Jann, 1983, 2002). Again, ideally, a distinction can be made between a cooperative contact culture, a flexible bargaining culture and a formalized regulatory culture (Jann, 2002, p. 442 et seq.). Thus, the Scandinavian group of countries, mirroring its consensus-oriented democratic tradition, displays distinctive cooperative features in its administrative practice. In contrast, flexibility, limited formalization and ad hoc solutions have been shown to be characteristic of the Anglo-Saxon type of flexible bargaining culture (ibid.). Finally, typical for the Continental European formalized regulatory culture are the high degree of juridification of administrative action and the formalized direction of administrative activities through regulation and programmes. As, however, significant reform-driven changes have occurred in the European administrative systems (see Chapter 4), and as the levels and sectors of administration have to be distinguished, a 'flawless' classification according to these three types of administrative culture is only partly possible.

A final classification to be mentioned here refers to the differences between the countries with regard to the scope and content of state activity. This differentiation is important for a comparison of administrative systems because the tradition and structure of a welfare state, in which the national administrative system is embedded, has a significant impact on the administrative activity in a particular country. From this perspective, country (group) differences in the dimensioning of the public sector, the key areas of administrative activity, in addition to the affinity or aversion towards specific administrative reform concepts (e.g., privatization, elements of competition etc.) can be explained. Following the reasoning of Esping-Andersen (1990), three ideal types of welfare state can be distinguished:

- the conservative type;
- the social democratic type;
- the liberal type.

These 'Three Worlds of Welfare Capitalism' (ibid.) are characterized by distinct differences in the organization of state activity, which can be seen particularly in funding, performance standards and persons entitled to benefits, and redistribution effects (cf. Ullrich, 2005, p. 23 et seq.). The decisive factor for typological classification is found in the extent of the decoupling of social security from the job market and the relaxing of the obligation for securing one's livelihood through gainful employment (so-called 'decommodification'). Universal state benefits (without means-testing), social security benefits, and the redistribution of wealth are less important in liberal welfare state types (e.g., USA, United Kingdom, Switzerland) than in other types of states.

By contrast, in the social democratic type (e.g., Sweden, Denmark, Norway, Finland, Netherlands), universality is considered the highest organizational principle and therefore there is a high effect of redistribution. The conservative welfare state type (e.g., Germany, Austria, France, Italy, Belgium) is characterized by a guarantee of social security while simultaneously maintaining status differences and a lower effect of redistribution. In line with Leibfried, there may be added the rudimentary welfare state type that is strongly based on non-governmental family support and is characteristic for less industrialized countries with a low average income (Spain, Portugal, Greece; cf. Leibfried, 1992; Ricciardi, 2010). Finally, as a more recent category – albeit rather heterogeneous – the type of the post-socialist welfare state has been discussed where different elements (liberal, conservative, social democratic) are combined, but without one of the three Esping-Andersen–type models dominating (e.g., Poland, Hungary; cf. Kollmorgen, 2009, p. 65 et seq.).[2]

Table 2.1 summarizes the typologies mentioned, including the ones used here, with their respective distinctive features:[3]

2.1.2 Models of public administration in Europe

The previous chapter made clear that country groups and classifications according to particular types of administrative profile can be differentiated in comparative research depending on cognitive interest and the criteria of analysis. The typological approach used by us is based on the comparison-related criteria of a vertical administrative structure on the one hand, and the administrative culture-based character on the other. The resulting five country profiles of European administrative systems (with further subgroups) are elaborated more closely below (see also Table 2.2).

The Continental European Napoleonic model

The Continental European Napoleonic model (France, Italy, Spain, Greece, Portugal) is marked first by the common Roman-French legal tradition and the importance of statutory law. The understanding of state and administration is defined by the principle of legality (*principe de légalité*), and is reflected in a comprehensive codification of legal norms and an extended administrative judicature. As on the European Continent as a whole (including Germany), public administration represents an institutional legacy of absolutism and was controlled by a constitutional monarch until the end of the nineteenth century. As to the Napoleonic tradition, the reforms that were effected under Napoleon Bonaparte's spell during the early nineteenth century, were ground-breaking (cf. Wright, 1990). At first these reforms

Table 2.1 Typologies of comparison in public administration

Author/s	Cognitive Interest (Geographic Reference)	Comparative Dimension	Country Groups	Country Examples
Kuhlmann and Wollmann (this volume)	Comparison of admin. systems/ reforms (Europe)	Admin. tradition; political-institutional features of admin. structures	Cont. Europe Napol.	F, I, E, P, GR
			Cont. Europe federal	D, A, CH
			Anglo-Saxon	UK, IRE
			Scandinavian	S, N, FIN, DK
			Eastern European	H, PL, CZ
Painter and Peters (2010)	Classification of admin. traditions (international/ global)	Legal tradition; relationship state– society; admin. organization civil service (+ geograph. location)	Anglo-American	UK, USA, IRE, NZ
			Napoleonic	F, I, E, P, GR
			Germanic	D, A, CH, NL
			Scandinavian	S, N, FIN, DK
			Latin American	RA, BR, ME
			Post-colon. South Asian/ African	IND, EAU
			East Asian	J, ROK, RP
			Soviet	CN, VN, CEE- countries
			Islamic	TR, UAE, IR
			Napoleonic	F, I, E, P, GR, B
Kickert (2011)	Explanation of NPM reforms (Continental Europe)	Admin. tradition; relationship state– society; democracy type	Germanic	D
			Small European states	A, CH, NL, B
			Southern European states	I, E, GR, P
Demmke et al. (2007)	Comp. civil service systems (Europe)	Features of public personnel (recruitment, promotion, legal status)	Anglo-Saxon	UK, IRE, M
			Continental European	F, A, D, NL, B
			Mediterr./South European	E, I, P, CY
			Scandinavian	DK, S, N, FIN
			Eastern European	BG, CZ, PL

Table 2.1 *(continued)*

Author/s	Cognitive Interest (Geographic Reference)	Comparative Dimension	Country Groups	Country Examples
Jann (1983, 2002)	Comp. of admin. action as problem-solving process (Western Europe)	Problem-solving action of admin.; interaction with citizens	Cooperative contact culture	S
			Flexible negotiation culture	UK
			Formalized regulatory culture	D
Esping-Andersen (1990)	Comp. of welfare states/state action (Western Europe)	State activity (financing, benefit standards, redistribution, decommodification)	Conservative	D, F, I, B, A
			Social democratic	S, DK, FIN, N
			Liberal	UK, USA, CH

Note: See endnote 3 for country codes.

Source: Authors' own summary.

shaped the French administration and then 'spilled over' to the Benelux countries and into Italy and Spain. The Napoleonic tradition (cf. Peters, 2008; Ongaro, 2009; Kickert, 2011) is characterized by a strong centralized government, a comprehensive, political culture-rooted acceptance of (centralized) governmental regulatory authority and a powerful centralized bureaucracy. The largely sectorally defined authorities of the bureaucracy usually extend from the central to the local levels while its centralist embodiment and personification can be seen in the central government-appointed prefect (*préfet*). Within this, the subnational and local levels are functionally subordinate, so the principle of territorial administrative organization and institutional subsidiarity is not well developed.

Within the Continental European Napoleonic tradition, a sub-category termed Southern European states can be identified (cf. Kickert, 2011, p. 107 et seq.) and to which the countries of Italy, Portugal, Greece and Spain can be assigned. Though these administrative systems are basically marked by a formally dominant legalistic tradition and structure, their administrative practice is shaped by exceptionally strong politicization, clientelistic relations and political party patronage with regard to recruitment to the civil service (Sotiropoulos, 2009, p. 408 et seq.; Kickert, 2011, p. 107 et seq.). One explanation for this lies in the significant role of political parties in Southern

European countries because they have a strong influence on the allocation of administrative posts and also on the remuneration and promotion modalities in public administration. Accordingly, 'political allies' are preferably singled out for support (Kickert, ibid.). While in principle the rule-of-law applies and formal personnel recruitment in public administration is guided by qualification requirements, in practice these guidelines are often ignored. In fact, the influence of political clientelism and party patronage becomes the more dominant, the higher in the administrative hierarchy the respective positions are placed (ibid. p. 108).

The Continental European federal model

The Continental European federal model (Germany, Austria, and Switzerland)[4] displays an essential commonality with the Napoleonic systems because of the strong legalistic orientation of administration and the rule-of-law culture following the Roman law tradition. Besides, German administrative tradition has its roots in the Prussian state, which subsequently also shaped the Austrian administration. The legislative-political purpose of the codification of laws was historically to limit the administration controlled by the monarch (Wollmann, 2002a, p. 495). A crucial difference from the Napoleonic group is, however, the important role of the subnational-decentralized level and the principle of subsidiarity. Traditionally, the central government level's bureaucracy is significantly weaker and numerically 'leaner', whereas great political-administrative importance is attached to the subnational-decentralized institutions. Thus, the strong position of local government must be emphasized as a crucially distinctive feature. In the organization of the administrative system, the territoriality principle and an orientation towards the territory-related form of organization (multi-purpose model; see further below) dominate (Wollmann and Bouckaert, 2006).

A first differentiation within this group of countries can be made concerning the conception of statehood and the status of the civil service. Thus, civil servants in Germany and Austria are traditionally viewed rather as 'servants of the state' and as hierarchically superordinate to the societal domain. In contrast, for one, civil servants in Switzerland (although with some regional differences) are perceived more as 'employees of the people' and less superordinate in the social hierarchy (cf. Brändli-Traffelet, 2004). Thus, the relation between the public and the social spheres is seen as distinctly less hierarchical. Second, Switzerland is characterized by an administrative culture shaped by the coexistence of three ('ethnic') nations and language communities (German, French, Italian) as well as by a direct-democratic tradition that also influences administrative practice (Schedler, 2008, p. 149 et seq.). Third, a stronger competitiveness on the subnational administrative levels (e.g., tax competition between local governments) and greater local autonomy make for a significant difference when compared to Germany and Austria (cf. Linder, 2009; Jäkel and Kuhlmann, 2012).

The Scandinavian model

The Scandinavian model countries (Sweden, Denmark, Norway, Finland) display significant overlap with Continental European federal countries in their administrative profiles since these countries are also rooted in the Roman law tradition (cf. Pierre, 2010; Wollmann, 2013). However, there is a crucial difference in the Scandinavian administrative profile (as opposed to the other systems with a Roman law tradition) concerning the openness of the recruiting and career system in the public service and the explicit accessibility of the administrative system by the citizens (freedom of information, external transparency, citizen participation, user democracy). Further commonalities with the Continental European federal nations are the subsidiary principle in which responsibilities are allocated to the central and local administrative levels. These countries possess a highly decentralized administrative structure with, by tradition, politically and functionally strong local governments and a high degree of autonomy of action of local authorities (as reflected, for example, in the municipal tax revenue; Wollmann, 2004). They therefore operate – despite their unitary state structure – as being even more 'decentralized' in some cases than federal countries (in particular those with intra-state federalism, such as Germany and Austria; cf. Pollitt and Bouckaert, 2004) within the Scandinavian administrative profile.

The Anglo-Saxon model

The countries with an Anglo-Saxon (and Anglo-American) administrative model (United Kingdom, Malta, Ireland) are classified within CPA as belonging to the public interest or civic culture tradition (Wollmann, 2000b; Heady, 2001; Halligan, 2003; König, 2006). Based on liberal and utilitarian philosophies of the state, this tradition is characterized by an instrumental concept of statehood. At its centre is the acting 'government', rather than the 'state' being extolled as a 'value in itself'. Thus, one often speaks of a 'stateless society' (Dyson, 1980). Embedded in a civic culture and individualist tradition, the cognitive and normative differences between the state and the social-economic sphere have not become very pronounced in the British administrative system. The crucial separation of the public and private legal sphere in Continental European administrations (see above) is largely unknown in the countries with a tradition of public interest. In light of this, the transfer of concepts and ideas between public and social market spheres is also far smoother. Thus, for example, managerial principles of action of NPM are deeply rooted in the administrative culture (König, 2006). Consequently, the NPM-reformed administration (see below) has since become a further common distinctive feature of Anglo-Saxon and Anglo-American administration spheres (see Halligan, 2003). Furthermore, the dominance of Common Law has traditionally been a characteristic of the legal and administrative concept in these countries, since the 'law of the land' is still based on judge-made law rather than on statute law (La Porta et al., 1999, p. 10). Administrative action in Continental Europe first and foremost pertains to the implementation of legal provisions as enacted by parliament. By contrast, legislative acts by Anglo-Saxon/Anglo-American parliaments have more the character of political programmes, so the administration has to find suitable ways and means to implement them.

One explanation for the endeavours to limit the powers of bureaucracy and the scope of action of the state can historically be found, in the United Kingdom, in the emergence of the doctrine of 'parliamentary sovereignty'. Hence, the Anglo-Saxon administrative model is characterized by the modern development of parliament and democracy that preceded the formation of a professional civil service; thus, the functions of the bureaucratic system were determined from the outset by the political regime (König, 2006, p. 24). This is also reflected in the parliament exercising control over the administration and holding it 'politically accountable', with administrative courts typically remaining absent. Hence, in the Anglo-Saxon context, bureaucracy has historically developed under the spell of the political domain and has remained so to this day.

The Central Eastern and South Eastern European model

Subjugated under the rule of the Soviet Union after 1945, the administrative structure in the Central Eastern and South Eastern European countries came (notwithstanding the different country-specific pre-communist administrative traditions) to be shaped all but uniformly by the imposed Stalinist state organization model. The double subordination of state administration under a centralized party rule and the abolition of the separation of powers were emblematic of this organization model (Wollmann and Lankina, 2003). In terms of administrative typology, this has also been labelled the 'Soviet Tradition' (cf. Painter and Peters, 2010, p. 27 et seq.). In order to ensure the 'unity and indivisibility of state power', the subnational administrative units (councils, representative bodies, commissions in the counties, cities and municipalities) acted as local bodies and offices for the state (Wollmann,

1997a, p. 262; Kuhlmann, 2003, p. 219 et seq.). In contrast to the traditional Continental European model of bureaucratic administration, the socialist cadre administration (cf. König, 1993) was also characterized by the partisanship, that is, the submission to the Communist Party of the public personnel (cf. Dimitrov et al., 2006, p. 205) and by an at best rudimentary adherence to legally binding norms and procedures, bordering on what has been called 'law nihilism' (cf. Pohl, 1991, p. 236 et seq.).

After 1990 when the communist regime in Central Eastern Europe was swept away, the system transformation of these countries was essentially effected by the abolishment of the (post-Stalinist) socialist state organization and by the (re-)introduction of the Continental European constitutional, state and administrative model (König, 1993). Yet the legacy of the Soviet Tradition in the individual countries developed quite differently. In some countries, an all but complete break with the previous socialist institutional setting has been effected. In others, however, the imprint and legacy of socialist administration has persisted to a significant degree, thus entailing serious problems for the functioning of administration.

It has been argued that, in general, the 'administrations in Central and Eastern Europe. . .are moving towards western Continental European administrative models' (Goetz, 1995, p. 541). However, this development has taken place against the background of country-specific political-institutional conditions and pre-communist administrative traditions at different speeds and with different emphases. Hungary and Poland, for example, are representative of the subgroup of countries of the Eastern European administrative profile, which – due to their geopolitical past[5] – have historically been shaped in particular by the Continental European and especially by the Austrian or Prussian administrative model (cf. Wollmann, 1995, pp. 566, 572; Wollmann and Lankina, 2003). After these countries' independence in 1919, the administrative organization was shaped by a 'distinctly centralized system in accordance with the French model' (Kaltenbach, 1990, p. 85). This institutional development was dramatically arrested in 1945 as a result of the communist takeover of power. In the wake of the system change in 1989, Hungary has arguably made the most progress in the (re)establishment of the Continental European constitutional and administrative model as this had already been initiated by 'reform-oriented communists' during the 1980s and was accelerated by the expected and then implemented accession to the EU. Notably in Hungary, the proximity to the German model is pronounced, as evidenced not least by the introduction of constitutional jurisdiction and the constructive vote of no confidence (cf. Dimitrov et al., 2006, p. 207 et seq.).

Table 2.2 Administrative profiles in Europe

Administrative Profile/Group of Countries	Administrative Tradition	Administrative Structure
Continental European Napoleonic (F, I, P, GR, E)	Rule-of-law (*Rechtsstaat*), legalism Southern European subgroup: clientelism, party patronage, politicization	Unitary-centralized; weak local government (decentralization in F, I, E since 1980s/1990s)
Continental European federal (D, A, CH)	Rule-of-law (*Rechtsstaat*), legalism Switzerland: weaker separation of state and society; weaker public service, legalism	Federal-decentralized; strong local government
Scandinavian (S, N, DK, FIN)	Rule-of-law (*Rechtsstaat*) culture, transparency/contact culture; accessibility of administration for citizenship	Unitary-decentralized; strong local government/civic self-determination
Anglo-Saxon (UK/England)	Public interest culture, pragmatism	Unitary-centralized; strong (since 1980s weakened) local government
Central Eastern European (H, PL, CZ)	Socialist cadre administration ('Stalinist' legacy); since the system change, re-establishment of pre-communist (rule-of-law) traditions	Unitary-decentralized; strong local government (recentralization since 2011 in H)
South Eastern European (BG, RO)		Unitary-centralized; weak local government

Note: See endnote 3 for country codes.

Source: Authors' own summary.

This can be distinguished from a South Eastern European group of countries (including Bulgaria and Romania). These countries were under the centralized rule of the Ottoman Empire and Tsarist Russia up to the end of the nineteenth century and 1919 respectively in terms of their administrative history. Moreover, their transformation after 1990 was initially determined by the post-communist elite.

2.1.3 Comparative local government

In many European countries, the discharge of legally regulated tasks and services is largely, if not predominantly, carried out by decentralized and in particular local levels. As a result of recent decentralization processes (see Chapter 4, Section 4.2), the role of local governments has been further strengthened, a role that is also reflected in the EU's recognition of local self-government now codified by the Treaty of Lisbon (see below). Thus, local government activities now represent a significant share (about 16 per cent) of the entire gross domestic product of all EU member states as well as of the total of public expenditure (about 34 per cent).[6] From a political and democratic perspective, local self-government fulfils an important stabilizing and legitimizing function within the overall national government systems and in the supra-national setting as well. This is because they offer the opportunity for citizens to get directly involved in political decision-making and ensure spatial proximity for political problem-solving (Bogumil, 2001, p. 17). Eurobarometer surveys show (cf. Special Eurobarometer 307, 2009, p. 9) that the citizens' trust in local and regional public institutions is significantly higher than in national parliaments and governments. In the effective functioning and the acceptance of a constitutional democratic government in European countries, therefore, local self-government plays a crucial role.

In light of this, comparative local government research has now become an important part of CPA and is positioned at the interface between local government research and administrative science. Three dimensions in particular are often distinguished and highlighted in the comparative study of local government systems (cf. Page and Goldsmith, 1987; Wollmann, 2004, 2008; Heinelt and Hlepas, 2006; Kuhlmann, 2006a, 2009a; Goldsmith and Page, 2010; Loughlin et al., 2010):

- functional profile, that is, the scope and salience of functional responsibilities that are assumed by local territorial bodies from the vertical distribution/fusion of functions between local and central government (separate versus fused systems; dual versus monistic function model) and financial autonomy;
- territorial profile, that is, the territorial structure and related territorial viability of local government (Northern European versus Southern European model);
- political profile, that is, the structure of local democracy (representative versus direct-democratic), the relationship between council and local executive authorities (monistic versus dual) and the electoral procedure of the head of administration (direct versus indirect).

Functional profile: distribution and scope of responsibilities, fiscal autonomy

Vertically, that is, in terms of the relationship between the local and central government levels, the local government systems can be differentiated first as to whether state authorities and local self-governments execute their responsibilities separately and largely independently from one another, or second, whether the levels interact strongly, leading to a mix of state and local responsibilities (Bennett, 1989). The first administrative type has been termed the 'separationist model', and is traditionally characteristic of the British (and Swedish) administrative tradition (cf. Bulpitt, 1983). The concept of a vertical separation of state and local government goes hand in hand with a monistic or uniform conception of local government responsibilities according to which the tasks, once they are assigned to the local government level, become 'fully-fledged' local government tasks (Wollmann, 2008, p. 259 et seq.; see also Chapter 4, Section 4.2).

In contrast, typical of the Continental European countries are 'fused systems', or 'administrative integrated models' (Baldersheim et al., 1996).[7] These are characterized by state and local self-government tasks not being carried out separately, but instead integrated administratively ('mixed'). They are hereby based on a dual conception of local government functions according to which the local authorities carry out local self-government responsibilities proper, as well as state tasks assigned ('delegated') to them by the state (the so-called 'Janus-faced character' of local government). Historically based on an 'invention' of post-revolutionary French municipal legislation in 1790 (cf. Wollmann, 2008, p. 41), the dual model entered the German-Austrian local and administrative tradition via the Prussian municipal charter (*Preußische Städteordnung*) of 1890. During the late nineteenth century this model weighed on the institutional development of local government in Central and Eastern European countries and again after 1990 when it influenced the local government legislation as adopted in Hungary, Poland and in the Czech Republic (cf. Wollmann, 1995; Wollmann and Lankina, 2003, p. 94 et seq.). Within the fused systems, a further conceptual differentiation can be made between the so-called 'state-centred integrationist model', in which the state administration carries out the self-government functions of the local governments in addition to its own tasks, and the 'local-administration–centred integrationist model', in which, as previously mentioned, the local governments perform 'dual' functions in carrying out their self-government tasks and the ones that the state has 'delegated' to them. France can be considered a prototype of the 'state-centred integrationist model' (until decentralization in the early 1980s), since the state authorities, through their local offices, were strongly involved in the conduct of local government tasks. In contrast, the 'local-administration–centred integrationist model' can be found in the German and Austrian local government tradition.

Aside from the distinction between separationist and integrated/fused systems and between monistic and dual task models, an analytically promising and viable typology of local government functions can also be based

Table 2.3 Fiscal autonomy of municipalities in selected OECD countries

Country	Proportion of Own Taxes (Without Social Contributions) in Overall Municipal Revenue in % (2009)
Sweden	63.6
Switzerland	59.2
Slovak Republic	50.3
France	44.6
Spain	43.4
Norway	41.9
Czech Republic	41.2
Germany	39.6
Italy	37.4
Denmark	33.7
Portugal	33.6
Poland	30.9
Hungary	22.8
United Kingdom	12.9
Netherlands	8.3
Greece	6.6

Source: OECD (2011).

on the scope and content of functional responsibilities and on the extent of autonomy (local discretion) that the local authorities have in carrying out the tasks.

A pertinent quantitative indicator of the scope and content of local government functions can be seen in the local expenditure quota in the overall public spending and in the local employment quota in total public sector employment. As an indicator for the scope of 'local discretion', the proportion of local tax revenue in the total local revenues (see Table 2.3) can be plausibly used. This indicator points to significant differences that exist, in financial terms, among the local authorities in exercising local autonomy. For example, the financial autonomy of Swedish local governments is particularly high because they are funded largely (64 per cent) from their own (income) tax revenue and, at the same time, have a significant influence on the local tax rates. For post-Thatcher England, in contrast, the opposite is true (with 13 per cent of their overall local revenues stemming from their own taxes), and in Hungary (with 23 per cent). With a proportion of 45 per cent of their own taxes in the overall local government revenues, the French local authorities have a higher local fiscal autonomy than their German (40 per cent) or Italian (37 per cent) counterparts (OECD, 2011; see Table 2.3).

Functionally strong local government systems such as Germany, Sweden, and, historically, the United Kingdom show an orientation towards the principle of territoriality,[8] which guides the distribution of administrative responsibilities (the so-called multi-purpose model; cf. Wollmann, 2004). In contrast, functionally weak local government systems are characterized by the principle of functionality (single-purpose model) under which mono-functionally operating units of deconcentrated state administration have priority (traditionally the Napoleonic systems). In some cases the actual operating strength and autonomy of local governments deviate considerably from their formal legal/constitutional status. Hence in many countries, local self-government now possesses a constitutionally codified status (Germany, Sweden, France, Italy, Hungary); in part, however, the actual scope of responsibilities is limited (France, Italy). Conversely, it was true for the United Kingdom until the Thatcher era that local government did not have a constitutional status (which is still the case), but enjoyed very extensive autonomy and a broad responsibility profile (which has since become largely eroded). On the legal level, a general competence principle applies to Continental Europe and Scandinavia, according to which the municipal councils are responsible (at least formally) for all matters relating to the local community. This stands in contrast to the British *ultra vires* principle by which the local governments only carry out those responsibilities that have been explicitly assigned to them by parliamentary legislation and that can be revoked at any time. The *ultra vires* principle was, however, attenuated by the local government legislation of 2000 and aligned more closely with the general competence clause typical of the Continental European local government tradition (see Chapter 3, Section 3.4).

Territorial profile: Northern and Southern European model

The criterion of territorial structure of the municipal level is closely connected to the functional profile, which can plausibly be seen as constituting an important institutional condition for the viability and operational capacity of local government. In line with Norton (1994), Baldersheim et al. (1996), John (2001, p. 25 et seq.) and Wollmann (2008), one can, on the one hand, identify the so-called Southern European type characterized by a small-scale local government structure with a multitude of small municipalities and by the absence of territorial reforms. On the other hand, the so-called Northern European type has been distinguished as being marked by territorially (and demographically) large-scale municipalities resulting from extensive territorial reforms (see Chapter 4, Section 4.3). Examples for the Southern European type can be found in particular in countries with a Continental European Napoleonic tradition (France, Spain, Italy, Portugal

Greece[9]), whereas the United Kingdom exemplifies the Northern European model, which also includes the Scandinavian countries. The countries shaped by a Continental European federal tradition can, in contrast, be largely assigned to the Southern European type (Switzerland, Austria; in Germany: the *Länder* of Rhineland-Palatinate, Baden-Württemberg, Bavaria, Schleswig-Holstein as well as most of the East German *Länder*; by contrast the *Länder* of North Rhine-Westphalia and Hesse, fall under the Northern European type).

Political profile: local democracy and leadership

In order to specify the political profile of local government, the democratic decision-making rights of citizens on a local level, the (internal) institutional arrangement of local government decision-making, and its politico-administrative leadership structure should be highlighted. This holds true particularly for the relationship between the local executive and local council ('horizontal dimension', see above; for an overview, see Loughlin et al., 2010). With regard to the first criterion, local government systems with a predominance of representative democracy-based institutions (traditionally, United Kingdom, Sweden since 1974, Germany until 1990, and France) can be distinguished from local government systems that possess strong direct democracy-based elements, such as binding local referenda (Switzerland, German *Länder* since 1990, Hungary, Italy, Sweden until 1974, Austria, Finland, Czech Republic). Under the latter criterion, monistic and dual systems[10] may be discerned (Wollmann, 2004, p. 151 et seq.).

In monistic systems, all decision-making powers, including the 'executive' direction and control of local administration, lie with the elected local council or, more specifically, with sector-responsible council committees. For this reason, in comparative terms, one speaks of government by committee systems (United Kingdom, Sweden, Denmark). In such systems, 'strong mayors' are generally unknown, and they have come to be criticized for a lack of political and executive leadership and for the sectoral fragmentation of administration.

In dual systems, by contrast, responsibilities are divided between the executive leader/mayor and the legislative/council with the local executive branch being equipped with its own decision-making powers (France, Germany, Italy, Hungary, Spain, Portugal, Greece, Poland; cf. Heinelt and Hlepas, 2006, p. 33). This 'strong mayor' form of local democracy (Mouritzen and Svara, 2002) is made even stronger in some countries through the direct

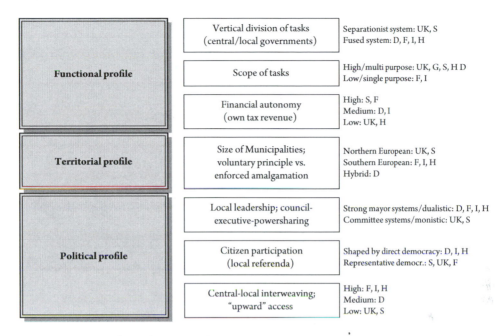

Functional profile	Vertical division of tasks (central/local governments)	Separationist system: UK, S Fused system: D, F, I, H
	Scope of tasks	High/multi purpose: UK, G, S, H D Low/single purpose: F, I
	Financial autonomy (own tax revenue)	High: S, F Medium: D, I Low: UK, H
Territorial profile	Size of Municipalities; voluntary principle vs. enforced amalgamation	Northern European: UK, S Southern European: F, I, H Hybrid: D
Political profile	Local leadership; council-executive-powersharing	Strong mayor systems/dualistic: D, F, I, H Committee systems/monistic: UK, S
	Citizen participation (local referenda)	Shaped by direct democracy: D, I, H Representative democr.: S, UK, F
	Central-local interweaving; "upward" access	High: F, I, H Medium: D Low: UK, S

Note: See endnote 3 for country codes.
Source: Authors' own diagram.

Figure 2.2 Comparing local government systems

election of the mayor (Germany, Italy, Hungary; cf. Wollmann, 2009). Furthermore, a major source of political power of local governments can be observed in the access of local political actors to higher levels of the political-administrative system. This access (Page and Goldsmith, 1987; Goldsmith and Page, 2010) can result from the accumulation of mandates (*cumul des mandats*), patronage-based relationships, as well as from the logic of political careers emblematic of Southern European local government systems (France, Italy, Greece, Spain). However, such access may lead to a blending of levels or even to a 'colonization' of the state by local actors (as in the case of France).

Figure 2.2 summarizes the main criteria for a comparison of local government systems.

Several of the comparative categories listed in Figure 2.2 are based on an earlier typology proposed by Hesse and Sharpe (1991), who divided local government systems into three types (see Table 2.4). However, this classification does not take into account the horizontal distribution of power between the local council and executive, or the territorial profile.

Table 2.4 Traditional types of local government systems from a comparative perspective

Feature of Comparison	North Middle European Group	Franco Group	Anglo Group
Constitutional status	High	High	Low
State–local relation/control from above	Low/Medium	High	Low
Functional responsibilities	High	Low	High
Local discretion	High/Medium	Medium	High
Political strength/community identity	High	High	Low
Country classification	Core group: N, S, DK Sub group: A, CH, D, NL	F, I, B, E, P, GR	UK, IRE[a]

Note: a. Of the non-European local systems, CA, AU, USA, NZ belong to the Anglo Group. Country codes may be found in endnote 3.

Source: Authors' own summary (following Hesse and Sharpe, 1991).

2.1.4   Civil service systems[11]

Civil service systems and formal politicization of public administration

The dimension of personnel in public administration was taken up during previous decades in research comparing civil service systems, with the focus of this being on ministerial bureaucracy (see Bekke et al., 1996; Alam, 1998; Bekke and van der Meer, 2000; Halligan, 2003; Raadschelders et al., 2007; Derlien and Peters, 2009). This strand of CPA, on the one hand, addresses the historical development, the legal and institutional organization and the cultural base of public personnel systems. On the other hand, it analyses the recruitment and career patterns of public employees, their qualification trajectories, their role perception and understanding, as well as including the issue of party-political neutrality or political dependence of ministerial civil servants.

The scope of the public workforce and the status of the public service as an employer are usually determined in a country-comparative perspective by numerically comparing employment in the public sector to the total employ-ment of a country (see also Chapter 3, Section 3.6.1). In a European com-parison, the extended civil services of the Scandinavian countries (Norway: 29 per cent; Sweden: 28 per cent), of France (22 per cent) and of Hungary (19 per cent) stand in contrast to the 'lean' civil services in Germany (10 per cent), Austria (10 per cent) and Switzerland (7 per cent). In the Scandinavian countries, the more expansive (social-democratic–shaped) welfare state shows in the number and percentage of public employees (see Section 2.1.1 above). In the case of France, the public service has, in the course of the twentieth century, become one of the most numerically expanded and at the same time one of the most powerful in the world (Alam, 1998). The United Kingdom (15 per cent), Italy (14 per cent), Greece (14 per cent) and Spain (13 per cent) occupy a middle position (cf. OECD, 2009).

In addition to the quantitative criterion of personnel numbers, CPA uses the 'openness' and 'closedness' of public service systems as a qualitative dimension for differentiation (cf. Auer et al., 1996; Alam, 1998). This is strongly connected with a country's above-mentioned state and administrative tradition. Open personnel systems or 'position-based systems' are characterized by a rather position-related recruitment, open access routes to public service, and greater permeability between the public and private employment sector. Typical for closed personnel systems or 'career-based systems' are career-related recruitment, the principle of seniority and lifelong appointment, and a separation between the public and private employment spheres and the low permeability from one to the other. Although the two models have become ever more blurred in reality as a result of reforms (see Chapter 4, Section 4.5), an approximate classification of the European public service systems can still be made (with an eye on the situation in 2007–08) (Table 2.5; cf. Demmke et al., 2007, p. 12 et seq.).

Traditionally, the exemplar Continental European public service (Germany, Austria, France, Spain, Belgium) is characterized by a closed career-based personnel system, which typically features a separation between public service law and general labour law, a seniority-based career system, low accessibility for lateral entrants, and a closed recruitment policy. In contrast, in the Anglo-Saxon civil service type, there is no explicit difference between the private sector and the public sector. The employment relationships of civil servants are not regulated by a specific public service law (as distinct

Table 2.5 Career- and position-based systems in Europe

Personnel Systems[a]	Country Examples
Career-based system	A, B, BG, D, F, GR, H, LT, P, PL, RO
Position-based system	CZ, DK, E, EST, FIN, I, NL, SLO, S, UK
Not assignable	N

Note: a. Country classification according to whether the features of a career-based system or a position-based system are predominant (see more detailed explanation in Demmke et al., 2007, p. 13 et seq.) See endnote 3 for country codes.

Source: Authors' own summary, following Demmke et al. (2007, p. 13).

from private labour law) or statute, but are contract based (Ridley, 2000). Generally they are subject to free collective bargaining and do not include a strict career trajectory, but are instead position-based. In addition, private and public employment spheres are more permeable, promotion and pay schemes are more performance-oriented, and recruitment paths for lateral entrants are more open. This, however, does not prevent the formation of a prestigious administrative elite.

Furthermore, regarding the status of the civil servant, differences exist between countries. In Continental Europe, this is typically based on public service law and unilateral appointment, subject to public law by official decision, and in general for life. This must be distinguished from the British definition of a civil servant, who is employed as a Crown servant in a civil position, and is remunerated from funds exclusively and directly approved by parliament. However, this applies to only 450 000 Crown servants in the United Kingdom; all other public employees are contract staff (Demmke, 2011, p. 321). Hence, it becomes obvious that the proportions of civil servants in European countries vary greatly. In some countries, the public servant status is dominant and is considered as a regular employment relationship in the public service (France, Greece, Belgium). Other countries, in contrast, have mixed systems, in which the civil servant status is reserved only for a section of the public staff and thus have a 'two-tier' system of civil servant and contract staff relationships (Germany, Austria, Denmark, Spain, Hungary; ibid., p. 323). A third group can be identified as public service systems in which contract-based employment relationships prevail and where hardly any civil servants remain (Sweden, United Kingdom, Poland, and more recently Italy; see Table 2.6). However, it should be noted that in individual countries the proportions of civil servants differ significantly depending on levels and sectors.

Another distinguishing criterion with respect to the personnel-related components of administrative systems is the 'formal politicization'. This refers to the (party-) politically controlled appointment of administrative key positions up to the phenomenon of 'patronage of positions'. One extreme of this would be the United Kingdom with its traditionally 'apolitical' civil service (see below). The Swedish administrative system is also considered traditionally less formally politicized and that can be explained, in part, by the greater importance placed on professional expertise in the ministries and in the quasi-autonomous agencies (Peters and Pierre, 2004, p. 42 et seq.; Kopecký and Mair, 2012, p. 9). An extreme at the other end of the spectrum is the USA with its much referred to 'spoils system', which is characterized by the exchange of numerous high-ranking governmental positions subsequent

Table 2.6 Comparison of the proportion of civil servants in European countries

Member State	Proportion of Civil Servants	Contract Staff
Czech Republic	0% on the state level, 38% on the regional and country level	
Sweden	1%	99%
Latvia	6%	94%
Poland	6%	94%
United Kingdom	10%	90%
Ireland	13%	87%
Italy	15%	85%
Hungary	25%	75%
Cyprus	28%	72%
Slovenia	34%	66%
Germany	37%	59% (4% soldiers)
Spain	59%	27% (14% other staff)
Finland	59%	27% (14% other staff)
Austria	61% (federal level)	36%
Lithuania	67%	28% (5% other staff)
Malta	67%	33%
France	73%	15% (12% other staff)
Greece	74%	26%
Belgium	75% (federal level)	25%
Luxembourg	77%	23%
Slovakia	85%	10% (5% other staff)
Estonia	90%	7% (3% other staff)
Netherlands	100%	Some contract staff
Portugal	15%	85%
Romania	7% (two civil servant groups)	93%

Source: Authors' own summary, following Demmke (2011, p. 323, with further references).

to a change in government. Also characteristic for the Southern European civil service systems are the pronouncedly party-political recruitment and promotion practice in the ministerial administration to patronage and clientelism between political parties and the administration (Italy, Greece, Spain; cf. Kickert, 2011). An extended practice of patronage has been noted for France and Belgium as well (Müller, 2001), and has been traced back historically in part to the patrimonial absolutist development path of the formation of the state in countries shaped by a Napoleonic tradition (Manow, 2002, p. 39 et seq.; Schnapp, 2006, p. 341). In comparison, Germany is considered to have a medium-sized, albeit increasing formal politicization of ministerial bureaucracy (cf. Schnapp, 2006; Schwanke and Ebinger, 2006), now reckoned to be even higher than in Hungary (Kopecký and Mair, 2012, p. 9).

Power, influence and functional politicization of public administration

The influence of bureaucracies on political decision-making is one of the classic questions raised by CPA and can be dated back to Max Weber's theory of bureaucracy. The focus here is on ministerial bureaucracy, that is, on an administrative type that is close to political decision-making processes and has less to do with direct executive implementation or service-related administrative functions (an example is in the study by Page, 1992). From a comparative perspective the central question is which political influence and scope of action do senior ministerial officials possess in different countries (cf. Peters, 2009)? This variant of the politicization of administration that eyes the ministerial bureaucrats who are politically responsive, anticipate political rationalities and weigh on political processes is, in comparative administration research, also termed as 'functional politicization' (cf. Mayntz and Derlien, 1989; in contrast to 'formal politicization'; see above). The preferred empirical approach to capturing functional politicization is to survey senior bureaucrats with respect to their role perception and understanding, in particular to their attitudes towards the political aspects of their work (cf. Aberbach et al., 1981; Mayntz and Derlien, 1989; Derlien, 1994; Schwanke and Ebinger, 2006). This has resulted in an ideal-typical differentiation between 'classic bureaucrats' on the one hand, characterized by a simply executive, technical, and apolitical understanding of their role, and 'policy-makers' on the other, who influence policy formation processes and positively view the political aspects of their duties (for further subtypes, see Aberbach et al., 1981). In comparative research, the senior bureaucrats of countries like Germany, Austria, France, Sweden, United Kingdom and, among the CEE countries, Hungary, have been ascribed a high level of policy-making influence (cf. Page and Wright, 1999; Meyer-Sahling and Veen, 2012, p. 8). Contrastingly, the ministerial officials in Italy, Greece and Belgium have a lower level of influence on policy-making processes.

Apart from this field of comparative administration research, which exhibits some overlap with political culture research, new approaches have been embarked upon that attempt to identify the influence potential of ministerial bureaucracies on policy-making processes through the analysis of concrete organizational-structural arrangements. Such an approach takes up a (neo-)institutionalist perspective. In this context, Schnapp (2004) studied ministerial organizational structures and decision-making institutions in 21 industrialized countries. His central issue covers the extent to which organizational-structural arrangements of ministerial bureaucracies determine the opportunities of administrative actors in influencing policy-making processes. 'Bureaucratic power' is explained in terms of the

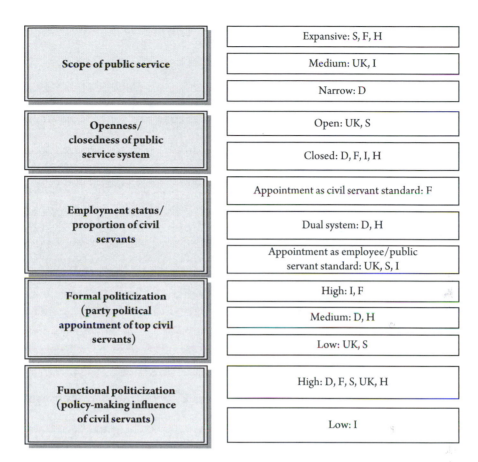

Note: For country codes see endnote 3.
Source: Authors' own diagram.

Figure 2.3 Comparative civil service systems

formal-organizational structure of administrative systems, by which action 'opportunities' and influence 'potentials' (i.e., the *possible* rather than the *actual* influence) are measured. The study concludes that the scope of action of bureaucracies is determined not just by formal administrative structures, but also varies according to the number and the concrete preference constellation of political veto players (Schnapp, 2004, p. 311 et seq.). Figure 2.3 summarizes the different features of analysis of comparative civil service systems.

2.1.5 Europeanization of public administration

In recent years, the change in national administrative systems as part of EU integration has developed into a favoured subject of comparative administrative science. Although the added analytic value and the empirical-methodological application of the concept of 'Europeanization' are still controversial (Goetz, 2006, p. 472), the administrative changes that are connected with the EU integration process in national contexts now play an important part in comparative research (Sommermann, 2002). In some of the available studies, administration is conceived of as an independent variable, whereas in others it is considered to be a dependent variable (Goetz, 2006, p. 472).

The aforementioned group of studies addresses the question as to which changes the EU integration process has triggered in the national administrative systems and how the latter have reacted to the supra-national impulse. One focal question relates to how the integration of national administrative systems in the European administrative space influences the scope of action, interaction structures and organizational arrangements of national ministerial bureaucracies. Another leading question is which institutional arrangements have been made on the level of member state ministerial bureaucracies for the respective country's coordination of EU policies (Kassim et al., 2000, with further references)? A further focus is the adjustment that national administrations have undergone and achieved in the face of the necessity for executing EU policies (Héritier et al., 2001; Knill, 2001).

The second group of studies analyses the relationship between administrative structure and administrative performance under the guiding questions of whether and how the EU integration and the resulting change in the administrative landscape have impacted on the performance of national administrations. So the influence of administrative-organizational setting on implementation deficits in the execution of European law has been comparatively studied in selected policy areas (Falkner et al., 2005).

Regarding the EU-incurred changes at the central government level, EU integration, it has been hypothesized (Moravcsik, 1994), has strengthened the executive while weakening the parliaments in the national political systems. There are now, however, a series of counter-arguments that point to de-parliamentarization as being neither inevitable nor occurring in all countries to the same extent. Rather, the national legislatives react very differently to the integration impulse (cf. Benz, 2004a; Kropp, 2006, p. 283 et seq.). Moreover, the understanding of their roles by parliamentarians and professional administrators varies in different Europeanized policy areas (Kropp and Ruschke, 2010, p. 669 et seq.). It has furthermore been argued that within the national central government, the ministerial administration benefits the most from EU integration, so that Europeanization presents itself first and foremost as bureaucratization (Goetz, 2003). Civil service bureaucrats are increasingly becoming multi-level players (which does not apply to the government proper to the same extent) and they 'use' Europe to enforce their own sectoral-administrative interests. They are strengthened in this by the bureaucratic nature of the EU decision-making system.

Comparative studies have also shown that EU integration promotes the development of privileged core executives within the national systems. These executives take over the EU-related coordination of ministerial rule and administration beyond departmental boundaries (Dimitrov et al., 2006). EU integration can thus be ascribed an institutionally concentrating effect in the inter-governmental setting within the national member states, as 'Europeanization' has ushered in the building up of central government units; this applies particularly to the finance ministries (cf. Maurer, 2003) that have become key actors in the coordination and bundling of European policies. However, there are substantial differences among member states. Thus, there exists what has been somewhat ironically called 'confraternities' of vertically interacting sectoral specialists, in the national and supranational context 'below' the 'core executives'. These are strengthened by working relations between the EU Commission and the respective ministries (for Norway and Sweden, see Larsson and Trondal, 2005).

As for inter-governmental relations, a surge of centralization originating in Brussels in the relations between the central government level of member states and their subnational levels has been advanced as a hypothesis that would particularly raise problems with regard to European federal states and the decentralized unitary states that have deeply rooted local self-government traditions (Sweden, Denmark, Norway, Finland) (cf. John, 2001, p. 61 et seq.). On the one hand, it has been argued that the implementation of the directives of EU regional policy has led to the concentration of decision-making powers in the ministerial administrative apparatus. Moreover, an involvement in EU processes by the local actors responsible for the implementation of EU policies takes place only in the margins (Hughes et al., 2004). On the other hand, it has been pointed out that during the course of the liberalization of the EU single market, traditionally protected local markets and supplier monopolies (e.g., in the area of public utilities etc.) have been broken open. As a result, the formerly wide scope of local government responsibilities has in some cases been significantly curtailed (Grunow, 2006). The allocation of resources within the cohesion and regional policy has only limited effect on counteracting this demunicipalization and centralization trend. In addition, the decentralized–transnational exchange, which also influences the newly established forms of regional and quasi-federal (self-) administration in Europe, seems to be a rather moderate counterweight to the concentration and centralization tendencies triggered by the EU. It remains to be seen whether and to which extent the Treaty of Lisbon of 1 December 2009 in which the EU has, for the first time, legally recognized local self-government,[12] is going to secure or even strengthen[13] the status of local government in the EU's multi-level system.

2.2 Institutional policies and administrative reforms

2.2.1 Conceptualizing institutional policies

Administrative reforms generally result from targeted institution-related policy interventions.[14] As such, they can be considered as a specific variant of policies, namely institutional policies, which are accessible to the analytic instruments of policy research on the one hand, but differ too in important respects from 'normal' substantial policies on the other. They can be assigned first and foremost to the group of 'normal' policies, to the extent that they, as in any policy area, consist of specific goals, subjects and objects of intervention, measures and activities as well as results and effects (Jann, 2001, p. 329). If understood in the narrower sense of the intentional shaping of structures and actions within a politico-administrative system, institutional policy refers to conscious and comprehensible decisions about institution building and on institutional change that are taken at the end of political processes (Benz, 2004b, p. 19). Administrative reform policy can be comprehended as the attempt by politico-administrative actors to change the institutional order (polity) within which they make and implement decisions. It can therefore also be termed polity-policy (Wollmann, 2000a, p. 199 et seq.; Ritz, 2003, p. 180). If administrative reform is viewed as policy, then it can refer to the entire policy cycle and thus examine its different phases from policy initiation/formulation and implementation to termination with subsequent evaluation/impact measurement and the possibility of the reformulation of policies. The rather 'loose coupling' between reform rhetoric (talk), action programme (decision) and actual changes (action) may well represent a functional and rational strategy in organizational reform processes (cf. Brunsson, 1989; Jann, 2006).

Administrative reforms can exhibit different forms and objectives, depending on whether they refer to changes between different organizational units/levels in the sense of 'external institutional policy', and internal modernization of administrations ('internal institutional policy') or to forms of citizen participation in administrative proceedings ('participatory reforms'). Accordingly, the respective constellation of actors, political arenas and reform effects may vary considerably. In Chapter 4, these different types, forms and objectives of administrative reforms will be addressed in more detail using the examples of selected European countries.

2.2.2 Types of administrative reform

If administrative reforms are viewed as institutional policy, then the distinction can be made between external (or outward-looking) and internal (or inward-looking) administrative reforms. Depending on which elements of institutional order are on the reform agenda and which regulatory areas of the institution are affected by the intended change, these reforms can be classified. Administrative reforms focusing on external relations (external institutional policy) are aimed at changing functional and/or territorial jurisdictions, membership rules and relations between organizations at different levels or sectors. In this, external actors are also always involved in the institution policy processes. These reforms are intended to change the 'shape' of the institutional order overall (Benz, 2004b, p. 20) and to redefine institutional boundaries. Internal administrative reforms, in contrast, are concerned with changes in the distribution of responsibilities and resources within administrative organizations and between internal administrative units as well as the reorganization of decision-making and cooperation rules.[15] If the external relations of administration are changed, then larger blocking or resistance can be effected more so than in cases of such reform measures that exclusively affect the internal relations of administration (ibid., p. 23 et seq.). In the area of external administrative reforms, three variants can be distinguished:

- Institutional changes in governmental multi-level systems (vertical inter-governmental administrative reforms) must be mentioned. These include reform approaches towards de- and recentralization, functional reform, regionalization and devolution up to a 'quasi-federalization'. This involves a change in the responsibility profile and decision-making powers in the inter-governmental relations between (central) state and regional/local territorial bodies. Fundamental constitutional and political reforms, as in the case of quasi-federalism (e.g., Italy) and devolution policy ushering in 'asymmetrical federalism' (e.g., the United Kingdom), may form the background for the administrative and functional changes in the multi-level system.
- Reforms should be envisaged that refer to territorial restructuring or 'territorial consolidation' in the subnational space. In this context, the redefinition of coordination and cooperation rules between different territorial bodies of a particular level should also be considered (horizontal inter-governmental administrative reforms/territorial consolidation).

This addresses different institutionalization variants between administrative cooperation and territorial fusion.

● Reforms that relate to the relationship between sectors, in particular the public, private and non-profit sectors (inter-sectoral administrative reforms) should be taken into account. These include privatization, outsourcing, public–private partnerships, and counter-currents towards renationalization/remunicipalization. By some, these reforms are termed 'horizontal decentralization' (cf. Bennett, 1989).

Internal administrative reforms take place within an administrative organization and relate primarily to the three areas of change: of organizational structures, procedural/management instruments and personnel. Since the 1980s, in all three, special importance has been placed on the international reform-guiding principles of New Public Management (NPM), the implementation of which needs to be examined in more detail in the following. It should be noted, however, that the internal modernization of administration also occurs by means of 'traditional' measures that can be traced back to earlier (i.e., pre-NPM) reform discourses (on this difference cf. Jaedicke et al., 2000; Bogumil et al., 2007; Kuhlmann, 2009a, p. 199 et seq.). Thus, the typology of administrative reform can be summarized as Figure 2.4 illustrates.

Since the emergence of the NPM movement in the 1980s, a number of comparative studies have dealt with the NPM concept diffusion, their implementation, and in some cases also with the effects of these administrative reforms (see among others, Naschold, 1995; Olsen and Peters, 1996; Flynn and Strehl, 1996; Kickert, 1997; Lane, 1997; Peters and Savoie, 1998; Naschold et al., 1999; Pollitt and Bouckaert, 2004; Wollmann and Schröter, 2000; Naschold and Bogumil, 2000; Christensen and Laegreid, 2001a, 2010; Wollmann, 2003b, 2003c). By turning its back on the concept of an expansive welfare state and the 'classic-bureaucratic' (Weberian) administration, the NPM reform movement, whose pioneers and international role models include primarily the Anglo-Saxon countries (United Kingdom, New Zealand), focused on two essential objectives. For one, NPM aimed at redefining and limiting the action radius of the state, strengthening market mechanisms, promoting competition and boosting the position of the citizen as customer. The thrust of this direction can be interpreted analytically as the macro-dimension of NPM (Schröter, 2011, p. 79). Second, the internal structures, organizational principles and personnel profiles of public administration were to be restructured according to the micro-economics–inspired model of a managerial state. This was to take place in particular by installing economic incentive mechanisms, implementing business management know-how, breaking up hierarchical structures, and

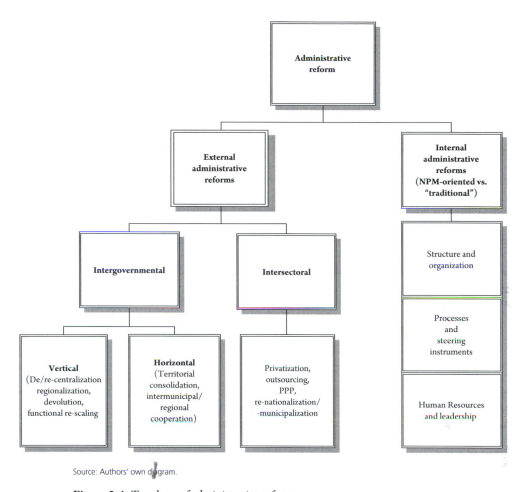

Source: Authors' own diagram.

Figure 2.4 Typology of administrative reforms

carrying out a clear separation of functions and roles regarding politics and administration. This bundle of measures can be considered the internal structural micro-dimension of NPM (ibid.) and results in the following model of NPM modernization in Figure 2.5.

The NPM reform movement was interpreted as a comprehensive convergence process of administrative systems due to the striking prevalence of the NPM discourse in the international context; it was seen to follow a sequential phase going from the welfare state via the neoliberal and managerial state to the 'guaranteeing' and 'enabling' state (Holmes and Shand, 1995; OECD, 1995). However, empirical research has challenged these rather normatively oriented convergence hypotheses as a result of more differentiated findings (see Chapter 4, Sections 4.4 and 4.5).

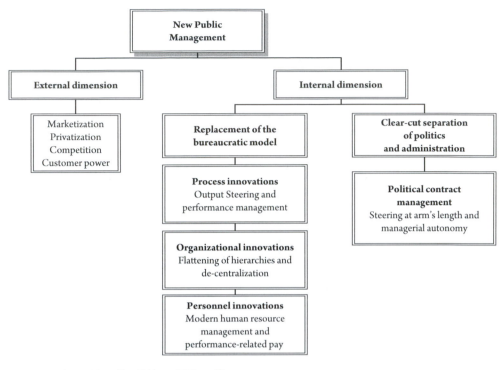

Source: Adopted from Kuhlmann (2009a, p. 45).

Figure 2.5 New Public Management as a reform model

2.2.3 Evaluating administrative reform policies

If the administrative reform discourse (talk), the reform programme (decision) and the concrete action are only loosely linked or even if they clearly diverge, the question regarding implementation and concrete effects of administrative reforms comes to the forefront all the more urgently. However, practice-related administrative reform policy and political evaluation research have so far paid (too) little attention to this issue of effects. The reason for this is related to the problems associated with conception and methodology as well as to issues of political rationality and (non-)desirability of such investigations. On the one hand, administrative reform programmes are associated with specific steering problems. These include the frequent unity of the subject and object of intervention, the initial intervention objective aiming at changes within the political-administrative system, and the importance of guiding principles and reform discourses that are often more (politically) important than the actual implementation of measures (cf. Jann, 2001, p. 330 et seq.; Benz, 2004b, p. 22). For the evaluation of the effects of administrative reforms, this means that this analysis, in contrast to the

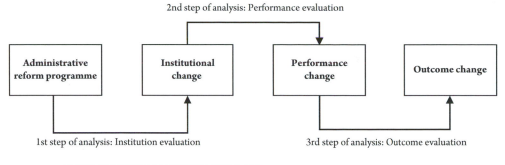

Source: Following Kuhlmann and Wollmann (2011, p. 481).

Figure 2.6 Three steps in the analysis of effects of administrative reform policy

evaluation of sectoral policies, is characterized by a more complex analytic architecture (Wollmann, 2000a, p. 199). In this way, impact analysis in the area of administration reform refers predominantly to institutional changes (e.g., new organization structures), and hence to the first step of analysis (see Figure 2.6). Far less empirical evidence exists, however, with regard to performance evaluation (second step); that is, concrete performance improvements/deterioration in administration such as procedural speed, and cost savings that result from reform measures. The issue that is conceptually and empirically least developed is the investigation into outcome effects of administrative reform (third step), referring to changes in the sphere surrounding the political-administrative system (e.g., enterprise establishment, reduction of unemployment etc.) and therefore characterized by a complex constellation of variables (cf. Kuhlmann, 2009b).

In addition to methodological and conceptual pitfalls (see Wollmann, 2000a, p. 201 et seq.; Kuhlmann et al., 2011), there are also limitations that result from the macro-structures of a country's politico-administrative system. Thus, the subject area of an administrative reform evaluation in the German federal system is extremely fragmented both vertically and horizontally and extraordinarily multifarious. In unitary countries, a central actor often plays a decisive role in the reform process including its evaluation (e.g., the National Audit Commission in the United Kingdom). By contrast, the initiation and implementation of administrative evaluations in Germany have proven to be complicated by the decentralized fragmented structure that is emblematic of the political-administrative system of the Federal Republic of Germany (for Austria, see also Pleschberger, 2009). So far – also in contrast to other countries – there has been at best little interest on the part of parliaments and audit offices to evaluate administrative modernization in the Federal Republic (cf. Färber, 2006, p. 116 et seq.). Yet, this disinterest is presumably due to the results of such studies, at least in cases where critical or even poor 'track records' are to be expected and that run counter to the actors' political image cultivation. A further difficulty lies in the general pursuit of several objectives by the initiators of administrative reforms (Pollitt and Bouckaert, 2004, p. 6), which are by no means free of contradictions (Boyne et al., 2003, p. 13 et seq.; Wollmann and Bouckaert, 2006; Kuhlmann and Wollmann, 2011). The objectives of administrative interventions are frequently ill defined and in many areas subsequent readjustments in different directions can be observed. The evaluation and weighting of individual dimensions can vary according to perspective and affiliation to different groups of stakeholders (cf. Connolly et al., 1980; Boyne et al., 2003, p. 14; Enticott, 2004). The simultaneous optimization of several objective dimensions, such as economic efficiency and proximity to citizens, is often precluded (so-called trade-offs).

If one, in spite of these restrictions, attempts to investigate administrative reforms in terms of their results and performance effects, it becomes necessary – as is generally the case for evaluations – to specify suitable evaluation criteria and indicators. The input-output model of the political-administrative system is known from the 'classic' approaches of policy analysis inspired by systems theory (cf. Easton, 1965, p. 112) and has also been incorporated by institutional and democracy research (cf. Scharpf, 1999). From this model, two fundamental dimensions of effects of administrative reforms can be distinguished: first, effects in the area of input legitimacy and, second, effects in the area of output legitimacy. Input legitimacy describes the dimension of citizens' participation and representation by means of the participation opportunities open to them in democratic processes. Output legitimacy includes the quality, efficacy and efficiency of task fulfilment. In addition to these criteria, there is a third, process-oriented dimension, which is conceptually informed by the throughput argument (Zürn 1998, 2000). This is concerned with the vertical and horizontal coordination performance that results from the interaction between different stakeholders of the decision-making and implementation processes. Three main dimensions can be derived from this and that can form the basis for the comparative administrative evaluation of effects (cf. also Pollitt and Bouckaert, 2011; Kuhlmann et al., 2011):

- effects in the area of 'output legitimacy': efficacy, efficiency, productivity;
- effects in the area of management and coordination: vertical and horizontal coordination, interlocking and unbundling of administration;
- effects in the area of 'input legitimacy': democratic control, political responsibility, participation, transparency.

Table 2.7 Analytical dimensions and indicators for evaluating administrative reforms

Performance Criteria	Analytical Dimensions/Indicators
	(1) Output legitimacy
Resources, costs, outputs	Expenditure (personnel, time, finances)
	Savings realized; amount of services 'produced'
	input-output-ratio
Legal quality/achievement of policy-objectives	Compliance with quality/auditing standards
	Legal correctness; legal disputes
	Proximity to citizens/customer friendliness/service quality
	Efficacy, problem solving, target group relevance
	(2) Coordination/throughput legitimacy
Horizontal and vertical coordination	Cross-departmental coordination
	Inter-municipal cooperation
	Cross-level coordination; friction losses
	Control/intervention 'from above'
	Willingness to follow/subversion/resistance 'from below'
	Vertical/horizontal interlocking/unbundling tendencies
	(3) Input legitimacy
Democratic control	Participation of the council
	Citizen participation; user democracy
	External transparency
	(4) Regional variance/disparities; differences in performance

Source: Authors' own summary, following Kuhlmann (2010b, p. 118).

Sweeping across these three areas of effects can be added the increase and decrease in performance differences and disparities in an inter-organizational/regional comparison as a dimension. This can be used to determine the extent to which specific reform measures (e.g., task decentralization) lead either to increased disparities between different administrative units or else to harmonization/unitarization. Put more simply, the evaluation matrix for administrative reforms may look as in Table 2.7 (cf. Kuhlmann, 2010b; Reiter et al., 2010; Kuhlmann et al., 2011, p. 53 et seq.).

2.3 Explaining administrative reforms: neo-institutionalist approaches

Neo-institutionalist theories have found growing attention and acceptance in the analysis and explanation of administrative reforms, transformations and also system persistence from a national and international comparative perspective. Therefore, this book highlights these theories as well. Examples of their use can be found, for example, in institutional transformation research (see Lehmbruch, 1993; Wollmann, 1995, 1996a, 1997a; Eisen, 1996a, 1996b; Kuhlmann, 2003); in administrative reform research, in particular on New Public Management (cf. Reichard, 2001; Schröter, 2001; Wollmann, 2002a; Pollitt and Bouckaert, 2004); in (comparative) local government research (cf. Röber and Schröter, 2004; Wollmann, 2004, 2008; Holtkamp, 2008; Kuhlmann, 2008, 2009a; Baldersheim and Rose, 2010a, p. 5 et seq.); in civil service research (cf. Peters, 1996; Raadschelders and Rutgers, 1996); and in administration-oriented Europeanization research (Kassim et al., 2000; Knill, 2001; Goetz, 2006). The different approaches of neo-institutionalism offer the opportunity to analyse administrative systems and reforms relating to their developmental formation factors ('starting conditions') on the one hand, and their impact mechanisms on the other. In this, institutions are assigned a focal analytic position as an explanatory variable. Common to all neo-institutionalist approaches is the conviction that institutions contain a structural suggestion as to actor behaviour (Dowding, 1995, p. 44). This results in having both an enabling as well as limiting effect in the political process, but without determining the behaviour of politico-administrative actors. The area of New Institutionalism in political and administrative science thus does not represent a simple reception of the classic institutionalist approaches (cf. Selznik, 1957; Loewenstein, 1969; Rokkan, 1970), which has been the focus of political theory since the times of ancient political philosophy and largely limited to fundamental constitutional structures (formal regulatory function of institutions). Neither does a neo-institutionalist perspective represent a complete rejection of behaviourist or political-sociological concepts in comparative political science. 'Rather', as Kaiser (1991, p. 191) points out, 'one can recognize here the aspiration of all variants of New Institutionalism to add an institutional perspective to contemporary social science theories – with varying "mixes"'.

What is undisputed today is the fact that there is no such thing as *the* New Institutionalism in political science (Edeling, 1999, p. 7; Kaiser, 1999, p. 196): 'The "new institutionalism" is not one thing but many' (Goodin, 1996, p. 2). Since the late 1970s, and in terms of the history of the theory, this can be explained by institutions having been 'rediscovered' as important determining factors of social action among a variety of social science disciplines – economics, sociology, political and administrative science, public law and others – independently of one another. At the same time, representatives of these variants of institutionalist theories took little notice of one another – despite similar theoretical positions – and communication between the different 'camps' did not, in effect, take place (cf. Edeling, 1999, p. 7).

In the following, three variants of neo-institutionalist approaches will be highlighted (cf. also Hall and Taylor, 1996; Kaiser, 1999):[16]

- the variant of rational choice or actor-centred institutionalism;
- the variant of sociological institutionalism;
- the variant of historical institutionalism.

These three neo-institutionalist approaches each contain different assumptions and models to explain institutional change and actor behaviour in institutional contexts. Put simply, rational choice institutionalism assigns the function of exogenous action control to actors who are seen to be essentially guided by utility-maximizing and by (bounded) rationality. Sociological institutionalism, in contrast, includes cultural features, normative frames and cognitive scripts in its concept of institutions. It is concerned with the neuralgic link between the formalized institutional rules and their socio-cultural anchoring 'in the minds' and behaviour of actors. Economics-oriented institutional approaches emphasize still more strongly the freedom of action of benefit-maximizing (egoistic) actors. In contrast, sociologically oriented approaches of the New Institutionalism prefer to be more concerned with the structural restrictions, normative frames and social rules that shape actor behaviour and limit their freedom of action. As such, New Institutionalism still contains – albeit with distinctions and to a lesser extent – the duality of economics (*homo oeconomicus*) and sociology (*homo sociologicus*), which Duesenberry alluded to in his often-cited dictum[17] (critically: Edeling, 1999, p. 8). Historical institutionalism especially homes in on not only the forces that shape institutions in the long term, but also on practised action and action-guiding cognitive-mental patterns that lead to path-dependent developments due to their persistence.

2.3.1 Rational choice or actor-centred institutionalism

In rational choice or actor-centred institutionalism (Mayntz and Scharpf, 1995; Scharpf, 2000; further Burns et al., 1985; Zürn 1992; Ostrom et al., 1994), institutions are seen as limitations of rational choices (Dowding and King, 1995; Peters, 1999, p. 43 et seq.). The starting point here is the consideration that rationally acting individuals would not be capable of cooperation in the absence of an institutional framework. By structuring the strategic action of groups and individuals, and enabling reciprocal predictability, institutions offer a way out of the cooperation dilemma in collective action situations. According to this view, they represent the external, social parameters of rational choices that 'take into consideration actors striving for an individual benefit when they make rational decisions in pursuit of their interests' (Edeling, 1999, p. 9). The underlying assumption is that actor behaviour is directed in principle at the maximization of individual benefits, based on a fixed repertoire of preferences (preference order) and building on a cost–benefit calculation that is (bounded) rational.

For comparative public administration, rational choice institutionalism is useful in analytic terms for several reasons. First, the freedom of choice of political and administrative actors can be conceived of as an independent variable. Freedom of choice can refer to, for example, the initiation (or prevention) of institutional reform programmes as well as to the implementation of measures (or the occurrence of reform resistance and blockades). Thus, the coming into existence (or not) of administrative reforms, and the retention of institutional patterns or their upheaval can be explained from the perspective of bounded rationality and benefit-seeking actors. It is particularly important in the comparative analysis of administrative reforms and discourses (see Chapter 4) to conceive of these freedoms of action and strategic calculations of actors as explanatory factors, and to separate this analytically from the institutional context. Actor-oriented institutionalism makes this possible by assuming an analytical and empirically useful separation of institutional structure and freedom of action and does not equate 'institution' with 'culture' and 'action' (see also Mayntz and Scharpf, 1995, p. 46).[18]

The behaviour of politico-administrative actors is thus not determined solely or largely by the institutional contexts in which they operate or the cultural circumstances within which they are embedded. Rather, it is largely dependent on their preferences and strategic calculations. As such, they must be considered a causal explanation of administrative reforms. From the perspective of actor-oriented institutionalism, the functioning of institutions, their reality, efficiency and performance, too, is dependent on the strategies and constellations of actors. Accordingly, reform processes should lead to very different results and performance effects in different contexts, depending on actor constellations, interests and 'political will and skill' (cf. Shonfield, 1965,

p. 63). Thus, actors can, for example, resist the implementation of particular reform measures, should these run counter to their preferences and interests (cf. Benz, 2004b, p. 22), and insofar as they form relevant advocacy coalitions (cf. Sabatier, 1993) within the given institutional context. In light of this, different results and effects of institutional reforms can be explained, in particular by different constellations of actors, modes of interaction, and by perceptions, preferences and skills of actors.

Some proponents of rational choice institutionalism (cf. Horn, 1995; Richter and Furubotn, 1996) apply the principles of neo-classical micro-economics, which were developed for the analysis of market behaviour, to the investigation of institutional arrangements. As part of this, institutional genesis is viewed as a process of economic optimization, and the rationality to be measured according to economic efficiency becomes the decisive criterion of institution building. Assuming similar benefit functions and economic circumstances, a converging trend towards a similar economic optimum can be plausibly expected (see further below).

2.3.2 Historical institutionalism

The concept of historical institutionalism (cf. Krasner, 1984; Immergut, 1992; Steinmo et al., 1992; Peters, 1999; Pierson, 2004) is based on the assumption that the preferences and choices of actors are pre-structured by institutional corridors established for the long term (cf. Peters, 1999, p. 63 et seq.). As applicable to administrative systems and reforms, this means that decisions are always to be viewed in the light of long-term institutional developments of the political-administrative system because these are effective as path dependencies and limit the policy alternatives viewed by the actors (Kaiser, 1999, p. 197). This assumption of a 'path-dependent' development clearly drops the focus on to the historically shaped institutional forces. These limit the scope of possibilities of administrative reforms and are the reason why institutions, and thus also national administrative models, appear to be 'relatively persistent features of the historical landscape and one of the central factors pushing historical development along a set of paths' (Hall and Taylor, 1996, p. 941; cf. also Baldersheim and Rose, 2010a, p. 10 et seq.). According to this interpretation, an administrative system can be considered as a configuration of collective actors with their own behavioural resources, objectives and interests, and one that has become entrenched during a process of institutionalization and whose modes of interaction are also largely institutionalized (Lehmbruch, 1996, p. 118). The politico-administrative actors move along a developmental path 'whose scope is determined to a considerable extent by the structures established in the past, handed-down situational interpretations and practised strategic patterns' (ibid., p. 119). Thus, it is the 'policy legacies' of current administrative reforms that shape the corresponding administrative system; as basic patterns of problem perception these legacies also tend to shape problem-solving in novel circumstances such as crises. The answers to newly emerging problems are pre-structured by existing institutional arrangements and historically ingrained patterns of problem-solving. The scope of options is thus limited by 'path dependency' (ibid.). For this reason, unintended consequences and dysfunctionalities may result if and when existing institutions and problem definitions prove to be unsuitable or inefficient in the face of novel challenges. Although historical institutionalism thus possesses a large amount of explanatory power in terms of institutional continuity, persistence and, at its best, incremental change, it nevertheless also offers conceptual possibilities for explaining transformation, reform and institutional upheaval. The corresponding model is the socalled 'critical juncture'. This 'crossroad' or 'turning point' arises during the course of the institutional path (viewed overall as a continuum) if and when significant and particularly external impulses such as social or economic crises should occur. These can then result in a departure from the 'old' path or lead to a new one being taken.[19]

In view of the remarkable persistence of national administrative systems and traditions also under similar external pressure (Europeanization, NPM discourse, globalization, economic crisis) historical institutionalism almost inevitably comes to mind as an approach. Depending on their corresponding historically shaped institutional contexts and administrative cultures, different European countries have viewed the concurring reform discourses (such as NPM) very differently. But historical approaches also lend themselves as explanations in terms of effects. Thus, identical or similar administrative interventions (e.g., decentralization or NPM) can bring about very different effects in the contexts of the individual countries because of country-specific historical path dependence. The reason for this lies in the fact that they each encounter different, pre-existing institutional arrangements and practised patterns of action. These in turn can have either a promoting or blocking effect on the envisaged reforms and the resulting changes in performance. Furthermore, application and utilization gaps in formally implemented reform instruments (such as management tools, controlling mechanisms, etc.) or performance deficits can possibly be traced back to the persistence and inertia of 'old' 'standard operating procedures'. These procedures are rooted in historically entrenched behavioural, thought and action patterns and, as institutional 'legacies', can retard or counteract reform processes and system change.[20]

2.3.3 Sociological institutionalism

Sociological institutionalism (DiMaggio and Powell, 1991, p. 9; Lepsius, 1995; Edeling, 1999, p. 12; Kaiser, 1999, p. 190) challenges 'methodological individualism'-inspired theories of rational choice as found in economics and sociology. In this approach, institutions are not conceived of as external limitations of rational choices, but rather as 'cultural phenomena' that provide cognitive scripts and normative frames (Lepsius, 1995; Kaiser, 1999, p. 190). The rational choice-inspired idea, under which institutional arrangements are considered merely 'boundaries for benefit-maximizing individuals who act according to a *logic of consequence*' (Kaiser, 1999, p. 194; original emphasis), is countered by the assumption that institutions also define a catalogue of rules of appropriate behaviour in the sense of a logic of *appropriateness*. On the one hand, for example, March and Olsen[21] view institutions as formal arrangements that provide a space where actors find a repertoire of behavioural rules (cf. Eisen, 1996b, p. 36). On the other hand, institutions also contain a 'dimension of orientation', which provides behaviour-structuring guiding principles relating to the purpose of coexistence in a community (Lepsius, 1995, p. 395). Put briefly, one might speak of a 'structural' and 'cultural' dimension (cf. Eisen, 1996a) or of the level of 'system' and 'actor' (cf. Göhler, 1987) of political institutions, which are conceptualized in sociological institutionalism in an 'extended notion of institutions'.[22] From this perspective, formal and informal structures (standard operating procedures) of institutionalized action, as well as collective spheres of meaning and cognitive frames, are viewed as sub-dimensions of institutions; they 'serve as a justification of the political institutions that enable its legitimacy and thus represent an essential basis for their stability' (Eisen, 1996b, p. 35). The functioning of institutions and their performance thus depend on whether and to what extent formal-structural rules are culturally 'enacted' and cognitively internalized. Notwithstanding its limits, noteworthy analytical benefit can be drawn from sociological institutionalism. For one, its 'broad' notion of institution offers the possibility for overcoming dualist models. The latter capture the influence of formal institutions on the one hand, and the current institutional reality on the other, both independently of one another and in separate research contexts. Overcoming such dualist approaches can enable a broader view of social reality in which both dimensions are interwoven and interact with one another. Regarding administrative reform processes and transformations, one can then consider to what extent the formal organizational changes are accompanied by cognitive and socio-cultural adaptation processes and by an alignment of the qualification skills of the actors. Thus, administrative reforms can be explained in light of the tension between the 'structural' and 'cultural' sub-dimensions of institutional reality (Eisen, 1996a, 1996b). Pivotal then is the question regarding the effects of the (potential) conflict between formal rules and cultural reality in administrative institutions. Thus, it is possible that an upheaval in the formal institutions as part of administrative reforms (e.g., decentralization of state tasks) is not compatible with existing cognitive-cultural characteristics, orientations and skills of actors 'on site'.[23] Despite the change and modification in the formal structures, the actors may continue their entrenched routines and modes of action and in this way evade the new rules and 'subvert' reform policy (cf. Benz, 2004b, p. 27). It could occur that the willingness or ability of actors to adjust to the new role requirements is so limited that new institutional rules ultimately do not result in any improvement or even engender dysfunctional effects. A decline in performance or efficiency of political-administrative institutions may be the outcome. If one assumes such a connection between actual performance and the cognitive-cultural acceptance of institutions (in the sense of the 'broad notion of institution'), then the action orientations, entrenched behavioural routines and qualification skills of the actors must be taken into account in order to explain the reform effects.

The transfer of formal structures and rules from one institutional context to another contains cultural 'risks of rejection' if it is not accompanied by cognitive-cultural adjustment processes and an internalization (enacting) of the new rules – at least in the long term (Offe, 1994, p. 46). These risks can lead to malfunctions and performance deficits. Examples of this can be found in NPM reform, such as in the rash adoption of management tools borrowed from the private sector (which particularly posed problems in Continental European public administrations), as well as in administrative transformation processes (e.g., in post-communist Central Eastern European countries). The use of a broad (socio-cultural) notion of institution thus enables the posing of the question as to whether the empirically observable administrative behaviour is shaped by a 'harmonious' interaction between cognitively internalized values and norms ('cultural dimension') on the one hand, and formal-institutional conditions ('structural dimension') on the other, or whether these two dimensions diverge (mismatch). In addition, with regard to administrative reforms and transformations, this allows for an examination of the question of whether formal rules and instrumental innovations are actually incorporated into standard operating procedures, hence into administrative routines, or if these merely exist 'on paper'.

As to their explanatory contribution to the study of administrative reforms, the three variants of New Institutionalism can be summarized in Table 2.8.

Table 2.8 Neo-institutionalist explanations of administrative reforms

Theoretical Approach	Basic Assumptions/Hypothesis	Explanation of Adm. Reforms
Actor-centred/rational choice institutionalism	Institutions limit/enable strategic choices of bounded-rational actors; narrow notion of institution; focus on order-ensuring functions of institutions; logic of benefit maximization and logic of consequence	Reforms result from strategic action/cost–benefit calculations of political and administrative actors, type/structure/power position of advocacy coalitions as reform shaping
Institutional economics	Efficiency/economic optimum as a core criterion of institution building	Institutional reforms as processes of economic optimization; convergence of national administrative systems
Historical institutionalism	Institutional development shaped by historical path dependency; change incurs high costs and is only possible under extreme circumstances (shocks); broad notion of institution	Action corridor for reforms restricted by existing institutions; persistence (inertia) of historically entrenched institutions; comprehensive reform an exception
Sociological institutionalism	Institutions as cultural phenomena; cognitive-cultural anchoring; logic of appropriateness; focus on orientation-ensuring functions of institutions; broad notion of institution	Administrative change due to normative pressure; imitation/isomorphism; cultural risks of rejection of new formal institutions; possible culture–structure mismatch following administrative reform

Source: Authors' own summary.

2.3.4 Convergence, divergence and persistence of administrative systems

In order to explain the convergence, divergence or persistence of national administrative systems (cf. Wollmann, 2000b, p. 22 et seq.; Schröter, 2001, p. 415 et seq., with further references; Kuhlmann, 2007a, 2009a; Christensen and Laegreid, 2010), we will draw on the above-outlined theoretical approaches of New Institutionalism. These offer different answers and explanatory models concerning the question of how institutions develop, what shapes institutions and how institutions and actor behaviour are causally related. In some cases, the hypotheses of the different variants of neo-institutionalism can be utilized to explain both convergence and divergence/persistence, albeit each with a different analytical focus.

The 'convergence hypothesis' is supported by the assumption that the forces of globalization (in particular, world market competition) and internationalization (within the European Union: alignment of legal regulations) will reach a high degree of 'external determinism'. National structures, which until this point have varied widely along with their historical defining factors, will lose more and more impact in the face of this determinism and will yield to an institutional, cognitive and normative alignment. The convergence hypothesis is also sustained by rational choice theory and its derivatives in New Political Economics and the economic theory of bureaucracy. These hypotheses view the significant administrative decisions made by leading administrative officials as being determined by their advantage-maximizing and disadvantage-minimizing calculations (cf. Dunleavy, 1991) which, in the face of similar external challenges, amounts to congruent decision-making.

Furthermore, the concept repertoire of sociological institutionalism, linked with concepts of policy learning, can explain institutional convergence. Thus, DiMaggio and Powell (1991) assume an adaptation 'by learning' up to an imitation of organizational models, so-called 'isomorphism'. This can occur as a result of force (coercive isomorphism), imitation (mimetic isomorphism) or normative pressure (normative isomorphism). From this angle, the convergence of administrative models may take place via the mechanisms of isomorphism relating to the development of administrative systems.

Normative isomorphism in particular emphasizes the explanatory power of ideas, discourses and concepts (cf. Wollmann, 2008, p. 18), which is also highlighted by discursive institutionalism (cf. V. Schmidt, 2008). This notion is closely related to sociological institutionalism, and is founded on the assumption that discourses and ideas thus impact national and international arenas of action, and that they acquire the attention, conviction and allegiance of relevant actors and actor constellations as conceptual and mental 'frames' (framing; cf. Rein and Schön, 1977), providing a guiding framework for their decisions. An example of this is the dominance gained and held by New Public Management maxims since the 1980s in the international modernization debate and practice. The appropriation and propagation of these maxims by influential international organizations (such as the World Bank and the OECD) and their economist-driven advocacy coalitions (cf. Sabatier, 1993) is a powerful explanation for convergence within administrative reform policies in European countries and other global players.

The divergence hypothesis, in contrast, is theoretically associated with historical institutionalism. It is represented by positions that assume that – irrespective of the influence of globalization forces – institutional, cultural and normative factors anchored in political, state and administrative traditions of individual countries or country groups have a continuing determinative effect. These factors also define 'path-dependent' corridors for the further path of discourse and practice.

According to Pollitt (2001), a differentiated examination of convergence and divergence requires a closer look at the different phases of reform processes in the individual countries. With the aim of clarifying convergence, he also suggests a differentiation according to four levels or phases (cf. also Jann, 2006, p. 132), which prove useful for the analytical examination purposes pursued here:

1. Discursive convergence: concepts, guiding principles, discourses.
2. Decisional convergence: reform decisions, adoption of reform programmes and measures.
3. Practice convergence: actual implementation of measures, application of new instruments and structures.
4. Result convergence: results and continuing effects of reform measures.

A brief look at individual country examples is enough to show that discursive convergence, which has been at the centre of many comparative studies (OECD etc.), has by no means resulted in similar implementation measures and certainly not in convergent reform effects. In light of this, the country analyses in this book are also intended to show whether and to what extent specific convergent reform discourses (see also Chapter 4, Section 4.1) have led to similar or markedly different, converging or diverging administrative models in Europe (Christensen and Laegreid, 2010).

NOTES

1 This 'broad' conception of administrative culture includes formal rule systems and the informal, historically entrenched cognitive-cultural action dispositions of administration. It must thus be distinguished from a 'narrow' conception of administrative culture that is limited to the attitudes and thinking patterns vis-à-vis administration as part of the general political culture of a particular country (cf. Jann, 1983; Thedieck, 1992, p. 46 et seq.).

2 A further typology of welfare state refers to the different types of funding (tax funded versus contribution based). While the so-called Beveridge Systems, which are characterized by strong tax funding, might be classified, according to Esping-Andersen, as liberal and social democratic, the so-called Bismarck Systems, which are based primarily on contributions from social insurance schemes, might be classified as conservative (cf. Schmid and Frech, 2004).

3 Country codes: A = Austria; AU = Australia; B = Belgium; BG = Bulgaria; BR = Brazil; CA = Canada; CH = Switzerland; CN = China; CY = Cyprus; CZ = Czech Republic; D = Germany; DK = Denmark; E = Spain, EAU = Uganda; EST = Estonia; F = France; FIN = Finland; GR = Greece; H = Hungary; I = Italy; IND = India; IR = Iran; IRE = Ireland; J = Japan; LT = Lithuania; M = Malta; ME = Mexico; N = Norway; NL = Netherlands; NZ = New Zealand; P = Portugal; PL = Poland; RA = Argentina; RO = Romania;

ROK = Korea; RP = Philippines; S = Sweden; SLO = Slovenia; TR = Turkey; UAE = United Arab Emirates; UK = United Kingdom; USA = United States; VN = Vietnam.

4 Painter and Peters (2010, p. 22 et seq.) term this group of countries 'Germanic', but also assign the Netherlands to this group. As, in our view, the unitary/federalism dimension represents an essential distinctive feature of administrative systems, the term 'Continental European federal nations' (excluding the Netherlands) seems more appropriate.

5 Large areas of Poland were annexed by Austria and Prussia as a result of the so-called Polish Partition of 1772; in 1867, Hungary became part of the Habsburg dual monarchy.

6 Furthermore, the approximately 91 200 municipalities and 1100 second-tier local governments in the EU-27 cover some 50 per cent of overall public employment.

7 The conceptual distinction between 'integrationist' and 'separationist' models was first introduced by Leemans in 1970 (cf. Wollmann, 2008, p. 259 for further references).

8 The multi-purpose model refers to a horizontal, territory-related administrative organization, in which a municipality as a territorial unit combines and executes all tasks relevant to the local community in its own responsibility. On the other hand, the single-purpose model represents a vertical, function-specific administrative organization, in which an area-oriented organizational structure exists from the (centralized) state to the local level, and the political responsibility lies outside of local government (see also Wagener, 1976; Benz, 2002; Wollmann, 2004; Wollmann and Bouckaert, 2006, Bogumil and Jann, 2009, p. 87; Kuhlmann, 2010b, p. 104).

9 As a result of the radical local-level territorial reforms that were carried out in Greece between 1997 and 2001 when the Capodistrias Plan came into effect, the country has conspicuously abandoned its historic 'Southern European pattern' of territorial structure (cf. Hlepas and Getimis, 2010; see also Chapter 4, Section 4.3).

10 These should not be confused with the above-discussed monistic and dual models of responsibility in the (vertical) relationship between central and local government.

11 The following two sub-sections are based largely on Kuhlmann (2010a).

12 Cf. Art 5, Para. 2: 'The Union shall respect the equality of Member States before the Treaties as well as their national identities, inherent in their fundamental structures, political and constitutional, inclusive of regional and local self-government'.

13 For this, see the emphatic joint declaration of German and French municipal umbrella organizations of May 2008, at http://www.rgre.de/fileadmin/redaktion/pdf/resolutionen/erkl_daseinsvorsorge_en.pdf; last accessed 28 February 2014.

14 This does not preclude the possibility that the results or effects thereof are also based on non-intentional effects of initiated reforms or emergent developments.

15 'Internal institutional policy' should not be equated with micro-policy (see Bogumil and Schmid, 2001, p. 103 et seq.; Benz, 2004b, p. 20 et seq.), even though there is considerable overlap. Micro-policy refers to the internal organizational, strategic conflict and consensus-building processes (as in Bogumil and Schmid, 2001) or to 'emergent' organizational development (as in Benz, 2004b). By contrast, the term 'internal institutional policy' introduced here refers to intentional inward-looking institutional reform measures in organizations (as opposed to outward-looking institutional reforms), which include, but are not limited to, micro-policy processes and emergent organizational development.

16 Peters (1999), in contrast, distinguishes between six different neo-institutionalist approaches: normative institutionalism, rational choice institutionalism, historical institutionalism, empirical institutionalism, international institutionalism, societal institutionalism and sociological institutionalism. Goetz, however, limits this to two approaches – 'rational' and historical-sociological – in his analysis of Europeanization logic in public administration (Goetz, 2006, p. 478 et seq.). Ultimately, it is a question of research interest as to which and how many approaches of New Institutionalism one chooses to refer to.

17 'I used to tell my students that the difference between economics and sociology is very simple. Economics is all about how people make choices. Sociology is all about why they don't have any choices to make' (Duesenberry, quoted from Edeling, 1999, p. 8).

18 Thus, the 'broad' concept of institutions used in sociological institutionalism (see below) raises serious problems for empirical institutional research, as it no longer allows for the differentiation between institution and culture necessary for an operationalization of relevant study variables (Kaiser, 1999, p. 196).

According to Mayntz and Scharpf (1995), attempts to 'culturalistically widen' the concept of institution lead to an abandonment of the central theoretical assumption whereby 'the institutional context enables and restricts action, but does not determine it' (ibid, p. 45). Instead, action is often explained in a crypto-deterministic manner, because the overarching concept of institution on the part of actors leaves at best a few idiosyncratic impulses that are hardly accessible to theoretical social-scientific analysis (ibid, p. 46).

19 The explanation for institutional change does, however, pose fundamental problems for historical institutionalism, problems such as regarding the question of the circumstances and constellations that may lead to a 'critical juncture' and the transition to a new institutionalization path (cf. Krasner, 1984; Hall and Taylor, 1996, p. 941 et seq.; Peters, 1999, p. 68 et seq.).

20 In this regard, there are obvious areas of overlap with sociological institutionalism (see below), which is why the two approaches are often viewed together (see Goetz, 2006).

21 March and Olsen's contribution is often cited as a 'manifesto' of neo-institutionalism (cf. March and Olsen, 1984, 1989).

22 The 'broad notion of institution' is based on this dual understanding of institutions as an (objective) structural and (subjective) cultural phenomenon (cf. Göhler, 1987), which is to be distinguished from the institutional understanding of the 'older' institutionalisms (see above).

23 In institutional administrative research, this hypothesis has been examined in particular with regard to the transformation process in East Germany (cf. Eisen, 1996a; Wollmann, 1996a; Kuhlmann, 2003). It was feared 'that West German institutional vessels. . .might run aground in East Germany' (Offe, 1991, p. 79), which did not, however, prove true for the administration (Kuhlmann, 2003).

3

Models and traditions of public administration in Europe: country profiles

 LEARNING OBJECTIVES

At the end of this chapter, you should:

- know and be able to compare the administrative systems and traditions in France, Italy, Germany, Sweden, the United Kingdom and Hungary;

- know the differences between these six countries with regard to state organization, administrative structure and public service;

- know the relevant indicators for quantitative administrative comparisons;

- have an overview of the scope of the public sector, the structuring and task profiles of public administration in a comparison of European countries.

In the present chapter, the different analytical concepts and categories for a comparison of administrative systems as outlined above will be applied to selected European countries. The aim here is to provide an overview of the essential features of state structures, national and decentralized-local administrative systems, including public service and personnel. As part of this, individual countries will be selected as representatives of the country groups listed in Chapter 2, Section 2.1.1) and will be analysed according to a uniform 'matrix':

- for the Continental European Napoleonic country group: France, and for the Southern European subgroup: Italy;
- for the Continental European federal country group: Germany;
- for the Scandinavian country group: Sweden;
- for the Anglo-Saxon country group: the United Kingdom;
- for the Central Eastern European country group: Hungary.

In the compact country profiles, the countries will be treated as representative examples of the respective country group and 'family'; however, in cases where it is required by the guiding question, other countries may briefly be referred to. The conclusion of this chapter comprises a comparison of administrative profiles regarding relevant structural, financial and personnel-related data.

3.1 The Continental European Napoleonic model: France and Italy

3.1.1 France

Basic features of government

In comparative government studies, France with 62 million inhabitants is classified as a semi-presidential system (cf. Steffani, 1995; Hartmann, 2005). Due to the powerful position of the directly elected state president on the one hand, France exhibits a series of features of a presidential hegemony. The president possesses a range of powers, partly with sole authority (the so-called *domaine réservé*), and partly in interaction with the prime minister, so that he 'shall ensure the proper functioning of the public authorities and the continuity of the State' (cf. Article 5 of the Constitution). On the other hand, during times of non-cohabitation,[1] ideological and political agreement regularly reigns between the state president and the parliamentary majority, and, thus, an 'interleaving' between executive and legislative exists. While the French political system functions according to the principle of majority parliamentarianism, a special feature of it is the historically and constitutionally weak position of parliament (so-called 'rationalized parliament'; Kempf, 2003, pp. 301, 316 et seq.). This weakness becomes evident in the appointment of the prime minister by the state president (even though this, in effect, occurs on the basis of the parliamentary majority), among other things. In terms of democracy type (cf. Schmidt, 2000), France is characterized as a 'mixed system', exhibiting elements of both the 'competitive democracy' and the 'consensus democracy'. Thus, in addition to the bicameral system consisting of the Assemblée Nationale and Sénat and a difficult-to-amend written Constitution, on the central state level further bargaining-democratic elements exist. These include the existence of a strong 'obligation to compromise' between both heads of the two-headed executive during cohabitation (Kempf, 2003, p. 307 et seq.). In such periods, the state president must take the majority constellations in parliament into account more strongly when considering his actions, and therefore becomes less autonomous and powerful in his decision-making. In contrast, competitive-democratic elements rise to the surface when there is no cohabitation and the state president can push through his policies without having to consider an opposing parliamentary majority. This was the case during major reforms such as decentralization in the 1980s. In addition, the competitive-democratic direction of the French political system is fostered by the absolute majority voting system and the resulting party political polarization in the National Assembly (*gauche – droite*).

State structure and administrative system

France is a unitary state and was considered one of Europe's most strongly centralized administrative systems until well into the 1980s (Kempf, 2003, p. 340; Pollitt and Bouckaert, 2004). The guiding principles of unity and indivisibility of the Republic (*une et indivisible*) and the state's sovereignty, both internally and externally (*Etat-nation*), has had a lasting effect on the development of institutions. Under its state and administrative tradition, France can be classified as the exemplar of the Napoleonic Continental European state and legalistic system (see above) in which the state is typically assigned a 'value in itself'. Its task is to define the public interest (*intérêt public*) and, following this logic and mandate, to provide comprehensive regulation of social and economic behaviour as well as to pursue economic activities itself (Mény, 1988). This is reflected in the fact that a large proportion of employees in France are in the public sector (approximately 22 per cent) and that the state quota (53 per cent in 2008) is one of the highest in Europe. Moreover, since the post-war period France has significantly extended its public sector, which is mirrored in the expansion of national and local administrative staff (see below).

In institutional terms, the French system is moulded by the tradition of executive centralism, whose roots can be traced back to the *ancien régime* (the 'old order'). The first decentralized institutions were created by the municipal law of 14 December 1789. After these institutions had been curtailed by the revolutionaries (in particular by the Jacobins), Napoleon Bonaparte transformed the institutional system into an executive-hierarchical instrument of centralized government and administration with the law passed on 17 February 1800 (Wollmann, 1999b, p. 194). To this day, a general administrative vertical structure of the central state has persisted, a structure that reaches from Paris to local levels and whose backbone in the 'territory' is the prefect (*préfet*) nominated by central government. The central state also has numerous deconcentrated authorities (*services extérieurs*) spread across the entire country. This model, in which the decentralized local self-government was functionally marginal and the state administration was dominant, survived into the 1980s. The French administration is thus traditionally oriented towards the principle of functionality and is related to the single-purpose model.

Although the French system formally possesses the possibility for comprehensive state control and centralist intervention on the subnational levels, the reality has been what was called 'tamed Jacobinism' (*jacobinisme apprivoisé*; Grémion, 1976). The Jacobinist centralized state exhibits a range of decentralized elements (Mabileau, 1996, p. 25 et seq.). Due to the widespread practice of accumulation of mandates (*cumul des mandats*) by which local mayors can also be members of upper-level representative bodies, including the National Assembly, the mayors have traditionally wielded a strong influence at upper administrative and political levels. Evidence of this is found in the legislative practice of the National Assembly, in which 50 per cent of the deputies consist of mayors (Hoffmann-Martinot, 2003, p. 166 et seq.). Moreover, the Sénat (France's Upper Chamber), which, due to the many *sénateurs* also being local mayors at the same time, has, over the years, proven to be a staunch defender of the institutional and territorial status quo at the subnational levels (Kempf, 2003).

Public administration at subnational levels and local self-government

The local government level and units (called *collectivités locales* or *territoriales*) are considered a part of the *'une et indivisible'* republic (Hoffmann-Martinot, 2006, p. 231 et seq.). According to the 'general competence clause', which was first introduced into French legislation in 1884 (Marcou, 2000, p. 3), the municipal council is responsible for all matters concerning the local community. Now local self-government has a constitutionally codified institutional guarantee, formulated in the first post-war Constitution of 1946 (and today laid down in Articles 34 and 72 of the French Constitution). With the exception of the three big (metropolitan) cities of Paris, Marseille and Lyon, a uniform system of 'municipal charter' exists, which was regulated first in the Code des Communes and later in the CGCT (Code Général des Collectivités Territoriales).

France's three-tier local government structure (*collectivités territoriales*)[2] includes the 27 *régions* (with Corsica), *départements* (101) and municipalities (36569). *Régions* have been introduced by the law passed on 5 July 1972 as a new administrative level and have, as a component of the decentralization reform of 1982 (see below), been recognized as a 'fully-fledged' local self-government level – with an elected regional council (*conseil régional*) and a (council-elected) executive (*président du conseil régional*). At the same time, however, its administrative profile is quite limited (as shown by numbers of staff and organizational structures). The *départements* can be historically traced back to a regional structure that was created 'from above' by the absolutist Bourbon kings so that they could effectively expand their rule. That is why they are fairly territorially homogeneous and cover very extensive areas (averaging approximately 640000 inhabitants). Initially during the French Revolution in 1789, and then again under the pressures of bourgeois liberalism in 1833 and 1871, the election of the *département* representatives (general councils – *conseils généraux*) and that of the general council presidents was codified. Until 1982, however, the prefect still remained the executive of the *départements*. Characteristic of the municipal level is its enormous territorial fragmentation and small-scale nature, which has been termed a 'municipal patchwork'. With its roughly 36600 municipalities, whose territorial structure generally reaches back to the Middle Ages because of largely failed municipal amalgamations (cf. Kerrouche, 2010, p. 162 et seq.), and whose average population lies at around 1600, France can be assigned to the so-called Southern European type (Norton, 1994). Ninety per cent of French municipalities still have fewer than 2000 inhabitants and only 1 per cent have more than 20000 inhabitants. The latter, however, comprises 40 per cent of the French population. In order to fulfil the increasing local services requirements, French municipalities have long since resorted to various association-type solutions (*intercommunalité*), the number of which has increased significantly since the 1970s. As a result, a new, intermediate institutional level has emerged below the *départements* but above the municipalities (cf. Chapter 4, Section 4.3).

The task profile and autonomy of French municipalities remained very limited until the 1980s as they were subject to the strict a priori state supervision (*tutelle*) by the departmental prefect. They generally had no administrative staff of their own and left the administrative implementation of their tasks to the departmental prefects and state authorities. As state and municipal local self-government tasks were thus not separate, but instead organizationally bundled, the traditional French administrative model can be classified as a fused system. If one further takes into account the deconcentrated public administration, with the prefect as a key figure who acted as the most important 'bundling authority', one can also speak of a 'state-centred integrationist model'. With regard to local services, the French model is a conspicuous case of early, functional privatization and contracting out. Although the doctrine of the 'common good' and 'public interest' (*intérêt général/public*) is deemed determinant for many areas of municipal activity and although the local governments also hold formal responsibilities (e.g., in the areas of water, sewerage, waste), these tasks were contracted out to a large extent to private providers as early as the nineteenth century in a first large wave of outsourcing. The model of public–private cooperation in the form of *gestion déléguée* (outsourcing) has become a dominant variant in the delivery of public utilities.

In France, too, the local level possesses a high political-democratic status, which is evinced, among other things, in the relatively high and relatively stable participation in local elections (around 70 per cent). By tradition, the principle of representative democracy has prevailed; hence the right of citizens to elect the municipal council is of major importance and has practically ruled out any additional procedures of direct democracy. In particular, the prominent position of the mayor is characteristic due to *cumul des mandats* (see above). Within the model of dual allocation of rights and responsibilities, the mayor holds extensive competences and not only combines the three functions of monocratic administrative management, council presidency and external local government representation, but is also the representative of the state at the local level (*agent d'Etat*). Albeit formally an indirect election, the French mayoral election system comes in effect very close to a direct election, because the first position of potential candidates on the party list is always assigned to the office of mayor (Mabileau, 1996, p. 65). Consequently, a de facto local presidential system has developed (Mabileau and Sorbets, 1989).

The practice of the *cumul des mandats* that has since long proved an intergovernmental political, institutional and cultural barrier for constitutional changes, has recently, at least in part, undergone a dramatic shift. When running for the French presidency in 2012 François Hollande made the abolition of the *cumul des mandats* a major electoral promise. After he won the presidential elections and the socialists gained the absolute majority of seats in the national parliament in the subsequent general elections, the reform of the *cumul des mandats* was placed onto the legislative agenda. On 9 July 2013 a bill prohibiting the executive position-holders of the municipalities, *départements* and *régions* (i.e., the respective mayors and deputy mayors as well as presidents and vice-presidents) from having a seat in the national parliament or in the Sénat was adopted by the absolute left-wing majority (and against the right-wing opposition) of the Assemblée. The fact that, in contrast to the executive municipal positions, elected councillors (on these three levels) will still be allowed to 'accumulate' a mandate on the national level in the future and that the reform will only become effective in 2017 reflects the compromises that needed to be made with powerful local elites (often called 'grands notables' or nicknamed 'barons'). Even if the bill was to be rejected or amended by the Sénat (in fact, on 19 July 2013 the Sénat adopted an amendment according to which the elimination of the *cumul des mandats* would not apply to the senators themselves) such veto or amendment will probably be overruled by the absolute majority of the Assemblée.[3] Thus, in all likelihood a crucial component of the *cumul des mandats* is going to be dismantled. In the words of the (socialist) Minister of the Interior Manuel Valls this would mark *'une véritable revolution démocratique'* and would, no doubt, remove a major political and institutional obstacle for future constitutional reforms.

Civil service and public personnel

The eminent role of the public service in the French politico-administrative system, as in society as a whole, has been repeatedly elaborated (see Alam, 1998; Meininger, 2000). The French state employs more than half of the overall public sector personnel, making it far and away the largest employer in the country. The political and social key position that the public service traditionally occupies in France can be explained, for one, by the sheer quantitative strength in terms of numbers, presence and visibility on all levels. Second, it has to do with the prestigious status of senior civil servants belonging to the powerful Grands Corps;[4] holding top positions in the whole range of public sector institutions, they are intimately involved in the process of political decision-making.

As is generally the case in the Continental European model, France is also characterized by the separation and hierarchical organization of the public and private legal spheres and employment sectors. The rules of access, training and career trajectory in the public service are separate from 'normal' (that is, non-public) professional careers. French administration is rooted in a long tradition of a professional civil service system, whose legal relationships are regulated in a public-law service statute (*le statut*). This stands in contrast to 'ordinary' employment to which general (civil law) labour legislation applies. The notion of a uniform employment status for public administration prevails and is mirrored in a broad generalization of the civil servant status (*les fonctionnaires/titulaires*) in the public service. This applies to 73 per cent of French public employees (Demmke, 2011, p. 323).[5] The French *fonctionnaires* have the right to strike and thus to defend their interests vis-à-vis public employers, if deemed necessary, by open confrontation. Moreover, the civil servants are legally allowed to participate in trade union activities, a right that is traditionally and extensively exercised by them (Lemmet and Creignou, 2002, p. 19 et seq.). In addition to the distinction of three areas of civil service (Fonction Publique d'Etat – FPE), health service (Fonction Publique Hospitalière – FPH) and territorial administrative service (Fonction Publique Territoriale – FPT), there is furthermore a sectoral differentiation in the form of the Corps systems. This holds true for the civil and health services as well as for the system of professional groups (*cadres d'emplois*) that applied to the local administration service. For the Corps or professional groups, the general statute for French public administrators provides specific statutes that include special regulations for recruitment, career progression and remuneration, among other things. It should be added that with regard to the status of public servants and their tasks, the French public service system does not distinguish between 'sovereign' (*régalien*) and 'ordinary' public tasks – in contrast to the German public service system in which such difference between 'sovereign' and 'ordinary' functions is observed (see Section 3.2).

The French public service is viewed as a closed personnel system (cf. Auer et al., 1996). Due to the Corps system and elitist training courses, recruitment is based on rigid selection procedures that are strongly selective and 'elitist', especially in the area of *haute fonction publique* (top civil servants) (Meininger, 2000). As part of this, selection takes place through the prestigious Grandes Ecoles and is linked to the Concours Général (a rigorous competitive selection procedure). Training courses and access routes to the civil service are separate from the ones available to local services. The postgraduate training for the Senior Civil Service takes place at the Ecole Nationale d'Administration (ENA) in Strasbourg, or – for lower-level executives – at the Institut Régional d'Administration (IRA), covering five regional locations. The key institution for education and training of local administrative staff is the National Centre for the Territorial Administrative Service (Centre National de la Fonction Publique Territoriale – CNFPT), which consists of 1700 members of staff and has its headquarters in Paris and 28 'deconcentrated' regional offices (*délégations régionales*) situated throughout the country. Whereas in some senior positions in the public sector, the so-called *pantouflage*, that is, a switch from the ENA/administration to the private sector is quite frequent (ibid.), career changes as well as personnel-related switching between the public and private sectors are generally difficult and rare. The promotion of civil servants occurs largely according to seniority (*ancienneté*), although performance bonuses are legally provided for as incentives.

Figure 3.1 shows the administrative system of France.

3.1.2　Italy

Like France, Italy can be assigned to the classic Continental European administrative model characterized by the Napoleonic state tradition, which includes a strong orientation towards codified law, Roman law tradition and

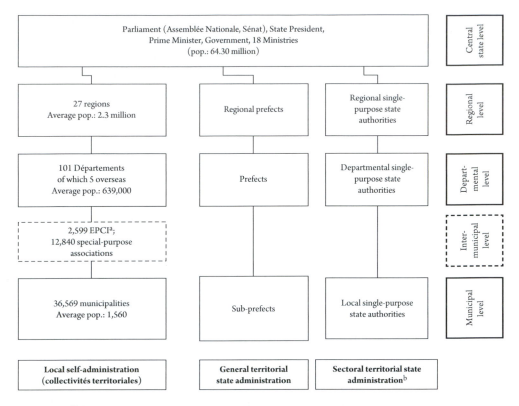

Notes:

a. Bodies of inter-municipal cooperation with fiscal autonomy (own taxes), but without the status of fully-fledged local governments.

b. *Services extérieurs de l'Etat* (under the authority of the respective ministries; territorial coordination by prefect); the area of public health (*hôpitaux publics*) is not shown separately in the figure.

Sources: Authors' own diagram. For further information see: http://www.insee.fr/fr/themes/document.asp?ref_id=ip1276#inter1; http://www.insee.fr/fr/methodes/default.asp?page=definitions/commune.htm; http://www.insee.fr/fr/methodes/nomenclatures/cog/; http://www.dgcl.interieur.gouv.fr/workspaces/members/desl/documents/intercommunalite/bilan_statistique/2012/bilan_statistique_au/downloadFile/file/BilanStat_EPCIaFP_Janv2012.pdf. Last accessed 1 March 2014.

Figure 3.1 Public administration in France (2012)

a centralized administrative organization with a weak local self-government level. Yet, it might be more appropriate to classify Italy – along with Spain, Greece and Portugal – as belonging to a joint Southern European (or Mediterranean) subgroup of Napoleonic Continental European administrative systems (Demmke et al., 2007; Sotiropoulos, 2009; Kickert, 2011, p. 107 et seq.). The reason for the 'Mediterranean' classification can be found in the particularities of the public service and of administrative culture that the countries of this subgroup share, particularly with regard to pronounced (party) politicization of the public service, clientelism in the appointment of administrative positions, and patronage in public service.

Basic features of government

When unified in 1861, Italy with its 60 million inhabitants was, notwithstanding the different traditions of its regions, turned into a unitary centralized state under the rule of the kingdom of Sardinia-Piedmont, with a Constitution oriented towards the French Napoleonic state model (Statuto Albertino). Under fascism, the unitary centralized organizational principle was intensified. After the end of the war, on 2 June 1946, a referendum abolished the monarchy. The new republican Constitution adopted by the constituent assembly came into force on 1 January 1948. Although the new Constitution was meant to break with Italy's centralist Napoleonic state tradition by establishing a decentralized (regionalized) unitary state, the creation of the 20 regions prescribed by it – five regions with 'special statute' (*regioni a statuto speciale*) and 15 with 'normal statute' (*regioni a statuto ordinario*) – remained initially to a large extent unrealized until the 1970s. It was only in the wake of a deep domestic political crisis triggered by corruption scandals and leading to the collapse of the worn-out party system (dominated by the Democrazia Cristiana) that decentralization was decisively propelled (cf. Brunazzo, 2010, p. 185 et seq.). The political rise of the separatist Lega Nord in Lombardy further ignited the debate about a federalization of the country. With the constitutional reform of 2001 – decided for the first time by national referendum – a major step was taken towards further decentralization, in particular by strengthening the legislative and functional responsibilities of the regions. According to the new Article 114 of the Constitution of 2001, 'the republic consists of municipalities, provinces, metropolitan cities, regions and the state'. All territorial bodies – from municipalities to the state (which is, *nota bene*, mentioned last in the constitutional provision) – are *de jure* put on an equal level. The constitutional reform of 2001 was seen by some as leading Italy's inter-governmental system towards 'quasi-federalization' (according to Bobbio, 2005, p. 29). By contrast, other voices, including the influential constitutional court (Corte Costituzionale), hold on to the traditional notion of the 'unitary' form of state (cf. Schefold, 2007, p. 27, with references). An even further-reaching constitutional reform, which would have transformed Italy into a fully-fledged federal state, did not, however, receive the necessary majority in the national referendum of 25–26 July 2006 (cf. Bull, 2007).

Italy has a parliamentary system composed of two chambers, the Camera dei Deputati and the Senato della Repubblica, a Chamber of Deputies with 630 members (elected for five years) and a Senate with 315 members.[6] Both chambers have almost identical responsibilities in the legislative procedure, making Italy the only European country to have such a system (also known as *bicameralismo perfetto*). As a result of the electoral reform of 2005, Italy has a system of proportional representation.[7] However, the law also awards a large premium to the winning party or coalition, in the Camera as well as in the Senato, that is, 55 per cent of the seats on national level for the former and 55 per cent in the latter on the basis of the election regions in the individual regions.[8]

The government is made up of the Council of Ministers (Consiglio dei Ministri) and the prime minister (Presidente del Consiglio dei Ministri). To form a government the prime minister, who is formally nominated by the state president, and the cabinet require the consent of both chambers. Both officials can be forced to retire by a vote of no confidence in at least one of the two chambers. Each minister is responsible for his or her department (the departmental principle). The prime minister is *primus inter pares*, without the authority to set policy guidelines. The state president is indirectly elected for seven years by parliament and by three representatives from each of the 20 regions. He or she can nominate the prime minister, influence the legislative process and, as a last resort, dissolve either of the chambers of parliament. The Constitutional Court (Corte Costituzionale) has significant judicial competences and has become an influential and respected constitutional player. It consists of 15 judges, a third of which are elected by the president, a third by parliament and a third by other upper courts.

In recent years Italy's political system has entered a critical stage in which basic constitutional and institutional problems and frictions ('bicameralism'; parliamentary system with a weak *primus inter pares* prime minister; the underlying '*porcellum*' electoral system; the inter-governmental architecture, particularly at the level of the province) have been aggravated by its rampant economic and budgetary plight. The political, constitutional and institutional crisis has manifested itself and climaxed in a rapid sequence of government changes: the resignation of Berlusconi's Popolo della Libertà (PdL)-led right-wing government was followed by the formation of a 'technocrat' (a sort of 'grand coalition') interim government under Mario Monti, which, in turn, was prematurely terminated in December 2012 when Berlusconi decided to 'pull out the plug' (*staccare la spina*) from the Monti government. The subsequent general elections held in March 2013 ended in a political stalemate as, resulting from the '*porcellum*' electoral system, the Chamber of Deputies came to be dominated by a centre-left Partito Democratico (PD)-led majority, while in the Senate Berlusconi's right-wing PdL prevailed. In order to overcome the threatening 'ingovernability' of the country, a 'grand coalition'-type (*larga intesa*) government, carried by the PD and the PdL, was formed under Prime Minister Enrico Letta who is a junior PD politician. The prime minister's political programme, which was initially supported by both coalition partners, aims at far-reaching constitutional and institutional reforms (reform of electoral system, possible move towards a semi-presidential system, remoulding the subnational levels). Prime Minister Letta vowed to attain these (ambitious) reform goals 'within 18 months', that is, by October 2014. Recently, however, Italy's political system and political process has again been tossed into deep turbulence and uncertainty: after the scandal-ridden ex-Prime Minister Silvio Berlusconi was finally convicted of fiscal fraud on 1 August 2013 by the country's highest court (Corte Suprema di Cassazione) and sentenced to four years of imprisonment, the PdL, in an all but desperate attempt to keep its founder and leader Berlusconi in the political arena and game, threatened to topple the Letta coalition government unless a 'political solution' was found to 'save' Berlusconi's political career. Berlusconi's smashing defeat in 2013 can be interpreted as sealing the end of 20 years of his domination of Italy's political arena.[9] On the basis of a spectacularly won vote of confidence (and the distinctive political victory over Berlusconi) Prime Minister Letta has obviously secured himself the government mandate to put into effect far-reaching constitutional and institutional reforms.

State structure and administrative system

As the decentralization of the historically centralized state model was stipulated in the Constitution of 1947, but was realized only gradually, the state administration initially continued to be shaped by its traditionally centralized (Napoleonic) administrative hierarchy. The persistent hierarchical structure was evidenced in the central ministries in Rome and their subnational administrative units, in particular at the level of the 100 provinces. For the latter, a key role was played by the prefectures, which were adopted historically from the French *département* structure, as well as the prefects (*prefetti*) appointed by and hierarchically subordinate to central government. Aiming to overcome this centralized state organization by transferring administrative tasks 'downwards', the 'administrative decentralization' (*decentramento amministrativo*) was introduced in the late 1990s. In the new Article 117, the Constitution of 2001 went so far as to stipulate that 'administration is generally a matter of the municipalities', thus introducing a presumption of general competence of municipalities, that is, of local self-government, for administrative tasks. However, on the level of the provinces, state administration continues under the responsibility of the central government-appointed *prefetto*. The strong organizational and function importance that state administrative authorities still have in the subnational area is expressed by the fact that even now, 55 per cent of the entire public personnel force are employed by the state, of whom most (especially teachers) are placed outside Rome at the provincial and municipal level.

As a result of the reform of 2001, the provinces were recognized and introduced as a level of local self-government (with elected councils) in their own constitutional right (Article 114 of the Constitution).[10] Consequently, the state province authorities, rooted in Italy's centralized administrative history, and the new provincial self-government bodies exist side by side on the territory of the provinces – similar to the traditional 'dual structure' of the French *départements*, thus adding another level of subnational self-government between the regions and the municipalities (*comuni*).

Public administration at subnational levels and local self-government

The strong position that the regions have on Italy's subnational level is based, for one, on the indirect influence they wield on national policy-making through the Senate, that is, the Upper Chamber. As most members of the Senate are elected within the bicameral system on the basis of regions, the Senate is ascribed the constitutional function of being 'representative of the regions'. The regions (alongside the members of the Chamber of Deputies and the Senate) also participate in the election of the state president, with 58 electors being designated by the regions. Second, and most importantly, the strong position of the regions can be attributed to the wide legislative responsibilities that have been granted to them by the constitutional reform of 2001 (see Chapter 4, Section 4.2). According to Article 117 of the Italian Constitution, the regions have legislative powers for all matters that are not explicitly reserved for national legislation. This applies in particular to so-called 'concurrent legislation' (*legislazione concurrente*), which hinges on a distribution of legislative competences (between the central state and the regions) according to which in many legislative matters the national legislator (that is Chamber of Deputies and the Senate) can only pass 'framework provisions'. It is left to the individual regions to fill in detailed provisions through regional legislation. An example of this is the legal regulation of social benefits where national legislation can define the 'essential standard' (*livello essenziale*), but important details need to be spelt out by each region individually. This has led to significant interregional differences in legislation and exacerbates the existing socio-economic disparities between regions. The tension between the constitutional imperatives (equality, etc.) of the unitary state and the often markedly different regional quasi-federal legislation has surfaced in numerous cases before the Constitutional Court. In its rulings the Constitutional Court has positioned itself as an advocate of the unitary state-related constitutional premises and of a correspondingly restrictive interpretation of the regions' legislative powers. Since 2000, the presidents (*presidenti*) of the regions, who until then were elected by the regional parliaments, are now being elected directly; an alteration that has significantly buttressed their political weight within regional politics and in relation to the central government in Rome.

The some 8100 municipalities (*comuni*) have an average of 7400 inhabitants with 71 per cent of them having fewer than 5000. The 110 provinces (with an average of 550000 inhabitants) traditionally constitute the lower state administrative level (headed by the central government-appointed *prefetto*) and, since the reform of 1994, the upper tier of local self-government. As explained above, first governmental decrees and subsequently, responding to a ruling of the Constitutional Court, constitutional legislation have been initiated, aiming to deprive the provincial level of its local self-government status and functions, as well as halving their number and hence enlarging the territorial range of the provinces as bearers of administrative state functions.

The persistent fragmentation on the municipal level might be explained by the fact that the mandate of the Constitution of 2001 (Article 118) to transfer administrative tasks to the municipalities has hardly been effected so far (cf. Schefold, 2007, p. 61). As a part of the comprehensive reforms of the 1990s, the direct election of the mayor (*sindaco*) was introduced in 1993, leading to a significant strengthening of their 'executive leadership'. As to administrative capacity, profound socio-economic disparities exist between the large and relatively wealthy cities in the north and the multitude of small municipalities. The functional importance of the subnational levels is embodied in their share of the total public expenditure. The regions spend about 20 per cent of the total public expenditure due to the financial commitments they have in connection with the public health system (Servizio Sanitario Nazionale) that was established in 1978. By contrast, the provinces and municipalities carry 10.4 per cent of the total public expenditure, the lion's share of which falls to the municipalities. The proportion of personnel employed by the local government levels compared to the entire public sector personnel shows a similar picture. Municipal and provincial employees account for only 14 per cent of the total number of public personnel, of whom 86 per cent in turn are employed by the municipalities and only 13 per cent by the provinces (in their local self-government function).

Civil service and public personnel

Italy's public service law, in force until the 1980s was characterized by unilateral appointment, career system, lifelong appointment, and so on, and was thus similar to German public service law and status. Since the 1980s, by legislative decree, the previous system has been made subject to private labour law and the collective bargaining made on this basis. An agency (Agenzia per la Rappresentanza Negoziale delle Pubbliche Amministrazioni – ARAN) acts as the representative of all public employers. The latter concludes collective agreements with the trade unions. Since the public law status of public employees has been replaced by private law labour contracts, disputes are now dealt with before civil law/labour courts. However, a 'two-track' and a 'mixed' system still persist (cf. Schefold, 2007, p. 82). Those public employees who are in charge of 'sovereign' tasks (public prosecutors, prefects, the police, etc.) continue to be considered as public officials under public law. This, however, now applies only to 15 per cent of public employees, whereas 85 per cent of them are private law contract staff (Demmke, 2011, p. 323).

As mentioned above, typically for Italy and the Southern European group of countries overall, the appointment of administrative (managerial) positions is characterized by a large degree of patronage. Furthermore, the political parties exert significant influence on recruitment and promotion in public administration. Although appointment and promotion in the public sector are regulated according to the Weberian model of formal access and qualification requirements, in reality, the practice is often quite different. Thus, the officially specified formal access regulations are often bypassed, for instance, by turning the fixed-term contracts into permanent contracts in the case of employees who attained an administrative position thanks to political or family 'connections' (cf. Cassese, 2002; for Spain: Alba, 1998; for Greece: Spanou, 2001). This mechanism also plausibly explains the expansion of public service personnel, which these countries have seen. Although various forms of such 'spoils systems', for instance, the political appointment of senior civil servants, are also familiar in other countries (France, Germany), it can conceivably be said that the extreme dimension, if not the 'excess', of political clientelism of party patronage and politicization in public administration are indeed a characteristic of the Southern European country group.

Figure 3.2 presents the structure of the Italian administrative system.

3.2 The Continental European federal model: Germany

Basic features of government

The Federal Republic of Germany (82 million inhabitants) belongs to the type of parliamentary systems that, despite a formal horizontal separation of powers, are characterized by a sort of de facto conflation of government and

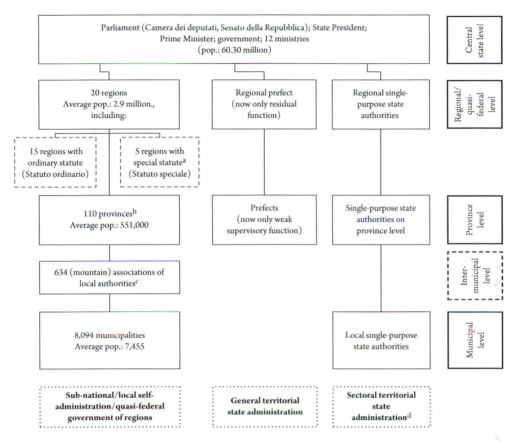

Figure 3.2 Public administration in Italy (2012)

Notes:

a. In regions with special statutes, the administrative organization varies in some cases.

b. Reduction of the number of provinces (from 100 to 50) has come under discussion, in late 2012, as one of the measures within the so-called 'spending review' initiated by the Monti government to reduce the costs of public administration. In the meantime (as of the beginning of 2013) the ultimate fate of the reform has become quite uncertain.

c. Without status of fully-fledged local government.

d. Subject to the respective ministries; territorial coordination by prefect; the area of public health (Servizio Sanitario Nazionale – SSN) with 171 local sub-units (*aziende sanitarie locali* – ASL) is not shown separately in the figure.

Sources: Authors' own diagram; further information from: http://demo.istat.it/bilmens2011gen/index02.html; http://www.comuniverso.it/index.cfm?Tutti%20i%20d&E2%t80%99Italia&menu=169; http://demo.istat.it/bilmens2011gen/index02.html; http://demo.istat.it/bil2010/dati/regioni.zip. Last accessed 1 March 2014.

parliamentary majority. Relatively strong within the national executive branch is the position of the head of government (Federal Chancellor), which has also been termed 'chancellor democracy' (cf. Rudzio, 2003, p. 283 et seq.). The 'monocratic chancellor principle', which includes the power to set policy guidelines (*Richtlinienkompetenz*), to form the government as well as the organizational authority of the Federal Chancellor, is intended to promote the consistency of the federal government and its capacity to act. The actual scope of the head of government depends, however, on the political circumstances, in particular on the coalition constellation (e.g., the smallest possible versus a grand coalition) and the position in his or her own party. In addition, in government practice, the 'chancellor principle' (*Kanzlerprinzip*), which is epitomized in the – rarely employed – *Richtlinienkompetenz* (policy-making power of the chancellor), is frequently in conflict with the 'cabinet principle' (*Kabinettsprinzip*) prescribing joint decision-making by the entire cabinet for specific decisions. Further conflicts can arise with the 'departmental principle' (*Ressortprinzip*) whereby each minister directs his respective department under his own responsibility within the guidelines set forth by the chancellor (cf. Bogumil and Jann, 2009, p. 90 et seq.). The German political system exhibits both competitive and consensus democracy-related elements. The former implies the strong position and high organizational degree of the political parties, and the dominance of party competition (with a tendency towards a 'political party state'). Consensus/bargaining democratic elements are in particular the federal state structure, specifically the variant of cooperative federalism with a pronounced horizontal and vertical interweaving of politics (*Politikverflechtung*). This shows up, inter alia, in the Federal Council (*Bundesrat*) model, in 'administrative federalism' (see below), in the system of inter-governmental revenue sharing (approximately 70 per cent of national tax revenue are 'shared revenues', *Gemeinschaftssteuern*), in financial equalization transfers, 'mixed' financing, federal level/*Länder* cooperation as well as in horizontal self-coordination of the *Länder* (Scharpf et al., 1976; Benz et al., 1992; Kropp, 2010, p. 49 et seq.). In addition, the strong position of the Federal Constitutional Court, the difficult-to-amend federal Constitution, the combination of proportional representation and majority voting, and an extended corporatism, all strengthen the bargaining-democratic orientation (Schmidt, 2000).

State structure and administrative system

Its vertical fragmentation and the many veto actors involved in the political process, have resulted in the German political system being classified as a 'semi-sovereign state' (cf. Katzenstein, 1987). For one, the *Länder*, that is, the *Länder* governments/executives, have a significant influence on federal legislation (hence identified by some as 'executive federalism') based on their veto powers in the Federal Council; at the same time their own legislative competences are becoming increasingly curtailed. This is because the federal government has made extensive use of the so-called 'concurrent legislative competence' (*konkurrierende Gesetzgebung*), which has, however, been relativized in part through the 'federalism reform' of 2006 (Kropp, 2010, p. 209 et seq.). Second, the *Länder* and local governments have a strong position within the German federal system because they are in charge of implementing most of federal legislation and federal programmes (as well as of the rapidly rising 'flood' of EU regulations and programmes), while the federal government can have its own administrative offices on the regional and local levels only in areas specifically enumerated in the federal Constitution (e.g., in the areas of customs, finance, water and shipping, federal defence administration and, as the organizationally most important exception, the Federal Labour Agency with regional and local field offices; cf. Article 83 and 86 of the Basic Law). Thus, Germany is characterized by a highly decentralized administrative system in which administrative functions are predominantly carried out on the subnational levels, particularly by local authorities. This manifests itself in the distribution of public sector personnel by government levels. While only 12 per cent of the entire public sector workforce are federal personnel, 53 per cent are employed by the *Länder* and 35 per cent by the local government levels.

Recently, several important changes have occurred in the multi-level system in the course of reforms of the federal system, changes that were pursued in an attempt to disentangle, decentralize and increase competition. With the so-called Federalism Reform I of 2006, the framework legislation of the federal government level was abolished. Parts of the concurrent legislation and legislative matters that had been previously regulated by the federal framework legislation were divided up between the federal level and the *Länder*. Furthermore, the approval requirement by the Federal Council for laws was changed to reduce the number of federal laws that needed approval, and joint tasks (*Gemeinschaftsaufgaben*) were newly regulated (Bogumil and Jann, 2009, p. 77). In this context, the previously uniform regulatory framework for *Länder* and municipal public employees was also eliminated so that, with regard to *Land* and municipal personnel, public service law, including public service salaries, pension schemes, and so on, are now largely the responsibility of the *Länder* (see Chapter 4, Section 4.5.4). In Federalism Reform II in 2009, the focus was on the codification of a debt ceiling (*Schuldenbremse*) and the introduction of a facultative provision on performance comparisons/benchmarking between the administrations of different levels (Article 91d of the Basic Law; Kuhlmann, 2011, p. 159).

Public administration at subnational levels and local self-government

The decentralized organization of the administrative system through the inter-governmental distribution of competences and strong local self-government is emblematic of German federalism. In this, the implementation variant prevails where the *Länder* carry out federal as well as *Land* legislation as 'their own' matter. Thus, they have a wide scope of action, but have to carry the resulting costs. In contrast, other variants, such as the so-called 'administration mandated by the federal level' (*Bundesauftragsverwaltung*) or the 'federal execution of federal legislation' (*Bundesvollzug von Bundesgesetzen*) are quantitatively less relevant. As each of the *Länder* individually determines its administrative structure, there are large variations among them. Because of this, one must distinguish between the three-tier and two-tier *Länder*.[11] The three-tier administrative structure comprises a central level (highest *Land* authority, higher *Land* authority), a meso-level (administrative district authorities, higher single-purpose *Land* authorities) and lower level (lower *Land* authorities, county administrations as a lower general purpose *Land* administration). This three-tier structure was first put in place in the *Länder* of North Rhine-Westphalia, Lower Saxony, Hesse, Bavaria, Baden-Württemberg, Saxony, Saxony-Anhalt and – in limited form – in Thuringia. In some cases, however, significant reforms have been undertaken in the meantime (e.g., transition to a two-tier system in Lower Saxony; cf. Chapter 4, Section 4.2). The general meso-level authorities (administrative district authorities) assume coordination and bundling functions in their territory, so that a reconciliation of interests between the different departments of the sectorally organized *Land* administration can occur. Other *Länder* have decided to do without meso-level authorities, so that they have two tiers (such as the *Länder* of Saarland, Schleswig-Holstein, Mecklenburg-Western Pomerania, Brandenburg, and since 2004 Lower Saxony). Only about one-third of the public personnel in these *Länder* constitute administrative staff in the narrowest sense; most of them do *not* work in the (core) administration proper, but specifically in the areas of education and science (about 50 per cent), the police force, public security, public order and legal protection (about 23 per cent; cf. Bogumil and Jann, 2009, p.99). Only to a limited extent do the *Länder* resort to having their own administrative sub-structure; instead they tend to 'delegate' the implementation of federal and *Land* laws to the local governments of the counties and municipalities. It has been estimated thus that between 70 and 85 per cent of implementation-requiring federal and *Länder* legislation (as well as the largest proportion of EU law; cf. Schmidt-Eichstaedt, 1999, p.330) is carried out by the local authorities. Furthermore, about two-thirds of all public capital investments are transacted by them (Wollmann, 2002b).

While, under the German constitutional tradition and doctrine, the local government levels (municipalities and counties) are considered, legally speaking, to be part of the *Länder* (which along with the federal level make up the 'two-layer' federal system), functionally they constitute a third politico-administrative level. Germany's politico-administrative system has traditionally been characterized by a multi-functional local government model. This multi-functionality is rooted in the scope of local government tasks and in the underlying 'general competence clause' laid down in Article 28 II of the Federal Constitution. Accordingly, the municipalities and (to a somewhat lesser degree) the counties must be 'guaranteed the right to regulate all matters relevant for the local community under their own responsibility within the limits prescribes by the laws'. In addition, besides performing their 'own' ('true') local government tasks (so-called 'own sphere of activity'), the local authorities can be put in charge of carrying out public tasks that are 'delegated' to them by the state, that is, by the *Land* or by the federal level (so-called 'sphere of delegated tasks'). Because of the organizational combination of genuine local government and delegated state tasks, the German administrative model can be termed a 'fused system', or more precisely, as a 'local administration-centred integrationist model' (cf. Wollmann, 1999b, p. 196, with further references). The 'true' local government tasks traditionally include a broad multi-functional range of charges including town planning and development, social and cultural tasks, and public services/utilities (*Daseinsvorsorge*, such as water, sewerage, public transport, etc.). Delegated tasks are typically related to public safety and public order such as environmental protection and building regulations, including planning permission procedures and the like. The territory-based model of local multi-functionality is further strengthened by the traditional feature of German local government being strongly engaged in the local economy and providing public services either by local government units and personnel (in house) or through municipal companies (municipal works, the *Stadtwerke*). In the engagement of local authorities in the provision of public services, the institutional variant of the *Stadtwerke* still prevails, under which the various services (energy, water, waste, traffic) are 'bundled' and has come to be considered a German peculiarity in the European context. By contrast, in the area of social services, the principle of subsidiarity is traditionally predominant, and so the provision of social services is largely undertaken by private, independent and/or non-profit organizations (*freie Wohlfahrtsverbände*). This has led to a de facto monopoly of large charities with pronounced corporate-like networks.

As to the territorial structure on the local government level, the *Länder* have exhibited wide differences in the exercise of their individual legislative power in determining the local-level territorial structure. The territorial structure of municipalities and counties that existed until World War II reached far back into the nineteenth century except for some early territorial reform moves undertaken in Prussia in the 1920s. After 1945, the old Federal Republic consisted of 24381 municipalities with an average of around 2000 inhabitants, 425 counties and 135 (single-tier) county-free cities (*kreisfreie Städte*), combining both municipal and county tasks. In the late 1960s and early 1970s, local government reforms were introduced and implemented in all the *Länder* of the (old) Federal Republic (see also Chapter 4, Section 4.3). Two of the *Länder* (North Rhine-Westphalia and Hesse) can be assigned to the Northern European type of territorial reforms, since large-scale amalgamations were effected, resulting (in the case of North Rhine-Westphalia) in 396 unitary municipalities (*Einheitsgemeinden*) with an average of around 45000 inhabitants. In most *Länder*, 'softer' territorial reform strategies more closely related to the Southern European territorial type were pursued. In the *Land* of Rhineland-Palatinate, for instance, the scale of amalgamation was minimal as it largely retained 2306 municipalities, averaging some 1700 inhabitants.

The legal regulation of the internal 'Constitution' of local government (i.e., the rights and responsibilities assigned to the different bodies and actors) falls, in the German constitutional tradition, to the individual legislative competence of each state. The local government statutes that were adopted after 1945 by the newly formed *Länder*, were significantly shaped by the respective regional local government tradition, but also influenced by the Allied Occupying Forces that intervened in the elaboration of local government statutes. The post-1945 local government statutes were largely moulded by the principle of representative democracy.[12] The South German *Länder* of Baden-Württemberg and Bavaria have institutionalized a 'powerful', directly elected executive mayor and a division of powers between council and mayor ('South German Municipal Charter'). By contrast, there are echoes of a parliamentary government system in the *Länder* of North Rhine-Westphalia and Lower Saxony. Borrowing from the British local government model, the 'North German Municipal Charter' is characterized by giving comprehensive powers to the elected local council, by assigning merely symbolic functions to the council-elected mayor and by creating the position of council-elected chief executive (*Stadtdirektor*) acting under the guidance and supervision of the local council.

Ever since the reforms of the municipal charters in the 1990s, there has been a considerable convergence towards the South German model of municipal charter (see Wollmann, 2008, p. 86 et seq., with further references; Bogumil and Holtkamp, 2013). This development notwithstanding, considerable differences still exist among the individual German *Länder*. The direct election of the mayor, which prior to the 1990s was in place only in Bavaria and Baden-Württemberg, has been introduced in all of the other German *Länder* – beginning with the *Land* of Hesse in 1990. This has also been connected to the all-new possibility of recalling a mayor by way of referendum. Heads of county administrations are now directly elected too (except in Schleswig-Holstein and Baden-Württemberg). Moreover, the 'twin peaks' (dual leadership) model has been abolished in those *Länder* that formerly had the North German model of municipal charter and in its stead an 'executive mayor' has been installed. The dual distribution of powers in both the chief administrative executive and the council is currently in place nationwide (Kuhlmann, 2009a, p. 274). Besides direct elections of the mayor and the recalls, the legal possibility to hold binding local referenda (based on popular citizen initiatives) was added to the municipal charters – even though procedural hurdles and regulations vary greatly from *Land* to *Land* (Wollmann, 2008, p. 74 et seq.). Overall, the frequency of local referenda in Germany is quite low.

Civil service and public personnel

The proportion of public sector personnel in Germany, compared to overall employment, is 10 per cent (in 2008), thus placing Germany among the group of OECD countries whose public administration, in terms of personnel, is small scale. If one also takes into account the rise in the number of part-time employees in the public service from 6.2 per cent to 25 per cent between 1960 and 2000, Germany can now be considered to have one of the smallest, as it were 'leanest' public services when compared internationally (Derlien, 2002, p. 232).

Traditionally, the public service personnel system is marked by a duality of status rights in that the distinction is made between civil servants (*Beamten*) and public employees (*Angestellte, Arbeiter*). On the one hand, in following the Continental European state tradition the 'civil servant system' (*Berufsbeamtentum*) and its 'traditional principles' (*hergebrachte Grundsätze*) have been adopted and anchored in Article 33 of the Basic Law (*Grundgesetz*) of 1949. The status of a civil servant is based on employment under public law, carries a lifelong appointment and a ban on strikes. The logic underlying this distinction is that 'sovereign' functions (*hoheitlich*; in French with a similar meaning, *régalien* – see Section 3.1.1 above) should be carried out only by civil servants. The 'sovereign' feature of public functions is defined by their exercise as possibly encroaching on the 'life and liberty' rights of citizens, typically those of building and environmental safety control, police, judicial functions and the like. A total of 37 per cent of public employees have such civil servant status (cf. Demmke, 2011, p. 323); of these, 60 per cent are employed on a federal and *Länder* level, and 12 per cent on a local government level. On the other hand, the employment relationships of employees and workers are based on private law and contracts; they have the right to strike. While such 'contractual' personnel, in principle, can be dismissed, their individual status, including their labour law protection from dismissal, depending on the duration of their respective employment, comes close to that of *Beamten* (see also Kuhlmann, 2006b). Some 59 per cent of public personnel are 'contractual' employees and workers, with the largest share in local administration. The German public service can be classified as a closed system (cf. Auer et al., 1996) since access for lateral entrants, career switching and personnel-related transitions between the public and private sectors are difficult and rare.

Through the Federalism Reform I of 2006 each of the *Länder* gained the all but sole legislative power and responsibility of their own to regulate the employment and career conditions as well as the salary/payment schemes of their personnel and that of the local authorities. As one of its major results, a growing differentiation and disparity has taken shape between the *Länder* regarding employment conditions and salary levels. While the 'rich' (typically Southern German) *Länder* have granted handsome salary hikes to their respective personnel, other (typically Eastern German) *Länder* (including Berlin), under budgetary pressure, were much more restrictive on this score. Consequently, the salary hiatus between public employees in 'rich' versus 'poor' *Länder* has widened to more than 10 per cent.[13] Consequently, political and judicial controversies have flared up and have triggered the call for returning to country-wide 'homogeneous' regulation, for instance concerning the salary scheme for civil servants and to thus undo the pertinent reform of 2006.[14]

Traditionally (and characteristically), the training of the administrative elite in Germany takes place in a strongly decentralized manner under the autonomy of the *Länder*, which have their own training centres for their *Länder* and municipal personnel. Lawyers are given priority in recruitment to the higher civil service, by virtue of the legalistic administrative culture. By the same token, the training for administration is strongly geared towards a legal curriculum and the acquisition of legal expertise.

Figure 3.3 illustrates the administrative system of Germany.

3.3 The Scandinavian model: Sweden

Basic features of government

Until the adoption of the new constitutional texts of 1975 (*regeringsformen*) the government system in Sweden (9 million inhabitants) was based on the Constitution of 1809 – the oldest, valid constitution in Europe. The political

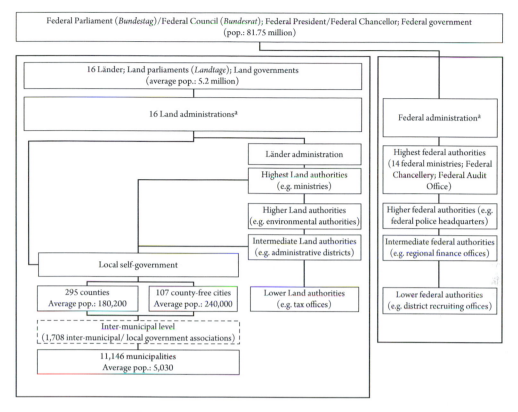

Note: a. The differentiation according to 'direct' and 'indirect' federal/*Land* administration is not shown separately in the figure (for this, see Bogumil and Jann, 2009, p. 88).

Source: Authors' own diagram; further (on local self-government): Bogumil and Holtkamp (2013).

Figure 3.3 Public administration in Germany (2012)

alignment, in particular the final introduction of the parliamentary system of government and the limitation of the king to representative duties in 1917, took place in a form – typical of the political culture of the country – of political agreements and constitutional customs. These were set down in the constitutional text of 1975 (which replaced the Constitution of 1809), whose *regeringsformen* – in contrast to most other European constitutions – did not completely capture the constitutionally relevant regulations, however.

Sweden is a decentralized unitary state and a parliamentary monarchy. Since 1971, the country has had a single-chamber parliament, the Riksdag, which consists of 349 members and is elected for four years on the basis of proportional representation. As the head of state, the King of Sweden has purely representative duties, no political powers whatsoever, and does not participate in political life. The Swedish government consists of the prime minister (*statsminister*) and the ministers (*statsråd*). The prime minister is elected by the Riksdag, and the ministers are nominated by him. By an absolute majority, parliament can express a vote of no confidence against individual ministers or against the entire government, thereby forcing their resignations. The ministers are generally assigned to one of the ten ministries (*departementet*), either as leader or as area director. The main duty of the ministries is the preparation of government decisions in the respective departmental areas. In contrast to most other states, however, the ministries are not permitted to issue directives to subordinate authorities (see below).

Because of the system of proportional representation, governmental coalitions have been typical in Swedish politics since 1945. These coalitions have usually comprised minority cabinets under the leadership of the Social Democratic Party (SAP). In a peculiarity of the Swedish political system, the individual legislative projects are generally prepared in the form of investigations (*utredning*) by independent commissions consisting of members of parliament, experts, scientists and stakeholders. The work of the commissions is supplemented by the so-called *remiss* procedure, in which administrative sections and stakeholders are encouraged to comment on the projects. The commission reports (SOU, Statens Offentliga Utredningar) often attract a wide public interest. Sweden's political culture is – irrespective of the conflicts between social democrats and conservatives – consensus oriented (consensus democracy). A major element of the political-culture–rooted consensus is the notion of socio-political solidarity in the form of the notion of *folkhemmet* ('home of the people'). This was politically fostered by the social democratic hegemony that reached beyond party-political electoral successes (with SAP as the dominant ruling party between 1932 and 1976).

State structure and administrative system

The government and its ministries traditionally have a remarkably lean organizational and personnel structure, reflecting Sweden's strongly decentralized state and administrative setting (cf. Pierre, 1995b, p. 142). The total number of ministerial employees is slightly higher than 2000. The Social Ministry (active in a key area of the Swedish welfare state) has only 100 employees. The higher state authorities (*myndigheter, ämbetsverk*), which are positioned beneath the small-scale government at the ministerial level, are responsible for the execution of central-state administrative tasks. They have a sectoral and, to some extent, a 'single-purpose' task role. As a special feature and peculiarity of the Swedish state organization, these higher state authorities enjoy a high degree of autonomy vis-à-vis the government as well as the parliament (cf. Petersson, 1994, p. 100). In formal terms, they are allocated to the individual sectoral ministries, but are not subject to their direc-tives (cf. Petersson, 1994, p. 100; Wollmann, 2008, p. 36; see also Chapter 4, Sections 4.2.4 and 4.5.2). The authorities are generally not located in the capital Stockholm, but in other cities (cf. Wollmann, 2008, p. 36). On the subnational regional level, the execution of state tasks lies with the public authorities (*länsstyrelse*) in the 20 provinces/counties (*län*), whose territo-rial structure reaches back to the seventeenth century – a further example of the unusual continuity of Swedish administrative structures. The head of the state provincial government on the *län* level is the county governor/head of the administrative district (*landshövding*), who is appointed by the govern-ment for six years.

Public administration at subnational levels and local self-government

Sweden's two-tier system of local government was created in 1862 by estab-lishing elected county representatives (*landsting*) on the territorial basis of counties on the one hand, and on the other, elected representatives (*fullmäk-tige*) were introduced into the 2200 local governments (*kommuner*) that existed at the time and whose territorial pattern reflected the existing church parishes (cf. Wollmann, 2008, p. 34 et seq.). The two local levels – the munic-ipalities (*kommuner*) and the counties (*landsting kommuner*) – played and continue to play a key role in the structure and the realization of the Swedish welfare state. For this reason, one can speak of '*den lokala staten*' (Pierre, 1994; Wollmann, 2008, p. 38f.), the 'local (welfare) state'. The decisive role played by the two local levels in the realization of the Swedish welfare state is reflected in the percentage of employees on both levels that combined amount to 83 per cent of the total of public sector personnel and of whom two-thirds are municipal personnel and one-third county personnel. By contrast, the state sector, that is, the ministerial level, the higher authorities/*myndigheter* and the state county/provincial authorities (*länsstyrelse*), accounts for only 17 per cent of all public sector employees. Of the entire public expenditure, the two local levels account for 41 per cent. Their financial and budgetary autonomy is reflected in the local government (income) tax, which is levied directly by the municipalities and counties from their citizens and covers the lion's share of local government expenditures. The large number of small municipalities that existed until the 1970s was reduced from around 2300 to 290 (with an average of 31300 inhabitants) as a result of two waves of territorial reform (cf. Häggroth et al., 1993, p. 14f.; Wollmann, 2008, p. 37; see also Chapter 4, Section 4.3.2). In the counties, the territorial boundaries largely date back to 1634 and so the deconcentrated state administration and local self-government exist side by side. Whereas the counties remained territorially unchanged for centuries they have, since the 1990s, come under pressure to modernize and have seen several regionalization experiments (see Chapter 4, Section 4.2.2).

Civil service and public personnel

On the central state level, the administration in the government as well as in the higher authorities (*ämbetsverk*) had a specific civil service tradition. This was based on the principles of professionalism and impartiality, but distinguished itself from the Continental European civil service tradition in terms of public employees – tellingly named *tjänsteman* ('service man') – being considered 'servants' rather than civil servants in terms of public service law (cf. Henningsen, 1986, p. 304). On local government level, a (voluntary, unpaid) layperson's administration prevailed in the municipalities, which were largely rural until the early twentieth century. This layperson's administration was replaced by full-time salaried administrative staff only with emerging industrialization and urbanization (cf. Strömberg and Engen, 1996, p. 267; Wollmann, 2008, p. 226).

Since the 1970s, the traditional legal difference between public sector and private sector employment has been increasingly levelled off. Although constitutional texts still speak of 'state service man' (*statstjänsteman*) as a special status, the relevant labour legislation now hinges on the uniform notion of *arbetstagare* (employee) without any distinction. To date, only 1 per cent of public personnel still have the 'old' civil servant status, while 99 per cent now are contract staff (Demmke, 2011, p. 323). The Swedish public service can thus be classified as an open/position-based system, in which a specific career path and a strict separation between public and private employment has become the exception.

Figure 3.4 illustrates the structure of the Swedish system of public administration.

3.4 The Anglo-Saxon model: United Kingdom[15]

Basic features of government

The United Kingdom (60 million inhabitants) is considered a prototype of a modern parliamentary democracy, in which not (in a formal separation of power) the legislative and executive powers, but rather (in a factual separation of power) the parliamentary majority and its government, on the one side, and the parliamentary opposition (with its shadow cabinet and leader of the opposition as the 'prime minister in waiting'), on the other,

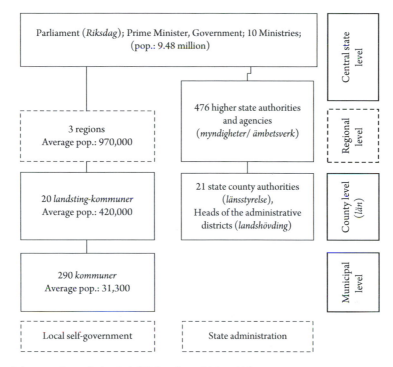

Source: Authors' own diagram; further: Dexia (2008); Wollmann (2010a, p. 225).

Figure 3.4 Public administration in Sweden (2012)

stand against each other. The United Kingdom does not have a written Constitution protected by a qualified majority requirement.[16] The 'unwritten' and 'unprotected' Constitution is the expression of the principle of parliamentary sovereignty codified in the Bill of Rights of 1689. According to this any constitutional issue can be settled by simple parliamentary majority (Wollmann, 1999b, p. 188) and parliament (de facto since 1911[17] – the House of Commons) is the centre of power. In parliamentarian practice, this means a clear privilege of the executive, in particular the prime minister (so-called prime ministerial government). The prime minister is not only assured of a loyal and disciplined parliamentary majority, but is also particularly powerful due to the cabinet structure (a Conservative- or Labour-led one-party government) and his pronounced personal patronage potential, for example, by appointing party members to government office. This strong position of the executive within the 'Westminster model' has also been pointedly termed 'elective dictatorship' as there are hardly effective counterweights (such as a constitutional court) and power-limiting institutions (such as federal structures or autonomous territorial bodies).[18] As radical reform initiatives and uncompromising programme changes are relatively easy to undertake within this model, the United Kingdom provides a prime example of a competitive or majority democracy. The power of the majority can assert itself against any existing resistance and hardly needs to take the veto positions of minorities into account. Although the claim of 'parliamentary sovereignty' has shown 'signs of disintegration' in recent political-institutional developments (see below), the history of administration in Britain can only be interpreted in the light of an understanding of constitution that provides for the ability to rescind any relativization of parliamentary supremacy by simple law, if necessary.

State structure and administrative system

The competitive orientation of democracy is confirmed in the constitutional doctrine of unlimited and indivisible parliamentary sovereignty that does not permit any vertical separation of powers; the United Kingdom is thus 'only conceivable as a unitary state' (Sturm, 2003, p. 227). According to this view, the sovereign parliament may transfer (devolve) the exercise of state authority to regional and local bodies, but cannot do so in the sense of an all-encompassing responsibility, as parliament is considered the only legitimate source of the exercise of power. Thus, decentralized institutions, as has occurred many times during British history, may be overridden at any time by a parliamentary majority of one vote.[19] Against this backdrop, a particular challenge to the Westminster system of government can be seen in the devolution policy, that is, the increasing transfer of sovereign rights to the parliamentary assemblies of non-English nations (Scotland, Northern Ireland and Wales). Such transfers have increasingly taken place since Tony Blair came to power in 1997 and have paved the way for an asymmetric devolution (Sturm, 2003, p. 227) or quasi-federalization (Wilson and Game, 2006, p. 82) (see below).

If the unitary organization of state and the unlimited power of the sovereign parliament represent the main features of the British government system, then the administrative structure exhibits pronounced decentralized elements. Thus, the central government in Westminster has been traditionally concerned with legislation and generally with 'governing' (high politics), which has also been termed the 'non-executant tradition of the British centre' (Sharpe, 1993, p. 248). By contrast, territorial bodies, in particular the counties and cities (districts, boroughs) were assigned to conduct all public tasks and the bulk of 'low politics'. In addition, as parliament did not allow the formation of a state administrative apparatus on the intermediary and lower levels (Sharpe, 1993), a vertical separational system developed; a system that has remained typical for British administrative tradition for a long time

(Wollmann, 2008, p. 30). This separation of central state and local government levels has also been termed 'dual polity' (Bulpitt, 1983). Characteristic of this is the central government not having installed any such territorial administrative units at regional level that might be comparable to French prefectures or German administrative district authorities. Instead, ministries established some single-purpose authorities of territorially and administratively inconsistent jurisdictions.

To understand administrative reforms in the United Kingdom, in particular the New Public Management (NPM) movement since the 1980s (see below), it is important to note that, since the post-war period, the centralization tendencies in the British administrative system have increased significantly. With the expansion of welfare state institutions and a massive nationalization policy, the traditional 'statelessness' (Dyson, 1980) was greatly relativized (Schröter, 2001, p. 419). During the 1980s, the public sector consumed almost 45 per cent of the gross domestic product and employed 21 per cent of the working population (OECD, 1998); approximately half the public personnel were employed by the central state level or by state-owned companies. In addition, as the social and health services were provided for almost exclusively at the local government level, a kind of Scandinavian model emerged in which local government as a public service provider held a de facto monopoly (municipal empires). On the central state level, the ministerial bureaucracy – albeit institutionally and also locally limited to Whitehall – had swollen into a monolithic apparatus, the reduction and disentangling of which was to become a major concern and target of subsequent reforms under Thatcher.

Public administration at subnational levels and local self-government

The principle of parliamentary sovereignty has also swayed the formation of the subnational administrative levels as it stipulates that regional and local authorities may carry out only such tasks that have been expressly assigned to them by parliamentary law. This maxim, known as the '*ultra vires* rule', contrasts with the 'general competence clause' typical of Continental European countries regarding the local self-government task model (see above). It contains – not only theoretical, but also in practice – the possibility that tasks, once assigned to decentralized institutions, can be withdrawn from them at any time by means of simple parliamentary law. However, the traditional *ultra vires* doctrine has been considerably attenuated under the banner of 'new localism', as proclaimed by the New Labour government. This was first embarked on by the Local Government Act 2000, according to which local authorities were endowed with the task 'to promote the economic, social and environmental well-being of their areas' (cf. Wollmann, 2008, p. 33; Wilson and Game, 2011, p. 32). With the explicit political goal of strengthening local self-government, the Conservative–Liberal coalition that was formed in May 2010 adopted the Localism Act on 15 November 2011. This granted local authorities a 'general power of competence' tantamount to a general competence clause.

As mentioned earlier, a regional administrative level is not an accepted component of the British administrative model, neither as a territorial state administration nor as regional self-government (Wollmann, 2008, p. 33). Only since the 1990s has the regionalization of administration gained increasing importance, beginning with the Regional Government Offices (RGOs) that were established in 1994 because state regional authorities tended to bundle together the regional offices of sectoral ministries. In connection with the devolution policy (see below) under New Labour Prime Minister Tony Blair, the regionalization movement intensified, albeit with a strong asymmetric orientation. The eight Regional Planning Bodies in England constituted merely a form of an administrative deconcentration of state administration[20] after the introduction of elected regional councils had failed. In contrast, remarkable steps of political regionalization have been undertaken in Scotland, Wales and Northern Ireland and each now has its own parliament with (in some cases, primary) legislative powers. As the integration of the non-English nations in the overall state has thus become increasingly fragile, the United Kingdom has developed into a disconnected union with a highly centralized centre (England) and an asymmetrically decentralized periphery with Scotland, Northern Ireland and Wales (Jeffery, 2009).

In the United Kingdom subnational tasks have traditionally been performed by local governments (counties/districts), which explains their share of approximately 56 per cent of overall public employment. Whereas Scotland, Wales and Northern Ireland have single-tier local government systems (unitary authorities), England has partly a two-tier system, in particular in rural areas and in Greater London, and partly a single-tier system, especially in urban centres and medium-sized cities. (1) In the two-tier system the 27 non-metropolitan counties constitute the upper level of local self-government, each with an average of 760000 inhabitants. The lower local self-government level is made up of the 201 non-metropolitan districts with an average of approximately 102000 inhabitants. Greater London also has a two-tier local government system with the Greater London Authority (GLA) on the upper level and 32 boroughs and the City of London on the lower level of local self-government. (2) In the single-tier system unitary authorities combine county and district functions (comparable to German county-free cities/*kreisfreie Städte*). In England, the centres of the large metropolitan areas (e.g., Manchester, Liverpool and Birmingham) are organized as unitary authorities, termed 'metropolitan districts',[21] and have an average of 308000 inhabitants. Moreover, 56 other unitary authorities exist outside the urban centres and average 209000 inhabitants.

These data highlight that the United Kingdom possesses pronounced large-scale local territorial structures and thus ranks as a front-runner of the Northern European type. The current local-level territorial structure is the result of repeated central government initiatives and several waves of incisive reforms that the English system of local government underwent during previous decades (cf. Chapter 4, Section 4.3).

The functional dimension of the British local government model is characterized by two opposing principles. The above-mentioned constitutional doctrine of parliamentary sovereignty and the *ultra vires* rule stand in contrast to the dual polity tradition. The latter has manifested itself in local governments traditionally having a broad range of tasks and exercising a significant degree of autonomy, notwithstanding their lack of constitutional protection. Modern local self-government was introduced in England by the Municipal Corporation Act of 1835 in the municipalities that were initially marked by the existence of a plethora of single-purpose organizations. As a result of these far-reaching territorial and organizational reforms, the local self-government units developed into an effective and multi-purpose administrative level.[22] Local tasks, including social services, most education, and a broad range of infrastructural services (water, energy supply etc.), were initially financed largely from local revenue (local rates). In 1920, revenue from these services still comprised 75 per cent of the entire local revenue. After 1945, however, the local government level lost important traditional tasks (water supply, sewerage, health services) and these were transferred to state structures (e.g., the National Health Service). At the same time, though, their responsibilities in the area of social services were expanded. Characteristic of the ensuing local government profile was the role of the local authorities as a quasi-monopolist provider of social services (Leach and Percy-Smith, 2001, p. 55 et seq.). Until the 1970s, the latter epitomized the primacy of the public sector in the expansion of the welfare state.

Contrary to the Continental European local government task model, the British system does not differentiate between delegated state and local self-government tasks. It thus represents a unitary (monistic) task concept, which, in turn, reflects the vertical separationist system (dual polity) – in contrast to the Continental European, fused system. Since the Conservative

Party government under Margaret Thatcher took office in 1979, the British local government system has experienced dramatic changes through centralization tendencies on the one side and privatization measures on the other. Consequently, the traditionally strong multi-functional local governments were jettisoned of numerous competences (hollowed out) and their autonomy considerably curtailed.[23] Hence, the separationist system has been crumbling (see below).

A distinctive strength of the British local government system can be illustrated in the very understanding and notion of local self-*government* – in contrast to the common Continental European term self-*administration* (in German: *kommunale Selbstverwaltung*; in French: *libre administration*), which, in both language and meaning, points to the 'administrative core' of local government tasks. Opposite to this, in the Anglo-Saxon understanding and definition and applied to the local level, 'government' also includes political decisions and the control of elected bodies such as local councils over the respective tasks, thus precluding a strong state-centred supervision. In British local government tradition, the elected local councils not only make all the relevant decisions, but are also directly responsible for the execution and control of the local administration. They do this primarily by establishing committees, which have decision-making and executive responsibilities for specific sectors of local government tasks (government by committees). However, the political profile of the British local government model has been historically considered as rather weak. The reason for this may be, for one, that the position of a strong executive mayor (such as that in the Continental European tradition) has been unknown – at least until recently. Second, within a dual polity setting, local political actors have been hardly able to influence national policy-making. Furthermore, community identity has barely developed on the local level, something that may be reflected in the low voter turnout in local elections. Only recently has this model been showing signs of transformation, as indicated by the introduction of direct-democratic empowerment of local citizens and by the move towards executive leadership in local politics.

Civil service and public personnel

Unlike Continental Europe, no explicit distinction between employment in the private sector and the public sector is – neither legally nor conceptually – made in the British public interest tradition. Public employees – in particular those in ministerial administration – have traditionally enjoyed certain privileges, such as a higher level of job security, lower weekly working hours, better social benefits, and so forth, compared to the private sector. In the areas of the military and the police, there were also some restrictions with regard to the right to strike and trade union activities. However, these provisions are neither laid down in specific public service law or statute for civil servants, separate from private labour law, nor are they recognized under Common Law (Bach and Winchester, 2003, p. 286). In the United Kingdom, employment relations of public employees are generally subject to free collective bargaining and contractual negotiations between parties, whereas different collective bargaining authorities exist for the different sectors of employment (e.g., the National Joint Council for Local Government Services for municipal employees). Furthermore, there is no strict career-track grouping, and private and public employment spheres are more permeable. This also represents a deviation from the Continental European format. A differentiation in terms of status is made only with regard to fields of activity for personnel, but not in terms of legal regulations of employment relations. Thus, the two large 'status groups' of workers (manual workers/industrial staff) and employees (non-manual employees/non-industrial staff) are distinguished, evincing a leaning towards the private sector (blue collar versus white collar staff) as well as the conceptual proximity of the public and private employment sphere.

The tradition of dual polity is also mirrored in the British public service. Thus, the civil service (in the technical sense) includes only the administrative staff on a central state level (ministries and agencies) and is therefore often used synonymously for central government. In contrast, local government employees, including teachers, are not part of the civil service but are public service employees. For this reason, the two levels of central government (civil servants) on the one hand and local government (public servants) on the other must be viewed as separate, both conceptually and with regard to employment relations (Bogumil and Kuhlmann, 2007, p. 143).

The origins of the modern British civil service reach back into the nineteenth century, when, following the Northcote-Trevelyan Report of 1854, a staff of administrative officers was created, 'who would ably carry out the functions of government' (Sausman and Locke, 2007, p. 190). These officers were to be selected according to ability and aptitude and recruited by means of open competition. Traditionally, the British civil service has been characterized by the principle of party-political neutrality and considered an impartial, permanent authority independent of political change and one that can serve any politically legitimate government (Sturm, 2003, p. 237; Page, 2010). The British ministerial bureaucracy is not allowed to appear in public in party-political function or identity, nor may a civil servant become a member of the House of Commons or the European Parliament (being a local councillor is, however, permitted). The absolute loyalty of the Whitehall ministerial bureaucracy vis-à-vis the current government, in particular vis-à-vis the respective minister to whom the best advice possible should be given, is an essential component of the role profile of the civil service (Page, 2010, p. 408). The higher ministerial elite (i.e., the Senior Civil Service) in particular is largely composed of Oxford and Cambridge University graduates (the so-called 'Oxbridge Elite'), who make up 80 per cent of the civil service. They are distinguished by a high social homogeneity, similar educational backgrounds at 'public schools' (that is, independent private elite schools), and professional exclusivity: 'senior civil service could be described as exclusive, clubby, and elitist' (Sausman and Locke, 2007, p. 190). Unlike the privileged position of lawyers within the legalistic administrative culture of Continental Europe, the British recruiting system is more open in terms of qualifications while also allowing for a variety of professional backgrounds (König, 2002), whereas generalists, in particular from the humanities, predominate (Sturm, 2003, p. 236). In 2004, the civil service comprised approximately 524000 people, while in the mid-1970s there were 750000, a fact that shows the traces left behind by Thatcherist retrenchment policy (Sausman and Locke, 2007, p. 192). The levers of power are, however, in the hands of a few hundred 'mandarins' (after the Chinese model) who form the heart of Whitehall, although only a sixth of them work in Inner London (Sturm, 2003, p. 236).

With a proportion of approximately 56 per cent in 2005, the local public service made up by far the greatest public employment sector, while the civil service (in central government) only accounted for 17 per cent and the National Health Service 26 per cent. Despite changing governments in London and the extensive reforms that have been pursued since the post-war period, the local public service in the United Kingdom has shown itself to be remarkably stable and until the 1990s, even an expanding sector of the public service. Because the local authorities are still responsible for school education, teachers are classified as local government employees, making up around one-quarter of local staff (Röber and Schröter, 2000). In the early 1950s, local governments still employed 1.4 million people, but this number grew to 1.8 million by 1962 and then reached almost 3 million in the mid-1970s. Only since the mid-1990s has local government personnel been reduced (by approximately 300000 employees) due to outsourcing and functional retrenchment.

Figure 3.5 summarizes the administrative system of the UK.

3.5 The Central Eastern European model: Hungary

What the Central Eastern and South Eastern European countries have in common is that their administrative structures were shaped by the central-

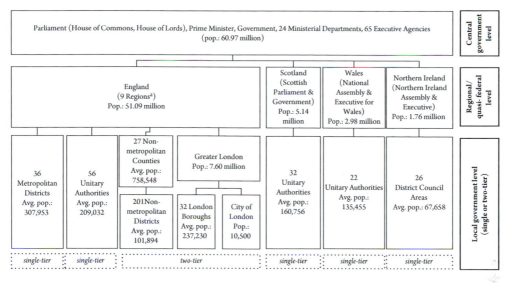

Figure 3.5 Public administration in the United Kingdom (2012)

Notes:
a. Since 2012, the English regions (except Greater London) no longer discharge any administrative functions. The area of the public health service (National Health Service – NHS) is not shown separately in the figure.

Sources: Authors' own figure; further information from: Office for National Statistics 2012 (http://www.ons.gov.uk/ons/guide-method/geography/beginner-s-guide/administrative/index.html; http://www.ons.gov.uk/ons/rel/kpversus/key-population-and-vital-statistics/no--34--2007-edition/key-population-and-vital-statistics.pdf; all last accessed 24 March 2012.

ized state organization model based on one-party rule between 1945 and 1990, that is, for almost half a century (Soviet Tradition; Painter and Peters, 2010, p. 27 et seq.). Within this, *grosso modo*, two groups of countries can be discerned by looking at their pre-communist administrative tradition and by the regime changes after 1990. On the one hand, there is the group (with Hungary, Poland, the Czech Republic and Slovakia) of Central Eastern European countries that in the nineteenth century and until 1919 were under the rule of the Habsburg Empire, or (such as parts of Poland) were annexed by Prussia. In these countries, following 1990, non-communist reform elites established decentralized constitutional and administrative models with concomitant local government structures (cf. Wollmann, 1995). On the other hand, a group of South Eastern European countries can be identified, for example Bulgaria and Romania, which were part of the Ottoman Empire or Tsarist Russia until the late nineteenth century or until 1919, respectively. They remained centrally ruled with their political and institutional transformation after 1990 determined primarily by post-communist elites.

Basic features of government

The rupture from the communist regime and the transformation into a democratic constitutional state occurred in Hungary (10 million inhabitants) as a 'negotiated transition' (Batt, 1991). The foundation of the new politico-administrative systems to a large extent was achieved through agreement between the democratic opposition and (in the late 1980s) the already reformed Communist Party of the country (cf. Wollmann and Lankina, 2003, p. 92 et seq., with references). The re-foundation of the Hungarian constitutional state in 1989–90 was largely based on a power-political consensus, which included radical decentralization and the introduction of local government (cf. Davies, 1995, p. 74).

While the post-communist Constitution of 18 October 1989 formally linked up with the (communist) Constitution of 1949, it proved in fact to be a completely new Constitution because of a radical recasting of the political structures. Also, following the most recent constitutional reform of 2011, which took effect on 1 January 2012, the parliamentary system of government in Hungary now has a one-chamber parliament whose 386 members are elected for a period of four years based on a combination of proportional representation and personality-based election. This is reminiscent of the German electoral system. Parliament elects the prime minister with the majority of its members; he in turn appoints his ministers without requiring approval by parliament. The prime minister possesses the power to decide the policy guidelines vis-à-vis the ministers. The prime minister (not the individual ministers) can be brought down through a constructive vote of no confidence where parliament withdraws its confidence by an absolute majority and at the same time elects a successor; this procedure is drawn from the German constitutional example. Overall, the prime minister has a powerful position in the Hungarian government system and can be compared to what, in the German case, has been called 'chancellor democracy' (cf. Dimitrov, et al., 2006, p. 208, with references). The state president is elected by parliament every five years, although he holds more extended powers than, for example, their German counterpart. He can dissolve parliament, has the right to submit legislative proposals to parliament and the right to examine legislative acts adopted by parliament on their substantive contents. In case of doubt they can, by means of a suspending veto, send the legislative act back to parliament for a renewed decision or submit it to the constitutional court. Parliament, in turn, can overcome the presidential veto by a majority vote. Since the constitutional reform of 2012, though, significant decision-making rights of parliament have been curtailed, primarily the parliamentary budgetary rights through the introduction of the so-called 'fiscal council'. Furthermore, the scope of rulings of the constitutional court has been reduced by the new Constitution, which has been strongly criticized in the 'Western' political media.

State structure and administrative system

The reconstruction of public administration launched after 1990 was marked from the very beginning by a profound contradiction. On the one hand, the almost unprecedentedly decentralized administrative model that was put into place aimed at providing the municipalities and settlements as a local government unit with a high degree of autonomy and with extended tasks, while at the same time keeping the central state supervision to a minimum. On the other hand, this pronounced autonomy of the decentralized local level was contrasted with, and counter-balanced by, the intention and practice of central government to have its own (deconcentrated) sectoral administrative units (the so-called 'decos' – deconcentrated state administration) on the regional and local levels (cf. Wollmann, 1995, p. 571). Thus, the centralized administrative strands inherited from the socialist state survived. This juxtaposition of, and tension between, local government institutions and state decos has had a lasting impact on the further development of the inter-governmental relations in the country.

Initially, administrative authorities were set up in seven regions (as well as the city of Budapest) formed explicitly for this purpose, with each being placed under the direction of a 'Commissioner of the Republic' (reminiscent of the French *préfet*) appointed by the prime minister. He was responsible for coordinating state activities in the region and for exercising legal supervision over the local self-government level. In a reform that followed shortly thereafter in 1994, the regions and their 'Commissioners' were abolished. Instead, in 1996 (meso-level) state authorities were created in the 19 existing counties (*megyék*) and in Budapest under the direction of appointees of the prime minister. Since state authorities now functioned alongside the counties' self-government bodies on the territorial basis of the counties (see below), a dual structure similar to the French *département* system has come into existence.

In 1996, the seven regional units were put in place as administrative spatial planning regions. These were modelled on the EU concept of NUTS[24] and aimed, with an eye on the desired accession of Hungary to the EU, primarily at aligning Hungary's inter-organizational setting with the supportive framework of the EU structural funds (cf. Wollmann and Lankina, 2003, with references).[25] As previously mentioned, running vertically parallel to the institutions of local government, Hungary's administrative system is marked by a pronounced spread of (sectoral) state administrative units. For one, this holds true for a significant number of higher state authorities, each of which is subordinate to the respective sectoral ministry and has a country-wide administrative jurisdiction, for example in labour market administration, health insurance funds and environmental authority. Furthermore, there are single-purpose state authorities (decos) on the level of the counties as well as, in part, the municipalities. They largely mirror the sectoral range of responsibilities of the higher state authorities and the guidance and supervision that sectoral ministries exercise right down to the local level.

In order to avoid functional overlaps and conflict, the full-time administrative heads of the small municipalities (traditionally called 'notaries') have been put in charge of carrying out functions of sectoral state administration in addition to the local self-government tasks (see below). In thus linking up with Hungary's pre-communist dual local administration scheme, which is, in turn, rooted in the Austro-German administrative tradition, the local authorities, besides fulfilling their own self-government functions, carry out tasks that are delegated to them by the state and stand under function-specific administrative supervision that goes beyond mere legal review.

Public administration at subnational levels and local self-government

Hungary has a two-tier local government system. The (lower) municipal level consists of 3175 local government units with an average of 3170 inhabitants each. Ninety-one per cent of them have fewer than 5000 inhabitants. The (lower) municipal level is further subdivided into 2863 villages, 265 towns and 23 cities with county status (comparable to Germany's county-free cities, *kreisfreie Städte*) (cf. Dexia, 2008, p. 365). With its 1.7 million inhabitants (representing 17 per cent of Hungary's entire population), the capital Budapest has a county-free special status and is divided into 23 city districts (cf. ibid.). The upper local government level is made up of 19 counties (*megyék*) whose territorial structure goes back to the Middle Ages. When, after 1990, local self-government was reintroduced at the county level, their representative bodies were indirectly elected by the municipal councils, before their direct election was installed in 1994 (see below).

The Local Government Act of 1990 was assigned a quasi-constitutional status in that its amendment requires a parliamentary two-thirds majority. Under this legislation, the municipalities, as the lower level of local self-government, were designed to become the pivotal point in the decentralization and democratization of the new state organization. The constitutional and political primacy that was ascribed to the municipalities in the 1990s is evidenced by the provision where initially only the municipalities had directly elected local councils, while the county councils were indirectly elected by the municipal councils, thus enjoying only 'derived' democratic legitimacy. With the reform of 1994, the counties were politically and functionally upgraded by the introduction of the direct election of their councillors and by an expansion of their tasks. Nevertheless, the counties continue to be neither legally nor functionally superior to the municipalities. Manifesting the democratic grassroots emphasis and high esteem of the lowest local level that was emblematic of the founding period, the local communities and 'settlements' were accorded the right to form new independent municipalities on their own initiative and free will. Consequently, the number of municipalities leapt from 1600 to over 3100 immediately following the regime change. Local territorial reforms have not been seriously considered since then.

Besides the elected local councils, the legislation provided for the direct election of the mayors who carry considerable weight in local government leadership. In the new Local Government Act, which was adopted under the Orbán government and came into effect on 21 December 2011, the ('quasi-presidential') direct election of the mayor was abolished; instead the mayor, in a 'quasi-parliamentary' manner, is now elected by the municipal council from among its members. The administrative leadership of local government lies with the above-mentioned full-time head of administration ('notary'), who is appointed by the municipal council based on a tender procedure. He wields the function of the administrative executive, while the mayor exercises the political leadership (cf. Temesi, 2000, p. 358 et seq.). The number of municipalities that have their own administration has decreased steadily from around 50 per cent in 1991 to 34 per cent in 2010, while the number of those that share the same 'notary' with another municipality or settlement has risen accordingly (Kovács, 2012). In view of the large number of small municipalities, from the earliest stage a broad range of forms of inter-municipal cooperation has evolved and been promoted by national legislation. This holds true for the 2003 law on multi-purpose associations as well as for the 1997 law on municipal associations and cooperation. Currently, around 2600 such inter-municipal formations exist for the joint provision of public services, and for joint administrative tasks (cf. Dexia, 2008, p. 369).

The broad task profile of local self-administration of municipalities comprises (primary) schools, social services, nursing and public utilities. In addition, they are responsible for tasks 'delegated' by the state. The reform of 1996 was targeted at improving the financial resources of the municipalities (cf. ibid., p. 366). The functional weight of local levels in the national administrative system is reflected in the fact that around 24 per cent of all public expenditures is made by them, with about 19 per cent being spent by the municipalities and around 5 per cent by the counties. Moreover, around 65 per cent of all public employees are personnel of the two local levels; this percentage is among the highest among European countries (cf. ibid., p. 64 with comparative figures).

Civil service and public personnel

Under the communist regime in Hungary – as in the other socialist countries – the employees of the state apparatus and other sectors were regulated by a uniform labour law (cf. Vesselin, et al., 2006, p. 216 et seq., with references). Subsequent to the regime change, legislation was passed in March 1992 in which a differentiation between the 'classic' career-based and the contract-based employment status was introduced (cf. Bossaert and Demmke, 2002, p. 9). The former category was meant to safeguard the professionalism, neutrality and non-corruptibility of public administration. Civil servant status is ascribed in particular to public employees who perform directing and executive ('statutory') functions, while all others are employed on a contractual basis. This pertains to, among others, teachers and the majority of municipal personnel (cf. Marcou and Wollmann, 2008, p. 152, with a comparative overview of the development of public service legislation in the other CEE countries). Thus, Hungary now has a two-track public service system in which 25 per cent of employees are civil servants and 75 per cent are contractual staff (cf. Demmke, 2011, p. 323).

Figure 3.6 summarizes Hungary's administrative system.

3.6   Cross-country comparison

In this section, the administrative profiles of the six countries will be compared and placed in a broader OECD context. For this, three relevant criteria will be highlighted according to which the OECD administrative systems and public sectors can be compared quantitatively:

- scope/'leanness' of the public administration;
- administrative structure according to levels;
- functional profile of administration.

First, Table 3.1 summarizes the major features of the state and administrative profiles that were identified in the previous sections. It should be noted that the referred-to features pertain to the traditional administrative profiles, and that reform-related changes that occurred during the previous decades (cf. Chapter 4) are not taken into account.

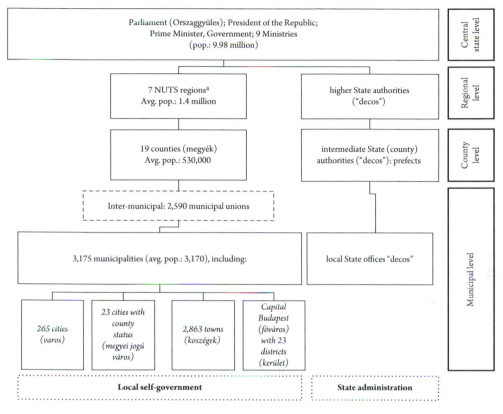

Note: a.   Without the right to self-government; abolished in 2012.

Sources: Authors' own figure; further information from Regional Atlas – Public Administration Structure of Hungary on 1 July 2009, http://portal.ksh.hu/regional_atlas_administration_structure, last accessed 14 May 2012; http://www.ksh.hu/docs/hun/hnk/Helysegnevkonyv_adattar_2011.xls, last accessed 2 March 2014.

Figure 3.6 Public administration in Hungary (2012)

3.6.1   Size and development of the public sector

The scope and extent of the public sector and public administration in a cross-country comparison are quantitatively reflected in two indicators in particular: (1) public expenditure quota (that is, the proportion of general public expenditure in relation to the gross domestic product – GDP); (2) public employment quota (that is, the proportion of public employees in relation to overall employment).

With regard to the development of the public sector in the international context, some significant trends can be gathered from Table 3.2. For one, between 1995 and 2009 public expenditures decreased in relation to the GDP in most OECD countries – with the exception of France, Belgium, Greece,

Table 3.1 Traditional state and administrative profiles in Europe

Country	Type of Government and Democracy	State Structure/ Administrative System	Subnational/ Decentralized Administration	Civil/Public Service
France	Semi-presidential; hybrid	Unitary, centralized-Napoleonic; rule-of-law culture (Roman-French)	Functionally weak, fused system, politically strong, Southern European territorial type	Career-based system/closed
Italy	Parliamentary; hybrid	Unitary, centralized-Napoleonic; rule-of-law culture (Roman-French)	Functionally weak, fused system, politically strong, Southern European territorial type	Career-based system/closed (until 1990s)
Germany	Parliamentary; hybrid	Federal, decentralized/ subsidiary; rule-of-law culture (Roman-German)	Functionally strong, fused system, politically strong, hybrid territorial type	Career-based system/closed
Sweden	Parliamentary; consensus-based democracy	Unitary, decentralized; rule-of-law culture (Roman-Scandinavian)	Functionally strong, separationist system, politically strong, Northern European territorial type	Position-based system/open
UK	Parliamentary/ majoritarian	Unitary, centralized, public interest-culture (Common Law)	Functionally strong, separationist system, politically weak, Northern European territorial type	Position-based system/open
Hungary[a]	Parliamentary/ hybrid	Unitary, decentralized; rule-of-law culture (Roman-German/ Austrian)	Functionally strong, fused system, politically strong, Southern European territorial type	Career-based system/closed

Note: a.   Refers to the period after 1989.

Source: Authors' own summary.

the United Kingdom, Ireland, Portugal, Spain, the USA and New Zealand, where the public expenditure quota increased. In the country group with a declining public expenditure quota the size of contraction differs considerably. It is more pronounced, for instance, in Germany (with a reduction from 55 per cent to 48 per cent) and in Sweden (from 65 per cent to 55 per cent)

Table 3.2 Public expenditure quotas by international comparison (%)

Country	1985	1995	2000	2009
Denmark	–	59.22	53.68	58.42
Finland	46.35	61.46	48.29	56.25
France	51.78	54.44	51.64	55.99
Sweden	–	65.10	55.09	55.16
Belgium	58.43	52.14	49.14	54.22
Greece	–	45.71	46.69	53.63
Austria	53.06	56.33	52.13	52.32
Italy	49.84	52.51	46.18	51.87
United Kingdom	45.92	43.90	39.05	51.64
Netherlands	57.26	56.45	44.20	51.40
Hungary	–	55.59	46.76	50.46
Ireland	–	41.12	31.27	48.90
Portugal	–	43.41	41.13	48.17
Germany	–	54.77	45.11	47.50
Norway	–	50.94	42.30	46.32
Czech Republic	–	54.47	41.82	45.93
Spain	–	44.44	39.12	45.80
Poland		47.71	41.08	44.40
Canada	48.3	48.48	41.11	44.05
USA	36.85	37.13	33.88	42.18
New Zealand	56.03[b]	41.56	38.32	41.91[a]
Slovak Republic	–	48.64	52.14	41.51
Australia	39.54	37.42	35.52	35.30[a]
Switzerland	–	35.00	35.10	33.74
OECD Average	–	–	41.94	46.24

Notes:
a. For the previous year.
b. For the following year.

Sources: OECD (2009, 2011) and authors' own summary.

than, for example, in Denmark (from 59 per cent to 58 per cent). Overall, the data show that the public expenditure quota, which can be observed internationally since the mid-1980s (cf. Naschold and Bogumil, 2000, p. 28 et seq.) continued to shrink, with a few exceptions, until 2000. Afterwards, this trend was reversed. Thus, since the 2000s, in most countries the public expenditure quota has – in some cases significantly – increased, plausibly mirroring a changed (post-NPM) concept of 'the State' and an abandonment of minimalist reform-guiding principles. Even in the United Kingdom, the public expenditure quota climbed from 44 per cent (1995) to 51 per cent (in 2009), a quite conspicuous increase in the face of the market-radical NPM drive during the 1980s (see Chapter 4, Section 4.4). Furthermore, different clusters of countries can be identified according to the size of the public expenditure quotas, which, in all six countries under consideration here, lie above the OECD average[26] (at 46.24 per cent in 2009). In the overall OECD context, three groups of countries can be roughly distinguished for the 2009 reference year:

● The group of 'high scorers' whose public expenditure quotas, despite, in part, massive reductions, still surpass 50 per cent (currently, however, below 60 per cent). This holds true for the Scandinavian countries (except Norway), France, Belgium, Greece as well as Hungary, Italy, Austria, the Netherlands and the United Kingdom.
● The middle group of countries that have public expenditure quotas over 40 per cent but well under 50 per cent include Germany, Portugal, Spain, the Czech Republic and Ireland.
● The group of 'low scorers', which have public expenditure quotas between 35 to 40 per cent. This comprises non-European countries (USA, Canada, Australia, New Zealand) as well as the Slovak Republic and Switzerland.

Serving as another important indicator for assessing the scope of state and administrative activities, the public employment quotas (cf. Table 3.3) show a less dynamic development and less congruence between the countries when compared to the public expenditure quotas. This may well be an expression of the persistence of public institutions and administrative units. With regard to public personnel development in relation to overall employment between 1995 and 2008, the OECD countries form two groups: a smaller group with increasing quotas and a larger one with declining ones. The former includes France, the United Kingdom, Finland, Belgium, Italy, Spain, Switzerland and the Slovak Republic as well as Turkey. The latter group comprises all other countries except for the Czech Republic where the quota has remained constant at 12.8 per cent. As to the amount of the public employment quotas in 2008, the countries can be divided into three groups. In our selection of six countries, only Germany and Italy come out below the OECD average (15 per cent), while the other four are above the average (see Table 3.3):

● The group of countries with a traditionally expanded public sector is composed of the Scandinavian countries, France, Hungary, the United Kingdom and Belgium. In these countries, the public employment quota amounts to between 20 and 30 per cent.
● In a second group of countries whose public sector is medium-sized, the public employment quota typically lies between 12 and 15 per cent, that is, at the average of OECD countries. To this category belong Ireland

Table 3.3 Public employment quotas in international comparison (%)

Country	1995	2008
Norway	31.2	29.3
Sweden	29.8	26.2
Finland	21.0	22.9
France	21.6	21.9
Hungary	–	19.5
United Kingdom	14.2	17.4
Belgium	16.9	17.1
Canada	17.9	16.5
Ireland	15.9	14.8
USA	15.4	14.6
Italy	14.2	14.3
Czech Republic	12.8	12.8
Spain	11.5	12.3
Portugal	13.0	12.1
Netherlands	13.1	12.0
Austria	11.8	11.4
Turkey	9.1	11.0
Slovak Republic	8.9	10.7
Poland	–	9.7
Switzerland	7.2	9.7
Germany	12.2	9.6
Greece	–	7.9
OECD-32	–	15.0

Source: OECD (2009, 2011) and authors' own compilation.

(from among the Anglo-Saxon group), Italy, Portugal and Spain (from among the Napoleonic group), the Czech Republic (from among the Central Eastern European countries), and the USA.

- A third country group with a still less extended public sector in which the public employment quota is as low as between 7 per cent and 11 per cent, includes Turkey, the Slovak Republic, Switzerland, Greece and also Germany.

Thus, by and large, public sectors in OECD countries have been both expanding and shrinking since the 1990s (cf. Table 3.3). This holds true also for the countries considered here, of which four show an increasing tendency in the development of their public employment quotas (France, Hungary,[27] the United Kingdom and Italy), while two show a decline (Sweden, Germany). If one compares the development of the public personnel in these six countries from 2000 to 2008, it can be seen that the most striking cuts were made

Table 3.4 Overall public employment by country comparison 2000–08

Country	2000	2005	2008	Difference	Difference
Germany	6 534 000	5 797 000	5 840 000	−694 000	−10.6
France	6 563 000	6 683 000	6 781 000[b]	+218 000	+3.3
Italy	3 640 600	3 635 500	3 611 000	−29 600	−0.8
Sweden[d]	1 208 900	1 239 800	1 267 400[c]	+58 500	+4.8
Hungary	837 700	874 400	822 300	−15 400	−1.8
UK	5 616 000[a]	6 107 000	5 995 000	+379 000	+6.7

Notes:
a. 2001.
b. 2006.
c. 2007.
d. 'General government sector' = governmental bodies, social insurance carriers, non-profit organizations with largely public financing/sponsorship.

Source: http://ilo.org/; last accessed 23 May 2012; and authors' own summary/calculation.

in Germany, with a reduction of over 10 per cent. Between 1993 and 2002 the personnel reduction amounted to some 25 per cent (cf. Kuhlmann and Röber, 2006, p. 99). Next come – clearly less pronounced – Hungary (−2 per cent) and Italy (−1 per cent). By contrast, the United Kingdom (+7 per cent), Sweden (+5 per cent) and France (+3 per cent) have expanded their public personnel since 2000 (see Table 3.4).

For France it should be noted that in 2007, State President Nicolas Sarkozy launched the ambitious reform programme of a comprehensive general review of public tasks (Révision Générale des Politiques Publiques – RGPP) targeted at cost saving. The aim, inter alia, was to achieve a reduction of 160000 positions in the public sector between 2009 and 2012 by replacing only every other vacant position ('*un pour deux*') during the retirement process. In the wake of the political change brought about by the election of the socialist president Hollande and of a left-wing majority in the National Assembly, the RGPP and its reform goals have apparently been sidelined. However, the personnel reform of the public service is bound, in the light of the country's deep budgetary crisis, to loom large on the political agenda of the new government.

In Italy the so-called 'technocratic' interim government under Mario Monti also moved – vis-à-vis the country's budget and debt crisis – to pass a reform package that, in Italian political jargon, was tellingly labelled (in Anglo-Saxon terminology) a 'spending review'. This reform programme was adopted on 7 August 2012 by both chambers of parliament and was aimed at cutting management personnel in public administration by 20 per cent and the 'ordinary' personnel by 10 per cent by 2014. However, the outcome of the general election both chambers held on February 24 and 25, 2013 has cast doubts on the further course and fate of these reform measures since the election results seem to be a long way from allowing a stable governing majority in both houses.

3.6.2 Administrative structures and levels of government

In order to comparatively assess the functional weight of public administration on the different levels of the politico-administrative system, the share of personnel employed by the (central) state in relation to the other administrative levels can serve as an indicator. Thus, the varying degrees of the (de-) centralization of administrative tasks in multi-level systems can provide a useful illustration. Table 3.5 reveals that the administrative systems of the countries under consideration here exhibit different degrees of decentralization. Hence, the previously mentioned limitation of state administration to ministerial and higher authority functions is numerically reflected in that in Sweden the share of state personnel is only 17 per cent. In the United Kingdom, the proportion of central state employees is also less than 17 per cent (in 2005). This share of central-level personnel seems remarkably low given the fact that England has passed clearly centralization-prone administrative reforms and its governance form is considered essentially to be unitary and centralized. The resolution of this apparent contradiction can be seen in the fact that, while the discharge of most public tasks has been transferred to the local authorities (as evidenced by the latters' high personnel numbers), they are regulated and controlled by central government in a more centralized manner than in any other European country. In Hungary, the share of state employees of only 35 per cent hints at a remarkable degree of functional decentralization. By contrast, in France the proportion of state employees is still over 50 per cent, suggesting that – irrespective of the decentralization initiated in 1982 and further promoted in 2003 – the presence, in terms of organization and personnel, of the central state of Napoleonic provenance is still very pronounced on the subnational levels. In Germany's federal system, the share of federal personnel is as low as 12 per cent, while that of *Länder* employees stands at 53 per cent. These figures illustrate the scant administrative role of the federal government and the significant administrative salience of the *Länder*. If one counts the latter (because of their quasi-state status) among the state sector, the proportion of 'state' personnel even amounts to 65 per cent. In Italy's quasi-federal system, the share of state personnel is as high as 55 per cent while that of employees of the regions is only 3.8 per cent. These figures reveal that in spite of the decentralization pursued since the 1990s, the country's (Napoleonic) central state has remained institutionally strong and visible in the subnational space. Moreover, the figures show that,

Table 3.5 Public employment by levels of government (%)

Country	Central/Federal Level			Regional/Länder Level			Local Level			Specific Sectors[a]		
	1985	1994	2005	1985	1994	2005	1985	1994	2005	1985	1994	2005
G	9.9	11.6	12.0	55.6	51.0	53.0	34.5	38.1	35.0	–	–	–
F	54.9	48.7	51.0	–	–	–	27.1	30.7	30.0	18.0	20.6	19.0
UK	21.9	21.4	16.8	–	–	–	55.0	53.0	56.0	17.6	20.8	26.0
S	–	17.3	17.0	–	–	–	–	84.7	83.0	–	–	–
I	–	63.0	54.7	–	–	3.8	–	14.0	13.6	17.0	19.0	27.9
H	–	35.0	35.5	–	–	–	–	65.0	65.0	–	–	–

Note: a. For UK: National Health Service; for France: *hôpitaux publics*; for Italy: *aziende sanitarie locali* and (since 2005) *enti pubblici*.

Source: Wollmann (2010a, p. 229), with further references) and authors' own summary.

while the regions have been strengthened in a 'quasi-federal' manner in their legislative, functional and financial responsibilities, they hardly carry out any administrative activities of their own.

The vertical architecture of administration in the subnational space exhibits remarkable differences among European countries. In principle, three levels can be distinguished:

- the federal or quasi-federal level;
- the local level;
- the inter-municipal units.

Federal or quasi-federal level

Following from its constitutional tradition that stretches back to the nineteenth century, Germany has a distinct federal decentralized state organization, in which the regions (*Länder*) possess independent political, legislative and administrative responsibilities of considerable scope. Since the 1990s, Italy has also come closer to a quasi-federal constitutional form due to the transfer of substantial functional and legislative responsibilities to the regions (*regioni*) that were established initially in 1948. In the United Kingdom, after the creation of autonomous regional parliaments and the 'devolution' of independent legislative and administrative responsibilities, Scotland, Wales and – to a lesser degree – Northern Ireland obtained the status of quasi-federal regions; by contrast, in England, the regions have kept the status of planning and administrative units. This has created an extremely asymmetric state organization (Jeffery 2009).

Local levels

The countries under consideration have two-tier local government systems – with the exception of France, where the regions were established in 1982 as a new level of the now three-tier local system (*collectivités locales/territoriales*). Thus, while the local government structure is generally made up of two tiers, in some countries a 'single-tier' local government form has been additionally put into place – one that combines the 'lower tier' municipal and the 'upper tier' county functions. This applies to the county-free cities (*kreisfreie Städte*) in Germany, to the unitary authorities in England and to the cities with county status in Hungary. This also holds true for Sweden's capital Stockholm and for France's capital Paris. Table 3.6 shows the distinctly different municipal structures and average size of the local authorities in the countries under consideration.

Table 3.6 Subnational administrative levels by comparison (status 2010–12)

Country/ Structure	Level	Term for Territorial Unit	Number	Pop. Avg.
Germany	Federal	*Länder*	16	5.2 m
	Local	Counties	295	180200
		Member-municipalities of a county	11146	5030
		County-free cities	107	240000
	Inter-municipal	Administr. associations, inter-municipal unions etc.	1708	n.s.
France	Local	*Régions*	27	2.3 m
		Départements	101	639000
		Communes	36569	1560
	Inter-municipal	*Syndicats*	12840	n.s.
		EPCI	2599	n.s.
UK	Quasi-federal	Regions (Scotland, Wales, Northern Ireland)	3	5.0 m (Scotland) 2.9 m (Wales) 1.6 m (Northern Ireland)
	Local (only England)	Metropolitan districts (single-tier system)	36	308000
		Unitary authorities (single-tier system)	56	209000
		Non-metropolitan counties (two-tier system)	27	759000
		Non-metropolitan districts (two-tier system)	201	102000
		London boroughs (two-tier system)	32	237000
Sweden	Local	*Landsting kommuner*	20	420000
		Kommuner	290	31300
Italy	Quasi-federal	*Regioni*	20	2.9 m
	Local	*Province*	110	551000
		Comuni	8094	7455
	Inter-municipal	*Comunità montane*	356	32700
		Unioni di comuni	278	n.s.
		Consorzi/Conveni	n.s.	16700
Hungary	Local	Counties (*magyék*)	19	530000
		Municipalities, including:	3175	3170
		Villages (*koszégek*)	2863	n.s.
		Towns (*vàros*)	265	n.s.

Table 3.6 (*continued*)

Country/ Structure	Level	Term for Territorial Unit	Number	Pop. Avg.
		Cities with county status (*megyei jogú vàros*)	23	1.7 m
		Capital Budapest (*fövàros*) with districts (*kerület*)	24	n.s.
	Inter- municipal	Cooperation associations	2590	n.s.

Note: n.s. = not specified.

Sources: Dexia (2008); Wollmann (2010a, p. 225); Bogumil and Holtkamp (2012) and authors' own summary and calculation.

Inter-municipal formations

In the countries where local-level territorial reforms have not yet been carried out and where a great number of small-sized municipalities prevail (as in France, Italy and in most German *Länder* as well as, since 1990, in Hungary; cf. Chapter 4, Section 4.3), inter-municipal formations have been established for the operative support of the small municipalities. Of these, France's *intercommunalité* (with 12840 *syndicats* and some 2600 *communautés*) is exemplary.

The salience of public administration in the multi-level system is also mirrored in the distribution of public expenditure according to administrative levels (cf. Table 3.7). In comparing the six countries under consideration, the share of the central state in public expenditure is the highest in France with almost 85 per cent and the lowest in Sweden with about 60 per cent. This illustrates the high degree of fiscal centralization in France and the high rate of fiscal decentralization in Sweden whose local government levels, with a share of 40.6 per cent of public expenditures top all other countries by far. In the German federal system, 24.6 per cent of public expenditure can be accounted for by the *Länder*, where personnel costs for teachers and police loom large. In 'quasi-federal' Italy, 19.6 per cent of the public expenditures, which include in particular financial support of the public health service (Servizio Sanitario Nazionale), is spent by the *regioni*. English local authorities come next, accounting for 29.5 per cent of public expenditure. This indicates that – despite the high degree of political centralization of the subnational levels in England – the activities of the local authorities that also cover the financing of schools are still 'very big business' (Wilson and Game, 2006, p. 139). In Hungary, some 24 per cent of public expenditures is made by local government, out of which the lion's share (18.5 per cent) falls to the

Table 3.7 Public expenditure by administrative levels (2005)

Comparison Criteria	Germany			France			Italy			Sweden		UK	Hungary	
	Munici-palities	Counties	Länder	Communes	Départe-ments	Régions	Comuni	Province	Regioni	Kommuner	Landsting kommuner	Single-tier authorities/ unitaries + two-tier districts, boroughs	Munici-palities	Counties
Per capita expenditure in €1000	1.5	0.3	3.2	1.2	0.8	0.3	1.0	0.2	2.3	4.9	2.4	3.9	0.8	0.3
Percentage of the level in overall public expenditure	11.7	2.4	24.6	8.2	5.4	1.9	8.8	1.6	19.6	27.1	13.5	29.5	18.5	5.1
Percentage of subnational expenditure in overall public expenditure	38.7			15.5			30.2			40.6		29.5	23.6	

Sources: Dexia (2008), Wollmann (2010a, p. 245).

lower local government level. With 15.5 per cent, France has the lowest proportion of subnational expenditures, where 1.9 per cent is accounted for by
the *régions*, 5.4 per cent by the *départements* and 8.2 per cent by the *communes*.

3.6.3 Functions and competencies

The European countries exhibit distinct differences with regard to the tasks
and functions assigned to public administration and the individual administrative levels. In order to identify and compare the importance of different types of tasks in public administration, two indicators can be used: the
distribution of public personnel and the distribution of public expenditure
according to areas of activity.

In a country comparison, social policy can be singled out as exemplary of the
functional variance of administration. In Scandinavian countries and in the
United Kingdom for example, social services are traditionally undertaken
by the local authorities, while in the Napoleonic unitary countries these
are largely assumed by the (deconcentrated) state administration (in some
cases, e.g. in Italy, also by church organizations). However, in the federal
subsidiarity-related systems such as in Germany, social services are traditionally delivered by voluntary or church-affiliated welfare organizations.
Another important policy field in which the implementation of tasks is differently organized is the sector of health services. The United Kingdom, Italy
and Sweden have public health systems. The United Kingdom's National
Health Service comprises 26 per cent of all public employees and Italy's
Servizio Sanitario Nationale 20.3 per cent. In France, too, public hospitals
constitute a self-standing sector with 19 per cent of all public employees.
By contrast, in Sweden the public health system is assigned to the counties
(*landsting kommuner*) as a local self-government task and is integrated into
the local workforce. In Hungary, important tasks in health services are ful-
filled by the local authorities. In a cross-country comparative perspective, the
'education and training' sector represents a particularly personnel-intensive
area. Its personnel (in particular teachers) constitute a significant proportion
of state employees in France, Italy and the German *Länder*, on the one hand,
and local government employees in Sweden, England and Hungary, on the
other.

The distribution of public expenditure according to areas of activity and
levels provides another significant indicator for identifying functional key
areas of public administration, showing that the areas of social security, education, and general public administration are particularly weighty in the
countries under consideration as well as in the overall OECD context (see

Table 3.8 Public expenditure by task areas and levels in percentage of GDP (2008)

Task Area	Germany			France		Italy		Sweden		UK		Hungary		OECD-29	
	Federal state	Länder	Munici-palities	Central state	Sub-national	Central state	Sub-national	Central state	Sub-national	Central state	Sub-national	Central state	Sub-national	Central state	Sub-national
General public administration	30.7	26.2	15.9	30.0	18.9	33.5	14.1	25.7	11.7	15.4	6.3	29.1	16.5	24.6	16.2
Defence	7.8	0.0	0.0	8.1	0.0	5.2	0.0	5.1	0.0	5.9	0.1	2.8	0.0	6.4	0.1
Public order and safety	1.1	9.0	4.5	4.4	2.9	6.1	1.5	4.0	0.9	4.4	9.5	6.2	1.4	4.9	2.9
Economic affairs	9.5	10.3	11.4	13.5	12.3	6.6	14.1	10.1	5.9	9.5	9.4	16.7	8.0	14.1	13.6
Environmental protection	0.2	0.5	5.2	0.4	6.8	0.8	4.8	0.5	0.9	0.9	4.2	1.6	3.7	0.8	6.4
Housing and community facilities	1.3	2.1	5.9	1.4	15.3	1.1	4.2	0.4	2.7	1.2	6.8	0.3	7.6	0.9	6.5
Health	0.0	1.6	1.7	0.9	1.1	13.3	45.2	4.5	26.9	17.3	0.0	6.7	15.2	9.0	8.5
Leisure, sports, culture, and religion	0.3	1.6	6.0	2.0	10.1	1.5	3.1	1.2	3.6	1.3	4.0	3.0	5.1	1.8	7.7
Education	1.2	25.4	17.0	19.3	16.5	13.0	8.3	6.3	21.4	12.1	32.0	11.0	29.4	11.0	22.7
Social security	47.9	23.4	32.6	20.0	16.1	19.0	4.7	42.4	26.2	32.0	27.7	22.7	13.1	26.4	15.5

Source: OECD (2011) and authors' own summary.

Table 3.8). The expenditures for general public administration are highest in France (regarding the central and the local government levels), in Italy and in the UK (at the central government level). By contrast, in Germany, public expenditure is highest in the area of social security (on both the federal and local levels). The same holds true for Sweden and Hungary on the central state level. In the United Kingdom, education (schools) proves to be the most important area of expenditure on the local level, similar to Hungary, where subnational education expenditure is also about 30 per cent of GDP. In Italy and Sweden, in contrast, the highest expenditure on subnational level is in the area of public health as measured by the proportion of GDP.

NOTES

1   Cohabitation, which has occurred three times in French history so far (1986–88, 1993–95, 1997–2002), is characterized by the head of state and the head of government belonging to different political parties. As the difference in legislative periods of state president (previously seven years) and parliament (five years) was abolished on the basis of a referendum in 2000 by amendment of the Constitution, and there has been a uniform five-year term of office, cohabitations have become less likely to occur and should thus further strengthen the element of democratic competition on the national policy level.

2   The terms 'local government'/'local government system' used in the following refers only to cities/municipalities (*communes*) and *départements*.

3   See *Le Monde*, 19 September 2013, last accessed 1 March 2014 at http://www.lemonde.fr/politique/article/2013/09/19/les-senateurs-refusent-de-se-voir-appliquer-le-non-cumul-des-mandats_3480203_823448.html.

4   In the public service, a differentiation is traditionally made between the 'ordinary' Corps and the so-called Grands Corps de l'Etat, which includes, inter alia: Conseil d'Etat, Inspection Générale des Finances, Cour des Comptes, Corps des Ponts, des Eaux et des Forêts; Corps des Mines; Corps Préfectoral; Corps Diplomatique. Overall, approximately 1000 Corps exist in the public and health service (Meininger, 2000, p. 191 et seq.).

5   However, due to financial problems, there has been an increasing number of staff whose employment relations are not governed by statute. Thus, the proportion of so-called *non-titulaires* on the level of the local self-governments now stands at 25 per cent (compared to 12 per cent in the civil service). These are far more flexible, in some cases 'precarious' employment relationships (such as *vacataires; emplois-jeunes, contrats emploi solidarité*, etc.).

6   Apart from seven senators that are currently appointed for life, senators are generally elected for five years on the basis of regions, with a minimum of seven per region.

7   The electoral system is based on a block-voting principle. It means that the voter cannot vote for a single candidate but only for the party or the coalition.

8   This electoral system in which the (party-political etc.) composition of the Camera reflects the national electorate, while that of the Senato that relates to different regional electorates has resulted in political inconsistencies and difficulties in the face of which this electoral system has come to be (somewhat drastically and pejoratively) nicknamed '*porcellum*' (alluding to '*porco*' = pig) in political discussion and in the media.

9   In a dramatic political showdown Prime Minister Letta, on 5 October 2013, posed the confidence vote, which for the continuation of his government needed to be approved by both chambers of parliament (Senato and Assemblea). Faced with the likely event that, in an unheard of rebellion within his own party (PdL), a significant number of the PdL senators led by Angelino Alfano (until then his most loyal and devoted political disciple, supporter and would-be successor) were going to approve the confidence vote against Berlusconi's will and 'command', in a downright desperate manoeuvre Silvio Berlusconi himself finally brought forward the motion, on behalf of the PdL senators, to back Letta's vote of confidence.

10 See Article 114: 'La Repubblica è costituita dai Comuni, dalle Province, dalle Città Metropolitane, dalle Regioni e dallo Stato'.

11 A special function in the administrative system not described here in detail is increasingly played out by the city states (Berlin, Hamburg, Bremen), which are federal *Länder* and municipalities simultaneously, and whose *Länder* governments (senates) thus take on *Land*-related and municipal responsibilities.

12 An exception since the post-war period in Germany is the introduction of the direct election of the mayor in Baden-Württemberg (since 1956) and in Bavaria (since 1952) in addition to the possibility of carrying out binding local referenda in Baden-Württemberg (since 1956). Moreover, numerous *Länder* in their municipal codes provide for direct-democratic town meetings for very small municipalities.

13 For data see http://oeffentlicher-dienst.info/vergleich/laender/; last accessed 1 March 2014.

14 See http://www.dgb.de/themen/++co++c740e04a-c41b-11e1-4c18-00188b4dc422@@dossier.html; last accessed 1 March 2014.

15 It should be recalled that Northern Ireland is part of the United Kingdom, but not part of Great Britain. If in the following England is not explicitly addressed or Northern Ireland not explicitly excluded, the term United Kingdom will be used.

16 However, there exist written constitutional foundations, such as the Magna Carta (1215), the Habeas Corpus Act (1679) and the Bill of Rights (1689), which have a constitutional status, even if they are 'only' simple laws that (theoretically) can be changed through a simple parliamentary majority. None have been integrated in a single constitutional document (Hartmann, 2005, p. 64).

17 In 1911 the veto powers of the House of Lords were abolished, so that the House of Commons decides de facto alone.

18 Lord Hailsham (1978); similarly, Richard Rose (1982): 'Crown in parliament can do everything that is not naturally impossible'.

19 Examples include the suspension of Stormont in Northern Ireland and the takeover of direct rule by the British government in 1972, as well as the dissolution of the Northern Ireland Assembly and the politically undesirable councils of six metropolitan areas and the Greater London Council in 1986 with the help of a parliamentary majority under Thatcher (Sturm, 2003, p. 227).

20 The regional planning institutions in the eight English planning regions were, however, also abolished following the change of government in 2010, as was the entire English regional planning system (cf. Kuhlmann et al., 2011, p. 218 et seq.). This shows a clear relativization of and a retreat from regionalization policy in England.

21 The metropolitan districts were, for a time, part of a two-tier system with six metropolitan counties on a supra-local level. These were abolished in 1986 as local self-government levels, so that the 36 metropolitan districts today act as unitary authorities (in the single-tier system) while also carrying out the former tasks of the metropolitan counties.

22 The counties that initially were administered by Crown-appointed Justices of the Peace were incorporated into the modern institutional development in 1888 by introducing elected county councils for the execution of their tasks. The districts were established in 1894 as a completely new level between the counties, and the towns or parishes. The latter two lost their tasks primarily to the districts, which thus today constitute the actual local self-government level (Wollmann, 2008, p. 29 et seq.).

23 It is revealing that the share of the local government's 'own' taxes in its total local revenues still stood at 40 per cent during the early 1970s while it dramatically dropped to merely 14 per cent during the 1990s (Wollmann, 2008, p. 238).

24 NUTS = Nomenclature des Unités Territoriales Statistiques. The classification of EU territorial units for statistics was developed in 1981 by EUROSTAT. NUTS is structured according to three different levels: NUTS 1, 2 and 3. Each EU member state is divided into one or several NUTS-1 regions and these in turn are divided into NUTS-2 and NUTS-3 units.

25 On the decision taken by the Hungarian government in 1999 (and still not effected) to transform these NUTS-related regions into regional self-government bodies, see further below.

26 Public expenditure quota for 2005: France: 55.9 per cent; Germany: 47.5 per cent; Hungary: 50.4 per cent; Italy: 51.87 per cent; Sweden: 55.1 per cent; United Kingdom: 51.6 per cent (cf. OECD, 2011).

27 In Hungary, the public employment quota rose from 19.2 per cent (2005) to 19.5 per cent (2008). For 1995, there are no OECD data available on Poland and Greece.

4

Administrative reforms from a comparative perspective

LEARNING OBJECTIVES

At the end of this chapter, you should:

- know the discourses on administrative reform policy in the context of OECD countries and their determining factors;

- know what differences and commonalities exist between the European countries with regard to administrative reforms in the multi-level system;

- be able to differentiate between the most important types of territorial reform in Europe and carry out a country classification;

- have an overview of New Public Management (NPM) reforms in the areas of privatization, internal modernization and public service;

- be able to classify and explain the development of European administrative systems as either convergent, divergent or persistent.

4.1 Reform discourses

Administrative modernization in European countries has been shaped by different reform discourse cycles over the past decades (see Jann, 2002). During the 1980s and 1990s, the NPM discourse in particular significantly influenced the reform agenda.

When tied in with the above-mentioned neo-institutionalist debate (Chapter 2, Section 2.3), the following factors can be identified (hypothesized) as shaping the patterns and profiles of the discourses on administrative reform policies (cf. Christensen and Laegreid, 2001a, 2010; Wollmann, 2003c, p. 231, with further references; Pollitt and Bouckaert, 2004; see also Figure 4.1):[1]

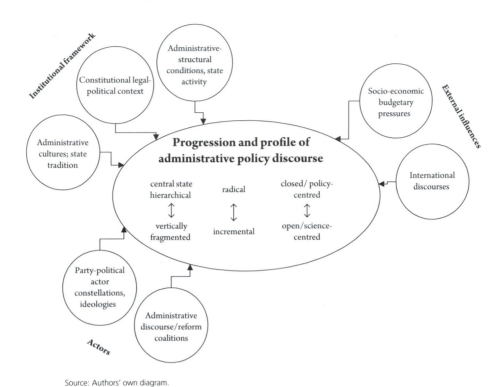

Source: Authors' own diagram.

Figure 4.1 Determining forces of administrative reform policy discourse

- Legal and political decision-making structures and procedures of the country (federal-decentralized versus unitary-centralized, majoritarian-competitive democracy versus consensual-consociational democracy) as institutional framework conditions (cf. Pollitt and Bouckaert, 2004, p. 41ff.)[2] that determine whether the discourse on administrative reform policy unfolds at the central state level or in a vertically decentralized and fragmented manner and/or whether it is geared to radical or incremental change.
- Administrative structural starting conditions of the country with which the administrative reform policy discourse is faced and whose country-specific features (scope of the state sector, degree of centralization, extent of state provision of services, administrative/bureaucratic model) are perceived as administrative reform pressure and need and can thus significantly sway the administrative reform policy discourse.[3]
- Institutional structures and basic cultural properties of state and administration (e.g., the rule-of-law tradition of Continental European countries versus the public interest/civic culture tradition of Anglo-Saxon countries; cf. König and Füchtner, 2000, p. 10 et seq.; Wollmann, 2000b, p. 4

et seq.; Pollitt and Bouckaert, 2004, p. 52 et seq.), which may determine the corridor of the administrative reform discourse.

- Socio-economic, in particular budgetary framework conditions that in a crisis situation can suggest urgent administrative reform action.
- (Party-)political actor constellations and their ideological, political, and so forth action interests and intentions.
- Administrative discourse and reform coalitions (cf. Wittrock et al., 1991, p. 43 et seq.; Sabatier, 1993, p. 116 et seq.) and potential rivalling discourse groups[4] that may be formed and sustained by politicians, administrative experts, scientists, think tanks, socio-economic stakeholders, management consultants and the like (cf. Derlien, 1996, p. 152). Access to and dominance within the discourse primarily depends on whether it is a closed, policy-centred or an open, science-centred one (Singer, 1993, p. 157).
- Opening of the national discourse arena to the international discourse and its increasing interweaving and cognitive congruence as so-called epistemic communities (cf. Adler and Haas, 1992, p. 367 et seq.), which may have a bearing on trans-/international learning, reception, imitation and exchange processes (policy learning)'(Rose, 1993; Sabatier, 1993).

The hitherto-made selection of countries will be supplemented in the following sections by including the USA and New Zealand in order to establish a fair and balanced account of the Anglo-Saxon countries that have taken centre stage in the current international discussion as frontrunners of the New Public Management (NPM) movement.

International discourse

The content of the international and transnational discourse on reform policy has been impinged upon by several factors: the latest modernization wave (known under the umbrella term of NPM) began initially in the Anglo-Saxon countries, in particular in the United Kingdom and New Zealand, and was almost exclusively put forward and disseminated in English-language publications. Thus, the discourse in these countries has strongly shaped the image of a new modernization movement moulding its 'Anglo-Saxon–centrist' and 'Anglophone' features (cf. critical: Wollmann, 2002a, p. 491).

During the early run of the international modernization discourse, influential international organizations, especially the OECD, were interested in downright canonizing NPM as a concept and strategy of state and administrative modernization, and propagating it as a modernization doctrine with global validity. As Frieder Naschold critically observed, 'this conception of the "one development path" [was] linked normatively to the issue of its effectiveness: the "one development path" – ultimately an idealized Anglo-Saxon model – [was regarded] as the most effective way to modernize the welfare state' (1995, p. 69). Thus, OECD/PUMA (the OECD's Public Management Service) took on a key role in an international 'discourse community', which primarily included government representatives, international consultants and (NPM-sympathetic) scientists (cf. Sahlin-Andersson, 2001, p. 59 et seq.; Pollitt and Bouckaert, 2004, p. 129).

Particularly the OECD, but also a group of researchers, have based their surveys and analyses on specific components and criteria that are regarded by them as constitutive for NPM. Consequently, these investigations tend to generate distorted results as only such dimensions of reality are perceived that conform to this analytical frame and scheme, whereas others are summarily analytically disregarded. The Anglo-Saxon–centred analytical 'lens' and language pattern is conceptually (if not epistemologically) predisposed (and biased) so as to ignore countries and administrative realities that do not 'fit' in terms of analysis and language.

Budgetary conditions

Since the late 1970s, all the countries under consideration (with the exception of the USA) have been beset by a budgetary crisis that evolved and hit at different times and with differing degrees of intensity. The budgetary crises have proven to be a decisive trigger for the countries' neo-liberal policy shifts. Economic, welfare state and administrative reform policy has gone hand-in-hand with this reorientation. This has occurred against the backdrop of an ever widening gap between public expenditures that were propelled essentially by the hitherto prevalent ('social democratic') welfare state principle, on the one hand, and the revenue that kept shrinking as a result of the economic crisis, on the other.

Actor constellation, politico-ideological context

The dominant impact of the budgetary framework conditions becomes manifest not least of all due to the fact that the neo-liberal policy shift was set off by the politico-administrative elites under conservative-led government majorities and coalitions, as well as under social-democrat–led ones. The United Kingdom and New Zealand are perfect examples of this: in the UK, the neo-liberal 'turnaround' was effected in 1979 by the incoming Conservative (Tory) government under Margaret Thatcher, a government that broke with the welfare state concept of the (old) Labour Party as well as with the earlier policy concepts of the 'old' Tories largely shared by them with the 'old' Labour. Shortly afterwards, when, in 1984, New Zealand's Labour Party took over the country's central government, replacing the conservative National Party, it immediately performed a spectacular neo-liberal policy shift. While in the United Kingdom the Tories had conducted (and won) their election campaign primarily with the demand to 'roll back the state', thus programmatically and propagandistically preparing the neo-liberal policy 'turnaround', in New Zealand the new Labour government embarked on its neo-liberal course without any prior programmatic or propagandistic preparation or advance notice. By contrast, in Germany, the Conservative–Liberal (CDU/FDP) coalition under Chancellor Helmut Kohl, which, in 1982, toppled the Social–Liberal coalition government under Helmut Schmidt, largely adhered to the traditional understanding of the German welfare state (*Sozialstaat*) – despite the neo-liberal rhetoric the conservative–liberal camp had entertained before taking over the federal government. A change in direction towards a neo-liberal welfare state policy and NPM orientation in administrative reform policy did not come about in Germany until the late 1990s under the Red–Green coalition and Chancellor Gerhard Schröder as a reaction to the increasing problems of national debt and budgetary consolidation that essentially resulted from the skyrocketing costs of German Unification.

Reform discourses and advocacy coalitions

The preparation and conduct of the discourse arenas and coalitions on administrative reform policy that have formed in the countries under consideration can be grouped and sorted out according to three types, that is: policy-centred, administration-centred or society-open.

The policy-centred discourse arena and coalition appears particularly pronounced in the United Kingdom and New Zealand. Here, under the conditions of their unitary-centralized (single level) constitutional system and a majoritarian decision system (Westminster model), the policy decisions on administrative reforms fall also under the political leadership of the head of government (in the United Kingdom) or under that of a key minister – such as the finance minister in the case of New Zealand (single actor; cf. Schmidt, 2000, p. 232 et seq.). The specific composition of such a policy-centred discourse coalition can depend heavily on the personal preferences (will and skill) of the key political actor. Former British Prime Minister Margaret Thatcher, for instance, kept the senior civil servants (mandarins) of her government apparatus rigorously on the sidelines of administrative reform policy discourse and preferred to take advice from prominent business leaders such as Derek Rayner and conservative think tanks. In contrast, New Zealand's finance minister surrounded himself, in an almost 'conspiratorial' manner (secretive elite; Halligan, 2003, p. 62), with neo-liberal economics graduates, in addition to senior civil servants from the Treasury. Whereas Thatcher's policy discourse was, at least initially, essentially based on general core beliefs in the general superiority of market and competition, the New Zealand discourse coalition was geared to providing conceptual ammunition for the imminent state and administrative reform and for packing it with a more rigorous theoretical foundation (in rational-choice, principal–agent theory etc.) than was the case in any other country.

Reflecting the prominent role of the president as a national actor, the administrative reform discourse in the USA – at least on the federal level – reveals a policy 'centring' that converges on the president. This has been strengthened by most presidents attempting to be identified with specific reform concepts in a high-profile and election-campaign–effective manner. This distinctly applied to the democratic presidency of Bill Clinton who made reinventing government his administrative reform policy slogan and trademark. The high esteem that private enterprise managerialism has since long enjoyed in the USA in the administrative reform discourse clearly also shows that in the USA, presidents seek pertinent advice from prominent business leaders. This was true for the Republican President Ronald Reagan (who appointed the reform commission headed by the businessman J. Peter Grace) as much as for the Democrats Clinton and Gore.

France exemplifies an administration-centred discourse coalition, which largely comprises senior civil servants from the Grands Corps. Their discussions are thus primarily conducted from within (cf. Pollitt and Bouckaert, 2004, p. 54) and their authority is not least of all based on the large intellectual, cognitive and normative homogeneity that connects the members of the Grands Corps in the areas of policy, administration and economy.

Sweden's administrative reform policy is largely carried by a society-open discourse arena and coalition, consistent with the country's traditional consensual policy style. Accordingly, the decentralists, traditionalists and economizers – with their respective specific locations in the different ministries and stakeholder groups (Premfors, 1998) – compete for opinion leadership and seek consensual reconciliation.

In Germany, in contrast to the UK's central-government–level and single-actor–centred administrative reform arena, the administrative reform policy arenas and discourses are rather fragmented in the country's federal decentralized (multi-level/multi-actor) policy system. Since the 1960s, a professional opening of the administrative reform policy discourse, which involves stakeholders and scientists in addition to administrative officials, has evolved. While the discourse and reform coalitions of the 1960s and subsequent years involved primarily administrative lawyers alongside administrative officials as traditional modernizers, since the early 1990s administrative officials, business economists and management consultants as well as NPM-sympathetic lawyers and like-minded political scientists have come to make up a reform discourse coalition where, in concept, the NPM modernizers set the tone.

4.2 Inter-governmental reforms: decentralization, regionalization and federalization

4.2.1 Concepts and definitions

The devolution of policy-making responsibilities and administrative functions on the subnational level has become the main thrust of the reform of state and administration in almost all advanced ('old') and 'new' democracies (Stoker, 1991, p. 7; Hoffmann-Martinot, 2006, p. 231; Wollmann, 2008, pp. 53, 253). The following focuses on two areas: first, on regionalization and federalization, and second, on the redistribution of tasks between the state and local self-government levels (decentralization and municipalization).

When powers are transferred to a regional, intermediate or meso-level located between central and municipal/local levels (see Sharpe, 1993), one can speak of federalization only if and when the recipient of the transferred functions possesses a democratically elected representation and to which autonomous legislative/norm-setting and policy-making powers are assigned (for an overview see Marcou and Wollmann, 2008, p. 138 et seq.). If the intermediate/meso-level is not accorded autonomous legislative and policy-making responsibilities, one speaks of (simple) regionalization. If regions are newly established, one can further differentiate between a 'hard' and a 'soft' formation of regions (cf. Bogumil and Grohs, 2010, p. 93). The former boils down to the creation of new regional territorial entities while abolishing related previous structures (e.g., 'old counties'). By contrast, 'soft' regionalization targets the creation of flexible, largely mono-functional regional cooperative forms in integrated spatial areas or in planning/grant-target regions[5] that do not have the status of territorial bodies and thus lack, as it were, the 'hard' institutional core. Furthermore, a definitional distinction can be made between the transfer of regional functions 'upwards' (bottom-up), for example, from county to regions, which has a centralizing effect, and the transfer 'downwards' (top-down), in other words, from a state authority to the region. This, then, has a decentralizing effect.

Decentralization and communalization (municipalization) as reform strategies pursued in a multi-level system refer to the devolution of responsibilities from the (central or national) state administrative level to the local self-government levels. The recipient then can be either the supra-local level (counties, *départements* etc.), that is, the 'upper' local government level or the local self-government level proper (municipalities, districts, *communes* etc.), that is, the lower tier of the local government structure. By means of this, two types of decentralization can be discerned, that is: a political variant and an administrative one.

In the case of 'political decentralization', political decision-making powers and responsibilities are transferred along with the respective administrative functions, in particular with regard to the specific tasks, while a direct intervention by the state administration in the form of supervisory control is ruled out. In the case of Germany, this type of political decentralization has also been termed 'real' or 'full' municipalization (Wollmann, 1997b; Burgi, 2009, p. 163; Kuhlmann, 2009a, p. 81; Kuhlmann and Bogumil, 2010, p. 14). This contrasts with 'administrative decentralization', which means that state tasks are transferred (delegated) to the local authorities to be carried out by them. However, elected local representatives/councils formally have neither influence nor control over the conduct of such delegated tasks, thus revealing its administrative logic. Moreover, the state authorities exercise an administrative supervision over the respective local activity that includes the merits, adequateness, and so on, of the action, therefore hinting at the 'administrative' and 'state-integrationist' logic of such delegated tasks. In reflecting such limitations and qualifications of 'administrative decentralization' in Germany, one speaks of 'truncated' or 'false' communalization (municipalization; Wollmann, 2008, p. 258 et seq.).

Finally, 'administrative deconcentration' needs to be defined clearly apart from (political or administrative) decentralization because it is an essentially administrative concept and notion referring to the transfer of state functions, including budgetary and in some cases human resources, from central state institutions (ministries, authorities) to subnational and local (deconcentrated) state or semi-state administrative units. In terms of definition and typology, again one can distinguish two forms: for one, the 'classic' deconcentration of national or central state administration in the form of territorially located state authorities and offices. As regional or local single-purpose

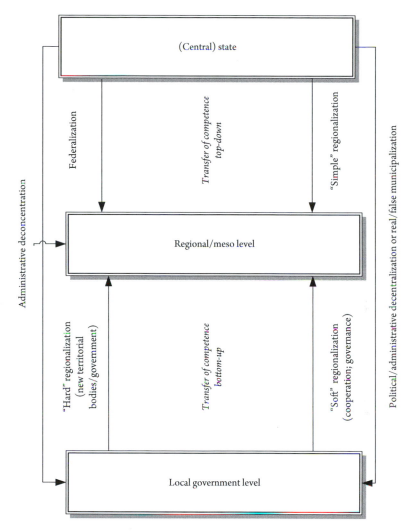

Source: Authors' own diagram.

Figure 4.2 Variants of state and administrative reform in a multi-level system

authorities, but also as administrative district authorities and prefectures, these have had a long administrative tradition in Europe. Second, there is the new NPM-inspired variant of state agencification, a topic dealt with in Section 4.5.

Figure 4.2 presents an illustration of the variants of state and administrative reform in a multi-level system.

4.2.2 Federalization, quasi-federalization, regionalization

(Quasi-)federalization

Historically, countries that have seen a 'federalizing' development share (except for the United Kingdom) the tradition of a unitary centralized state model largely with Napoleonic features. Thus, Italy's democratic post-war Constitution of 1948 was aimed at breaking with the historic centralized Napoleonic state model that extended back to the unification of 1861 and became even more centralized during fascism (for details, see Chapter 3, Section 3.1.2). The constitutional reforms of 1999 and 2001 brought the breakthrough to a regionalization, in which the regions were equipped with comprehensive autonomous legislative and operative powers. This has been interpreted by some as the transition of Italy to a 'quasi-federal state' (Bobbio, 2005, p. 29; cf. also Brunazzo, 2010, p. 185 et seq.). However, it should be noted that significant constitutional and political actors, such as the Constitutional Court (Corte Costituzionale), continue to adhere to the fundamental premise of a unitary (*unitario*) state. In addition, Italy's region-alism clearly has asymmetric features due to the salient (political, economic, etc.) differences between 'normal' and 'special' regions and within Italy as a whole. Following the definition of federalization presented above, according the term 'federalism' requires the existence of elected regional representative bodies and the assignment of autonomous legislative and political decision-making powers, and so Italy can be classified as a variant of 'federalization' (Palermo, 2005; but critically see Behnke, 2010). However, the new rights that have been granted to the regions to exercise regional self-government have been only hesitatingly implemented (Behnke, 2010, p. 314). Tellingly by 2009, four regions with normal statutes still had no new regional statute (as a quasi-constitution of the regional system of government); see Table 4.1.

Spain can be considered as another significant case of federalization of a politico-administrative system of Napoleonic provenance. By virtue of the regional existence of different cultural and linguistic nationalities (the Basque region, Catalonia, Galicia), the country undertook several attempts during the late nineteenth and early twentieth centuries to move towards a federal constitutional setting, as evinced in particular in the draft Constitution of 1873. However, the country later experienced an extremely centralized regime under the dictatorship of Franco (1936–75). Trying to take account of existing regional and even separatist tendencies, especially in the Basque region, Catalonia and Galicia, the (democratic post-Franco) Constitution of 1978 created 17 regions (*comunidades autónomas*) and granted them broad powers that have subsequently been further expanded (cf. Alba and Navarro,

Table 4.1 Adoption of regional statutes in Italy (2010)

Region	Year of Adoption	Region	Year of Adoption
Abruzzo	2006	Marche	2005
Basilicata	1971	Molise	1971
Calabria	2003	Piemonte	2005
Campania	1971	Puglia	2004
Emilia Romagna	2005	Toscana	2005
Lazio	2004	Umbria	2005
Liguria	2005	Veneto	1971
Lombardia	2008		

Source: Behnke (2010, p. 314, with further references).

2003, p. 198). However, a federal representative body, comparable to the Swiss 'council of cantons' (the Ständerat) or the German Federal Council (the Bundesrat), has not yet been established.

In view of the eminent political weight carried by the Basque region and Catalonia amidst the other *comunidades*, Spain has been called by some an 'asymmetric federalism' (Alba and Navarro, 2003, p. 199). Thus, in comparative literature, the country has been counted among the new European federal states (see Colino, 2009). Nonetheless, it should be noted that in the constitutional and political debate conducted in Spain, the term 'federalism' is often avoided and one instead speaks of a 'state of autonomous regions' (*estado de comunidades autónomas*).

The Belgian state, founded in 1831, initially also bore the traces of a unitary centralized Napoleonic state organization and largely retained this until recently. In order to cope with the growing tensions between the Walloon and Flemish population groups, a federalization of the country was initiated step by step. This gradual federalization was codified in the constitutional reform of 1993 under which three regions and three language communities were put into place. In 2001, this process further advanced with the so-called Lambermont Agreement. The transition of Belgium from a unitary state into a federal state ushered in a complex political structure not readily comparable to other federal states. Besides the three regions of Flanders, Wallonia and Brussels, three additional 'communities' were created having a Flemish-, French- and German-language basis and which are by no means geographically congruent with the other three regions. The regions now hold very broad legislative powers (cf. Hecking, 2003). However, irrespective of the country's radical federal restructuring, Belgium's existence and survival continues to be threatened by the fierce Flemish–Walloon conflict (cf. also Chardon, 2009).

Regarding the United Kingdom[6] it has always been assumed that Scotland and Wales constitute two separate 'Celtic nations' (Sharpe, 2000, p. 67), and some analysts have even spoken of a 'social federalism' (Sharpe, 2000). Until recently however, the notion of a unitary state, which is rooted in the principle of parliamentary sovereignty, has remained untouched. In the late 1990s, though, the New Labour government embarked upon an (historic) devolution policy by establishing elected regional parliaments (assemblies) in Scotland and Wales on the basis of referenda that were held in these two regions. Furthermore, following the Good Friday Agreement of 1998, parliamentary representation in Northern Ireland was restored under the name of Stormont (which, however, since 2000 has been suspended four times).[7] It is peculiar to the British variant of devolution that the new powers and responsibilities that were granted to the regional parliaments and executives are, under the time-honoured constitutional principle of parliamentary sovereignty, only 'delegated' powers and could thus be, at least legally and conceptually speaking, revoked and 'retrieved' by the House of Commons at any time (Kastendiek et al., 1999, p. 287; Sturm, 2003, p. 227). This, though, in political and realistic terms appears to be extremely unlikely.

With regard to devolution, a further distinction is usually made between an administrative, an executive and a legislative one.[8] The first variant that prevailed until 1997 (cf. Münter, 2005, p. 29ff.) is still largely rooted in the classic Westminster model, and pertains to the transfer of administrative tasks to regionally responsible cross-sectional departments operating on the national level, for example, in the form of territorial ministries (Scottish Office 1885; Welsh Office 1964–65; Northern Ireland Office 1972). 'Executive' devolution means the transfer of administrative tasks to regional bodies for autonomous implementation, that is, the legislative framework remains centralized in Westminster, while the elected representative bodies may undertake legislative adjustments to the regional circumstances via secondary legislative powers (Münter, 2005, p. 25 et seq.). This was the case, for example, in Wales until 2006 before the National Assembly of Wales was granted primary legislative powers through the Government of Wales Act of 2006 (e.g., in the areas of agriculture, fishing, forestry, culture, etc.). Such a transfer of primary legislative powers to regional parliaments is considered 'legislative' devolution (Kastendiek et al., 1999, p. 287). This has applied to Scotland since 1999 when the Scottish Parliament – by deviation from the *ultra vires* principle – was accorded a kind of general competence clause (Sturm, 2002, p. 58). Recently, through the Scotland Act 2012, the Scottish Parliament was

Table 4.2 Asymmetric devolution in the UK

Region/'Nation'	% UK Population	% UK GDP	Type of Devolution
England	83.6	85.7	Direct government by Westminster; no elected regional representation; no devolution
Scotland	8.6	8.1	Scottish Parliament with primary legislative powers in the majority of policy areas (except for foreign policy); general competence; far-reaching legislative devolution
Wales	4.9	3.9	National Assembly of Wales until 2006 only with secondary, after that with some primary legislative powers in areas determined by Westminster; extended legislative devolution
Northern Ireland	2.9	2.2	Northern Ireland Assembly with primary legislative powers in areas not reserved by Westminster (conceded/conditional/excluded rights); limited legislative devolution

Source: Following Jeffery (2009) with authors' own additions.

given further powers and fiscal autonomy rights. Thus, it remains to be seen whether the Scotland-wide referendum scheduled for autumn 2014 will result in a popular vote for Scottish independence.

The original intention of the Labour Government to also create elected regional councils in the eight English spatial planning regions by holding regional referenda remained unrealized after the North-East region rejected the proposal of a regional council by a striking majority of 78 per cent of the voters (Sturm, 2006, p. 137). Hence, England has also been termed the 'black hole' of British devolution (Trench, 2009, p. 342). Even if, with an eye on Scotland and Wales, one can speak of a 'quasi-federalization' (Wilson and Game, 2006) of the United Kingdom, there are good reasons to call it (highly) 'asymmetrical'. For one, it should be borne in mind that only 13 per cent of the total UK population reside in Scotland and Wales, while the overwhelming majority live in (still strongly centralized) England. Second, even between Scotland and Wales as the two 'quasi-federalized' regions, there are significant legal and other administrative differences (see Jeffrey, 2009; see also Table 4.2).

'Simple' regionalization and creation of regional counties

Although it is the cradle of the Napoleonic state model, France also abandoned the path-dependent entrenched unitary centralized state model when the historic decentralization was initiated in 1982 and then continued in 2003 (see below) through the transferring of state functions and responsibilities to the subnational levels. However, this development did not and does not represent a federalization – as in Italy, Spain and Belgium – but rather a regionalization. On the one hand, in 1982 the regions (*régions*) were accorded the status of territorial bodies (*collectivités locales*/today: *territoriales*) with fully-fledged local self-government (in France called *administration libre*) and were equipped with democratically elected, politically responsible representative bodies (*conseils régionaux*) and indirectly elected regional executives (*présidents du conseils régionaux*). On the other hand, however, the constitutional amendment of 2003 explicitly stipulated that the regions represent a subnational level of self-government that is hierarchically equal to the two already existing self-government levels (*départements* and *communes*) and that the regions are not superordinate to them (so-called *non-tutelle*).

The functional equivalence of the regions with the *départements* and municipalities (*communes*) shows in Article 72 of the Constitution of 2003 that, without any differentiation between the three levels, 'the local authorities are called upon to take decisions in the range of functions, which can be best rendered at their (respective) level'. This amounts to a 'general competence clause' with a dose of subsidiarity. Furthermore, it is stipulated, again without differentiation by levels, that 'the local authorities have a regulatory competence [*pouvoir réglementaire*] for the exercise of the functions'. Although the regions are formally on the same footing with the other two levels, in reality the exercise of the regions' regulatory competence has been quite significant (see Marcou, 2012, p. 13 with a remarkably broad account of such regulations by regions). But since these regional regulations, notwithstanding their growing extension, are based on and limited by explicit national legislative authorization, their issuance still clearly falls short of any kind of quasi-federal legislative power in its own right.

The largely undifferentiated 'general competence clause' and principle of *non-tutelle* have followed up and even further accentuated the traditional task competition and overlap (*enchevêtrement*) among the three local government levels. This has been criticized abrasively, also by the Comité Balladur. The regions remain limited in their administrative responsibilities and evinced in their minimal personnel staff: only 0.7 per cent of the total number of employees of the three subnational levels are regional personnel. Hence, the development of the regions towards any quasi-federal status has so far been consciously and deliberately prevented.

As a crucial component of the Reform Act (Loi de Réforme des Collectivités Territoriales), which was adopted on 16 December 2010 following a lengthy and controversial legislative process and that is to take effect on 1 January 2016, the status and the functions of the regions will change significantly. In a new inter-governmental concept, the *régions* and the *départements* on the one hand, and the municipalities and their inter-municipal cooperative formations (*intercommunalité*), on the other, will be organizationally accentuated as the two major subnational areas of activity (*pôles*). Under this structure, the position of the regions within the first *pôle* is to be emphasized, without, *nota bene*, relinquishing the principle of its general equivalence of all three subnational levels. In order to avoid the task overlap, the regions and the *départements* are to be stripped of the general competence clause and will instead be assigned specific tasks. However, after the conservative President Nicolas Sarkozy and his conservative parliamentary majority were replaced in May 2012, by the socialist President François Hollande and his socialist majority, the future fate of the reform project of 2010, which was politically identified with the Sarkozy presidency, has become uncertain.

In Italy, the lower sub-state levels (i.e., the provinces and municipalities) have thus far remained untouched despite the radical regionalization movement (quasi-federalization) and irrespective of its territorial fragmentation of reforms, a fact also explained by the inability of the Berlusconi government and its conservative majority to bring about reform. Faced with the pressure of the intensifying financial and euro crisis and at the EU's insistence, the new 'technocrat' government under Mario Monti finally put together a reform package that was targeted at reducing public expenditure (see also Chapter 3, Section 3.6.1). As one of the key elements, territorial reorganization on the levels of the provinces and large cities was included. Put to the vote in the two chambers of parliament with the help of the parliamentary leverage of a vote of confidence (*voto di fiducia*), the reform package was adopted as law on 7 August 2012 with a large majority (cf. *La Repubblica* of 8 August 2012). Inter alia, the law provides for the reduction of the number of provinces from 110 to 50 (with an average size of at least 350000 inhabitants).[9] For further development see Section 4.3.3 below.

In Sweden, which is a unitary yet distinctly decentralized country, the counties (*län*) constitute the territorial basis for both the lower level of state administration (*länsstyrelse*) and for the upper level of the two-tier local self-government system (*landsting kommuner*). While the county boundaries dating back to the seventeenth century remained unchanged until recently, the conspicuous (all but 'path-dependent') continuity and stability of the county landscape has been challenged by a debate about the need to introduce regions in Sweden (cf. Lidström, 2010, p. 61 et seq.). In a first (experimental) step in 1999, the regional counties of Skåne and Västra Götaland, now explicitly called 'regions' and no longer 'counties', were established to include the two major cities of Malmö and Göteborg as well as two neighbouring counties. These regional counties have directly elected regional assemblies (e.g., the region of Västra Götaland). In addition to their existing county functions, the new regions have been assigned the tasks of regional planning and development previously performed by the state authorities. Initially intended as an experiment to last until 2001, the scheme was extended until 2010. In this reform variant, the counties concerned are incorporated into the new regions, while the core cities (Malmö and Göteborg) retain their municipal responsibilities but lose their county functions to the regions. The creation of the regions ties in with the further decentralization of state tasks, as regional planning and regional development that was hitherto carried out by the county state administration (*länsstyrelsen*) has been transferred to the regional local self-government level. A third region was established on the island of Gotland. The three at first experimentally created regions have by now become a permanent structure.

In 2002, the government appointed a commission ('Responsibility Commission', Ansvars Komittén),[10] which presented its findings in 2007 after several years of consultation (cf. Lidström, 2010, p. 70 et seq.). In its recommendations the commission, inter alia, focused on the county level. Following up the earlier 'experimental' creation of regions, it proposed that the remaining 20 counties (averaging some 420000 inhabitants) be dissolved and replaced with six to nine regional counties (regions with directly elected regional parliaments (cf. SOU, 2007a, 2007b; see also Wollmann, 2008, p. 40 et seq.). Furthermore, the commission recommended that the tasks and responsibilities of the municipalities be retained and strengthened with a focus 'on the heavyweight welfare services and core planning functions' (SOU, 2007b, p. 10). However, the recommendations of the commission have still not been implemented (cf. Lidström, 2010, p. 76). Meanwhile, the Swedish regionalization policy has come under mounting criticism, as the subnational functional and institutional structures have become more complex and heterogeneous, and reminiscent of a 'regional mess' (Olsson and Aström, 2004; see also Stegmann McCallion, 2008).

In Germany, a new regionalization movement has evolved within the existing federal administrative structure. In this regard the creation of city-regional structures in urban centres (such as the region of Hanover, the Municipal Association [*Stadtverband*] of Saarbrücken, the Regional Association [*Regionalverband*] of Stuttgart and the like) needs to be distinguished from

Note: Since 4 September 2011; average population: from 91 056 to 204 875; average surface area: from 1288 km² to 2897 km².

Source: See http://de.wikipedia.org/wiki/Kreisgebietsreform_Mecklenburg-Vorpommern_2011, last accessed 6 March 2014.

Figure 4.3 Establishment of regional counties in Mecklenburg-Western Pomerania

the establishment of quasi-regional counties in less densely populated areas, especially in Eastern and Northern Germany. What both variants have in common is that the 'old counties' are being replaced by (quasi-) regional structures with local self-government status, in part by incorporating county-free cities (*kreisfreie Städte*) into ('regionalized') counties in what has been referred to as 'hard regionalization' (see above) (Bogumil and Grohs, 2010, p. 93). Exemplary of this is the *Land* of Mecklenburg-Western Pomerania where, after a highly controversial political debate, the *Land's* parliament passed a piece of *Land* legislation (the County Territorial Reform Act) through which, taking effect on 1 January 2009, five regional counties (averaging 350000 inhabitants) were to be created by fusing 12 existing counties and by incorporating six existing county-free cities (see Figure 4.3). But, upon the judicial complaint filed by some of the affected counties, the *Land's* Constitutional Court handed down a ruling in July 2007[11] that declared the Reform Act to be unconstitutional (on the grounds of procedural violations).[12] Subsequently, the *Land* parliament adopted a (revised) county reform act that, coming into force on 4 November 2011, retained the coveted status of a county-free city for the *Land's* capital and for the historical Hansa City of Rostock. The rest, though, held onto their initial determination to territorially reorganize the county level by creating 'regionalized' counties (with between 280000 and 160000 inhabitants) (cf. Gayl, 2010). Similar developments have also since occurred in other *Länder*.

In the Central and Eastern European reform countries, the initial emphasis was on the build up and consolidation of subnational political and administrative institutions on the levels of local self-government. The regional level of self-government came into focus only during a later reform phase. So, in Hungary, several steps have been taken since the mid-1990s to create regional units above and below the counties. First, this applies to the seven NUTS regions that were established in 1996 with an eye on EU Structural Fund support. Although in 2006 the government made an attempt to transform the NUTS regions into regional self-government bodies with elected councils, the project remained unrealized because the required legislative majorities did not come to pass. In the meantime, in 2012, the Orbán government abolished the NUTS regions. Second, the creation of so-called 'micro-regions' below the counties was pursued by which municipalities were expected to group themselves voluntarily for planning and development purposes. Initially, 138 and ultimately 174 such 'micro-regions' came into existence (cf. Kovács, 2012). By and large, these institutional initiatives did not achieve their aim to establish institutions on the regional level, disposing of decision-making, operating and coordinating capacity. Instead, the development amounted to a 'jungle of institutions on the meso-level', as was succinctly put by Kovács (ibid.).

In Poland, the system transformation was the result of a 'dilatory power compromise' (cf. Wollmann and Lankina, 2003, p. 100 et seq.), in which the victorious Solidarność gave priority to the build up of democratic institutions on the local level, while the communist elite was keen, first of all, to hold its ground in the 49 regional administrative authorities (*województwa*). During the communist phase, the latter were put in place as regional bridgeheads of centralist state and party rule. It was only in 1997 that, after several attempts, a comprehensive reform package could finally be decided on. Accordingly, the number of regions was reduced from 49 to 16. Similar to the dual structure of the French *départements*, the regions became the territorial basis both for the regional state administration (headed by the central government-appointed prefect, *wojewoda*), and for regional self-government institutions with directly elected regional councils (*sejmik*) and a council-elected leader (*marszalek*); (see Swianiewicz, 2003, p. 287; Brusis, 2010). The region reform of 1997 was largely driven by Poland's aspiration to join the EU and by its wish to improve the institutional preconditions to get EU funding for which the territorial rescaling of the regions to serve as NUTS-grant target areas was seen as crucial (cf. Wollmann and Lankina, 2003, p. 106).

Preliminary conclusion and comparison

It is clear, then, that a wide range of variants can be observed in the area of regionalization/federalization. Whereas the countries shaped by a Napoleonic legacy (with the exception of France) and the United Kingdom have headed towards federalization models, the 'simple' regionalization option was adopted in the Central Eastern European and Scandinavian countries. With regard to the former group, it has become evident that the reform development amounted mostly to distinct asymmetric forms, within which the powers and possibilities for action of the (quasi-)federal subjects have been distributed unevenly. This factor thus markedly distinguishes the new 'federal' states in Europe from the 'old' federal states (Germany, Austria and Switzerland).

Furthermore, simple regionalization exists in numerous facets that can be classified according to the features of the territorial versus functional principle and the degree of commitment (hard versus soft regionalization) (see Figure 4.4).

The powers are distributed either in a top-down (i.e., from the state to the regions or in a bottom-up manner (i.e., from the local government level to the region). The latter is generally associated with the introduction of completely new regional territorial units, mostly in the form of local government.

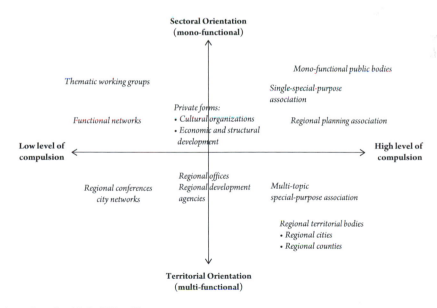

Source: Bogumil and Grohs (2010, p. 94).

Figure 4.4 Variants of 'hard' and 'soft' simple regionalization

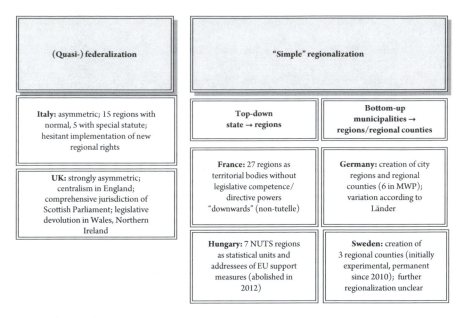

Source: Authors' own diagram.

Figure 4.5 Federalization and regionalization in Europe

Another variant in the group of 'simple' regionalizers belongs to the transition countries, whose regional organization was guided by funding-policy reasons and was rather based on the (spatial) classification of NUTS regions, mostly without 'breathing life into them'. Figure 4.5 provides a summary of federalization and regionalization in Europe.

4.2.3   Decentralization and deconcentration

As put forward above, a distinction can, first of all, be made between decentralization/municipalization on the one hand, and administrative deconcentration on the other. In the former, state tasks typically performed by single-function/special purpose units are transferred to and integrated into local self-government based on the multi-functionality principle. Thus, this reform strategy amounts to a strengthening of the territorial organization (multi-purpose model). By contrast, administrative deconcentration goes hand in hand with the expansion of sectoral state administration hinging on the principle of mono-functionality (single-purpose model). The deconcentrated administrative units and their respective tasks remain under the political control and responsibility of the state.

The distinction between a 'monistic' and a 'dualistic' task model that was introduced earlier (see Chapter 2, Section 2.1.3; see also Figure 4.6) can also

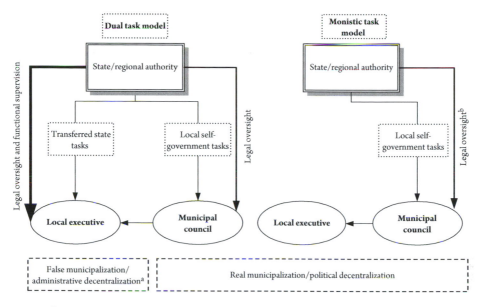

Notes:

a. Tends towards 'administrative deconcentration'.

b. The 'local self-government task according to instructions' as known in the monistic model is subject to state functional supervision and legal oversight.

Source: Authors' own diagram.

Figure 4.6 Task model and decentralization

be applied to the analysis of decentralization and municipalization strategies. Within the 'monistic' model, all functions that are assigned to the municipalities are 'real' local self-government tasks for which the elected local council is responsible. By contrast, in the dualistic task model, the municipalities have two types of tasks. For one, there are 'real' local self-government functions that are particularly derived from the traditional general competence clause. For these functions, the elected local council is responsible, as in the monistic task model. Second, the municipalities can be assigned the task of carrying out functions that are assigned ('delegated') to them by the state. The responsibility for the conduct of such 'delegated' functions lies with the local government's executive (mayor, etc.) and not with the elected local council. In this case, one may speak of a 'false' (in lieu of 'true') municipalization (cf. Wollmann, 2008, p. 259 et seq.) or of 'administrative' decentralization. By contrast, the monistic task model implies 'real' municipalization or 'political' decentralization (cf. Kuhlmann, 2009a, p. 81 et seq.; Kuhlmann, et al., 2011). The issuance of building permits, for example, can serve as a litmus test for showing the distinction between the two task models. In the monistic model, the issuing of building permits is a 'real' local government task that is ultimately decided by the elected local council (as in the case of Sweden). By contrast, in the dualistic model, this function is assigned to and carried out by the local government executive without any say so from the elected council (as in Germany; see Wollmann, 2008, p. 276 et seq.).

The transfer of functions in the case of 'false' municipalization or administrative decentralization has significant consequences for the municipalities regarding both the internal relations between the local council and local executive (mayor, county administrator – *Landrat*), and their external relation to the state. For one, in the internal relationship the local executive is solely responsible for the implementation of 'false' local tasks while the elected council has, at least formally, no influence in these matters. Second, in the external relationship, the local administration is subject to a functional/administrative supervision (in German, *Fachaufsicht*) that goes beyond the legal oversight (*Rechtsaufsicht*) and that also addresses the 'merits', and adequateness (in French, *opportunité*) of the activity concerned. By contrast, in cases of 'real' municipalization ('political' decentralization: see above), the elected local council is, internally, the highest decision-making body, while externally the municipality stands only under the legal oversight by the state authorities. Although in both regards the distinction has often become blurred in local practice, it remains relevant if and when conflicts arise (cf. Wollmann, 2008, p. 259 et seq., with references).

Decentralization policy is often premised on the assumption that the level to which public tasks are assigned and the one that is responsible for their implementation does have an influence on the performance (quality, etc.) of the delivery of public services. However, the findings and information available in the relevant literature on the effects of decentralization are highly contradictory (cf. De Vries, 2000; Pollitt, 2005; Treisman, 2007). Thus, there is evidence – partly theoretically derived, partly empirical – for positive as well as negative effects, as summarized in Table 4.3.

In view of these different, and in some cases strikingly contradictory assessments, pertinent studies come to the conclusion that differences in performance results are accounted for less by decentralization as such than by the concrete implementation of the decentralization programme (cf. De Vries, 2000, p. 200; Treisman, 2007, p. 21 et seq.) and by the specificity of the policy area (cf. Ostrom and Bish, 1977; De Vries, 2000, p. 200 et seq.; Kuhlmann et al., 2011).

Table 4.3 Advantages and disadvantages of decentralization

Effect Dimension	Advantages	Disadvantages
Effectiveness	Proximity to users/local knowledge; accuracy (Oates, 1972; Mill, 1991) Innovation/experimentation capacity	Insufficient specialization/functional power (Segal, 1997) Legality deficits due to local politicization of administrative action (Pettit, 2004)
Efficiency	Competition between small units increases efficiency (Tiebout, 1956; Oates, 1972) Savings through economies of scope	Decreasing economies of scale (Wagener, 1969; Alesina and Spolarole, 2003) Expenditure expansion at the cost of the central state (Rodden, 2002)
Horizontal coordination	Improved cross-functional coordination (multi-purpose benefits; Wollmann, 2006) Weakening of 'Fachbruderschaften' (confraternities)	Greater conflict intensity due to permanent cross-functional coordination processes Insufficient territorial coordination in undersized territorial units
Vertical coordination	Policy stability by local veto players (Tsebelis, 2002) Vertical balance of power; counterweight to central power (Weingast, 1995)	'Blame shifting' by the central state Lack of congruence between revenue and spending responsibility (connectedness) Coordination deficits between administrative levels
Democratic control/ participation	Greater participation; 'public spirit' (Dahl and Tufte, 1973) Transparency, accountability of decisions	Susceptibility to corruption (Bardhan and Mookherjee, 2006) Loss of transparency in 'false' municipalization
Uniformity/ equality	Local/regional variance enables more flexible offers Adaptability to local problem situations and preferences	Greater performance differences Equality of living conditions under threat Legal uncertainty due to different application of law

Source: Following Grohs et al. (2012, p. 127, with further references).

Sweden – a front-runner in political decentralization

Sweden ranks as a front-runner of political decentralization in Europe (see also Chapter 3, Section 3.3). The monistic task model is still in place in a remarkably 'pure' form, since the elected local councils are responsible without exception for all tasks assigned to local governments, and thus also for the above-mentioned building permit process example (cf. Wollmann, 2008, p. 204 et seq.). In drawing on the distinction that has been proposed in the Swedish debate between *lagstyrd* (legally-driven) and *folkstyrd* ('people-', or rather, 'policy-driven') decision-making, the decisions effected in the building permit issuance process are, on the one hand, framed by the existing pertinent legislation (*lagstyrd*), but are, ultimately and politically, reached by the local council (*folkstyrd*) (cf. ibid., pp. 131, 204).

In order to provide some guidance for extending the responsibilities and strengthening the autonomy of the municipalities in the wake of their massive territorial rescaling in the mid-1970s, the government inaugurated a reform programme dubbed the 'free local government experiment' (*frikommuner*). Between 1984 and 1991, for 40 municipalities a number of legal restrictions were (experimentally) suspended (cf. Strömberg and Engen, 1996, p. 284 et seq.). Inter alia, the responsibility for primary and secondary schools was turned over to the municipalities, the financial allocation system was deregulated (in particular through the increased transition from earmarked allocations to block grants) and the autonomy of counties and municipalities in decisions regarding their political and administrative institutions was expanded (cf. Montin, 1999). On the basis of a subsequent evaluation, a new local government act was passed in 1991, under which the powers of local government, in particular with regard to internal organization, were considerably enlarged (cf. Häggroth et al., 1993). Furthermore, the (initially 'experimental') legal deregulation scheme was widened, made permanent, and extended to all local governments. In addition, the tasks in the aforementioned sectors were politically and extensively decentralized, for example in the education system and in labour market policy (Premfors, 1998), where the local governments took over the functions from the now-dissolved central authorities (Montin, 1999; Pierre, 1995).

France – political decentralization and administrative dualism

In France (cf. Kuhlmann, 2008, 2009a, p. 82 et seq., 2009b; Reiter, 2010), the high degree of centralization was evidenced by the peculiarity that tasks that in traditionally (politically) decentralized countries like Germany and Sweden are local government responsibilities, such as city planning and social services, were, until 1982, carried out by France's state administration, particularly on the level of the *départements*. The main steps of decentralization in France can be separated into two phases. The first was triggered by legislation in the 1980s (the so-called Acte I).[13] The second (Acte II) began with the Constitution amendment of 28 March 2003,[14] and that was then followed by subsequent decentralization laws during the course of the 2000s. Initially, the system of the *départements* was fundamentally revamped in Acte I by transferring the executive function of the prefect to the (then still indirectly elected) president of the departmental council (*conseil général*). The latter then became the head of the newly established *département* administration. The power loss of the prefect pertained also to the abolition of the strict and comprehensive *a priori* state supervision (*tutelle*), which until then, was exercised by the prefect. The *tutelle* now has been reduced to a diluted form of (*a posteriori*) legal oversight.[15] During the process of 'real' municipalization and 'departmentalization', which also included regulatory powers of the departmental council (*pouvoir réglementaire*), the central state transferred numerous functions to the levels of local self-government (*collectivités territoriales*). Thus, tasks that were performed by the state authorities until 1982 were passed on to the municipalities (*communes*) as 'real' local self-government tasks in the steps of *political* decentralization. However, in certain areas, a dualistic task assignment remains in place where the mayor carries out assigned state tasks as an 'agent of the state' (*agent d'Etat*)[16] (e.g., registry matters, issuance of building permits in unplanned areas and so forth). However, generally speaking, the decentralization logic in France edges towards a monistic task model. By virtue of the constitutional amendment of 2003 (Acte II), decentralization attained a constitutionally codified status as Article 1 now stipulates that 'the organization of the French Republic is decentralized'. For the 'indivisible Republic', the introduction of a form of subsidiary principle on the constitutional level represents an unusual thrust.

Regarding the responsibilities of the *départements*, the most significant functional shift has, no doubt, taken place in the 'social action' (*action sociale*) sector, where comprehensive responsibility, including finances, has been transferred to the departmental councils (*conseils généraux*) (Reiter, 2010).[17] Through the legislation of 13 August 2004, further responsibilities have been passed on to the *départements*, such as tasks in the educational system (transfer of technical employees of the *collèges*), in infrastructure (20000 km of national roads, personnel transfer from state infrastructure authorities), in social housing and in the areas of culture and sports.

However, decentralization has not entailed a clear separation of levels in France (separationist model), but has instead resulted in an increase in administrative interweaving, overlaps and institutional competition (so-called *enchevêtrement*) in the subnational space. The Reform Act of 16 December 2010 was aimed at clarifying, adjusting and reducing such overlap and duplication of functions (see above).

At this point one should bear in mind that the degree and amount of deconcentrated administrative units of the central state administration in France remains extremely high. Tellingly, 95 per cent of state employees work outside the Paris ministries in the regional offices (*services extérieurs de l'Etat*) (Thoenig, 2005, p. 689). Although these territorial state authorities have lost influence and importance as result of decentralization (Borraz and Le Galès, 2005, p. 21 et seq.), they have remained significantly present in the subnational space and are still active 'at the grass roots level' (Thoenig, 2005, p. 689). In addition, their position during the course of the 1990s and 2000s has even been strengthened, despite decentralization. The reform programme of a '*renouveau du service public*', initiated under the socialist Prime Minister Rocard in February 1989, provided for extensive steps towards a (further) 'territorialization' of state administration through the installation of additional, locally operating administrative units. The budgetary, personnel-related, and so on, scope of action of these authorities was simultaneously enhanced (Rouban, 1999). A further transfer of tasks from the ministerial level to the regional state offices was initiated by the Deconcentration Act of 1992 passed under the socialist Prime Ministers Cresson and Bérégovoy. The shift of functions from the 'Paris headquarters' to the subordinate administrative state structures on the 'periphery' was driven along further in 1995 under the conservative Prime Minister Juppé as part of the reform programme 'Réforme de l'Etat et des Services Publics', which also included some relocations. At the same time, steps towards some reconcentration of state administration can be identified as components of the reforms in the strengthening of the coordinating role of the prefect in relation to the deconcentrated state functional administration. Current developments also pertain to the Finance Reform Act of 2001 (Loi Organique Relative aux Lois de Finances – LOLF), which inaugurated a new scope of action for the finance sector, resources management and budgeting within the state administration. These developments have amounted to a renewed gain in autonomy of the local state authorities in relation to the ministerial administration in Paris as well as to the prefects. The action space of the latter has been strengthened, while the control and steering capacity of the 'Paris headquarters' has been further weakened as a result of global budgeting on the basis of programme and performance targets (*finalités*) set between specific departments and subordinate authorities. By and large, as a result of decentralization and deconcentration, the costly doubling of personnel (*doublon*) and the 'dualism' (Marcou, 2010) of administrative functions have increased, a situation that was severely criticized by the Comité Balladur in 2009.

Italy – codified political decentralization and persistent centralism

Italy, as highlighted before, provides another example of the traditional centralized administrative model of Napoleonic provenance. A decisive step towards political decentralization of the country by strengthening local government was taken by adopting the so-called Bassanini Laws and the constitutional reform of 2001 (Behnke, 2010), in Italy also known as 'devolution' in adopting English terminology (cf. Brunazzo, 2010, p. 185 et seq.). This reform drive aimed at according broad responsibilities to the local government levels (*comuni, province*): the constitutional amendment of 2001 went as far as stipulating that the municipalities (*comuni*) have the right to perform all administrative functions except those that are explicitly assigned to other levels of government (cf. Article 118 I Costituzione, Article 13 I 'Testo unico delle leggi sull'ordinamento degli enti locali', the 'Tuel', of 18 August 2000). At the same time, the dualistic task model was reaffirmed (Article 3, V Tuel).

However, Italy's state and administrative practice is lagging blatantly behind this draft Constitution, as the state offices on the subnational levels, not least prefects (*prefetto*) on the level of the *province*, still play a significant role in the conduct of administrative functions (cf. Schefold, 2007, p. 66). In the 'dualism' of the (still preponderant) chain of state offices and (still sidelined) local government units the institutional imprint of the (Napoleonic) centralized state is evident. This state of affairs is shown in the share of municipal employees, which amounts to only 14 per cent of the number of public personnel, while state-employed personnel make up over 50 per cent (cf. Tables 3.2 and 3.4 in Chapter 3). Thus, although political decentralization is codified in the Constitution, it remains largely unrealized so far.

Hungary – initially far-reaching decentralization and recent recentralization

As was mentioned earlier (Chapter 3, Section 3.5), after the collapse of the communist regime and Hungary's return to democratic government, the build up of local-level administrative structures was marked by a contradiction. On the one hand, legislation of 1990 contained a decentralizing and municipalization impetus, about which has been pointedly said was 'extremely liberal by any international standard' (Davies, 1995, p. 74; Wollmann and Lankina, 2003, p. 93 et seq.). Around 65 per cent of all public personnel are still employed by the municipalities (in particular by large and medium-sized cities) and only 35 per cent by the (central) state, including state administration in the counties and deconcentrated, single-purpose state offices ('decos'). Thus, until recently, Hungary exhibited an extraordinarily high degree of decentralized local-government–level implementation of public functions and which, along with Sweden, tops all other European countries.

The build up of distinctly decentralized local government institutions was, from the very beginning, paralleled by a vertical organizational strand of 'decos'. While the 'decos' were an organizational and personnel resource for central government to have its own administrative structure in the subnational space, they were resented by the local authorities as a strategy and an attempt to 'recentralize' Hungary's pronouncedly decentral local-government–centred institutional fabric (see Wollmann and Lankina, 2003, p. 97, with references).

The recent adoption of a new Constitution ('Basic Law'), for which the conservative Orbán government could mobilize a broad parliamentary majority and which came into effect on 1 January 2011, is bound to profoundly remould and change Hungary's post-1990 inter-governmental setting by radically recentralizing the entire administrative system and by making the state's influence and control in the subnational space prevalent. The counties have been stripped of most self-government functions, while the central government-appointed 'prefects' have been given control over the conduct of public functions. The municipalities have been rid of important tasks (schools, health services), which have been taken over by the state (cf. Kovács, 2012).

Germany – 'false' municipalization with withdrawal of resources

Irrespective of the federalism-typical variance between the German *Länder*, the transfer (decentralization) of administrative functions from the state level to the local authorities has mostly been effected (based on the traditional 'dualistic' task model) in the organizational form of 'delegated' tasks (cf. Wollmann, 1997b, 2010a; Burgi, 2009, p. 163, 2010). As was explained earlier in some detail, in the 'delegated' task form, the conveyance of that function is the sole responsibility of the local government's executive (mayor, head of county, etc.) without any involvement of the elected council, while in relation to the state level, the implementation of 'delegated' tasks is subject to the 'functional' supervision by the state authorities and not just by a 'legality' review. Because of this two-fold restriction, the transfer of tasks in the 'delegation' mode is seen to fall short of 'real' municipalization and 'political' decentralization; instead, it has been interpreted as a 'false' municipalization or as an 'administrative' decentralization.

As a rule, such a transfer of tasks is directed at the counties and county-free cities with the majority of municipalities hardly being involved. Since the *Länder* are responsible for municipal legislation, there is, however, no uniform decentralization legislation that could be equally applied to all local

Table 4.4 Variants of administrative structure reform in German Länder

Administrative Decentralization (Example: BW)	Administrative Deconcentration (Example: LS)	Regionalization (Example: MWP)
Comprehensive false municipalization	Moderate municipalization	Transfer of *Länder* state tasks to regional self-administrations
Drastic streamlining of sectoral state administration	Expansion of single-purpose *Land* authorities	Establishment of regional counties (MWP: 12 ➔ 6)
Strengthening of the multi-functional county level as 'lower *Land* authorities'	Abolition of meso-level state authorities	Regionalization of state coordination function
Strengthening of meso-level state authorities	Hardly any upgrading of multi-functional self-administration	Reduction of sectoral state administration (in the two-tier model)

Note: BW = Baden-Württemberg; LS = Lower Saxony; MWP = Mecklenburg-Western Pomerania.

Source: Authors' own compilation.

governments. For the sake of simplification, three variants of administrative structure reform will be distinguished in the following (see Table 4.4); it should be added, too, that such (functional) reforms may take place along with (or without) related territorial reforms (see below) and that only in a few *Länder* (e.g., Baden-Württemberg) have they been linked with *Land* policy-imposed efficiency gains.

Since the early 2000s, in almost all *Länder*, a 'new wave' of 'functional reforms' has been set off, that is, a wave of decentralizing public tasks from the state level to the local government level, particularly to the municipalities (cf. Bull, 2008; Kuhlmann, 2009a, p. 119ff.; Kuhlmann and Bogumil, 2010).[18] Insofar as the addressees of such transfers are the municipalities, one speaks of 'municipalization' or in Germany of 'communalization' (*Kommunalisierung*, as in German the term '*Kommune*' comprises both 'municipalities' as well as 'counties').

The *Land* of Baden-Württemberg proved to be frontrunner and prime example of this new wave of 'functional reform', which, insofar as the transfer of state functions was related to local authorities, was carried out in the organizational form of 'delegating' tasks to them. Hence, it was an 'administrative' decentralization or 'false' municipalization rather than political decentralization or 'real' municipalization. The complete dissolution of 350 of the total of 450 existing single-purpose administrative authorities of the

Land administration was the core element of that reform. The tasks and the personnel of these single-purpose state authorities have instead been transferred to 35 county administrations and nine county-free cities as well as to the four administrative district authorities (Bogumil and Ebinger, 2005). The costs of the transfer of tasks and personnel to the local authorities were initially covered entirely by the *Land* budget. However, as these transfer payments of the *Land* are being reduced by 3 per cent every year, the *Land* government expects a so-called efficiency gain (*Effizienzrendite*) of about 20 per cent over the next five to seven years. The generation of this 'gain' has been imposed on the local authorities. In Germany, 'municipalization' (Baden-Württemberg being a case in point) has, on the one hand, led to a simplification of the subnational institutional landscape and to a reduction of the density of authorities and of the number of institutional actors in the multi-level system. At the same time, it has resulted in a distinct functional upgrading of the local government level, particularly of the counties and county-free cities. On the other hand, the expanding volume of tasks of the local authorities must be dealt with by ever-decreasing resources (evidenced by the reduction of local government personnel by almost 40 per cent since the early 1990s). This development is bound to entail deficits in the implementation and the quality of public services and cast doubt on the undertaking of further municipalization (Bauer et al., 2007; Ebinger, 2010; Richter, 2010).

By contrast, an example of administrative deconcentration can be observed in Lower Saxony, which is the only *Land* to have effected a 'system transition' from a three-tier to a two-tier system (Bogumil and Kottmann, 2006, p. 63). By the administration modernization act in Lower Saxony of 5 November 2004, the four meso-level administrative district authorities of Brunswick, Hanover, Lüneburg and Weser-Ems were dissolved and the meso-level administrative districts were completely abolished effective 1 January 2005 (cf. also Reiners, 2008). At the same time, a significant deconcentration of the administrative functions that were previously 'bundled' by the four (now dissolved) meso-level administrative district authorities was effected. Although Lower Saxony had initially intended to transfer 70 per cent of the now available tasks as 'delegated' tasks, that is, by way of ('false') municipalization to the counties and county-free cities, the decentralization effects have remained minimal. Following the abolition of the four meso-level administrative district authorities only about 10 per cent of their functions have since been 'municipalized', whereas the task profile of the single-purpose state authorities has been noticeably expanded. On the one hand 121 *Land* authorities (including the four meso-level administrative district authorities) have been abolished. On the other hand, however, 21 new single-purpose authorities have been put into place and the vast majority of tasks of the erstwhile meso-level administrative district authorities have been transferred to single-purpose state authorities or ministerial administration rather than being 'muncipalized'. Thus, the reform has resulted in a significant expansion of deconcentrated, sectorally organized *Land* administration instead of strengthening decentralized local self-government.

United Kingdom/England – hollowing-out of the monistic task model and recentralization

Historically, England has been a prime example of the monistic task model. While local governments could carry out only tasks expressly assigned to them by parliamentary law under the *ultra vires* doctrine (see Chapter 3, Section 3.4), once the functions were accorded to them, they passed as 'real' local government tasks to be discharged by local government, thus making it a 'political' decentralization (cf. Wollmann, 2008, p. 259 et seq.). Although the monistic local task model still remains formally valid, since the 1980s the decision-making scope (discretion) of local councils has been hollowed out by an extremely dense network of directives (guidances notes) and intervention powers of central government (cf. Kuhlmann, 2006a; Wollmann, 2008, p. 200 et seq., with references; Reiter et al., 2010). Furthermore, due to its dominant strategy of administrative deconcentration (agencification, quangoization; see Section 4.5.2 below) and its corresponding recentralization of its administrative system, the United Kingdom presents an aberration. The traditional profile of politically responsible and functionally strong local governments has been weakened and hollowed out in a manner that is unique in Europe (Stoker, 1999).[19] This strategy was directed at transferring tasks that were traditionally located within the remit of local authorities to state agencies or so-called 'quangos' (quasi non-governmental organizations)[20] thereby manifesting a pronouncedly centralizing effect of the reform. 'One of the notable features of the UK public sector reforms of 1987–1997 was that, unlike the parallel reforms in many Continental European states, most of the decentralization under the British Conservative administration was administrative rather than political' (Pollitt et al., 1998, pp. 6–7). This strategy reveals a profound mistrust on the part of the Conservative government vis-à-vis local authorities whose majority was dominated by Labour. Central government, which, in the dual-polity tradition was limited to Whitehall, is now institutionally anchored in the local sphere by its own agencies and quangos. It has thus increasingly crowded out and disempowered multi-functional local government. The scope of quangoization that has occurred can be seen in the existence of 5000 of such state and semi-state quangos in the United

Table 4.5 Quangos in the United Kingdom (1996)

Quango Type	Number (1996)
Executive	
NDPBs	301
Non-recognized Northern Ireland NDPBs	8
NHS bodies	788
Non-recognized local quangos	4653
Advisory	
NDPBs	674
Total number of executive and advisory quangos	6424

Note: NDPBs = non-departmental public bodies.

Source: Skelcher (1998, p. 13, with further references).

Kingdom in 2001, directed by 50000 central-government–appointed board members. This contrasts with only 500 local councils with a total of 23000 elected council members at the district and county levels (Winchester and Bach, 1999, p. 32).[21] Table 4.5 shows the state of quangoization in the United Kingdom in the mid-1990s, including central state as well as local-level organizations.

The coalition government formed in May 2010 by the Conservatives and Liberal Democrats began to reduce the number of existing quangos. In doing so the Conservatives aimed at cutting back the public sector and slashing the public deficit. To date, around 80 (of a total of about 1000) quangos have been dissolved. A recent government document identified 177 further 'candidates for abolition'.[22] Moreover, the Localism Act, which came into effect on 15 November 2011, is intended, inter alia, to largely replace the traditional *ultra vires* doctrine by introducing a general power of competence and to thus upgrade the task profile of the local authorities (cf. see Chapter 3, Section 3.4). However, it remains to be seen whether or not the recentralization trend will be halted or reversed.

Preliminary conclusion and comparison

Decentralization and municipalization are European-wide trends of administrative reform. Only in the United Kingdom (England) and more recently in Hungary, can distinct recentralization tendencies in the relation between state and local level be found. Thus, the general trend of administrative development in European countries points to an increase of the responsibilities and of the action space of the local authorities with the state handing over functions 'downwards'. Ultimately, the model of strong multi-purpose local government continues to advance. However, the mode and the effects of decentralization/municipalization differ significantly. In Sweden, for example, comprehensive political decentralization has proceeded and the monistic task model has been further buttressed by this. By contrast, in Germany the recent administrative structure and functional reforms have resulted in 'administrative' decentralization and 'false' municipalization, thereby further accentuating the traditional dualistic task model. On top of this, as the share of delegated state tasks continues to grow, the elected local councils are under threat of further losing influence in their internal relation with the local executive. By this same token, externally the local administrations has fallen ever more steeply under state (functional) supervision and is becoming, as it were, 'statelized' (cf. Wollmann, 2008, p. 259 et seq.). However, the transfer of further state tasks to the local authorities and the concomitant enlargement of the local task profile also holds the potential of a progressive municipalization of state tasks. This is because the implementation of these tasks lies with the directly elected mayor or head of county (*Landrat*),[23] who is strongly integrated into the local political context in possible defiance of state functional supervision and influence, thus fostering some political municipalization. Also, France and Italy, where the far-reaching steps of political decentralization have been codified, are still holding on to the dual task model and retaining a strong presence of state administration in the subnational space, although the state supervision of the local authorities has meanwhile been significantly diminished. Figure 4.7 summarizes decentralization and municipalization in Europe.

Predominant type of decentralization (current reforms)

	Political/real	Administrative/false	Re-centralization
Dual	France Italy	Germany	Hungary
Monistic	Sweden		United Kingdom

(left axis label: **Task model**)

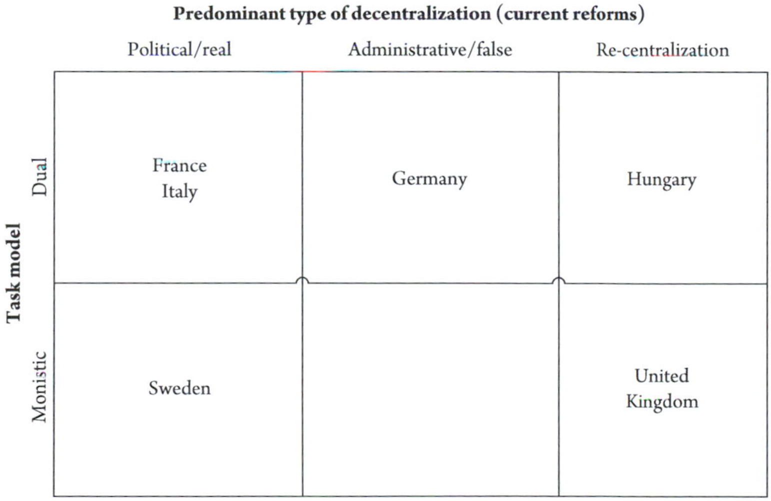

Source: Authors' own diagram.

Figure 4.7 Decentralization and municipalization in Europe

4.2.4 Cross-country comparison: convergence, divergence, persistence and explanatory factors

Convergence

The country analyses have shown that reforms have been placed on the administrative reform agenda throughout European countries. With only a few exceptions this trend prevails towards decentralization/regionalization and towards transferring responsibilities and functions to the lower levels of the politico-administrative systems. For one, the development of the meso-level points to a progressive regionalization. Thus, particularly the previously unitary-centralized countries in the Napoleonic country group, that is, Italy, Spain and Belgium, have experienced a paradigmatic shift and a distinct approximation (convergence) towards federal constitutional arrangements, albeit with differences in the results and the scope of reforms. These countries are marked by a (quasi-federal variant of regionalization, in which autonomous legislative and administrative responsibilities have been bestowed on the regions' powers. While they differ in this from 'ordinary' regions, they still stand aloof from a fully-fledged federal status. The United Kingdom, too, shows an approximation towards a federal system thanks to the devolution in Scotland and Wales. However, due to the remaining distinctly centralized organization of the England's administrative setting, which was termed the 'black hole' of British devolution, this resultant quasi-federal construction is highly asymmetric, thus making for a patent difference from both the traditional and the new federal states in Europe.

With regard to decentralization policy below the meso-level, that is, in the local space, a convergence of European administrative systems towards a multi-functional, politically responsible and institutionally ensured local self-government level can be observed. Traditionally, this was a characteristic of the North-Middle European country group, including Sweden, the United Kingdom and Germany. Although the transfer of functions to the local level has varied considerably in extent and scope, and different approaches in the political upgrading of local government have been pursued, as a general rule, a clear tendency (convergence) towards a functional and political strengthening of local self-government in Europe can be identified.

Persistence/divergence

Thus, from an (empirically somewhat more remote) macro-perspective, isomorphic and convergent developments in the European administrative multi-level systems can be distinctly recognized. Looking closer, however, one must, undoubtedly, differentiate and modify the assumption of convergence, in particular with regard to specific reform trajectories and reform results (practice/result convergence). To begin with, one should note distinctly differing or diverging cases among the observed general trends. Thus, in the country sample under consideration, the United Kingdom (England) illustrates an exceptional European case in view of the far-reaching disempowerment of its local authorities and of the ensuing departure from the model of functionally strong, local self-government. Lately, Hungary, too, has moved in this direction. In the Napoleonic country group, France represents a divergent case insofar as it has opted for a simple regionalization (in lieu of some federalization) of its meso-level. Its regionalization policy, in which the regions were merely granted autonomous decision-making and administrative responsibilities as well as democratically elected representative bodies (*conseils régionaux*), is clearly different from the (quasi-)federal variant in other countries where, inter alia, fully-fledged norm-setting powers are accorded to the regions. Another developmental pattern of regionalization can be observed in connection with the functional upgrading of existing counties in a, thus far, two-tier local government system. Such upgrading, which resulted from the territorial amalgamation of counties, finds its expression by the employment of the term 'region' instead of county. This applies, for example, to Sweden and Denmark (see Section 4.3). Thus, the European countries have chosen very different reform paths, so that 'convergence' can be observed within particular country groups rather than on an all-encompassing European scale. Furthermore, below the meso-level, decentralization policy shows distinct variance. The pronouncedly political form of decentralization within the further strengthened monistic task model in Sweden is conspicuously different from the largely administrative decentralization or 'false' municipalization in Germany within the retained traditional dualistic task model.

Explanatory factors

Drawing on the sociological institutionalism, the described convergence in decentralization policies can be seen as the result of institutional 'imitation' (mimetic isomorphism). Countries have 'copied' reforms undertaken by other countries because these have proven successful or at least influential elsewhere or because refraining from the international trend would have been considered as inappropriate behaviour. According to the normative isomorphism, the national actors have thus followed a 'logic of appropriateness' (see Chapter 2, Section 2.3) in doing what appeared to be expected and normatively desired. Furthermore, the sociological institutionalism points at the externally generated, albeit not strictly speaking, legally compelling coercion to embark upon decentralization (coercive isomorphism). This is exemplified by the EU policy (e.g., structural funding), which has prompted, in particular, the previously centrally ruled countries to install decentralized/ regional institutions, or else face direct or indirect sanctions. Thus, recently, significant impulses have come from the EU to establish regions. For one, the EU Council of the Regions (CoR) and the ensuing participatory opportunities of the regions have evoked and intensified the wish of individual EU member states to be able to exert more influence on the EU policy system by buttressing the regional level. Moreover, as manifested in the examples of Poland and Hungary, the creation of regions that dovetail NUTS regions of the EU structural funding policy are seen by these countries as a precondition of improving their chances to apply for and be granted EU funding.

In line with economic institutionalism, it can be argued that the national actors in Europe react to similar external challenges with similar institutional strategies, as these hold the promise of maximizing institutional benefit and creating an approximation to an (economic) optimum (for the theoretical foundations see Chapter 2, Section 2.3). For this, first, functional reasons and necessities can be identified that have induced European countries, along convergent paths, to put into place new planning and action arenas on the meso-level. An example of this was the introduction of regions as territorial entities in France (1982) and Poland (1999). Second, the integration and concentration processes resulting from Europeanization and globalization can be named as factors that create external pressure on national administrative systems. Thus, particularly the traditionally, centrally governed countries have to strike a balance in order to ensure the stability of the expanding supra-national construction of the EU 'from below' and thereby to also legitimize this internally against the backdrop of their still inadequate democratic legitimization. From the perspective of economic institutionalism, it can be argued that for the actors, a rational optimization strategy involves compensating EU-induced centralization and concentration on the supra-national level through decentralization/regionalization and deconcentration in the national/subnational context, leading then to convergent developments.

As has been shown, some countries have experienced massive upheavals and in some cases almost paradigmatic institutional changes. Neither the narrow economic interpretation nor the isomorphism theoretical scheme of sociological institutionalism appears to have been able to provide an adequate explanation for this. Instead, the interest constellations of the relevant actors must be considered as pertinent determining factors and independent variables highlighted by actor-centred institutionalism. Thus, for one, federalization and regionalization has been driven by the resolve of the relevant actors to achieve a space for political and cultural self-determination in individual regions as well as for population groups characterized by ethnic, linguistic and political identities. This has applied particularly to Spain and Belgium, but also to Italy (especially in the regions with special status, such as Alto Adige/South Tyrol and Sicily) and to the United Kingdom (with regard to Scotland and Wales).

The influence of political and administrative actor constellations and of individual actors on administrative processes can also be exemplified in the German case. Thus, the pioneering role resumed by the *Land* of Baden-Württemberg in the pursuit of functional reforms (by way of transferring *Land* functions to the local government level) can be largely explained by the coalition formed between the *Land's* then Minister-President Erwin Teufel and the heads of counties (*Landräte*). The resultant reform was essentially based on a political compromise and 'bargain' in which the *Land* renounced the carrying out of a territorial reform at the local level, including the counties, while the local government actors, particularly the heads of counties, agreed to accept a major transfer of tasks, including the commitment to generate an 'efficiency gain' (see above). In the case of Lower Saxony, by contrast, the *Land* government aimed first of all at bolstering its own political profile by abolishing the meso-level district administrations, resulting in a highly fragmented, top-heavy structure of single-purpose *Land* administrative authorities.

Finally, France should be mentioned as exemplifying the explanatory power of actor-centred institutionalism. A strong elucidation as to why the socialists who traditionally have a Jacobin-egalitarian and consequently centralist inclination, turned in the early 1980s to embrace (and, with some success, implement) a decentralization policy can plausibly be seen in the interconnection and interweaving of France's national and local political arenas and their actor networks. The national legislature has been often influenced by local interests that became ever more pronounced in the post-war period as the practice of the *cumul des mandats* in which the local mayors simultaneously are elected members of the National Assembly or of the Senate further advanced (see above).[24] A similar pattern can be recognized in the decentralization process of Acte II of 2003 (see Kuhlmann, 2009a, p. 86 et seq.).

Still another set of factors for explaining the persistence or divergence in the development of European administrative systems can be sought in historical institutionalism. For one, institutional path dependencies and legacies can be surmised from the local task models and the related municipalization strategies. Thus, adherence to the monistic task model and the continual decentralizing character of Sweden's administrative policy hints at its historical legacy and practice, one that has not been fundamentally questioned by the recent economization discourses. In Germany also, a historical path dependency can be seen inter alia in the fact that the duality of the local government model, which was established in Prussia and has its roots in German-Austrian administrative history (cf. Wollmann, 1999a, p. 51 et seq., 2010a), is still vigorous. This also applies to the French, Italian and Hungarian local government levels, but attempts to remould Germany's traditional cooperative federalism into a competitive federal model, as advocated by some and suggested by the theory of economic federalism are also likely to fail in the face of the persistence of traditional structures and the institutional interweaving that reach back to earlier institutional decisions and junctures (Kropp, 2010, p. 34 et seq.).

4.3 Territorial reforms

4.3.1 Concepts and definitions

Below the national or federal levels, the European countries, as a rule, have two-tier local government systems (see Chapter 3, Section 3.6.2, Table 3.6). The upper level is termed counties (*Kreise, landsting kommuner, province* etc.) and the lower-level municipalities (boroughs/districts, *Gemeinden, kommuner, comuni*).[25] The following illustration refers primarily to the lower ('classical') local government level, but also can include the 'upper' level.

In most European countries, the municipal level was historically characterized by a small-sized and fragmented structure, which often extends back to the late Middle Ages, and originated in the territorial landscape of parish communities. On the one hand, a group of countries can be identified in which national governments acted to reinforce the administrative efficiency of local government by way of territorial and demographic extension (enlargement in scale). While the democratic potential of the local government level was meant to be retained, if not enhanced, the improvement of the administrative-economic performance (*efficiency*) was given priority as a crucial frame of reference (cf. John, 2010, p. 106 et seq. for the United Kingdom). This strategic thrust, also termed 'up-scaling' (cf. Baldersheim and Rose, 2010a, p. 20, 2010b) was a basic guideline of the territorial reforms that following World War II were carried out in England/UK, Sweden and also in some German *Länder*. In the international comparative literature, one therefore speaks of a Northern European reform model (Norton, 1994, p. 40).

Table 4.6 Territorial reform patterns in Europe

Northern European Reform Variant: Up-scaling	Southern European Reform Variant: Trans-scaling
UK, S, DK, German *Länder* (NR-W, HE)	F, I, many CEE-*Länder*; German *Länder* (Rh-P, SH)
Increase in scale; amalgamation	Fragmented municipal structure retained; further fragmentation
UK: Avg. pop.: metrop. districts: 310000; non-metrop. districts: 100000; counties: 760000	F: 37000 communes; avg. pop. 1700
Efficiency; administrative-economic improvement	Background: local government task implementation by state administration (Napoleonic countries)
Background: functionally strong local government systems; often social democratic spirit; rationale zeitgeist/ planning euphoria	Voluntariness: amalgamations only with local government consent
Implementation ultimately by means of binding legislation	Massive local resistance against territorial reform
Subordination of local self-government to parl. decision-making powers	Inter-municipal formations as a substitute (*intercommunalité*; associated municipalities; administrative cooperation)

Source: Authors' own presentation.

In contrast with this Northern European country group, stands a group of countries in which the small-sized fragmented territorial structure of local government whose origin often dates back to the eighteenth century has largely remained unchanged. Reform attempts that the governments in these countries, too, embarked upon during the 1970s largely failed, as these reform measures were made dependent on the consent of the municipalities concerned and, as such, local approval was not obtained. Since France and Italy are prominent examples of this country group, the comparative literature refers to these as the 'Southern European' reform model. In these countries, strategies (termed 'trans-scaling' by Baldersheim and Rose) have been pursued that aim at ensuring the operative viability even of the very small-scale municipalities, by establishing inter-municipal bodies (in French: *inter-communalité*). The creation of such institutionalized forms of inter-municipal cooperation and institutional symbioses can be seen as a response to and a 'substitute' for the lack of formal territorial reforms through municipal amalgamation. Table 4.6 summarizes the reform patterns in Europe.

From the outset, in the transformation of the Central and Eastern European countries from centralized communist regimes to democratic constitutional governments, great importance was also attached to the territorial and organizational restructuring of the subnational level for the development of democratic and efficient decentralized structures. Given the aspired accession to the EU, the concepts and process of the territorial restructuring of the government levels in these countries have been strongly influenced by the territorial NUTS scheme as promoted by the EU (see Chapter 3, Section 3.5). The territorial reform profile of the transformation countries approximates partly the Northern European and partly the Southern European reform type (cf. the country studies in Horváth, 2000; Swianiewicz, 2010). One group of countries follows a Southern European reform pattern in that it was decided to do without municipal amalgamations despite the existing fragmentation of the municipal level and whose further fragmentation was even permitted (e.g., Hungary, Czech Republic). By contrast, in another group of countries the governments, immediately following the system change, implemented far-reaching local territorial reforms conforming to the Northern European reform profile (e.g., Bulgaria, Lithuania). This presumably reflected the intention to territorially 'modernize' the municipal level with an eye on the desired accession to the EU.

4.3.2 Northern European reform patterns: territorial amalgamation, enlargement in scale, administrative efficiency

United Kingdom: 'sizeism' and reform-political breathlessness

The United Kingdom epitomizes the Northern European territorial reform group. The instrumental grip of the central government level on the local level has been determined by two factors. First, it was derived traditionally from the principle of parliamentary sovereignty in that parliament had the right to decide on any institutional changes on local government level by means of legislation – including territorial re-scaling (see Chapter 3, Section 3.4). Second, in dealing with local governments, central government has long since been guided by an 'almost obsessive predominance. . .to production efficiency' (Sharpe, 1993, p. 252; cf. also John, 2001, p. 102 et seq., 2010, p. 106 et seq.).

This logic of action instructed the early territorial reform thrust of 1888 and 1894 under which England's subnational levels were radically revamped in order to adapt them to the policy needs of the central government (cf. Wollmann, 2008, p. 30 et seq.). First, in 1888, elected county councils were established in the 62 historical (largely rural) counties/shires while single-tier county borough councils were provided for in 62 larger cities. Subsequently, in 1894, some 1200 district councils were created within the counties as a completely new lower level of local government. The duality of (two-tier) county councils (with district councils within the counties) and (single-tier) county borough councils became the territorial basis for the Victorian local government model (which was greatly admired abroad) and constituted its territorial and organizational basic structure well until the 1970s.

Since then, the local government system has experienced several ground-swells of radical territorial and organization changes, in which the decision-making power of parliament and the instrumental grip of the central level on the local level again became manifest. In the far-reaching reform move of 1974, for one, the district/borough councils were territorially merged through a drastic reduction of their number from 1250 to 333, while at the same time raising their population size to an average of 170000 inhabitants – a size far beyond any comparison and parallel in Europe (cf. Norton, 1994, p. 41; Wilson and Game, 2006, p. 58 et seq.) and was criticized as sizeism (Stewart, 2000). Second, the county councils whose borders reached back to the medieval shires were rescaled by cutting their number from 58 to 47 and by lifting the population average to 720000 inhabitants. Finally, the almost century-old single-tier system of the county borough councils was abolished, while the two-tier system was expanded to now encompass the entire local government system. Consequently, even large cities such as Birmingham were reduced to the status of a district council. This downgrading was fiercely opposed and bitterly resented by Birmingham and other affected big cities.

Subsequently the British local government system experienced a series of further upheavals. In 1986, the Conservative government under Margaret Thatcher rescinded a central element of the 1974 reform. The (two-tier) structure of 36 metropolitan county councils that had been put into place in 1974 was undone. Consequently, the downgrading of large cities, such as Birmingham, to metropolitan district councils (within two-tier counties) was reversed. This was greatly welcomed by the large cities, which thus regained their previous single-tier status. At the same time, unmistakably for party-political motives, the Thatcher government dissolved the Greater London Council, which was governed by the Labour Party and figured as an active opponent to the Thatcher government. Thus, London's two-tier local government system that was introduced in 1965 was done away with and the single-tier status of the 32 London boroughs restored.

In the early 1990s, the Conservative government under John Major triggered still another drastic territorial and organizational turnover. In England's urbanized areas, the two-tier system of districts/boroughs and counties that had been installed under the 1974 reform was gradually erased. Instead, by territorially, organizationally and functionally integrating counties and districts/boroughs, step by step 56 so-called (single-tier) unitary authorities were created, each averaging about 209000 inhabitants (cf. Wilson and Game, 2006, pp. 68–9).

As a result, at that time large-scale local government structures were in place in almost all urbanized areas, with the 36 metropolitan district councils or the 56 unitary authorities having an average of 308000 and 209000 inhabitants respectively. Today, the two-tier scheme exists only in distinctly rural areas. But, even there, the population average is remarkably high (over 100000 in the non-metropolitan districts, and almost as many as 760000 in the non-metropolitan counties; see Chapter 3, Section 3.4, Figure 3.5).

Under the New Labour government of Tony Blair, the abolition of the Greater London Council that had been imposed by the Tory government in 1986 was reversed, as had been promised in the election campaign. Based on the referendum held in 1999, the Greater London Authority was set up as a (two-tier) London-wide local government structure while retaining the 32 London boroughs. At the Greater London level, the London Assembly was introduced as the 'parliamentary' body and, at the same time, the directly elected Mayor of London was designated as the executive.

The many institutional shifts and ruptures that the local government structures in England have endured have been criticized, in that 'breathless has been the pace of change over the past 30 years' (Leach and Percy-Smith, 2001, p. 236). The resulting 'diversity, fragmentation and perhaps sheer messiness of British local government' (ibid., p. 13) has been ascribed to an 'endless piecemeal tinkering with the system and the absence of wholesale reform' (John, 2001, p. 103).

Sweden, Denmark: territorial anchoring of the local welfare state

In Sweden, historically a predominantly rural country, industrialization and urbanization set in as late as the 1930s, that is, much later than, for example, in the United Kingdom or Germany. Against this background the territorial reform of municipal level that was launched by the government in two phases (1952 and 1974) aimed at enabling the municipalities to act as a key local agent of Sweden's welfare state (*den lokala staten*). In Sweden, too, the national parliament has the power to carry out territorial reform of the local government level without the approval of or, indeed, even contrary to the wishes of the local population. Consequently, the number of municipalities

Table 4.7 Population figures of Swedish municipalities (2007)

Population	Number of Municipalities	Proportion in %
Less than 10 000	72	24.8
10 001–20 000	101	34.8
20 001–30 000	36	12.4
30 001–40 000	28	9.7
40 001–60 00	19	6.6
More than 60 000	34	11.7
Total	290	100.0

Source: Lidström (2010, p. 63).

was drastically reduced from 2282 (with an average of some 2800 inhabitants) to 290 (with an average of 31300 inhabitants; cf. Häggroth et al., 1993, p. 12; for details see Table 4.7).

The territorial organization of Sweden's 20 counties (*landsting kommuner*), each with an average of 420000 inhabitants, has remained unaffected by this territorial reform drive. However, the three largest cities in the country (Stockholm, Gothenburg and Malmö) have been allotted a status (comparable to the German county-free cities and the English unitary authorities) that combines municipal and county tasks. Since the late 1990s, a reform debate hinging on a regionalization has gained momentum where also the (time-honoured) existing county boundaries have been questioned (for an overview, cf. Olsson and Aström, 2003; Lidström, 2010; further, see Section 4.2.2 above).

Denmark too provides a prime example of the Northern European territorial reform type (cf. Mouritzen, 2010). In a first reform step in 1970, the total number of 1386 municipalities (*kommuner*) was reduced to 271, while the number of 26 counties (*amter*) was cut to 14. In 2007, another even more radical reform followed suit, resulting in 98 municipalities with an average of 55400 inhabitants (cf. Dexia, 2008, p. 249; Vrangbaek, 2010). Thus, Denmark's municipalities have leapt to an average population size that, while staying clearly behind the unparalleled population size of British local government ('sizeism'; Stewart, 2000), otherwise ranks at the top of the European local government systems. Furthermore, the 14 counties were amalgamated and transformed into five new 'regions', whose organization is oriented on the NUTS regions of the EU system (cf. Dexia, 2008, p. 250).

Up-scaling in Southern European and transformation countries: Greece, Bulgaria, Lithuania

Until the 1990s, Greece fell in line with the Southern European territorial pattern with its historic fragmented territorial structure of 5825 municipalities (averaging 1900 inhabitants). At the meso-level, 50 prefectures were in place that, founded in 1833 as meso-level of state administration in conformity with the French *département* model, carried out the bulk of public tasks, as well as being in line with the Napoleonic state model.

During the wave of massive territorial-organizational reforms triggered in the 1990s, the state prefectures, in 1994, were transformed into 50 meso-level (prefectural) self-government bodies with elected representation (cf. Hlepas, 2003, p. 230 et seq.). Moreover, the so-called Capodistrias reforms have conspicuously abandoned the Southern European trajectory of the small-size, fragmented local territorial structure and have spectacularly all but embarked on a 'Northern European' reform pattern. Consequently, the number of municipalities has been drastically reduced by large-scale amalgamations from 5825 to 1034 (now averaging 10750 inhabitants). They are now made up of 914 cities (*dimos*) and 120 municipalities (*koinotita*; cf. Hlepas, 2003, p. 231 et seq., 2010, p. 233 et seq.; Dexia, 2008, p. 327; Getimis and Hlepas, 2010). In the meantime, an even further-reaching territorial reform is on the political agenda and this may receive further impetus by the reform pressure from the country's current financial crisis.

Among the transformation countries, Bulgaria is an example of territorial up-scaling of the 'Northern European' type. As early as 1991, a territorial reform was decided on and implemented, one that resulted in the creation of 264 municipalities with an average of 29090 inhabitants (cf. Dexia, 2008, p. 199). In 1994, Lithuania followed suit by cutting the number of 581 municipalities to 56 with an average population of 55000 inhabitants (cf. Beksta and Petkevicius, 2000; Dexia, 2008, p. 442). Alongside England and Denmark, this is the highest population average among European countries. In the meantime, however, a political debate emerged in Lithuania, in which the municipalities that resulted from the 1994 reform have been criticized for being 'over-sized' and therefore a corresponding 'reform of the reform' has been called for (cf. Dexia, 2008, p. 443).

4.3.3 Southern European reform model: inter-municipal cooperation and trans-scaling

France: 'Inter-municipal revolution' as a pragmatic path towards territorial consolidation

Due to the huge degree of small-size fragmentation of its local territorial structure and to its remarkable historical continuity, France is the 'classical' example of the Southern European territorial pattern (cf. Norton, 1994, p. 40). The territorial structure of the 37000 municipalities (*communes*), with an average of 1600 inhabitants, dates to the French Revolution of 1789 and historically extends even further back because it is largely rooted in parish communities. This territorial setting has remained essentially unchanged to the present day. In 1971, parallel to the 'North European' reform initiatives, the French government undertook the legislative attempt (Loi Marcellin) to overcome the historically fragmented, territorial structure of the municipalities by amalgamating them. However, this reform attempt completely failed as the reform legislation, premised on the 'voluntary' principle (*volontariat*), made the realization of territorial reform dependent on the consent of the affected municipality and its population; such 'voluntary' consent could, however, hardly be achieved under this circumstance.

In view of the path-dependent, persistent territorial fragmentation of the municipalities, France proceeded, in a sequence of developmental stages, to establish a multi-layered and complex institutional system of inter-municipal cooperative bodies (called *établissements publics de coopération intercommunale, EPCI*), which has become a typical feature of France's subnational institutional world (*intercommunalité*; Kuhlmann, 2010c). On the basis of national legislation of 1890 and 1959, the municipalities at first institutionalized their cooperation in the form of mono- and/or multi-functional bodies (*syndicats à vocation unique* and *syndicats à vocation multiple*). Subsequently, in 1966, a new institutional form of inter-municipal cooperation, the so-called urban associations (*communautés urbaines* – CU), was introduced by legislation. This form was marked in particular by providing the associations with taxation rights of their own (*à fiscalité propre*), thus strengthening their institutional, functional and budgetary integration, while still retaining their member municipalities (cf. Marcou, 2000). Under binding legislation (*par la loi*), a rare exception of the voluntary principle, urban associations (*communautés urbaines*) were created in the four metropolitan areas of Marseilles, Lyon, Lille and Strasbourg; subsequently another ten and more recently (in 2008) another two *communautés urbaines*[26] were (voluntarily) established. Meanwhile, these 16 urban associations have risen to become functionally and financially integrated local government units in France's most important urban/metropolitan areas. Although the member municipalities have preserved their political autonomy, this development can still be seen as marking France's 'pragmatic route towards achieving territorial reform despite the failure of amalgamations'[27] (Marcou, 2010, p. 41).

Another major legislative and institutional-political step was taken in 1999 by the adoption of a law (Loi Chevènement), which has been regarded by some as ushering in a 'true inter-municipal revolution' (*veritable révolution intercommunale*; Borraz and Le Galès, 2005; cf. Kerrouche, 2010, p. 170 et seq.; see also Kuhlmann, 2010c). This law was designed to simplify the 'mushrooming' of the *intercommunalité* by laying down in statute three types of inter-municipal formations (differentiated by size and settlement structure and endowed with a taxing power of their own according to which the municipalities should be grouped in the future. As a result of this process, which was promoted by financial incentives along with gentle pressure from the prefects, by 2011, 191 agglomeration associations (*communautés d'agglomération* – CA) and 2387 associations of local authorities (*communautés de communes* – CC) were established. The total number amounts to 2599 inter-municipal formations (EPCIs) with taxing power. Sixty-nine per cent of all municipalities are clustered under one of these three types of association (Table 4.8).

Notwithstanding the remarkable institutional consolidation of the *intercommunalité*, its continuing weakness is seen for one in the fact that it further complicates, rather than facilitates, the subnational network of action.[28] Second, the lack of a direct election of the decision-making bodies of the *communautés* has been criticized as a serious political and democratic deficit (cf. Wollmann, 2008, p. 45; Kuhlmann, 2009a, p. 90 et seq.). The debate surrounding an extensive reform of the subnational institutional system received fresh impetus when President Sarkozy, in October 2008, appointed a high-ranking commission that was chaired by ex-prime minister President Balladur and named after him (Comité Balladur). In submitting its reform recommendations in March 2009 (cf. Comité Balladur, 2009), the Commission proclaimed the ambitious, strategic goal that 'the inter-municipal bodies would be transformed into fully responsible municipalities, enabling France to possess a reasonable number of strong municipalities'.[29] Accordingly, the Comité proposed a whole range of reform steps (for details, cf. Marcou, 2010; Némery, 2010; Wollmann, 2010b; Kuhlmann, 2010c).

Following a long and controversial legislative process, a Reform Act (Loi de Réforme des Collectivités Territoriales) was passed on 16 December

Table 4.8 Development of inter-municipal cooperation in France 1993–2011[a]

Form of Cooperation (EPCI)	1993	2000	2003	2011
Development of EPCI with taxing authority				
Communautés urbaines (CU)	9	12	14	16
Communautés d'agglomération (CA)[b]	–	50	143	191
Communautés de Communes (CC)[c]	193	1533	2195	2387
Syndicats d'agglomération nouvelle (SAN)	9	9	8	5
Districts[d]	252	241	–	–
Communautés de villes (CV)[e]	3	–	–	–
Total number of EPCI with taxing authority	466	1845	2360	2599
Development of the 'extent of coverage'				
Proportion of local governments in EPCI in the total number of local governments in %	13.8	58.0	80.9	95.5
Proportion of the population in EPCI in the total number of the population in %	26.7	61.3	81.1	89.9

Notes:
a. Not included: forms of cooperation with allocation funding from the individual local governments (*syndicats à vocation unique* – SIVU; *syndicats à vocation multiple* – SIVOM, *syndicats mixtes*); total number for 1999: 18 504.
b. Introduced by the Loi Chevènement in 1999.
c. Introduced by the act of 1992.
d. Transformation into CU, CA or CC envisaged (Loi Chevènement 1999)
e. Reintroduced by the act of 1992; transformation into CU, CA or CC envisaged (Loi Chevènement 1999).

Sources: Kuhlmann (2009a, p. 92); further: Direction Générale des Collectivités Locales – DESL 2004, 2011; authors' own summary.

2010, envisaging far-reaching changes in France's subnational institutional system. Inter alia, the members of the representative bodies (*conseillers communautaires*) of the individual inter-municipal formations (*communautés de commmunes, d'agglomération, urbaines, métropoles*) from 2014 on shall be directly elected in member municipalities that have more than 3500 inhabitants. However, the member-municipalities with fewer than 3500 inhabitants (and this is the majority) will retain the existing electoral procedure of indirect election by the municipalities' councils (*conseils*). This 'split' electoral procedure reflects the political conflicts and compromises on which the legislation was based. Furthermore, taking up the recommendations of the Comité Balladur, the establishment of so-called *métropoles* is stipulated. In the Reform Act, the eight *communautés urbaines* (CU), established by legislation in 1966, will provide the territorial basis of the *métropoles* that comprise the most densely populated large cities with surrounding municipalities (Lyon, Lille, Marseille, Bordeaux, Toulouse, Strasbourg, etc.). In addition, another four inter-municipal formations (*communautés d'agglomérations*) with more than 500000 inhabitants were identified as *métropoles*. As a result, practically all metropolitan areas in France will be organized as *métropoles*. The *métropoles* will not be established as new autonomous territorial bodies, as proposed by the Comité Balladur, but rather as a constellation of member cities and municipalities following the traditional logic of the *intercommunalité*. However, further institutional and functional integration will be achieved by assigning them important tasks of their (formally continuing to exist) member-municipalities as well as functions of their respective *département* and *région*. The inclusion and transfer of departmental and regional functions thus makes for a remarkable innovation. The new model of *métropoles* would embody an organizational logic similar to the German county-free cities (*kreisfreie Städte*) and the English unitary authorities. The new design of the *métropoles* would amount to the functional and vertical integration of even three levels (*communes, département, région*).

Finally, the Reform Act provides for a simplified procedure for the amalgamation of municipalities to create 'new municipalities' (*communes nouvelles*). On this, however, the voluntary principle (*volontariat*) is retained (under which, it should be recalled, the legislative attempt of 1971 to instigate territorial reforms was largely doomed to failure).

While the Reform Act of 2010 stipulated that the key provisions of the reform come into effect by 2014–15, in the meantime the fate of the reform project that bears the handwriting of the last period of the Sarzoky presidency and of his conservative parliamentary majority seems uncertain. France's new (socialist) President François Hollande who was elected in May 2012 and the new (socialist) parliamentary majority appear to be set to rewrite the agenda and legislation on France's subnational institutional structure and to undo, at least in part, the legislation shaped by his predecessor's government and majority.

Italy, Spain: growing fragmentation and increasing reform pressure

Italy's reform pattern also corresponds to the Southern European type. As such, legislation passed in 1990 was geared towards bringing about voluntary territorial reform of the 8100 municipalities (*comuni*), with an average population of 7400,[30] as well as the 110 provinces (*province*), with an average population of 550000. The results, however, were 'laughable, as the number of municipalities did not decrease and that of the provinces even increased' (Bobbio, 2005, p. 38). In light of this, the legislation passed in 1990 and 2000[31] was targeted at encouraging the local governments to establish inter-municipal formations for cooperation in several institutional variants (cf. Dexia, 2008, p. 409). First, there was the founding of the *unioni di comuni* (comparable to the institutional form of French *intercommunalité* and also German joint administrations *Ämter*). Their number increased from 50 to 278 between 2000 and 2008 and includes 1240 (or almost 20 per cent of) municipalities with a total of 3.9 million inhabitants. Furthermore, the establishment of *comunità montana* for the (expansive) mountain areas was made statutory, which now include 4201 (or half of the) municipalities with a total of 10.8 million inhabitants. Moreover, the municipalities entered into a number of cooperation agreements (*consorzi*).

Furthermore, a new law (Legge Galli) came into effect in 1994, under which the territorial and institutional fragmentation of water supply was to be overcome. On this basis, so-called 'agencies with optimal territorial scope' (= *autorità di ambiti territoriali ottimali* – ATO) were created in the regional vicinity of the individual *province* as a variant of obligatory inter-municipal cooperation (Citroni, 2010). In the meantime, 91 such agencies have been created in the water sector and in 2006 the ATO scheme was expanded to include waste removal (cf. Iannello, 2007; Lippi et al., 2008; Dreyfus et al., 2010).

The euro crisis and pressure on the part of the EU have prompted the previous Italian 'technocrat' interim government under Mario Monti, as well as the 'grand coalition' (*larga intesa*) under Enrico Letta to push for local-level territorial reforms. The Monti government set upon a strategy (revealingly with the Anglo-Saxon label 'spending review'), which aimed at cutting the costs of the existing political and administrative structures. In November 2012, a couple of (governmental) decrees[32] were adopted that, for one, abolished the elected councils of the *province*. Thus, the introduction of self-government at the provincial level was to be reversed. Second, the number of *province* (with regard to the remaining deconcentrated state functions) was to be reduced from 86 to 51. Third, those *province* in which the ten largest cities (Roma, Torino, Milano, Venezia, Genova, Bologna, Firenze, Bari, Napoli and Reggio Calabria) are located were to be amalgamated, by binding legal provisions, with these cities to form a *città metropolitana*. However, whilst the respective *province* were to be integrated in the *città metropolitana*, their (small-scale) member municipalities were still to be retained. These new *città metropolitana*-type local government units were, as a rule, to be represented by the mayors of the member cities, whereby the metropolitan mayors would generally be those of the affected large city. In their institutional structure, the Italian *città metropolitana* are reminiscent of France's *communauté urbaine*.

On 4 July 2013 the Constitutional Court, which got involved in the matter by the complaints of some *province*, declared the governmental 'decrees' to be unconstitutional, as such radical change in the *province* (as constitutionally entrenched entities) would require constitutional legislation. In an immediate response to the court ruling the Council of Ministers, on 5 July 2013, approved a pertinent constitutional draft law, which manifested Prime Minister Letta's and his government's determination to put the radical political, institutional and functional transformation and reduction of the existing *province* into effect as soon as possible.

In line with the Southern European pattern of territorial organization, Spain has also experienced the emergence of inter-municipal formations for the operative support of municipalities. Besides the consequential introduction of the regions (*comunidades autónomas*) as a 'quasi-federal' subnational level (see Section 4.2.2 above), following the end of the Franco dictatorship and the foundation of a democratic and constitutional state in 1978, the reconstruction of local self-government took place initially under the traditional two-tier local government structure (cf. Alba and Navarro, 2003, p. 203). On the lower tier, the 8111 municipalities (*municipios*), with an average population of 5430 and two-thirds of which having less than 1000 inhabitants, have a Southern European territorial profile. The upper level comprises the 50 *provincias*, whose representative bodies (*diputación provincial*) are not elected directly, but rather indirectly by the municipal councils (cf. Dexia, 2008, p. 590). To date, the regions, which decide on the territorial structure of the municipalities, have not only refrained from territorial reform, but since 1980 have even increased the number of municipalities. The creation or acceptance of local authorities that would be strengthened by territorial consolidation is obviously not in the interest of the regions wary of their influence (cf. ibid., p. 214). Instead, in part mono- and in part multifunctional inter-municipal formations (*mancomunidades*) have been set up (currently about 1000), into which around 75 per cent of all municipalities are grouped (cf. Dexia, 2008, p. 591). Furthermore, four of the regions (currently 81) have installed *comarcas* that are responsible for the inter-municipal implementation of tasks transferred to them by the regions.

Transformation countries: Hungary, the Czech Republic

Among the group of Central and Eastern European transformation countries, Hungary and the Czech Republic exemplify the Southern European territorial pattern. In Hungary, the local government legislation adopted in 1990 granted extensive autonomy to the lower local level by establishing local government units ('settlements'). The local populations quickly activated this right to reverse the territorial amalgamation of the local level that had been enforced under the communist regime (cf. Temesi, 2000, p. 347; Soós, 2003, p. 245; Wollmann and Lankina, 2003, p. 95). As a result, the number of municipalities in the wake of the regime change jumped in a short space of time from 1584 to 3175 local government units with an average population of 3170, of which almost a third had fewer than 500 inhabitants. While the local government system was significantly strengthened both functionally and politically by subsequent reforms, in particular that of 1994 (see Section 4.2.3), the territorial structure of the two levels remained unchanged. In reaction to the existence and continuation of the multitude of small and very small municipalities, different forms of inter-municipal cooperation were legislatively encouraged and put into place, thereby falling in line with the Southern European pattern. This holds true first for a law passed in 1997, which was intended to boost the mono-functional inter-municipal cooperation. To date, around 2590 such forms of cooperation have come into existence (cf. Dexia, 2008, p. 369). Second, a law passed in 2003 targeted the institutionalization of the multi-functional cooperation between municipalities (cf. Pfeil, 2010, p. 255 et seq.). The government has now initiated the establishment of 162 such multi-functional inter-municipal formations, into which 97.5 per cent of all municipalities are grouped (cf. Pfeil, 2010, p. 256).

The Czech Republic is another distinct example of territorial fragmentation on the local government level (cf. Illner, 2003, p. 68 et seq., 2010, p. 219 et seq.; Dexia, 2008, p. 231). Due to the spontaneous formation of municipalities following the system change of 1990, the number of municipalities rose from 4120 to 6196 local government units (cf. Illner, 2010, p. 223) numbering an average of 1640 inhabitants, two-thirds of which have fewer than 500 inhabitants (cf. ibid., p. 224). Although the need for local government territorial reform has long been a subject of political debates, the government has thus far failed to undertake any serious reform initiatives (cf. Dexia, 2008, p. 232). The establishment of inter-municipal forms of cooperation in the Czech Republic is also aimed at providing operative support to the smallest municipalities, whose size impedes any real efficiency. To date, 474 such inter-municipal bodies have been created, to which 4680 (or 70 per cent) municipalities belong (cf. ibid., p. 230 et seq.).

4.3.4 Reform hybrid: Germany between territorial amalgamation and inter-municipal cooperation

The reform strategies pursued in Germany can be assigned in part to the Northern European model and in part to the Southern European one. The reason for this lies in the constitutionally entrenched power of each of the *Länder* to decide their 'own' territorial reform policy that reflects the different settlement structures and varying party-political constellations. In procedural terms, the *Länder* governments prepared the elaboration and implementation of their respective reform concepts by appointing reform commissions, by public hearings and by a so-called voluntary phase. During this phase, the municipalities affected were given the opportunity to 'voluntarily' adjust themselves to the envisaged territorial changes. If an agreement on the part of the municipalities could not be reached, the *Land* parliament – in line with the 'Northern European' reform model – decided by means of statutory law. A radical reform variant can be found in the strongly urbanized *Länder* of North Rhine-Westphalia and Hesse, which, at the time, were governed by the social democrats. This reform variant was targeted at creating so-called 'integrated' municipalities (*Einheitsgemeinden*) through the comprehensive amalgamation of municipalities. In both *Länder*, the number of municipalities was drastically reduced by over 80 per cent. In North Rhine-Westphalia, this resulted in the formation of municipalities with an average of 46000 inhabitants (cf. Laux, 1999; see also Table 4.9).

By contrast, a somewhat Southern European reform variant was embarked upon in the (more rural) *Länder* of Rhineland-Palatinate and Schleswig-Holstein, by largely forgoing the amalgamation of the existing small municipalities and by, instead, introducing inter-municipal formations (comparable to the French *intercommunalité*) for the operative support and coordination of the municipalities concerned. Hereby, one can distinguish between two variants of inter-municipal formations. First, there are the inter-municipal unions (so-called *Ämter* or *Verwaltungsgemeinschaften*), such as in Schleswig-Holstein where the directing boards of the inter-municipal formation are appointed indirectly by the member municipalities. Second, there is the example of Rhineland-Palatinate, which 'invented' the institutional innovation of the *Verbandsgemeinde*, a kind of 'double-decker municipality'. In this, the previously existing municipalities (*Ortsgemeinden*) are preserved as fully-fledged local self-government units with their traditional responsibilities, such as budgetary and local planning rights. At the same time, the *Verbandsgemeinde* also constitutes a fully-fledged local self-government entity with directly elected councils. Functionally, they are responsible for overarching tasks (e.g., land use planning) and the operative support of their *Ortsgemeinden*.[33]

The majority of *Länder* have opted for a 'mixed' ('hybrid') variant, lying, as it were, between the Northern and Southern European reform types. This, on the one hand, implies a clearly more restrained reduction of the number of municipalities through territorial consolidation (for example, in Baden-

Table 4.9 Municipal structures in Germany

Land	Number of Municipalities		Change 1990–2010		Avg. Population 2010[a]	Number IMF[b] 2010	Proportion of IMF[b] – Member- Municipalities 2010 in %
	1990	2010	Change Abs.	In %			
Brandenburg	1739	419	−1320	−76	6052	53	64.7
Meckl.-Vorp.	1149	814	−335	−29	2064	78	95.0
Saxony	1626	485	−1141	−70	8701	99	51.7
Sax.-Anhalt	1270	345	−925	−73	6991	45	73.9
Thuringia	1699	951	−748	−44	2407	121	87.1
New *Länder*	7483	3014	−4469	−60	3517	424	81.5

Land	Number of Municipalities 2010	Avg. Population 2010[a]	Number of IMF[b] 2010	Proportion of IMF[b] – Member- Municipalities 2010 in %
BW	1102	9755	270	82.6
Bavaria	2056	6089	313	48.1
Hesse	426	14256	–	0.0
Lower Sax.	1024	7785	137	71.8
NRW	396	45447	–	0.0
Rhinel.-Pal.	2306	1755	163	97.9
Saarland	52	19942	–	0.0
Schl.-Holst.	1116	2542	87	92.6
Old *Länder*	8478	13446	970	49.1

Note:
a. Population figures of county-free cities are included in the calculation.
b. IMF = Inter-municipal formations (administrative associations; *Amt, Verwaltungsgemeinschaft*, etc.).

Sources: German Federal Statistical Office 2010 and authors' own calculation/compilation.

Württemberg and Bavaria by 67 per cent and 71 per cent, respectively), resulting in an average population size of municipalities of around 8000 inhabitants. On the other hand, inter-municipal formations (labelled often as administrative associations, *Verwaltungsgemeinschaften*) have also been set up as a 'dual structure' to support their associated smaller municipalities. At the same time, during the late 1960s and early 1970s the counties were also territorially rescaled, thus cutting their total number country-wide from 425 to 237 (arriving at an average population size of 60000 inhabitants) (cf. Laux, 1999, p. 176).

After 1990, the East German *Land* governments also turned to territorial reforms of the counties as an important step towards installing efficient local government structures.[34] This amalgamation of counties resulted in a reduction of their overall number from 189 to 87, leading to an average population size of over 100000 inhabitants (cf. Wollmann, 1997a, p. 284 et seq.). However, despite having to cope with a multitude of small and tiny municipalities, the *Land* governments initially decided to without municipal territorial reforms altogether. The reason for this was, first of all, to politically respect the just recently regained local democracy, not least in the smaller and smallest municipalities, but also to avoid, for the time being, the conflict that potentially goes with municipal territorial reforms (cf. Kuhlmann, 2009a, p. 116 et seq.). Thus, they preferred a Southern European reform strategy, as it were, by leaving the existing territorial structure of municipalities unattained and by, instead, introducing inter-municipal formations that, following the West German example, had the function of providing operative and cooperative support to their member municipalities (cf. Wollmann, 1997a, p. 284 et seq.). As a consequence of this early reform process, the *Land* of Brandenburg, for example, had 1739 municipalities (with an average of 1800 inhabitants) of which 97 per cent were grouped into 123 inter-municipal formations (*Ämter*) (cf. Wollmann, 1996a, p. 94 with data on Brandenburg and other East German *Länder*).

In the meantime, a new round of territorial reforms was set off in the East German *Länder*, typically involving the territorial reform of municipalities by means of amalgamation and a corresponding reduction in the number and scope of inter-municipal formations (cf. Kuhlmann, 2009a, p. 116 et seq.; Wollmann, 2010c). This reform wave was kicked off by the *Land* of Brandenburg. Following a controversial political debate and in the face of continuing local resistance, the *Land* parliament decided to carry out a municipal territorial reform to come into effect on 1 January 2005. Consequently, the number of municipalities was diminished through municipal amalgamation from 1479 to 419 (in 2010) and the inter-municipal formations (*Ämter*) from 152 to 53. Accordingly, the share of '*Amt*-free' municipalities rose to 35 per cent (which had previously been at 3 per cent). Thus, the *Land* of Brandenburg's territorial reform trajectory picked up a somewhat Northern European territorial reform pattern in the direction of 'up-scaling'. Similar (i.e., Northern European) territorial reforms were, in the meantime, embarked on in Saxony-Anhalt, Thuringia and Saxony (cf. Kuhlmann, 2009a, p. 118; Wollmann, 2010c).

The most recent example of reform can be seen in the *Land* of Saxony-Anhalt, where, accompanied by sharp political and judicial conflicts, the parliament decided to cut the number of municipalities from 1030 (with an average of 2000 inhabitants) to 219 (with an average of 10900 inhabitants) by municipal amalgamation taking effect on 1 January 2011. About half of the municipalities are now organized as 'integrated' municipalities (*Einheitsgemeinden*), while the other half are grouped into inter-municipal formations (*Verbandsgemeinden*). It deserves mentioning that Saxony-Anhalt's previous variant of inter-municipal format (that is, the administrative association, *Verwaltungsgemeinschaft*) was replaced with the variant of *Verbandsgemeinde*, that is, the 'double decker municipality' whereby Saxony-Anhalt followed Rhineland-Palatinate's 'invention'. Currently, the *Land* of Brandenburg is also considering a new local government reform, which may well result in the formation of larger municipalities, possibly including the 'double decker model' of the *Verbandsgemeinde*.

In the meantime, Rhineland-Palatinate, as the first West German *Land*, initiated local-level territorial reform.[35] This was limited, however, to a territorially rescaling of 28 municipalities outside the *Verbandsgemeinden* and the 163 *Verbandsgemeinden* themselves (with an average population of 10000 for the former and 12000 for the latter) until the local elections in March 2014. By contrast, a reform of the 2258 municipalities within the *Verbandsgemeinden* as well as the counties has so far not been considered.

4.3.5 Cross-country comparison: convergence, divergence, persistence and explanatory factors

Convergence, divergence, persistence

Finally and in summary, the development of territorial structure of the subnational levels will be discussed as to whether, to which extent and why it exhibits convergent or divergent patterns (for an overview and further country analyses cf. also Hulst and Montfort, 2007; Baldersheim and Rose, 2010c; Swianiewicz, 2010). With regard to territorial and population size, the municipalities still show large, and in some cases even palpable differences. This is particularly conspicuous in the population size (between 1640 and 139000) as well as, for example, in the proportion of municipalities with fewer than 5000 inhabitants (between 96 per cent and 2 per cent or 0 per cent, cf. Table 4.10). Thus, territorial structure does not signal convergence but, on the contrary, reveals persistent differences and divergence. However, within certain country clusters cross-country trends (convergence) can be recognized.

On the one hand, countries possessing the Northern European reform profile (England, Sweden, Denmark, some German *Länder*) demonstrate convergence among each other insofar as in some cases large-scale amal-

Table 4.10 Territorial structures of municipalities in Europe

Municipalities	Avg. Population of Municipalities	Avg. Area of Municipalities in km²	% of Municipalities with <5000 Inhabitants	Number of Municipalities with >100 000 inhabitants
Czech Rep.	1 640	13	96	5
Cyprus	1 660	18	95	0
France	1 720	15	95	37
Slovakia	1 870	17	95	3
Hungary	3 170	29	91	9
Austria	3 510	36	91	5
Luxembourg	4 080	22	81	0
Latvia	4 340	123	91	2
Spain	5 430	62	85	58
Estonia	5 930	199	80	2
Malta	5 970	5	54	0
Germany	6 690	29	77	81
Romania	6 800	75	35	27
Italy	7 270	37	71	43
Slovenia	9 560	97	48	2
Greece	10 750	128	53	8
Finland	12 660	813	52	6
Poland	15 390	126	25	39
Belgium	17 910	52	14	8
Bulgaria	29 090	420	11	11
Sweden	31 310	1 552	4	13
Portugal	34 380	299	20	23
Netherlands	36 890	94	2	25
Ireland	37 310	612	37	15
Denmark	55 480	440	3	6
Lithuania	56 570	1 088	2	5
UK	139 480	562	Non-relevant	68
EU-27	5 410	47	82[a]	500

Note: a.   EU-26.

Source: Dexia (2008).

gamation of existing small local governments has been effected, resulting in demographically enlarged municipalities (up-scaling; Baldersheim and Rose, 2010a). In a reform wave that has set in since 2000 Southern European Greece as well as the Central Eastern European EU-accession countries of Bulgaria and Lithuania have moved closer to the Northern European territorial reform profile. This has been additionally pushed by the financial and euro crisis and the pressure from the EU. However, these countries, albeit within an overall convergent development, still reveal significant, and in part, glaring differences in the average population size of their municipalities – from 140000 (England) to 10700 (Greece).

On the other hand, convergence becomes apparent within the group of countries belonging to the Southern European reform pattern (France, Italy, and the majority of the Central and Eastern European countries) in that (almost) no territorial reforms on the municipal level have been realized by way of amalgamation, thus leaving their historically fragmented territorial structure unchanged, while putting in place a layer of inter-municipal formations for their operative support (trans-scaling; Baldersheim and Rose, 2010a; see also Hulst and Montfort, 2007). While these countries display an overall (convergent) Southern European pattern, their average population size is significantly different (e.g., with 1720 inhabitants in France and 7250 inhabitants in Italy). Whether the financial crisis and the EU-induced pressure will prompt the 'Southern countries' to move more closely towards Northern European-type up-scaling, thus resulting in convergence, yet remains to be seen. Indications of this can be noticed in Greece's territorial reforms and Italy's recent, albeit still not realized, pertinent reform legislation. In their local level territorial reforms, the German *Länder* present a mixed (hybrid) picture in that most of them have a somewhat Southern European reform profile, while two (North Rhine-Westphalia and Hesse) have a Northern European one. Due to the recent reform wave that has gained momentum since 1990, the East German *Länder* have moved towards the Northern European reform pattern through amalgamating their municipalities and diminishing the inter-municipal formations. Figure 4.8 summarizes these findings.

Explanatory factors

The question remains as to which factors have impinged on the respective convergence or divergence (see Table 4.11). The dynamics of the territorial development that in the Northern European countries was directed at the 'enlargement in scale' of the local government units was essentially driven by the fact that in these countries the parliaments have, constitutionally and politically, the power to enforce a local government territorial structure envisaged through binding legislation, with reference to the overriding 'common good', even in the face of rejection or resistance by the affected (small) municipalities. This parliamentary decision-making power harks back to institutional history and political culture in the multi-level system of these countries, according to which local government level was assigned a crucial role in the realization, on the local level, of the national welfare and intervention state. The understanding and willingness to subordinate local

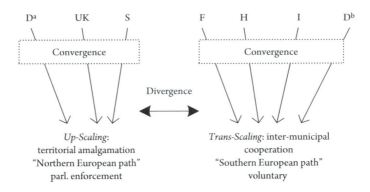

Note:
a. For example, NR-W, Hesse, Saxony, Saxony-Anhalt, Brandenburg.
b. For example, Rhineland-Palatinate, Schleswig-Holstein, Baden-Württemberg, Thuringia, Mecklenburg-Western Pomerania.
Source: Authors' own diagram.

Figure 4.8 Convergence and divergence of territorial policy in Europe

Table 4.11 Theoretical explanations for territorial reforms

Factor	Explanation	Neo-institutional Theoretical Approach
Fiscal, economic demographic pressures	Striving for functional optimization; rational/ efficient problem-solving	Economic institutionalism
(Party-)political preferences/ raising institutional-political profile/shows of strength	Policy-/vote-seeking; party differences; actor constellations; veto players	Actor-centred institutionalism
Reform convictions: efficiency/ productivity versus creation of local identity	Prevalence of discourse ideologies, framing	Sociological (discursive) institutionalism
Reform traditions: parliament enforcement versus voluntary principle	Historic-cultural anchoring of decision-making styles	Historical institutionalism

Source: Authors' own compilation.

self-determination ultimately to the parliamentary decision-making powers is entrenched in the political and parliamentarian culture of these (not surprisingly largely Protestant) countries.

One determining, conceptual driving force (framing) of territorial reforms was to enhance the improvement of the operative planning, action and coordination capacity of the local authorities through their territorial and demographic 'enlargement'. This impulse came to bear on the reform wave of the 1960s and 1970s, inspired by the 'rationalist' zeitgeist, as well as in the recent round of reforms. The different scope and speed of reforms reflect and are influenced by the different goals and intentions of the relevant (party-) political actors (in the sense of actor-centred institutionalism).

By contrast, the continuity and persistence of the local government territorial structure in the Southern European countries can be largely accounted for by the path-dependent constitutional, political and political-cultural assumption that territorial changes by way of amalgamating existing municipalities can be achieved only with the consent of the affected local government units and their population This 'voluntary' principle (*volontariat*), which has proven to be an on-going obstacle to territorial change in local political practice, is premised on the conviction, rooted in institutional history and political culture, that the realization of the welfare state is essentially assigned to the (Napoleonic) centralized state administration. At the same time, the function of the local government level is first of all focused on serving as the political arena and site for the local citizens to define, express and 'live' their local identity. In addition, the 'voluntary' principle is anchored in the institutionally guaranteed influence exercised by (for example, in France) the local mayor as defender of the territorial status quo also on the national level (for a detailed comparative country analysis, see Baldersheim and Rose, 2010c).

A rupture or even a deviation from a 'path-dependent' institutional trajectory occurs if and when the relevant actors (in the sense of actor-centred institutionalism) feel prompted to perform a political or institutional 'act of strength', for instance in a situation that they deem to be a deep crisis of the existing territorial or organizational structures. This kind of situation can be triggered by urgent external pressures, such as an economic or fiscal crisis (e.g., the current budgetary and debt crisis in the Southern European countries) or demographic problems. For example, the territorial reform drive in the East German *Länder* has been propelled by the perception that the existing small municipalities were increasingly 'bleeding empty' demographically, politically, economically and financially. In addition, the operative and political functionality of inter-municipal formations has been increasingly called into question because of their high coordination, cooperation and transaction costs. In France, similar assessments and motives guided the reform project of 2010, one that hinged on the functional, financial and democratic strengthening of the *communautés* as a pragmatic move towards a territorial reform 'without explicit amalgamation' (Marcou, 2010), thus making for an all but gradual deviation from the path-dependently prevalent *intercommunalité*. The

Italian government, too, saw the need to react to the mounting budgetary crisis and pressure from the EU Commission by putting together its reform package of 2012. Table 4.11 summarizes the explanatory factors.

4.4 Reforming public administration between state and market: privatization and remunicipalization

4.4.1 Concepts and definitions

The readjustment of the relationship between state/public administration, market and civil society has always been one of the key issues of administrative reform. In Western Europe, a number of reform phases and reform discourse cycles can be discerned (cf. Jann, 2001). Internationally, during the 1960s and early 1970s, an expansion of state activity and the development of the modern welfare state were observed, resulting in the growth of public tasks and administrative functions, a fact evidenced by the rising public expenditure and public employment quotas (see Figures 3.2 and 3.3, Chapter 3). From the early 1980s on, the Anglo-Saxon–inspired NPM doctrine focused its attention on reducing and restricting the action radius of state and local government administrations to 'core tasks' and halting the expansion of public tasks and expenditure through privatization, outsourcing and delegation. Theoretical justification for the minimalist state and the superiority of the market in the provision of services was derived in particular from the public choice literature (cf. Downs, 1957; Niskanen, 1971; Dunleavy, 1991) and New Institutional Economics, including transaction cost analysis, principal–agent theory, property rights (Williamson, 1985; for a summary, see Reichard, 2002; Schröter, 2011, p. 82 et seq.). Major reform drivers were the deepening economic crisis and strategic political elections that resulted in a mounting dominance of the neo-conservative and neo-liberal discourses of Thatcherism in the United Kingdom and Reaganomics in the USA. Against this backdrop, in the Anglo-Saxon and Anglo-American world the political concern was with deconstructing rather than with reconstructing the state.

In Continental Europe, the EU policies that were directed at ensuring market liberalization and freedom of competition have become a crucial catalyst for privatization and market liberalization measures. Thus, the EU competition policy amounted to a paring back of the state to its core functions and limiting it to an 'enabling' function, whereas 'providing' was to be generally reserved for external (private sector or non-profit) actors (Wollmann, 2002b). The 'establishment of a common market' (Article 2 of the EC Treaty), which was formally realized in 1992 with the creation of an internal market with free movement of persons, goods, services and capital became a primary task of the European Union (Löwe, 2003, p. 187). The importance of the internal market is not limited to just creating a common market, but also to the value that is given to this objective indicating the primacy of the market and of competition overall (ibid., p. 188). The influence of the EU has been particularly evident in the so-called 'services of general economic interest', of which particularly the public utilities (in Germany labelled '*Daseinsvorsorge*'[36]) (energy, water, waste, public transport) are counted (cf. also Waiz, 2009, p. 41 et seq.).

An additional impulse for market liberalization has come from national initiatives and funding programmes targeted at promoting public–private partnerships (PPP). Examples in Germany include federal programmes, such as the competition 'Learning Regions' ('Lernende Regionen'), the Federal–*Länder* Joint Initiative, 'The Social City' ('Soziale Stadt') and the structure policy-related programmes of the *Länder*, as for instance in North Rhine-Westphalia. In addition, in 2001 and based on British experiences, the SPD party group in the German Bundestag set up a project working group that identified PPP projects as elements to improve efficiency and to modernize the state (Sack, 2006). On the *Länder* level, the Red–Green coalition government in North Rhine-Westphalia pushed ahead with a PPP initiative of its own, one that also promoted pertinent projects (see Sack, 2006, with further references).

However, since the international financial crisis, which made the general public dramatically aware of the negative consequences of an overly deregulated politico-economic system, critics of liberalization and privatization have received increasing attention. Thus, calls for a reregulation of the market by the state and even for a renationalization or remunicipalization of privatized functions and activities have become more vociferous. Hence, in the post-NPM phase a strategy shift towards a 'comeback of the public' has taken shape (see further below). A new wave of privatization in the public services sector (and beyond) appears to be triggered in the budgetary crisis-ridden Southern European countries, which face increasing demands by the European Commission, the European Central Bank and the International Monetary Fund, embodied in the so-called Troika, to sell public assets, including municipal facilities and companies in order to reduce the public 'sovereign' debts (for the conception of sequential phases 'over time' see Polanyi, 1944;[37] Millward, 2005; Röber, 2009; Wollmann and Marcou, 2010; Clifton et al., 2011; Wollmann, 2011, 2013; Hall et al., 2013).

For the analysis of NPM-inspired and EU-driven market liberalization and public sector modernization policies, it is useful to distinguish between two variants (see Libbe et al., 2004, p. 60 et seq.). The variant of 'functional privatization' pertains to the transfer of public tasks, for which the state and/or local governments either have a (legally codified) enabling responsibility or which they assume voluntarily, to private-commercial or non-profit actors by employing various forms of contractual policy. In institutional-economic terms, this results in a separation of principal (state/local government) and agent (executing organization), whereby the connection of the 'providing agent' to the public actor takes place by means of a contractual arrangement, such as concession, leasing or operating contracts. Such a retreat by local governments from the implementation responsibility by passing on tasks to third parties has been variously described, more or less accurately, in the literature (contractual PPP, outsourcing, subcontracting, delegating, contracting out etc.). The NPM concept and the EU policy generally amount to a reliance on contracting out/outsourcing rather than on self-production.

Functional privatization should be distinguished from 'organizational privatization', in which the legal and/or ownership status of public enterprises and institutions is changed and which can take place formally or materially (see below). Moreover, attention should be paid to more moderate forms of reorganization that are aimed 'only' at institutional unbundling and agencification while retaining the public-law–based structure.[38] Thus, three sub-types of organizational privatization and outsourcing can be distinguished (cf. also Reichard, 2006):

- *Organizational autonomy.* This refers to administrative units becoming more autonomous in terms of budget and/or organization while still retaining public legal forms, for example, by the founding of municipal/autonomous, publicly owned enterprises or institutions of public law. The affected organizational areas of the core administration are thereby transformed into legally non-autonomous (internal administrative) enterprises, institutions or establishments.
- *Formal privatization.* In this, public enterprises/institutions are transferred to a private law form (e.g., by founding a private or public limited company, cooperative, etc.), but without a change in ownership. Here, the municipal companies are legally and organizationally autonomous, but remain economically in the ownership of the state/local government.
- *Asset privatization.* This refers to the partial or complete sale of public property, enterprises, plants and other infrastructural facilities to private parties. This designation also includes private equity participation in public institutions (e.g., as part of public–private companies). The complete sale of local enterprises and institutions to private parties, which

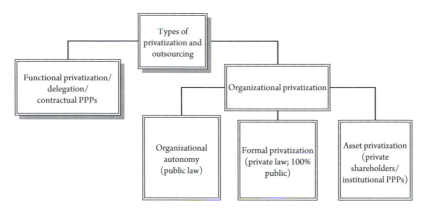

Source: Adopted from Kuhlmann (2009a, p. 153).

Figure 4.9 Privatization and corporatization

(in contrast to functional privatization, see above) cannot be reversed, at least not unilaterally by the public sector, thus arguably represents the most consequential and far-reaching step towards market opening and liberalization.[39]

In summary, all these types can be illustrated in the following classification of privatization and outsourcing policy (Figure 4.9).

4.4.2 Privatization of public corporations

From the 1980s, privatization of the state and local government economy sector has been a primary modernization objective in all OECD countries (cf. OECD, 2003, 2008; Christmann, 2004; Mayer, 2006; Bieling et al., 2008; Wollmann and Marcou, 2010; Pollitt and Bouckaert, 2011). With this, the strategy change has been particularly pronounced where – such as in the United Kingdom – the state's ownership and operation of a large segment of the economy coincided with party-politically accentuated neo-liberal government objectives, or – such as in New Zealand – with the pointedly neo-liberal policy change of the Labour Government implemented during the course of the acute economic crisis (see Section 4.1).

United Kingdom

In the United Kingdom, a declared policy goal of the Thatcher government was to privatize, preferably in their entirety, the public utilities and nationalized enterprises, not least in order to thus weaken the trade unions and to promote a kind of 'people's capitalism' (Schröter, 2001, p. 421). The United Kingdom is the European country where the pertinent ownership experienced the most rapid transformation and where privatization was the most radical. It has thus become a forerunner and – despite all subsequent negative developments – a role model in the EU, leaving a distinct mark on European liberalization policy. The radical privatization programme resulted in privatizing around three-quarters of previously nationalized enterprises, including industrial enterprises (such as British Steel), but also service providers, such as British Telecom, the British Airport Authority, water providers and waste water disposers, electricity companies and, finally, the state railways. Problematic and unintended consequences of this policy – in addition the lack of competition in many areas – included, in some cases, considerable reduction in performance and quality, in particular in the grid-based services. This proved particularly perilous for the state railways, where a massive lambasting of this form of privatization arose following the fatal accident at Hatfield in 2000 caused by damaged tracks that had not been repaired by the now-dissolved private infrastructure company Railtrack although it had been aware of the problem.

In hindsight, privatization in the UK has been interpreted as the 'paradigm of a history of failures' (Drews, 2008, p. 46). On the top of this there were very substantial redundancies, such as in the electricity sector, where between 1990 and 2001 approximately 58 per cent of jobs were lost (from 140000 to 60000; cf. Lippert, 2005, p. 79). Moreover, social polarization deepened, for example as the result of a huge price hike in electricity services since 2005 and in the slipstream of a growing number of cut-offs of power and water supplies for indebted private households (cf. Dickhaus and Dietz, 2004, p. 48). There was little evidence, however, for privatization-related increases in productivity (cf. Pollitt and Bouckaert, 2011), which can be accounted for by the lack of competition in many areas of privatization. The increasing loss of popular support for privatization policies may well have been one of the reasons why, in the late 1990s, New Labour renounced 'privatization at any price', although the market orientation was generally preserved. Emblematic for the British privatization approach, and also in a certain sense seminal for European administrative reform policy overall, is the massive build-up and expansion of a new regulation bureaucracy consisting of, politically and organizationally relatively autonomous, mono-functional authorities and agencies (e.g., Office of Communications – Ofcom – and analogously Ofgem, Ofwat and ORR, the Office of Rail Regulation). In addition to a rebureaucratization through reregulation effect, these newly created authorities have had a rather small influence on the private companies concerned (as the example of Railtrack clearly showed) just as the regulation authorities exercise insufficient political control and responsibility (cf. Schröter, 2001, p. 422).

On the subnational and local government level, the sale of large portions of social housing to the respective tenants (1995: 1.5 million houses) and the privatization in the area of public transport should be mentioned. Through this, an extensive market liberalization occurred following the 1985 Transport Act, during the course of which numerous local bus companies were formally and materially privatized (Christmann, 2004, p. 233). By contrast, waste disposal still remained within the remit of local governments, albeit linked to delegation to private companies (concessions; see further below). The 14 active electricity providers that operated on the regional level were also subject to complete asset privatization, so that almost the entire British electricity sector is now under private ownership (Drews, 2008, p. 50). The sequence of the most important privatization steps in the UK is shown in Table 4.12.

Sweden

While the Anglo-Saxon political culture and state tradition offer some fairly fertile soil for sowing a comprehensive privatization policy, the corresponding reform steps in Continental Europe and Scandinavia have progressed at a more moderate pace, even though, in the end, their outcome has been quite significantly different. This different change pattern is, for one, accounted for by the varied 'starting conditions' of the reforms. In Germany, for instance, the number of state-owned (nationalized) enterprises, to begin with, was smaller by far than in the United Kingdom. The varied welfare state traditions (see Chapter 2, Section 2.1) that impinge on the reform trajectory make a difference as well. In the case of Sweden, for example, radical privatization approaches stand in opposition to politico-culturally–rooted convictions of a fully blown (social democratic) welfare state (*folkshemmet*). Thus, following the economic slump in Sweden in the 1980s, it is true that the country saw a neo-liberal policy reorientation, in which some observers recognized the beginning of a 'system change' (Premfors, 1998, p. 151). In particular, the right-of-centre government under Bildt (1991–94) aligned itself with a privatization discourse by explicitly referring to the radical role models of the United Kingdom and New Zealand. However, this policy shift did not result in British-type market-radical privatization measures, but rather instead in a 'competition-oriented modernization' that took account of the particularities of the Swedish model and was flanked by socially compatible regulations (Schalauske and Streb, 2008, p. 215). Following the formal privatization of several state-owned enterprises (post office, telecommunications) and the market opening in the electricity sector in the early 1990s, several asset privatizations were carried out that, since the country's accession to the EU in 1995, were, at least to some degree, impinged upon by the

Table 4.12 Privatization of public enterprises in the United Kingdom according to sectors

Sector	
Telecommunication	
1981	Separation of post and telecommunications (Post Office, British Telecom)
1984	Conversion to a plc, partial privatization of British Telecom (sale of 51% of shares)
1991	End of the 'duopol' phase; gradual market opening
1991	2nd share issue of BT (remaining state holding: 21.8%)
1993	3rd share issue of BT (remaining state holding: 0)
1998	Almost complete market opening through liberalization of the area of Carrier Selection (near and far)
From 2000	Sale of majority stake in foreign telecommunication companies
2001	Complete market opening through removal of monopoly rights of directory enquiries
Post office	
1981	Separation of post and telecommunications
2000	Postal Services Act 2000 (establishment of a regulatory authority, new licensing system)
2001	Conversion of Royal Mail to a plc
2006	Complete market opening
Railways	
1996	Privatization of the infrastructure enterprise (Railtrack)
1997	Complete privatization of the railways
2000	Accident at Hatfield
2002	Founding of Network Rail
Gas	
1986	Privatization of British Gas
1997	Breaking up of British Gas into British Gas plc and Centrica
1998	Complete market opening
Water	
1989	Privatization of water supply in England and Wales
From mid-2000	Endeavours towards vertical disintegration
2001	Ofwat agrees to such an application by Welsh Water
Electricity	
1990	Privatization of generation and distribution companies and of regional distribution companies
1990	Liberalization of the industrial sector
1998	Complete liberalization
Since 2005	Massive price increases

Sources: Drews (2008, p. 43 et seq.) and authors' own summary.

adaption to EU directives. When in 2006, the conservative and so-called 'Alliance for Sweden' under the leadership of Fredrik Reinfeldt returned to power, it put forward an extensive privatization programme through the sale of six state-owned enterprises (Dansbo and Wallner, 2008, p. 29 et seq.). Of these, the banking group Nordea and the credit institution SBAB have since been privatized (Schalauske and Streb, 2008, p. 222). Moreover, the market liberalization policy of the European Commission and the growing presence and competition of nationally and internationally operating utility companies has mounted pressure on the local government sector of public utilities (energy, water supply, waste disposal, etc.). Public utilities have traditionally been at the core of the multi-functional task profile and understanding of Swedish local government. Chiefly, local authorities governed by right-of-centre majorities have set upon selling their local enterprises to national and international companies, thus retreating noticeably from the corresponding local government activities (cf. Strömberg and Engen, 1996, p. 267; Montin and Amnå, 2000, p. 8). Nonetheless, in spite of these cuts, the Swedish welfare state model has been largely preserved. In the course of the 'competition modernization', public enterprises that are by international comparison highly competitive have emerged (for instance, the energy giant Vattenfall, which is still 100 per cent publicly owned), without any major social conflict arising. The most important reorganization steps in Swedish state-owned enterprises can be summarized as follows (Table 4.13).

France

In France, the interventionist state tradition (*dirigisme*) and a strong public sector (*service public*) with a social integration function have impeded privatization. Furthermore, France is marked by a significant discontinuity in the entrepreneurial activity of the state (Mayer, 2006, p. 104), a situation that can, in part, be explained by a strong party-political bent on privatization policy. Thus, conspicuously contrasting with policy then prevalent in the UK, France's socialist government under President Mitterrand decided, in the early 1980s, to carry out far-reaching nationalizations, particularly of five profitable industrial and banking groups. This policy was, however, immediately reversed when the conservative President Chirac took office (1984–88). The ensuing privatization of a total of 66 public enterprises (adding up to more than 900000 employees) was followed once again by a retraction of privatization plans when, in 1988, the socialists returned to power. Subsequently, in 1993, privatization was once again placed on the political agenda with the comeback of a conservative government (Schröter, 2001, p. 427). Typically, so-called 'silent privatizations' (*privatisations silencieuses*; cf. Mayer, 2006, p. 113) took place by the engaging of private capital

Table 4.13 Privatization and reorganization of public enterprises in Sweden according to sectors

Sector

Telecommunications

1980	Founding of Teleinvest AB
1981	Comvik AB receives approval to operate an analogue mobile communications network
1982	Spectrum licences for two further mobile communications operators
1985	Abolition of the telephone monopoly
1988	Complete abolition of the statutory device monopoly
	Abolition of the de facto network monopoly
1990	Establishment of Statens Telenämnd
1992	Televerket loses final regulation powers
1993	Regulatory authority Telestyrelsen replaces Statens Telenämnd
	Beginning of formal privatization: conversion of Televerket to Telia AB
	Adoption of the telecommunications act to promote competition
1997	Directive (97/33/EC) as the basis of liberalization in EU member states from 1998
2000	Beginning of asset privatization

Post office

1991	The private operator City Mail enters the market
1992	Abolition of the post monopoly
1993	Abolition of the transport monopoly
1994	Postal Act: conversion (formal privatization) of the post office into the public limited company Posten AB (1993: 1684)
1997	Many new market entries by smaller companies
1997	First European 'postal directive': 97/67/EG
1998	Amendment of the Postal Act (SFS 1998:483)

Railways

1988	Transport Act: vertical separation of the monopoly company SJ; transferral of responsibility for unprofitable long-distance traffic to regional authorities
1990	First market entry by a private operator (BK Tåg)
1990	Liberalization of regional freight traffic
1991	First EU rail directive: 91/440/EWG
1996	Complete liberalization of freight traffic
2001	Separation of SJ into six autonomous areas; beginning of asset privatization by selling three areas
2003	Deep crisis: SJ is saved from bankruptcy by the state

Electricity

1991	White Paper on industrial policy for growth
1992	Formal privatization: conversion of Statens Vattenfallsverk to Vattenfall AB
	New state authority Svenska Kraftnät takes over responsibility for the operation of the national grid
	White Paper on an electricity market with competition

Table 4.13 *(continued)*

Sector	
Electricity	
1996	Complete deregulation of the Swedish electricity market
	Directive on internal market in electricity (96/92/EG)
1998	Electricity Commercial Act comes into force
	New regulatory authority STEM commences work
2003	New EU directive on internal market in electricity (2003/54/EC)

Sources: Schalauske and Streb (2008, p. 6 et seq.) and authors' own summary.

to finance public enterprises or by selling indirect state enterprises (which was explicitly illegal). Between 1978 and 1986, the Haut Conseil du Secteur Public registered 160 cases of such illegal asset privatization (cf. ibid.). Also, because of legal hurdles, the public monopolies were initially excluded from privatization, and the market was gradually opened in the 1990s, beginning with La Poste, followed by France Télécom (1997) and Air France (1997), thereby contributing directly to fulfilling the Maastricht criteria.[40] Moreover, there were extensive partial privatizations (*privatisations par morceaux*), including Elf-Aquitaine, the insurance company CNP, the oil company Total, the chemical company Rhône-Poulenc, the motorways (Autoroutes du Sud de la France), the Banque Nationale de Paris (BNP) and the steel company Usinor-Sacilor. Since the electoral victory of the Conservative Party (UMP) in 2002, the market-liberal policy orientation in France has become further accentuated. Since then, additional public enterprises have been converted, by way of formal privatization, into public limited companies and in some cases subsequently sold (by way of asset privatization). This, among others, pertains to the (previously 100 percent state-owned) energy giant EdF-GdF, whose initial shares were sold on the stock market in 2005, and to the airport authority Aéroports de Paris (Beckmann, 2008, p. 132). In addition, the legally prescribed majority of state ownership in Air France and France Télécom has been reduced to a minority position. Later on, particularly since the conservative President Sarkozy came to power in 2007, the privatization movement has gained further momentum and has reached into the social systems, such as the privatization of hospitals and education (ibid.). Yet, the Post Office, which was transformed through formal privatization into a private-law entity on 1 March 2010, and the railways are still in public ownership.

To sum up, in terms of market liberalization, France can arguably be considered by far as the most hesitant and restrained country in which European liberalization requirements have been implemented at the latest possible time (ibid., p. 126). This can be explained, for one, by the political strategy explicitly pursued by France's national government to prepare the former state monopolies to become successful competitors, if not 'national champions', on the country-wide, European and international markets. Another reason arguably is the public pressure, wielded not least of all by the public-sector–related trade unions, to secure employment relations, pension plans, and so on.

On the local government level, public–private companies (*sociétés d'économie mixte locales* – SEMLs) have become increasingly important in France. In the 1980s, 100 of such companies were founded each year (Santini, 1990, p. i), so that one even speaks of an 'SEML reflex' (ibid.; Kuhlmann, 2009a, p. 161). In some local government tasks, the SEMLs have come to prevail in service provision. In 2008, there were 1094 SEMLs with a total of 51 000 employees. Since the groundswell of new start-up companies in the 1980s, an organizational consolidation and a somewhat slight decline has set in due to organizational concentration (Grossi et al., 2010). In France, a series of legal 'disciplinary measures' related to organizational PPPs, have ensured privileged access by public decision-makers. In contrast to Germany, public agencies are generally required to be majority shareholders in SEMLs and also to hold the majority of votes/seats on the supervisory boards.[41] Through the legislative amendment of 2 January 2002, the maximum share of public owners in SEMLs was raised from 80 per cent to 85 per cent (with the minimum share remaining at 50 per cent), thus lowering the minimum of non-public investors to 15 per cent (cf. Deporcq et al., 2003, p. 36). The fact that 63 per cent of the capital invested in the SEMLs is in the hands of local government bodies and only 21 per cent of private shareholders and banks[42] clearly evidences the preponderance of local government in the French variant of institutional PPPs. To some degree, the local authorities also deliver the public services themselves (*en régie*) by way of quasi-autonomous 'public-commercial establishments' (*établissements publics à caractère industriel et commercial* – EPICs).

Italy

In Italy, the beginning of a targeted national privatization policy that coincided with the decentralization movement (see Section 4.2.3), was and is connected with the country's economic and political crisis as well as with the EU-induced privatization pressure. Until the early 1990s, Italy was marked by a comparatively extended economic activity by the state, for example, in the food and steel industries. Measured by the volume of revenues gained from privatization, the privatization programmes that were adopted and have been carried out since 1992 by various coalition governments were the most comprehensive ones among OECD countries during that decade (Mayer, 2006, p. 160). Initially, formal privatizations were inaugurated under the Amato government and, among others, related to the state holdings and enterprises IRI, ENI, ENEL[43] as well as to railways (Ferrovie dello Stato Italiane – FS). These measures were also intended to depoliticize the management of the enterprises and to curtail party-political influence. This phase was followed by a transition to asset privatizations, at first between 1993 and 1994, under the government of the non-partisan former Central Bank governor Ciampi, later under Berlusconi (1994), Dini (1995–96), Prodi (1996–98) and d'Alema (1998–2000). The Italian privatization policy, increasingly shaped by the EU convergence criteria and consolidation requirements, particularly by its single market policy, developed more and more into a 'supranationalization' of privatization.[44] Initially, the key asset privatizations on the national level were the sale of banks and insurers, including the Credito Italiano, IMI and Comita. They further included the sale of the public enterprise Nuovo Pignone and the state-owned INA. Thereupon, privatizations of network companies and public utilities providers (*servizi di pubblica utilità*), which had until then been organized as monopolies, were arranged. Thus, in 1995, the partial asset privatization of the state-owned energy company ENI took place, although it had previously already sold around 140 holdings between 1992 and 1995 (cf. Benedetti, 1996, p. 47). In 1997, the asset privatization of Telecom Italia, the restructuring of the state railways (in accordance with European requirements, that is, separation of infrastructure and transport within a holding), and (in 1999) the IPO of the electricity company ENEL were carried out. As a result, the privatization policy reached an interim peak in the mid-1990s with a revenue volume of 18 trillion lire in 1996 and a further 40 trillion lire in 1997. Subsequently, in 1997, it consolidated at a peak level of 25 trillion lire, resulting from a further retreat of state ownership, inter alia from the BNL bank and the airline Alitalia, as well as through a further partial sale of the public holding ENI (Mayer, 2006, p. 195 et seq.).

Until the early 1990s, the public utilities (water, sewerage, waste, public transport, energy) were delivered in Italy – as in Germany, Scandinavia and the UK – largely by public institutions. Traditionally, Italy has had a well-developed municipal economy sector, mostly in the organizational form of the so-called *municipalizzate* (comparable to Germany's municipal multi-utility works, *Stadtwerke*). This dates back to the legislation of 1903 (Citroni, 2010; Grossi et al., 2010). The *municipalizzate* under which the various services segments typically are institutionally bundled (multi-utility) have been traditionally, for the most part, in public ownership. In the early 1990s, though, national legislation that was part of Italy's decentralization policy, ushered in further organizational diversification and the outsourcing of companies (corporatization). Consequently, now around 50 per cent of municipal staff are employed in outsourced companies (Grossi and Reichard, 2008, p.604). On the one hand, the massive formal privatizations ('outsourcing') have taken place showing a clear preference for private-law limited companies (*società per azioni* – SpA) in a process that has also been referred to as a 'radical change from municipality to local public group of companies' (Grossi, 1999, p.6). To date, around 58 per cent of all municipal companies in Italy are organized as SpA (Grossi and Reichard, 2008, p.605). As a result of the increasing transition to the private-law form, the number of municipal private-law limited companies doubled between 2001 and 2006, that is, from 405 to 1024 (cf. Confservizi, 2006; Grossi and Reichard, 2008, p.604). On the other hand, asset privatizations have gained importance (Lippi, 2003, p.163; Bobbio, 2005, p.43) as augmented through partial or complete sales, such as in the municipal energy sector. As a result of the increased attraction and involvement of private capital and investors, 30 per cent of the municipal enterprises are now operated as public–private companies (Grossi and Reichard, 2008, p.602). In 40 per cent of municipal private-law limited companies (*società a responsabilità limitata* – SrL), private investors even hold the majority of shares (Kuhlmann and Fedele, 2010). In the energy sector, only in a few cities (e.g., Turin, Venice, Brescia) are the *municipalizzate* entirely in municipal ownership, while in the majority of the municipalities national or multinational energy corporations are also (as a rule, minority) shareholders (Wollmann et al., 2010b). By and large Italy's local energy companies (*municipalizzate*) have defended their position on the energy market and even managed to expand it in some cases (see further below).

Germany

In the mid-1990s, the combined effect of European influence, financial constraints (resulting from German Unification) and a growing ideological opening towards market competition, triggered a privatization policy also in Germany, albeit significantly later than in the Anglo-Saxon world. In 1982, there were still 4070 companies in Germany where public authorities held the capital or voting majorities, including those of municipal transport and public utilities, *Land* development companies (*Landesentwicklungsgesellschaften*) as well as industrial enterprises, in whose assets the *Länder* were involved (Deckwirth, 2008, p.65). On the federal level, the post office (Bundespost) and state railways (Bundesbahn), but also a wide range of major industrial enterprises (Volkswagen, VEBA, Salzgitter AG, etc.) were held in federal (co-)ownership. When the Conservative–Liberal coalition under Helmut

Kohl came to power in 1982, it first drew up a list of objects and enterprises earmarked for privatization. As an initial conspicuous move, in 1989 the ('debundling'-type) separation of the federal postal system (Bundespost) into the areas of postal service (Post), postal banking (Postbank) and telecommunications (Telekom) was effected. While the privatization dynamics remained comparably small at the beginning of the Kohl era, they gained momentum in the mid- and late 1990s. For one, around 8500 state-owned factories (*Volkseigene Betriebe* – VEB) of the former German Democratic Republic were to be privatized after 1990 by a trust company (Treuhandanstalt – THA) established for this purpose. Second, Telekom and Bundespost went public (in 1996 and 2000, respectively). Whereas consumer prices decreased at Telekom, postal charges for private customers saw a significant hike. In both sectors, massive redundancies occurred with 110000 jobs being cut at Telekom within a ten-year span (Wehner, 2005, p. 37)[45] and some 30000 jobs slashed at the Bundespost between 1999 and 2004. Moreover, the density and coverage of services and branches at the Bundespost was significantly reduced.[46] Overall, the privatization programmes of the 1990s and the related liberalization laws that were adopted with large parliamentary majorities in the field of telecommunications, postal services, railways and energy went far beyond what had been envisaged at the beginning of the Kohl era (Zohlnhöfer, 2001, p. 365 et seq.; Deckwirth, 2008, p. 68). The privatization-friendly policy continued also after the Red–Green coalition government under Chancellor Schröder came to power in 1998. Similarly, the 'grand coalition' government formed in 2005 by the Christian Democrats and Social Democrats and headed by Chancellor Angela Merkel adhered to this overall privatization-friendly policy line. The same applies to the successor (Christian–Liberal) coalition government that was formed in 2009 and was again headed by Chancellor Merkel.

The rise and continuity of privatization policy on Germany's recent policy agenda are arguably evidenced by the revenues achieved by asset privatization. While these revenues in the overall public budget (federal, *Länder* and local government) totalled 1.9 billion Deutschmark in 1970 and some 4.4 billion DM in 1980, they rose to about 31 billion DM in 1995, and reached a peak in 1998 of almost 53 billion DM (Röber, 2009). Thus, one might argue, during this period and at least on the national level, Germany has come close to the 'market-radical' NPM-driven group of 'minimizing' countries of which the Anglo-Saxon countries are exemplary.

On the local government level, the provision of public utilities (water, sewage, waste, public transport, energy), in Germany called '*Daseinsvorsorge*', has historically and traditionally been a local government task carried out largely by public/municipal institutions, first of all in the traditional form of (multi-utility) municipal/city works (*Stadtwerke*). The 'local markets' within which the provision of public services has traditionally taken place with the *Stadtwerke* in an all but 'monopolist' role have, since the 1990s, come under the market-liberalization and competition pressure from the EU (Trapp et al., 2002; Wollmann, 2002b). Moreover, due to the budget crisis, an increasing number of local governments felt compelled to out-source or privatize the provisions of their tasks. As in other European coun-tries, this involved for one, outsourcing or formal privatization, evinced, for example, in the fact that about 50 per cent of municipal employees are now employed in outsourced municipal companies (Grossi and Reichard, 2008, p. 604).

The total number of municipal enterprises in Germany is estimated to be around 4000, whereby every German city with more than 50000 inhabitants has an average of around 20,[47] and the larger cities having an average of 90 companies each (ibid.). The outsourcing movement in German local gov-ernments can be described primarily as a transition to the private-law legal form (formal privatization), which has also pointedly been called a 'flight from municipal-owned companies. . .towards municipal-controlled compa-nies' (Reichard 2001, p. 89). The most common legal form is the GmbH (*Gesellschaft mit beschränkter Haftung*, analogous to private limited company) amounting to 73 per cent of all municipal companies (Richter et al., 2006, p. 63).

Private sector investors hold shares in almost 40 per cent of municipal com-panies and have even a majority share position in about one-tenth (11 per cent) of all surveyed German municipal companies (Universität Potsdam/ KGSt, 2003). By contrast, the municipalities have minority shares in 20 per cent of the municipal energy companies (Libbe et al., 2004). Against this backdrop, the degree to which the provision of public utilities has already moved towards asset privatization becomes evident. However, strong vari-ances stand out between sectors. The energy sector, for example, is known to be economically profitable and is therefore particularly attractive for asset privatization, whereas in public transport, as a service area chronically in need of subsidization, the acquisition of assets is consequently less coveted by private investors (cf. ibid., p. 76 et seq.; Scheele and Sterzel, 2000, p. 16 et seq.). In the water sector, the provision by the municipalities themselves or by their companies (*Stadtwerke*) traditionally prevails, while the proportion of purely private companies is still very low (3.5 per cent of the total of about 6000 water companies) (BGW, 2005, p. 15; Kuhlmann, 2009a, p. 175; see Table 4.14).

Table 4.14 Legal forms/ownership of local general public services in Germany

Legal Form/Ownership	Water	Energy	Public Transport
Public legal form (in % of companies)			
Municipal enterprise	22	–	2
Public institution	5	–	–
Special purpose association	2	–	–
Total public legal forms	29	–	2
Private legal form (in % of companies)			
GmbH (private limited company)	47	57	58
AG (public limited company)	24	43	40
Total private legal forms	71	100	98
Ownership (in % of companies)			
100 per cent local government[a]	55	29	68
Municipal majority interest[b]	38	54	28
Municipal minority interest[b]	7	17	4
Total	100	100	100

Notes:
a. Direct and indirect interest.
b. Majority interest: municipal shares 50 to <100%; minority interest: municipal shares <50%.

Sources: Libbe et al. (2004, p. 78, with further references) and authors' own compilation.

Hungary

Hungary's institutional starting condition, that is, in the transformation from a communist centralized structure to a democratic and decentralized constitutional state, was decisively moulded by the legacy of a socialist state and socialist state economy in which practically all public and social services were owned, operated and rendered either by the state and its subnational agents or by units of the state economy. After 1990, this structure was dissolved. In the ensuing institutional transformation, different trajectories and patterns of change were embarked upon, depending on sectors and levels.

For one, the privatization of the industrial sector of the socialist state economy was tackled through asset privatization, that is, by partially or entirely selling the state-owned companies to private investors who appeared most suitable (cf. Tittor, 2008, p. 285). To carry out this fundamental transition of major segments of the industrial sector from state to private ownership, a state privatization agency APV (Állami Privatizációs és Vagyonkezelő Rt.) was created for which the trust agency (Treuhandanstalt) that was instrumental in East Germany's economic transformation served as a model (ibid., p. 287 et seq.).

Second, the telecommunication and energy sectors became important fields of regulation and privatization policy (in accordance with similar developments in other European countries; ibid.; for a detailed study cf. Valentiny, 2007).

Under the communist regime, the public utilities (water, sewerage, waste, public transport, etc.) were in state ownership but formally in the responsibility of the representative bodies (councils) of the subnational levels. These tasks were transferred, by the local government legislation of 1990, to the some 8000 municipalities and 19 counties, whereby simultaneously the ownership of the respective institutions was passed on to the local governments (cf. Teller and Somogyi, 2005, p. 46).

As a result of the municipalization of ownership and functions in this broad scope of tasks, the municipalities were confronted with huge operating and financial problems that they have attempted to handle through various strategies. For one, to deliver these public services, in particular water, sewerage and district heating, the municipalities made use of so-called 'budgetary institutions' (*költségvetési intézmények*) (cf. Temesi, 2000, p. 366; Horváth, 2008, p. 233). These are municipally operated units for which the municipality is directly responsible for administrative, personnel and financial tasks. Second, the municipalities outsourced tasks to companies, which – comparable to the *Eigengesellschaften* in German local government – remain in municipal ownership, but are organized as private-law companies (as public or private limited companies). Under financial pressure, many municipalities began to create ('mixed') public–private companies (institutional PPPs) by involving private sector investors and capital (cf. Dexia, 2008, p. 369). In some cases, however, the municipalities – under budgetary pressure – considered it necessary to completely sell public service facilities and companies to private investors. This applies in particular to the water sector (cf. Temesi, 2000, p. 367; Soós, 2003, p. 248 et seq.; Horváth, 2008, p. 233). While the nearly 400 city works are still predominantly owned by the local authorities, in the biggest of them for instance (in Budapest) international water companies have acquired a 25 per cent share. Overall however, the 'budgetary institutions' still prevail (with over a third) vis-à-vis private-law limited companies (with just under a third) and the privatized companies with a tenth (figures for 1996–98; cf. Teller and Somogyi, 2005, p. 48).

This situation may, however, have changed significantly as a result of the far-reaching administrative reform that was decided following the new Constitution ('Fundamental Law') of 25 April 2011. These recent reforms have entailed a significant political and administrative recentralization of the country and a 'comeback' of state administration on the subnational levels, to the functional detriment of the municipal level (see above). In public and social services, important functions that the municipalities had been endowed with since 1990 have been 'taken back from the municipalities and counties' by the state, in particular in the fields of (higher) education, social protection, youth institutions, health institutions, and so on. It remains to be seen whether and to what degree the 'recentralized' state of the new political regime will impact the institutional landscape in the provision of public utilities.

Preliminary conclusions and comparison

For the comparative analysis of privatization policy in the European countries under consideration, the simplified typology of 'marketizers/minimizers', 'modernizers' and 'maintainers' that has been suggested by Pollitt and Bouckaert (cf. Pollitt and Bouckaert, 2004, p. 172 et seq.)[48] shall be drawn on for the following summary interpretation. The first group (minimizers) includes those countries that have undertaken particularly far-reaching asset privatization measures on the national level and have thereby drastically slashed the (economy-related) public sector. By contrast, the group of modernizers comprises those countries that have embarked upon marketization and competition, but have largely forgone extensive asset privatization and minimalist dismantling of the state. The group of 'maintainers' encompasses those countries that have essentially maintained the status quo. With regard to privatization policy, though, this does not apply to any of the countries under consideration, so this category has not been taken into account here (cf. Figure 4.10).

If one places the rate of the (asset) privatization of state-owned companies on the national level in the European countries under consideration in relation to the starting conditions of these reforms, in particular in the scope of national (public) economy, the following country classification can be made, as shown in Figure 4.11.

4.4.3 Functional privatization and contracting out

The transfer of public tasks to external 'vicarious agents', also termed purchaser–provider split or principal–agent relations following NPM terminology, marks a further focal area of action of administrative reform in the European countries. This refers to the awarding of (partial) services via contracts to external providers (outsourcing/contracting out), whereby the enabling responsibility remains with the public institution. This has also

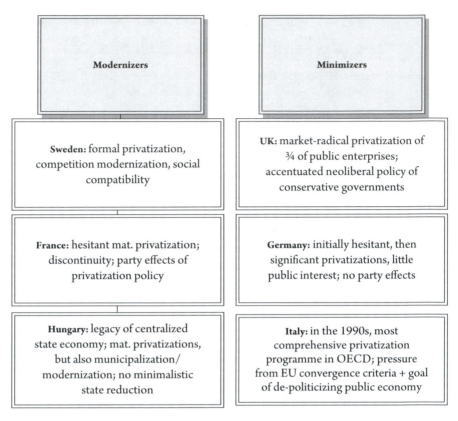

Source: Authors' own diagram.

Figure 4.10 Modernizers and minimizers in privatization policy

been interpreted as a transition to the 'enabling state' (cf. Schedler and Proeller, 2000). As functional privatization frequently involves the outsourcing of execution and service functions, the subnational and local administration units that hold the responsibility for these tasks often take centre stage as arenas/levels of action. Typically, the concepts of outsourcing, marketization and competitive tendering have been particularly pronounced in countries in which the social (and health) services had been hitherto almost exclusively publicly provided (United Kingdom, Sweden).

United Kingdom

In this regard, the United Kingdom can again be considered as a downright pioneer. Until the 1970s, the local government sector held a de facto monopoly position in the provision of services. This was shaped by the philosophy of the Labour Party, which governed the country immediately following World

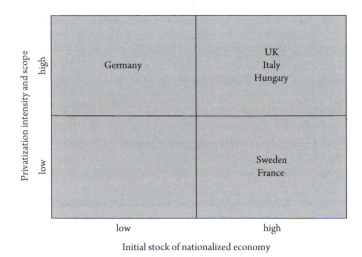

Source: Authors' own diagram.

Figure 4.11 Initial conditions and intensity of asset privatization by country comparison

War II, that the efficiency of the expanding modern welfare state would best be ensured if it was conducted primarily by public personnel (Wollmann, 2008). In social services, for example, the idea that the public sector was best suited to the task (referred to as its self-sufficiency, cf. Stewart, 2000, p. 51) was supported by having the relevant personnel, in particular the social workers, professionally trained (cf. ibid., p. 46 et seq.). Under the conservative government led by Margaret Thatcher, this traditional local organizational model was changed by legally obliging the local authorities to put out numerous local public services (waste removal, canteens, street cleaning, maintenance, etc.) to tender in market competition (compulsory competitive tendering – CCT). In this, private and non-profit service providers as well as the respective administrative units (in-house) of the local governments could participate. Thus, the local authorities proceeded to avail themselves of external (private and non-profit) service providers through outsourcing pertinent services and to appropriate the concept of a purchaser–provider split. For example, residential care is provided to a growing extent by so-called independent, that is, private and non-profit, providers. Whereas in 1970 63 per cent of residential care places were organized by local authorities, this figure dropped to 14 per cent by 2002 (cf. Wollmann, 2008, p. 128, with further references). From the outset, however, such outsourcing of services was guided hardly at all by strict competition as much as by partnership, trust and cooperation (for an instructive example, cf. the Contract Strategy formulated by Lancashire County Council; ibid.). The retreat of local governments

Table 4.15 Job reductions in British local authorities in the wake of CCT

Task Area	1990	1998	2000	Change 1990–2000	
				In thousands	In %
Education	1431	1204	1300	–131	–9.2
Social services	417	395	388	–29	–7.0
Police	199	207	204	5	2.5
Construction	114	61	59	–55	–48.2
Others	806	712	739	–67	–8.3
Total	2967	2579	2690	–277	–9.3

Sources: Bach and Winchester (2003, p. 294) and authors' own calculations/summary.

from the direct provision of services is also expressed in the fact that between 1998 and 2003, the number of local government employees in residential care fell by 21 per cent and in domiciliary care by 6 per cent, while the direct on-site social work (area office, field work staff) also shrank by 6 per cent.

CCT was abolished under New Labour and replaced by the Best Value system (see Section 4.5.3); consequently within one year alone (2000–01) the number of tenders dropped by 23 per cent (Wegener, 2004). However, even under this new system, the local authorities were obliged to compare their services with private providers and outsource them (Reimer, 1999, p. 157 et seq.). As a result of this competitive tendering, since the early 1990s, around 300000 local government jobs have been cut which has primarily affected the area of manual workers (canteen catering, waste removal, leisure and sports facilities, industrial cleaning, road construction and maintenance; see Table 4.15). On top of that, market competition led to a downgrading of the labour relations in local government services, in particular through the slashing of wages and social benefits (holiday and sick pay), expanding temporary and short-term contracts, enhancing employment insecurity and 'multiple jobholding', and raising the workload (ibid.; see also Section 4.5.4).

Sweden

Since the 1980s Sweden too has pursued the reform concept of functional privatization as a purchaser–provider split. Similar to the United Kingdom, in the original political and ideological understanding of the Swedish welfare state the public sector was chiefly responsible for the provision of services. The local governments' responsibility pertained mainly to the almost exclusive provision of social and public services by the local authorities and their employees themselves. The realization and practice of the modern Swedish welfare state was thus essentially assigned to the 'local state' (*den lokala staten*; Pierre, 1994).

Under the budgetary crisis pressure, Sweden also adopted the NPM-guided reform idea of commercialization, diversification of providers and external outsourcing of services in market competition. This was to ensure the transition from a direct performance to an enabling function by way of various competitive elements such as operator models, unbundling, service vouchers or user fees (cf. Rieger and Naschold, 1997, p. 17). The competition authority Konkurrensverket was established on 1 July 1992 to boost and monitor the opening up to competition. Exactly one year later, a competition law (the Konkurrenslagen) came into effect, essentially ruling out competition-restricting forms of cooperation (Roseveare et al., 2004, p. 9 et seq.). Under the two slogans of the right-of-centre government 'Break the local (government's) service monopoly' and 'Freedom of choice revolution in the municipalities!' (van Otter, 1999, p. 96), social services (e.g., care for the elderly and disabled, etc.) were awarded through competition to private-commercial and non-profit providers in a growing number of local authorities. Previously, these services had been almost entirely rendered by local government personnel. Thus, since the early 1990s a number of local governments have begun to turn to private or non-profit service providers or to utilize local vouchers, for example, in schooling (cf. Wollmann, 2008, p. 132 et seq.). Such liberalizing strategies were applied predominantly in local governments with right-of-centre majorities. Overall, however, the Swedish reform strategy – in contrast to the British approach – is characterized by a more moderate use of market forces and by planned and regulated competition that opens up a broader range of options for beneficiaries (e.g., through school and kindergarten vouchers, etc.). In the meantime, private-sector commercial and non-profit providers have been able to acquire increasing shares in these new markets, although they still play, at best, a supplementary role alongside the local government and regional institutions (Schröter, 2001, p. 435). Thus, local government employees, and in particular local social workers, still provide the lion's share of local services, that is, around 90 per cent (cf. SKF/SCB, 2004, p. 116).[49]

France

France deviates markedly from the other countries under consideration insofar as most of the public services (public utilities) have long since been outsourced ('delegated') to private providers by concession contracts. The model of functional privatization or contractual PPP (*gestion déléguée*) has been established in the French local government system for a long

Table 4.16 Functional privatization in the French water sector (2000)

Service Segment	% of Municipalities	% of Population
Water supply		
Direct execution	48	21
Delegation	52	79
Wastewater disposal		
Direct execution	62	48
Delegation	38	53

Source: Hansen and Herbke (2004, p. 300).

time[50] – going back historically to the nineteenth century – and has been termed 'French-style privatization' by foreign observers (Citroni, 2010). Since the 1980s, this variant of service provision has spread further, although more in connection with the decentralization-related expansion of tasks rather than as a result of NPM (see Section 4.2.3). Many municipal companies that had been established in some municipalities vanished and private providers have acquired a leading role (*'un rôle leader'*; Lorrain, 1995, p. 105), for example in the water sector (see Table 4.16), which is divided up among three large private companies. This action has been referred to as a 'generalization of delegation' (Duval, 2006). In the supply of drinking water alone, the private share rose from 30 per cent in the mid-1950s to 60 per cent in 1983, and finally to almost 80 per cent by 1999 (Guérin-Schneider and Lorrain, 2003, p. 46; see Table 4.16). In the area of waste removal, only 13 per cent of enterprises are run by local authorities' governments, while a large chunk is 'delegated' to private companies, in particular to the two large companies Veolia Environnement (formerly: Compagnie Générale des Eaux) and Suez Environnement (formerly: Lyonnaise des Eaux). The opening of the market in the provision of public services (water, waste, public transport) has occurred primarily through an expansion of concession contracts to private providers (*exploitants*). In this process, however, the local governments retain the enabling responsibility and, in principle, remain owners of the companies and facilities. The companies with which the local governments make concession contracts belong almost entirely to the same large corporations (*grands groupes*); this evinces the high degree of concentration and integration on the part of the service suppliers in contrast to the institutional fragmentation on the (local government) demand side.

A further area of the outsourcing of service provision is the social services. Following the expansion of the third sector in France beginning in the 1960s, non-profit organizations (*associations*) became more and more important in the field of 'social action' (*action sociale*). Since the early 1970s, the rapid growth of non-profit organizations (*associations*) has been referred to as a regular 'baby boom' of NPOs in France (ibid.). Thus, between 1970 and 2000, an average of 48500 NPOs were founded every year, representing a total growth of about 1.3 million new *associations* in France since 1975. In the late 1990s, this was termed a 'welfare mix' (Archambault, 1997, p. 181 et seq.).

Italy

In Italy, as in Germany, social services were typically provided by independent organizations, in particular Catholic charity organizations, but also – such as in the area of elderly care – by the families themselves. During the 1970s and 1980s attempts were made by left-wing council majorities to strengthen the role of the local authorities in service provision in accordance with the Scandinavian model. However, the non-profit organizations initially retained their dominant position as service providers (Fargion, 1997, pp. 142 et seq., 76f.; Bönker et al., 2010). Thus, even before the NPM debate of the 1980s there existed a mix of municipal service providers, in particular in the larger cities, and (largely church-related) non-profit organizations (Bobbio, 2005, p. 43). In the meantime, a massive functional shift to private-sector providers took place in this sector, a shift that some have viewed as the 'triumph of privatism' (ibid.). This development has ushered in the intensification of the already existing fragmentation of Italian social policy and disparity in social services, in particular in terms of the North–South division. With regard to internal services (facility management, IT, canteens, etc.), a growing trend towards functional privatization and contracting out/outsourcing has been shaped (Grossi and Reichard, 2008, p. 603; Dipartimento della Funzione Pubblica, 2006). Doubt has been voiced as to whether the (albeit strengthened) local executives are in a position to control this new 'networked local government', characterized by partnerships, contracts and various contractual arrangements, and which threatens to increasingly become institutionally 'frayed' (Meneguzzo, 1997; Magnier, 2003, p. 193).

By contrast, the area of public services (public utilities) provision is marked by the interplay between the above-mentioned institutional spin-offs (corporatization) with organizational and asset privatization rather than by functional privatization (see above). For example, in the drinking water sector, EU norms and national legislation, in particular under the 1994 Act No. 36 (the so-called Galli Act) paved the way for competitive tendering and concession contracts with private actors. However, the local authorities have so far only made reluctant use of these privatization options (see Table 4.17). Hence,

Table 4.17 Operating structure in the Italian water supply (1999)

	Operation of Aqueducts	Water Supply	Wastewater Treatment	Sewerage	Overall
Municipality	3714	4534	3644	6340	6463
	(80.1%)	(84.6%)	(85.8%)	(95%)	(82.6%)
Munic. enterprise	83	88	60	59	107
(municipalizzate)	(1.8%)	(1.6%)	(1.4%)	(0.9%)	(1.4%)
Consortium	400	329	170	100	528
	(8.6%)	(6.1%)	(4%)	(1.5%)	(6.7%)
Public body	28	19	33	8	53
	(0.6%)	(0.4%)	(0.8%)	(0.1%)	(0.7%)
Joint stock	130	144	148	100	215
company	(2.8%)	(2.7%)	(3.5%)	(1.5%)	(2.7%)
Other	280	246	190	70	460
	(6%)	(4.6%)	(4.5%)	(1%)	(5.9%)
Total	4635	5360	4245	6677	7826

Source: Citroni (2010, p. 202, with further references).

in the water sector, up until 2007 only four out of 91 'optimal territorial districts'[51] (ATOs) utilized competitive tendering and concessions (Lippi et al., 2008, p. 632). Overall, at least with regard to this task area, there has thus been a 'slow progress of concessions across the national territory' (ibid., p. 628). This is not least of all due to the distinctly localized Italian culture and the strong position of the multi-functionally organized local economy, in particular in the North (and less pronounced in the centre and the South; ibid.).

Germany

In Germany, social services are a preferred field of activity for contracting out to external providers. It should be recalled that in Germany, based on the principle of subsidiarity, local social services are traditionally provided by non-profit organizations, that is, they are 'outsourced', thereby showing that Germany's administrative history has a commonality with Italy's. Thus, while 'outsourcing' has long since been the usual mode of service provision, the large non-profit welfare organizations (*freie Wohlfahrtsverbände*) that have engaged in the provision of these services have operated in distinctly corporate networks and developed downright 'monopolies' (Grohs, 2010). Against this backdrop, the pertinent national (federal) legislation aimed at removing the existing legal primacy of welfare associations and at 'pluralizing' the provider sector. Since then, market opening processes have gained momentum especially in the area of (outpatient) care services, of which, for example in East

Table 4.18 Functional privatization in the area of outpatient care services in Germany

Year	Proportion of the Total Number of Care Services %					
	East public	Indep. organizations	Commercial	West public	Indep. organizations	Commercial
2001	1.0	38.2	60.8	2.3	49.3	48.4
2003	0.7	36.8	62.5	2.0	48.7	49.3

Sources: Statistisches Bundesamt (2003c, 2005) and authors' own summary.

German *Länder*, more than 60 per cent are performed by private-commercial providers, with the local authorities hardly playing a role (see Table 4.18).[52]

However, outsourcing through contracting out has also become increasingly important in the field of public services (*Daseinsvorsorge*, that is, in EU terminology: services of general economic interest, including 'voluntary' local government tasks in cultural and sporting activities). Besides the 'classic' concession models practised in the energy sector, the local authorities increasingly apply operator models in waste management (e.g., waste incineration plants), construction (e.g., school buildings) and the operation of swimming pools, libraries, museums, theatres and sports and tourist facilities. With regard to new capital investments, the construction of the corresponding facilities are financed either entirely privately or in a mixed, public–private form while the actual operation is subsequently contracted out to private companies, whereby – such as in waste incineration plants – contract periods are set for up to 30 years. Such forms of long-term 'delegation' (or contractual PPPs) are becoming more and more frequent among German local governments due to their financial dearth and investment backlogs. According to a 2005 study conducted by the German Institute of Urban Affairs (DIfU) on behalf of the PPP Task Force of the Federal Ministry of Transport, Building and Housing (BMVBW), a regular PPP boom has set in since 2004, with such contracts having doubled when compared to previous years. Thus, the DIfU identified around 160 long-term local PPP infrastructure projects for 2005, which, in addition to co-financing, included the subsequent operation (in some cases for over 20 years) and the maintenance by private companies (cf. DIfU/BMVBW 2005, p. 4).

Hungary

In Hungary, too, under growing financial pressure and prompted by NPM-inspired outsourcing and marketization concepts, the municipalities have proceeded to outsource public services to private providers through concessions and contracts. In doing so, Hungary's municipalities have availed themselves of outsourced providers on an average higher than other Central and Eastern European countries (cf. Kopányi et al., 2000; Briški, 2003, p. 93 et seq.; Soós, 2003, p. 248; Struyk, 2003, p. 19; OECD, 2008, p. 29 et seq.).

A prime example of the progressing functional privatization can be found in water supply sector (cf. Tittor, 2008, p. 296). Until 1990, there were 33 state-operated regional water companies under the control of a 'central water authority'. After 1990, the overseeing of the water supply became a compulsory local government task, while the infrastructural facilities came under municipal property. To date there exist a total of 377 local government-owned 'extremely fragmented' (ibid.) water supply companies, which have outsourced water provision by means of long-term (15-to-20-year) concessions to private, and, in particular, foreign companies (Veolia, Suez, RWE, E.ON, etc.). Thus, Hungary's pattern of public service provision can be encapsulated as the transformation from a centralized state structure to an initially decentralized local government system, one that has subsequently been opened to market principles and is now increasingly experiencing functional privatization, especially through outsourcing and concessions to private sector companies.

Moreover, mention should be made of the construction of highways/motorways (cf. OECD, 2008, p. 29), of public transport, burial services, social services and health care (cf. Temesi, 2003, p. 31) that have also been marked by 'contracting out' and functional privatization, albeit in different legal forms. Thus, the responsibility at the local government level for health care has resulted in the local authorities collaborating with the respective medical doctors on a contractual basis in 80 per cent of cases (cf. Füzesi et al., 2005, p. 282). Also in the provision of social services – for example, care of the homeless – far more than 50 per cent of all tasks are assigned to non-governmental organizations (NGOs) via contracts, as they are considered to be more experienced as well as being more cost-effective (cf. Hrast et al., 2009, p. 108). Other examples of collaboration between local governments and NGOs pertain to the operation of local cultural facilities, such as libraries and community centres, or other social tasks (home care, drug prevention, etc.; cf. Jenei and Kuti, 2003, p. 146). Contracts with external service providers are often commissioned following a tendering process whereby, in drawing up the contracts, the local authorities often do not avail themselves of external assistance or of careful scrutiny by the local administration or by the municipal council (cf. Baar, 2001, p. 118). Overall, contracts with external actors make up around 15 per cent of all expenditure (cf. Kopányi et al., 2000, p. 38). Thus, 'contracting out' and functional privatization are a widespread strategy in Hungary, more so even than in other Central and Eastern European countries (cf. Baar, 2001, p. 103).

Preliminary conclusions and comparison

To summarize, country comparison shows that, on the one hand, there existed quite different traditions of public service tasks and starting conditions of reforms, something especially apparent in the area of the local welfare state and public utilities (water, waste disposal, energy, etc.). In several countries, these were provided for exclusively by local authorities (UK, Sweden), in others largely by 'third sector' (non-profit, NGOs) organizations (e.g., social services in Germany and Italy) and still in others by the state sector (e.g., Hungary and other ex-socialist countries, prior to 1990). Despite these differences, on the other hand, a significant trend has taken shape towards functional privatization, outsourcing and delegation across countries evinced in a general movement away from a service-production–focused role of local government and towards its 'enabling' responsibility and profile (cf. Figure 4.12).

4.4.4 Is the pendulum swinging back?

Since the beginning of the 2000s, a trend reversal has been taking shape towards the 'return of the public' – obviously as a response to the negative effects of privatization and to 'market failures' as evinced by the world-wide financial crisis. This trend reversal has surfaced in reregulation, remunicipalization and repurchase of assets. In attempting to come to grips with the global economic and financial crisis, national governments and supranational organizations have fallen back on state regulation with the public sector. Moreover, public institutions have come to reassess and 'rediscover' them as relevant actors and agencies. Moreover, the assessment that in providing public utilities public enterprises are, as a rule (at least) on a par with private sector providers comes out in most available studies (see the broad overview in Mühlenkamp, 2013, p. 18).[53] The balance sheet becomes even more favourable for public/municipal provision if the 'transaction costs' of the outsourcing of services (costs of monitoring, contract management etc.) are taken into account,[54] not to speak of the negative 'welfare effects' of privatized service provision and the positive ones (social, ecological etc.) of public/municipal provision (see Florio, 2004, p. 341[55]). Against this background, the neo-liberal battle cry 'private is better than public' has lost much of its force and credibility, while the state and the public sector appear to have seen a (positive) reappraisal and 'comeback' with the 'pendulum swinging back'.

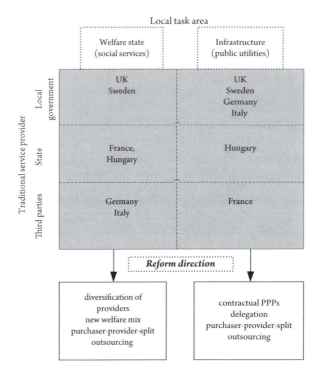

Source: Authors' own diagram.

Figure 4.12 Initial conditions and direction of functional privatization by country comparison

On the local level, strong indications of such reversal trend towards a 'remunicipalization' of service provision and related local-level activities can be identified, although admittedly empirical evidence still remains scattered (cf. Röber, 2009; Engartner, 2009; Verbuecheln, 2009; Wollmann and Marcou, 2010; Wollmann, 2011; Kuhlmann and Wollmann, 2013; Hall et al., 2013; Wollmann, 2013). In some regions, citizens have come to increasingly value public sector service provision higher than private sector provision. In Germany, for instance, this trend is evidenced by a growing number of local referenda in which the privatization of public services and facilities is rejected (for a recent overview see Mehr Demokratie, 2012, p. 42ff.). Thus, local petitions and referenda were initiated to block the privatization of municipal enterprises and infrastructure facilities being considered or already decided on by the local councils. For instance, in the cities of Düsseldorf, Hamm, Steinheim and Münster, as a result of successful local referenda, the *Stadtwerke* remained in municipal ownership. Besides, referenda have been directed not only against the (asset) privatization of municipal facilities, but also against (functional) privatization. Internationally, if not globally, this trend is propelled by the emergence and formation of social and political movements of which Attac[56] (and its involvement in national referenda) is exemplary.

On the European level, mention should be also made of the European petition 'Water is a human right', which was initiated under the 'right of petition' procedure that has been introduced in the context of the Treaty of Lisbon in 2009. According to this 'right of petition' 'any citizen of the European Union. . .shall have the right to address, individually or in association with other citizens or persons, a petition to (the European) parliament on a matter which comes within the European Union's fields of activity and which affects him, her or it directly'.[57] The petition, which was initiated in April 2012, aimed at requesting the European Commission 'to propose legislation, implementing the human right to water and sanitation and promoting the provision of water and sanitation as essential public services for all'.[58] By June 2013 the petition was signed by some 1.5 million citizens and, in surpassing by far the procedurally required 1 million signatures, adopted. The immediate effect of this EU-wide 'referendum' has been to politically question, if not delegitimize, any further privatization moves at least in the water sector and perhaps even beyond.

In the following the energy and water sectors will be singled out as cases in point to provide more empirical evidence of this post-NPM development. In these two grid-based services, the municipalities in most countries have the right to grant (time-limited) concessions to the enterprises that want to establish and use such grids. As currently many of these concessions contracts expire, a 'window of opportunity' is opening for the municipalities to renegotiate the concessions contracts and to possibly remunicipalize the services.

Energy

The energy sector offers a good example of current trends of remunicipalization (cf. Wollmann et al., 2010b; Libbe et al., 2011; Wollmann, 2011). Local government energy companies in Italy, for example, have managed to defend and even expand their position on the Italian market despite privatization pressure. Some large cities have even purchased shares in the (formally privatized) energy giant ENEL and are extending their production and distribution grids. The municipal energy companies in Milano and Brescia, for instance, merged in 2008 to form a stock-market–listed energy company ('A2A'), generating 3.9 per cent of the entire national electricity production. In addition, further small-scale municipal companies are producing around

14 per cent of electricity. In Italy, the generation of electricity by nuclear power was ruled out as early as 1987 and this was supported by a national referendum in June 2011. Because of this, the municipal energy companies, which rely largely on renewable (in particular hydro-) energy sources, have been gaining in importance (cf. Wollmann, 2011).

In Germany, since EU-promoted market liberalization of the energy sector began in the mid-1990s, the municipal energy companies, which had mostly operated in the organizational form of multi-utility *Stadtwerke*, faced competitive pressure from the 'big four' private sector energy giants (E.ON, RWE, EnBW, Vattenfall). Temporarily, even the 'demise of the *Stadtwerke*' (*Stadtwerkesterben*) was predicted (for details cf. Wollmann et al., 2010b, p. 177). However, the *Stadtwerke* learnt not only to hold their ground, but even to strengthen their market position. For one, they managed to adapt to the new competition rules. Furthermore, they were protected by the legal provision that energy companies with fewer than 100000 customers were exempt from the requirement to 'unbundle' the energy generation, transmission and distribution functions. As a result, a remunicipalization movement in the energy sector gained impetus. For one, local authorities founded new municipal energy companies or bought back previously privatized assets and grids. Moreover, they decided not to renegotiate the expiring concession contracts, thereby providing an opportunity for remunicipalizing the facilities. In a 2011 survey, one-third of all local governments stated that remunicipalization in the area of energy supply was planned, while only 2 per cent indicated their intention to pursue further (partial) privatization (cf. Institut für den öffentlichen Sektor, 2011, p. 6 et seq.).[59] The large majority (94 per cent) welcomed remunicipalization as a chance to retain or regain local-level influence and control over local energy provision (ibid., p. 8; see Figure 4.13).

Seventy-four per cent of the respondents indicated that a prime reason for remunicipalization was to achieve additional revenues (see Lenk et al., 2011; Reichard and Röber, 2012; Meyer-Gohde et al., 2013). The town of Ahrensburg in Schleswig-Holstein provides an illustration (Box 4.1).

Under the EU's pressure to enhance competition in the energy sector, the 'Big Four' proceeded to relinquish their (minority) shares in municipal multi-utility companies (*Stadtwerke*).[60] A spectacular example occurred in 2009 when a consortium of *Stadtwerke* repurchased the shares held by E.ON in municipal companies, amounting to 3 billion euros and resulting in the establishment of the so-called Thüga Holding.[61] In the meantime Vattenfall, the Swedish state-owned energy giant, too, saw itself induced by the EU's pressure to sell its *Stadtwerke* holdings.[62] In 2010, 700 of 1372 municipal

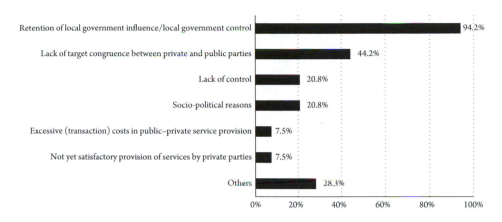

Note: n = 120; multiple responses possible.

Source: Institut für den öffentlichen Sektor (2011, p.8).

Figure 4.13 Reasons for remunicipalization efforts in energy supply

---

BOX 4.1

AHRENSBURG ACCELERATES

The town of Ahrensburg terminated its concession contract with E.ON in 2006. Under the programmatic slogan *'Ahrensburg gibt Gas'* ('Ahrensburg accelerates') the town took gas supply back into municipal operation and repurchased the distribution grids from E.ON. The latter was reluctant to sell as it resented losing customers and revenue. On its part, the local authority expected to have annual revenues of about 1.5 million euros by operating its own gas company.

The example of Ahrensburg was observed with great interest by other local authorities in Northern Germany, which considered remunicipalization measures as well. However, in view of the fact that additional capital investments are necessary for repurchasing the assets and so on, and setting up a municipal company (around 11 million euros in the case of Ahrensburg) the further course and volume of remunicipalization measures remains to be seen.

---

utilities were active in supplying energy and one-third of them in electricity production, thereby adding up to around 10 per cent of the country's entire electricity generation (cf. VKU, 2009). The role of local governments and their *Stadtwerke* in energy supply has gained additional dynamics by the decision of the Federal Government in June 2011 – in reaction to the Fukushima nuclear reactor disaster – to abandon nuclear power electricity generation by 2022. Thus, the German municipalities and their energy companies, which have always been pioneers in the use of energy-saving and renewable technologies (in particular co-generation), are facing new energy-related challenges and opportunities.

In France, the energy market continues to be dominated by the electricity giant Electricité de France (EdF), of which 80 per cent is still in public ownership and where 75 per cent of the electricity is produced by nuclear power. At the same time, the municipalities and their 230 local energy companies also play quite a visible role in (local) energy policy. As their position has been strengthened by decentralization, French local authorities have been able to expand this role (cf. Wollmann et al., 2010b). For one, since the 1980s a local energy (-saving) policy has become more and more accepted. Some local authorities have begun to create their own (alternative) energy generation systems that were better adjusted to local conditions, for example by using small waterfalls for power generation and relying more on co-generation and wind energy (ibid.). Second, they have increasingly used their supply grids as sources of revenue, since, weighing in as *autorités organisatrices* on the concession contracts, they are able to influence the amount of charges, pricing and service-related parameters.

In the United Kingdom, where the local energy sector was entirely nationalized in 1946 and entirely (materially) privatized in 1989, the local authorities have been left with hardly any role in energy supply. However, some resurgence of energy-related policy activities of local governments can be observed here, too. In fact, the Conservative–Liberal coalition government that was formed in May 2010 explicitly urged the local authorities to contribute to the national policy objective of raising the proportion of renewable energies in overall consumption to 15 per cent by re-engaging themselves in local energy matters.[63] Meanwhile a number of local authorities, such as in Sheffield, Leeds and Bradford, have initiated such energy-related projects.[64] In addition, local authorities have begun to take back previously outsourced tasks into their responsibility (insourcing). According to a survey conducted in 2010 by the Association for Public Service Excellence (APSE[65]) in 140 local authorities in England, Scotland and Wales, almost 60 per cent indicated that they already carried out or had prepared or planned such insourcing; just 20 per cent responded that they had never outsourced services (cf. APSE, 2011, p. 11). Such insourcing comprises a broad spectrum of tasks, including waste removal, recycling, social services, education, housing and maintenance (ibid., p. 15 et seq.). In their responses 'a need to improve efficiency and reduce service costs' was the most cited reason for insourcing (ibid., p. 11).

Water

In Italy, the water sector also exemplifies strategies that run counter to the privatization trend (Citroni, 2010; Wollmann, 2011). The conservative Berlusconi government paved the legislative way for a far-reaching privatization of the water supply by means of the Ronchi Decree in 2009. This move, however, was stopped by the national referendum of 11 June 2011 when an overwhelming majority rejected the privatization of the water supply. The political campaign that preceded the referendum was primarily supported by the Forum Italiano dei Movimenti per l'Acqua, a broad (largely left-wing) movement, consisting of 150 local governments and a variety of political groups.[66] This movement reflects the degree of politicization (and in some cases, ideologization) that the refusal of a 'privatization of water' had reached. As a result of the referendum, the advances of international private sector water companies appear to have been halted.

In Germany, too, where since the 1990s large companies such as Veolia, Suez, RWE and E.ON 'bought into' municipal utilities (*Stadtwerke*) from the 1990s and thus made inroads into the hitherto predominantly municipal water supply, a counter-movement has evolved. In Stuttgart, for example, which sold its waterworks to the EnBW in 2003, a local referendum was held in June 2010 demanding that the waterworks be remunicipalized. Responding to the referendum, the city council decided to buy back the waterworks in 2013 following the expiration of the concession contract.[67] A fierce political controversy was ignited in the city state (*Land*) of Berlin on a possible remunicipalization of the water company. In 1999, 49.9 per cent of the waterworks had been sold to Veolia and RWE. In July 2012, the *Land* of Berlin decided to buy back the RWE shares at a cost of around 654 million euros; furthermore, the repurchase of the 24.95 per cent share held by Veolia is currently under consideration.[68]

In France during the past few years, the municipalities and local administration have also begun to switch from the delegation of services (*gestion délé-guée*) to delivering them on their own (*en régie*). One reason for this is their wish to become independent of the *grands groupes* (Veolia, Suez, SAUR) and to regain more political influence on the water sector. It should be recalled that in France, despite a 'generalized delegation', the lion's share of drinking water networks (still 99 per cent at the end of the 1980s; cf. Lachaume, 1997, p. 67) continues to be owned by local authorities which, as *autorités organisa-trices*, are legally entitled to opt out of concession contracts after they expire and to manage the services themselves (*sortir de la délégation*). In addition, Paris – as a pace-setter for other municipalities – remunicipalized its water supply in 2010 with the city of Grenoble providing for another spectacular example of this movement (Box 4.2). As the result of this development, the proportion of the French population whose water supply is managed by the

---

BOX 4.2

GRENOBLE

In the city of Grenoble the provision of water, until 1989, operated by a municipal unit (*en régie*), was (materially) privatized in 1990 and subsequently, in 1997, transformed into a 'mixed' company (institutional PPP, SEML). Following a decision taken by the municipal council on 20 March 2000 water provision was remunicipalized. Today, the Régie des Eaux de Grenoble (REG) is organized as a public body (*établissement public à caractère industriel et commercial* – EPIC), which is entirely in municipal ownership. At the same time, the wastewater disposal was 'inter-municipalized'; thus, it is now established on the (inter-municipal) level of the Communauté d'Agglomération Grenoble-Alpes Métropole (La Métro). In some regions, these measures have led to regular chain reactions, in which one local authority makes a first move and then others follow suit, so that in fact a trend towards remunicipalization appears to be taking shape.

---

municipalities themselves (*en régie*) rose from 18 per cent in 1970 to 28 per cent in 2008 (Bordonneau et al., 2010, p. 134).

Other sectors

In other pertinent fields, privatization measures or contracts with private sector actors have been unravelled as well. In the area of waste management this has even been termed as an 'orange revolution' (Engartner, 2009, p. 70; Verbuecheln, 2009). For example, the city of Bergkamen in North Rhine-Westphalia, which, after having bought back its electricity grid in the mid-1990s, turned to also remunicipalizing waste disposal in 2006 (Schäfer, 2007; Dreyfus et al., 2010). A large number of other German cities followed this example (Gruner et al., 2009; Verbuecheln, 2009). According to a study conducted in 2009, as many as 10 per cent of German local authorities planned to remunicipalize their waste disposal at that time (Ernst & Young, 2007, p. 16). In 2009, 44 cases were identified in which the remunicipalization of the waste disposal sector was on the political agenda (Gruner et al., 2009; Dreyfus et al., 2010). In France, local school canteens (*restauration scolaire*) are another well-known example of remunicipalization (e.g., in Le Havre, where remunicipalization reacted to a serious performance deficit on the part of private provider). According to a survey, the majority (63 per cent) of school canteens in large French cities are now operated by local authorities themselves, while only 37 per cent are 'delegated' or put out to tender (*marché public*; cf. Dexia Crédit Local/AMGVF, 2004; Kuhlmann, 2009a). For a broad international overview see Hall et al. (2012, 2013, p. 207ff.).

4.4.5 Cross-country comparison: convergence, divergence, persistence and explanatory factors

Convergence, divergence, persistence

The privatization, marketization and commercialization ('commodification') of public services have turned out to be significant 'mega-trends' of administrative reforms in both European and international contexts. The privatization of nationalized and municipalized economic, service and infrastructure enterprises and the transition from (largely) public to increasingly private-commercial service provision with a simultaneous limitation of public institutions to an 'enabling function' can be considered generally converging developments within European countries and their administrative systems over the past 20 years. In addition to the formal and, in many cases, also asset privatization of state-owned enterprises, there has been an upsurge in spin-offs of municipal companies and companies organized under private law (corporatization; Grossi and Reichard, 2008) on the local government level across Europe. Moreover, the purchaser–provider split and the incorporation of private service providers via service level agreements (functional privatization) have proven to be convergent modernization trends in European administrations. As a result of this development, in many European countries the public sector has not only shrunk numerically (see Chapter 2, Table 2.3), but has also become, in terms of sectors, more differentiated and more fragmented. This is because numerous external, mono-functionally operating 'vicarious agents' have become involved in the providing of public services, while the state and the local authorities have withdrawn from the direct production of public goods.

The hierarchical 'steering' via core administration has decreased, while contracted out and privatized service areas have been added and now constitute an increasingly unclear formation of private or semi-public (para-governmental/para-municipal) 'satellites'. In the countries under consideration, the landscape of actors in the conducting of public tasks has become notably differentiated and the model of the 'enabling state' has become prevalent. For the European local government systems, the 'shift from a system of local government to a system of local governance' (Stoker, 1999, p. 41), which has been identified in the United Kingdom, can be considered overall to be characteristic. In this respect, France, due to its 'delegation tradition', has had a head start, whereas the other countries have exhibited corresponding convergent development patterns in this direction. However, converging developments also result from the effects of the 'satellite formation' (cf. Lachaume, 1996, p. 67; Kuhlmann, 2009a, p. 167), as this has led to a growth in management and control problems, transaction costs and transparency deficits through-out. New Institutional Economics with its principal–agent theory, a theory that is often used to justify privatization, can provide an excellent contribution to the theoretical explication of this (cf. Reichard, 2002).

Irrespective of the general European convergence in the privatization debate and (partial) privatization practice, notable differences exist in scope, intensity and type of the implementation of measures between the individual countries (but also within countries between sectors and administrative levels). The United Kingdom can be viewed as a prime example of a market-radical privatization model, one that has strongly centralizing features due to the simultaneous 'disempowerment' of the local authorities as monopoly-type providers of numerous services. Accordingly, the UK along with New Zealand – has been assigned to the group of marketizing and minimizing countries ('that have gone further and faster down the roads of marketizing and minimizing'; Pollitt and Bouckaert, 2004, p. 179). These have been most strongly guided by liberalization ideas and NPM concepts in the modernization of the public sector.

Under the labels as designated by Pollitt and Bouckaert, Sweden and France can be classified as 'modernizers', as privatization has occurred more moderately and is embedded into the respective existing administrative culture and welfare state tradition. In Sweden, the modernization of the welfare state has been implemented primarily by means of opening up competition and by the diversification of providers, which had been flanked by social regulations and element of user democracy. The privatization of state-owned enterprises did not occur to the same extent as in other European countries, and asset privatizations continue to be the exception rather than the rule. In France, the opening up of competition on the national level also took place only gradually and quite late, a timeline related to the attempt to retain traditional structures according to the French *service public* legacy to defend these against resistance if necessary. Also in the local sphere, special legal provisions have been stipulated allowing for privileged access of public actors to partially privatized ('mixed') companies (*societés d'économie mixte locales* – SEMLs). Due to the long-standing practice of outsourcing through concessions, radical steps towards functional privatization are not necessary, so that this can also be referred to as modernizing (in the sense of the Pollitt and Bouckaert typology).

In the early 2000s, Germany was designated by Pollitt and Bouckaert as a maintaining, and, to some extent, modernizing country that implemented NPM-induced changes in a more adaptive sense, essentially due to the persistent politico-administrative structures. However, with a view to the national privatization policy of the 1990s, Germany should no longer be assigned to this group. For one, subsequent to the comparatively moderate privatization plans at the beginning of the Kohl era, privatization pressure intensified so rapidly that today, of all the large state-owned infrastructure enterprises, only the DeutscheBahn is still 100 per cent in public (state) ownership, the IPO of which was only prevented (temporarily) by the financial market crisis and not by a lack of national political will. Irrespective of the political hue of the governments and (in contrast to France, Italy and the United Kingdom, for example) without any notable resistance by the trade unions, Germany has developed into an 'eager outperformer' (Deckwirth, 2008, p. 87) of European liberalization requirements since the mid-1990s. Three major liberalization acts (railroad 1994, Telekom 1996, postal system 1997) were passed based on a broad national privatization consensus. Against this backdrop, there is evidence that Germany – at least with an eye on the national level – has turned from a maintainer into a marketizer/minimizer, a fact that is also supported by the significant drop in the public employment from 12.2 (in 1995) per cent to 9.6 per cent (in 2008). As such, Germany ranks at the tail end of OECD countries, that is, distinctly behind Sweden (26.2 per cent in 2008) and France (21.9 per cent), but also markedly behind Italy (14.3 per cent), the United Kingdom (17.4 per cent) and Hungary (19.5 per cent), and more or less level with Poland (9.7) and Switzerland (9.7; cf. OECD, 2011; see Chapter 3, Table 3.3). For Germany's municipal economy, which remains pivotal for public service tasks (*Daseinsvorsorge*), the classification as a marketizer/minimizer should be qualified insofar as, although liberalization and privatization have taken place there as well, the local electricity, gas and water providers are still largely in public ownership and partially privatized companies are even being bought back, so that the persistence (maintaining) of traditional provision structures is more pronounced here.

Albeit following the cautious initial (formal) privatization steps undertaken in the early 1990s, Italy exhibits a similar profile as having the most extensive privatization programme in Europe – measured in terms of revenues from privatization – and effected during the course of the decade. In contrast to Germany as an 'outperformer' and 'anticipator' of European requirements, in Italy EU policy has been one of the key triggers and decisive driving forces behind privatization, ranging from private sales to large-scale IPOs. Following the withdrawal by the state from industrial companies, the banking and insurance sectors and finally step by step from the large infrastructure enterprises, the Italian denationalization policy reached its peak in the mid- to late 1990s. Although the Italian state remains substantially active in the business sector and the transition from *Stato imprenditore* to *Stato regolatore* does not appear to be completed (Mayer, 2006, p. 205), Italy can be rightly assigned to the group of marketizing/minimizing countries given the privatization scope of the past two decades. This is confirmed by the fact that the public employment numbers in Italy are at 14.3 per cent (2008) and thus are much lower than that of Sweden and France, and even slightly lower than in the United Kingdom (OECD, 2011).

In addition to scope and intensity, the instruments and forms of privatization in the European countries differ, amounting to a 'divergence within convergence'. Whereas in Sweden formal privatization still predominates nationally and functional privatization has advanced on the local level, there has been a far greater extent of asset privatization in the United Kingdom, Germany and Italy. This difference becomes apparent when considering state-owned enterprises – in particular infrastructure companies. This is also evinced in the municipal economic sector, where there is a greater reliance on public–private companies and private share ownership. To that extent, the privatization policy in these countries is more radical, going hand in hand with a sale of public property, a sale that cannot be unilaterally rescinded. France, by contrast, exhibits similarities to Sweden, to the extent that it relies rather on a purchaser–provider split – albeit linked to over 100 years of concession culture – and thus retains the possibility of deciding unilaterally to take back enterprises *en régie*. Figure 4.14 summarizes.

Explanatory factors

The above-described discursive and institutional convergence in the privatization policy of European countries has exogenous and endogenous

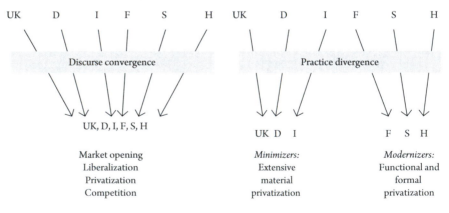

Source: Authors' own diagram.

Figure 4.14 Discourse convergence and practice divergence of privatization by country comparison

determining factors, which point to the explanatory approaches of New Institutionalism outlined at the beginning of this book. In addition to the signs of economic crisis and growing financing problems of the welfare state as decisive macro-economic triggers of the international privatization discourse,[69] EU policy represents a significant convergence-promoting (exogenous) lever in the reform area here considered.

The theoretical approach of sociological institutionalism comes into play here, according to which isomorphic adaptations occur as the result – inter alia – of (external) pressure – 'coercive isomorphism' – thus, in the case of the EU as an adaptation to legal obligations. Although the EU cannot decree the privatization of public enterprises, the European Commission is entitled to issue appropriate directives and regulations to the member countries in cases of violations of public companies against competition rules. This then generates direct coercive pressure. Thus, on the one hand, use has been made of the possibility to liberalize infrastructure areas through sectoral European regulations (e.g., EU Directive on Electricity, EU Directive on Commercial Waste, etc.). Moreover, the regulations set out in the treaty on the internal market, on European competition law, on European procurement law (Schmidt, 2008; Töller, 2010) and the case law of the European Court of Justice, that is, the legislative domain of negative integration, are relevant in the sense of coercive pressure (Schmidt, 2004, p. 18 et seq.; Töller, 2010). These regulations have led to a growth in privatizations by competitive tender because municipal enterprises often fail to enter into the tendering process due to the uncertain outcome or because private companies receive concessions. Similarly, this is true for the prohibition of state aid as contained in Article 87 et seq. (cf. also Blauberger and Töller, 2011), which has resulted in an increase in efficiency pressure towards privatization and the gain of market shares by private companies resulting from the cessation in subsidies to public enterprises.[70]

By contrast, normative pressure has been generated by the European Commission in those areas of activity where before it had lacked regulatory powers of its own. This is because, first, municipal actors are advised to apply specific techniques (OMC [open method of coordination], benchmarking, peer review) for 'mutual learning'. Second, the imitation of particular organizational variants (privatization) and procedures (competition-centred management) in the provision of services is promoted by the Commission's dissemination of normative concepts regarding the preferred means of providing services of local public service tasks and by the exertion of its influence via framing (Rein and Schön, 1993; Quack, 2005). The overarching neoliberal reform discourse cycle of the 1980s and 1990s was thus significantly promoted by the EU and offers a key explanation for the persuasive power created by the slogan 'private is better than public' that has gone beyond countries and sectors, albeit with differences (see further below).

On the one hand, the convergence of the privatization movement can therefore be interpreted as an exogenous and top-down development, which was initiated or at least accelerated by the EU institutions (so-called downloading; cf. Dyson and Goetz, 2003) and that is characterized by coercive or normative pressure. 'Adjustment by coercion' applies to the countries examined here, in particular to Italy and France, to a limited extent to Sweden and Hungary, and in the case of Germany, to the energy and partially to the waste sectors. In the latter case, privatizations have been sparked off directly and indirectly by EU policy (directives, sector-specific regulations, state aid policy, economic effects of internal market policy, convergence criteria of the economic and monetary union).

On the other hand, there have also been bottom-up processes (uploading) within the context of European policy, induced by individual member states (endogenously) and which had diffusing and, in the end (exogenous), 'Europeanizing' effects. This is particularly true for the United Kingdom. Whereas Margaret Thatcher was considered to be anti-European (Mergel, 2005, p. 198 et seq.), the influence of the British privatization model on the EU – and mediated by the EU to its member states – has been significant (Drews, 2008, p. 41). In virtually all areas of public infrastructure, the United Kingdom was a forerunner within the EU regarding the processes of commercialization, privatization and liberalization. This has led to the British model – in spite of all its flaws – becoming the yardstick for reorganizational processes in other countries and for the discourses and principles on the European level with the European Commission even explicitly referring to the dynamics in the United Kingdom (Dickhaus and Dierz, 2004, p. 46). Similar bottom-up developments were also initiated by German politics, which likewise proved to be a promoter of an accelerated European liberalization movement. Thus, the EU was by no means the sole trigger of privatization processes in the area of infrastructure enterprises, but has rather facilitated and even accelerated the already on-going negotiations for the breakthrough. (Deckwirth, 2008, p. 87). This shows how the EU is 'used' ('usage of Europe'; cf. Goetz, 2006) to legitimate specific national policy preferences in one's own country on the one hand, and to influence the political course at the European level on the other.

The strong influence of EU policy-making on national/local institutional developments can also be observed in the more recent post-NPM developments. Thus, the readiness and motivation of local authorities to engage themselves in the provision of public services has been fostered by changes in EU regulations regarding the role and position of local governments in the European inter-governmental setting. In the EU (and concomitantly in the national) contexts the status and function of the local government level has recently been strengthened, as in the Treaty of Lisbon of December 2009 (see above). Furthermore, and particularly relevant for the delivery of 'services of general economic interest', in a protocol to the Treaty of Lisbon (which has the same legal status as the Treaty itself) it has been stipulated that regarding these 'services of general interest' the EU explicitly recognizes 'the essential role and the wide discretion of national, regional and local authorities in providing, commissioning and organizing services of general economic interest, as closely as possible to the needs of the users' as well as 'the diversity between various services of general economic interest and the differences in the needs and preferences of users that may result from different geographical, social or cultural situations'. This means that the EU has significantly mitigated its programmatic single market mandate and claim by virtually allowing local exceptions and possibly even local markets. Furthermore, in certain policy fields, the local government level has been recognized as an important actor both by the EU and by the national governments. This applies prominently to environmental protection and energy-saving targets.[71] For implementing the stipulated energy- and climate-preserving policies the local authorities have been recognized as crucial actors.

However, the observed patterns in the European reform discourse are also endogenously caused by the formation of 'actor coalitions' in the countries under consideration. This observation can be theoretically captured with the concept of actor-centred institutionalism that focuses on the behavioural preferences of veto players and the action strategies of actors, in particular the electoral objectives (policy- and vote-seeking) of national parties and local political actors. In Germany, this can be seen, for example, in the ideological change in both major popular parties, whose governments found support from a broad privatization consensus after 1982, and were flanked by a limited mobilization on the part of the trade unions (except for the Postal Workers' Union), thus leading to a 'privatization-friendly' veto player configuration. The privatization policies of the different governments could be linked with their predecessors more or less seamlessly so that notable party difference is not apparent. In Italy, there has also been a broad political-ideological privatization consensus among the relevant political actors on the national level – although here this has occurred in the face of resistance from the trade unions. This consensus was based on the use and legitimization of privatizations as a political strategy in order to break the requisition of state-owned enterprises by the parties (*consociativismo*; Berti, 1998) and to loosen the close relationships between enterprise management and the political classes, which had been in a deep legitimization crisis in the early 1990s due to numerous corruption allegations. From an actor-centred perspective, privatization policy can thus be explained here on the grounds of the action preferences of political actors meeting the electoral objectives (vote-seeking) of the governing parties.

Nevertheless, analysis has shown that the countries followed different NPM paths and can be assigned to different reform types (divergence within convergence), thus pointing to a continuing and, in some cases, even a strengthening of the differences between them. One principal explanation – again linking back to actor-centred institutionalism – involves the political and administrative actors. These have access to significant freedom of choice, such as in the initiation as well as in the prevention of privatization measures and in the (non-) implementation of European directives. There has been considerable leeway in European countries regarding the question of whether and to what extent the privatization logic of NPM is taken up and implemented. As such, the radical nature of British privatization measures can be explained largely by the political show of strength of the Thatcher government that faced hardly any opposition by veto actors, and the market-liberal political ideology, thereby in turn affecting Europe as a whole. By contrast, the liberalization of the German municipal economy has happened less incisively due to an actor constellation consisting of the federal government, EU Commission and local governments, and because remunicipalization has even been encouraged. In addition, the withdrawal of privatization plans or the repurchase of municipal enterprises or facilities on the local level is often driven by strategic electoral considerations of local political actors (vote-seeking), for which a successful referendum against a privatization measure decided by the local council represents a heavy blow to be avoided at all costs. Thus, political actors seek and use the opportunity to regain political control over the quality and price-setting of service provision and to pursue social, ecological, and so on, objectives (welfare effects), for instance by way of cross-subsidizing structurally and chronically deficient service sectors (such as public transport). In doing so, they act upon and play out a 'political rationality', which (ideally) is oriented on the common good and best interest of the community.

The specific configuration of actors has also considerable explanatory power with regard to the more moderate or hesitant privatization measures in the cases of France and Sweden. For the former, there was 'lively' resistance against privatizations, so that this could only be pushed through in difficult compromise constellations (cf. Beckmann, 2008, p. 126). In the latter case, there was hardly a basis of consensus for asset privatizations – disregarding exceptions – so that more moderate, competition-oriented modernization has been aimed for, although it can, however, find support from broad political alliances (thus in Sweden; cf. Schalauske and Streb, 2008, p. 215). Overall, the variations in the privatization policy of European countries can thus be traced back first to a national or local veto player configuration and the political preferences of actors (Mayer, 2006, p. 275), in which party differences only play a limited role, as shown in the examples of the United Kingdom and Germany. Second, the variance in privatization between the countries can be explained in terms of their respective administrative and public sector cultures, which have had an influence on the path of possible privatization steps. This is true for the consensus-supported culture of the Swedish *folkshemmet* and the society-integrating *service public* in France as much as for the German local government tradition of municipal utilities (*Stadtwerke*) or the locally rooted *municipalizzate* in Italy that have exhibited a remarkable persistence and survival capacity despite privatization pressure. Hence, despite all the privatization dynamic and EU-related diffusion processes, the assumptions of historical institutionalism can be confirmed, according to which administrative-cultural legacies and public sector cultures bring about path-dependent institutional developments and effect persistence or divergence. With a view to the conceptual considerations as covered in Chapter 2, Section 2.3, the theoretical explanation of national reform paths in the area of privatization policy can be summarized in Table 4.19.

Table 4.19 Theoretical explanations for reform development in the area of privatization

Factor	Explanation	Neo-institutionalist Theory Approach
Exogenous explanatory factors (supra-/international)		
EU policy; opening of the internal market	Coercive isomorphism, normative pressure, framing, usage of Europe	Sociological institutionalism
Economic and fiscal crisis		
2 NPM discourse dominance		
3 Post-NPM discourse		
Endogenous explanatory factors (national/local)		
Pro- and anti-privatization coalitions; political alliances	Policy-/vote-seeking; veto player configurations	Actor-centred institutionalism, veto player theory
Administrative and welfare state traditions	Path-dependencies, lock-in effects, critical junctures	Historical institutionalism

Source: Authors' own compilation.

4.5 Modernizing administrative organization, procedures and personnel

4.5.1 Concepts and definitions

As described above (cf. Section 4.1), since the 1980s the internal modernization of administration has been strongly wrought by the international reform
doctrine of New Public Management. The demand was to transform the
rule-based administration, which had been accused of budget maximization
and encrusted bureaucracy, into a 'customer-friendly service enterprise' that
could be managed in a performance- and cost-oriented manner (Hood, 1991;
Reichard, 1994; Schedler and Proeller, 2000). For this, tools from output
steering, target agreements, controlling systems and economic performance
incentives have been introduced, hierarchical structures have been disbanded
and a clear division of function and role between politics and administration
has been implemented (for details, see Bogumil et al., 2007, p. 23 et seq.).
Efficiency and effectiveness were to be increased by decentralizing responsibility for resources and a corresponding redesign of the organizational structure (large commercially inspired departments, results centres), procedures
of performance management (accrual accounting, product catalogues, performance indicator systems, reporting) and a performance-related personnel management. The steering of internal administrative processes as well as
the parliamentary control of administration were now to take place on the
basis of contracts and target agreements. By means of competition mechanisms, in particular performance comparisons, benchmarking and 'customer
power', the new system of administrative management was to be 'energized'
(cf. Kommunale Gemeinschaftsstelle für Verwaltungsmanagement, KGst,
1993). As part of the international NPM movement, this bundle of measures
represents the internal structural micro-dimension of NPM (see Chapter 2,
Section 2.2.2). Figure 4.15 highlights the major features of the classic Weber
administrative organization vis-à-vis the reform proposals of NPM in the
area of internal modernization, which uses the criticism of 'classic' administration as a starting point.

Although a broadly convergent NPM-inspired reform discourse is apparent, there are significant differences among the countries in terms of the
implementation and use of the various reform instruments. These differences will be dealt with in more detail in the following. In terms of European
administrations, it can be generally stated that a radical NPM-guided and
top-down implemented managerialization of the public sector, as was characteristic of the United Kingdom (and similarly in New Zealand), has not
taken place in the majority of administrations: 'Only New Zealand rivals

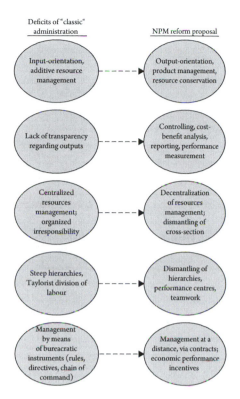

Source: Authors' own diagram.

Figure 4.15 Comparison of classic administration and NPM reform proposals

the British commitment to this style of public sector reform' (Stoker, 1998, p. 374). By contrast, the implementation of NPM concepts that has taken place in Continental Europe has been significant, but by no means revolutionary (Bouckaert, 2006; Kuhlmann, 2009a). However, this does not mean that reform activities, such as in the areas of delegation of responsibility, the formation of autonomous administrative units, performance management or performance-related pay in the public service, have been minimal. The countries have simply adapted to the respective administrative-cultural context and have less of the 'hyperactive quality' (Stoker, 1998, p. 374) that was criticized in the British reform approach.

It should be noted in this connection that a broad understanding of NPM has led in many cases to the neglect of other, more traditional and sectoral reform steps that go back to earlier (pre-NPM) reform discourses, as these were 'absorbed', so to speak, by NPM (Jaedicke et al., 2000, p. 57). In the German context, for example, this relates to the citizens' one-stop shops (*Bürgerämter*), which are not an NPM invention, but rather developed in the early 1980s in an entirely different context (cf. Liedtke and Tepper, 1989). In practice, however, the 'classic' reform approaches are difficult to separate from NPM-inspired measures; quite the opposite as both are frequently combined and amalgamated. This should be taken into account in the following comparison of administrative modernization, again with a special focus on the six representative countries of the different European administrative profiles. In this, three reform areas are of interest:

- organizational structures;
- procedures and steering tools;
- personnel.

4.5.2 Organizational structures

Ministerial administration: agencification

The modernization of organizational structures in public administrations in Europe had been strongly shaped by the notion of decentralization,[72] the flattening of hierarchies and institutional autonomy of organizational units. Inspired by the NPM idea of a clear separation of roles and functions between political-executive leadership on the one hand and administrative implementation on the other, the agency model in particular has become widespread on the ministerial level in a number of countries (Döhler and Jann, 2007, p. 8 et seq.; Bach et al., 2010, p. 15 et seq.). Given the rise in the establishment of such quasi-autonomous administrative units (executive agencies) during the past two decades, there has been talk of 'agency fever' (cf. Pollitt et al., 2001; Christensen and Laegreid, 2005). The functions of the agencies assume implementation and regulation tasks that had previously been located within the ministries. Administration is to become 'depoliticized', giving politics more strategic and steering capacities. As such, the agencies should be steered by the political leadership (ministers) 'at arm's length' – and no longer by the classic-bureaucratic means of hierarchical command (Talbot, 2004; Bach et al., 2010, p. 55 et seq.). For this, instruments have been borrowed from the area of business management/administration (product budgets, service-level agreements, performance indicator-based controlling, etc.; see Chapter 2, Figure 2.5).

The NPM-inspired agencies must be distinguished from the regulation agencies that were established during the course of EU internal market liberalization as a counterpoint to privatization and competition opening. They mark the often-cited transition from a service-providing state to an enabling and regulation state, whose role is no longer to provide or produce, but only to

Table 4.20 'Classic' authority versus 'modern' agency

Agency in the Broad Sense: Authority	Agency in the Narrow Sense: 'Modern' Agency
Structural autonomization	Steering by means of target and performance agreements
Public law status	
Own task profile	Extended scope of action for the management of administrative resources
Own resources	
Subject to ministerial steering and control (not legally independent)	Separation of policy formulation (ministerial administration) and implementation (agency)

Source: Bach et al. (2010, p. 13).

ensure fair competition in the new markets that had not existed previously (Döhler, 2008, p. 276). To do this, the state employs quasi-autonomous regulation agencies whose apolitical nature is supposed to enhance the credibility of regulative politics (Pollack, 1997; Bach et al., 2010, p. 21). On the other hand, the mono-functional orientation of agencies is geared towards decreasing information procurement and information processing costs, which are accrued in classic administrations in highly specialized regulation fields (McCubbins and Page, 1987, p. 417). Nevertheless, with regard to the functionality and steering problems, NPM and regulation agencies exhibit a number of commonalities (cf. Bach et al., 2010, p. 28 et seq.). See Table 4.20 for a summary of classic and modern agency functions and definitions.

With regard to agencification in the countries of interest here, the distinct difference in use and implementation of this 'modern' variant of administrative deconcentration (see Section 4.2.3) must be viewed in close connection with the national politico-institutional starting conditions. The initially very hesitant reception of the agency concept in Germany can be explained by the existing high degree of administrative deconcentration and political decentralization within the administrative-federal system characterized by the principle of subsidiarity. In Germany, administrative implementation is already located at subnational levels (*Länder*, local governments), so that one might speak of a deconcentration/decentralization head start when compared to unitary-centralized countries such as the United Kingdom, France or Italy (Wollmann, 1996b). From the point of view of the existing institutional 'layering' between ministries and implementation administration reaching back to the late nineteenth century, the German federal administration can be considered 'agencifiable' only to a limited extent (Döhler, 2007, p. 13). However, the number of institutions on the federal level that are classifiable as 'agencies' has also increased since the post-war period (for empirical data, cf. Bach and Jann, 2010, p. 457 et seq.).

The example of the United Kingdom paints a different picture. Here, under Margaret Thatcher, the entire ministerial administration was restructured (deconcentrated) from 1988 onward during the course of the so-called 'Next Steps' initiative. Since then, the British 'radical approach' has been considered a prime example of agencification in Europe. With the aim of breaking up the highly centralized ministerial bureaucracy in Whitehall, and in the evident political intent of Thatcher to weaken the British Civil Service (and its Labour-friendly trade unions), the implementation tasks hitherto located within the ministries were transferred to more than 100 Next Steps Agencies comprising around 80 per cent of public personnel employed on central-state level (Schröter, 2001, p. 422). In 2002, around 350000 people were employed in Next Steps Agencies (Lodge, 2007, p. 60). These are managed by a chief executive – often recruited from private industry – who is largely autonomous when it comes to issues of resource management, hiring/firing/payment of personnel, task implementation, and so on. In this, the central management tool is the so-called framework agreement, which is entered into by the minister and the chief executive and that specifies the key points of performance (budget, time frame, reporting modalities, performance indicators, etc.). The Next Steps Agencies can be also distinguished in terms of a range of features, among other things with regard to their size (between 30 and 65000 employees) and their tasks (e.g., Passport Agency; Child Support Agency; Prison Agency, etc.; cf. Lodge, 2007, p. 57 et seq.). Measured by the number of existing agencies, agencification in the United Kingdom reached its peak in the late 1990s, although since then, there has been a slight decrease (see Figure 4.16).

During the course of agencification, the British Civil Service was subjected to strongly centrifugal tendencies with the result that the central-state administration today is highly deconcentrated, if not fragmented, and overarching steering is extremely difficult (Christensen and Laegreid, 2001b, 2010; Lodge, 2007). In reaction to this, a number of agencies have since been abolished and there has been a call, which is being debated under the catchwords of 'joined-up governance' or 'whole-of-government reform' (ibid.), to reintegrate agencies into ministerial administration.

In the other countries examined here, the agency concept has been taken up in a far less 'radical' manner. In Sweden, this is linked to the fact that the total of 234 agencies (*ämbetsverk*; cf. Tiessen, 2007, p. 141) that make up the largest part of the state administration (99 per cent of state employees; cf. Alam, 1998, p. 103) have more than a 200-year history in some cases, so that this may also be considered to be a 'modernizing head start'. In France for many years (see Section 4.2.3), the state administration has also been highly

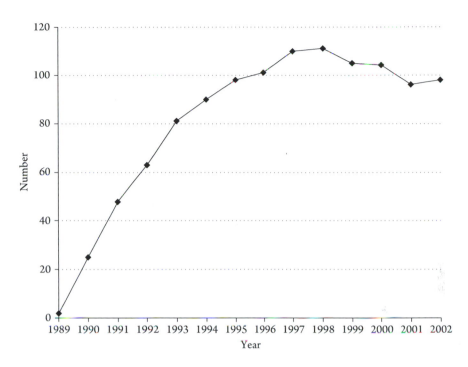

Source: Following Lodge (2007, p. 59, with further references).

Figure 4.16 Number of Next Steps Agencies

deconcentrated and equipped with numerous classic local implementation units (*services extérieurs de l'Etat*), whose de facto freedom of action is not insubstantial. Thus, the institutional necessity for an additional unbundling and 'territorialization' of the French state is rather limited. Until recently, however, the approaches of output and contract management connected to the agency model have only been used sparingly. By contrast in Sweden, the agencies adopted management by results (*målstyrelse*; cf. Sundström, 2004) in the early 1990s, so that the tools of global budgeting, contract management, decentralized results and resource responsibility and performance measurement have been in practice for almost 30 years. In France, however, a reform thrust was propelled only when the institutional law on public financing came into force in 2001 (Loi Organique Relative aux Lois de Finances – LOLF). As a result, the output responsibility and budget autonomy of the deconcentrated state authorities might be strengthened towards an agency model (see further below).

In Italy, where the deconcentration of state administration is also not insubstantial (Wollmann et al., 2010a), the NPM idea of agencification has been welcomed, albeit – as in France – rather cautiously. It should be recalled that the first agencies in Italy had already been founded during the time of the Kingdom of Piedmont.[73] Following the 'privatization' of employment relations in the public service (see further below), the collective bargaining agency Agenzia per la Rappresentanza Negoziale delle Pubbliche Amministrazioni (ARAN) and two further central regulation authorities, inter alia in the environmental sector, were initially established in the early 1990s. An agencification more closely aligned to the British Next Steps reforms then took place under the Ministerial Reform of 1999, which was targeted at instituting several executive agencies on the central-state level, including four in the fiscal department. Overall, however, there is no agency fever in sight in Italy either. Moreover, case studies of ten agencies (cf. Fedele et al., 2007) concluded that their managerial control only functions to a limited extent. Although they now have wide-ranging freedom of action in resources management, in 2006 only the fiscal agency was fully contractualized while performance management hardly existed (ibid.).

Hungary is also characterized by a moderate application of the agency concept. Initially, due to the transformation processes in the early 1990s, new agencies were formed, in some cases in a chaotic manner, in which each ministry put together its own group of agencies. Nevertheless, the number of agencies on the central level has hardly gone beyond 60, even under the influence of pro-NPM cabinets and EU accession. Thus, a clear trend towards agencification cannot be observed (cf. Hajnal and Kádár, 2008, p. 26 et seq.). Instead, there has been a development over the past few years, and in particular since 2006, towards a reintegration of agencies in their respective ministries, a consolidation of specialized agencies in a single authority and a limit to agency autonomy (cf. Hajnal, 2010, p. 21 et seq.). In addition to fiscal savings, the aim was to strengthen political control of the administrative structures, which in this respect corresponds to the post-NPM trend of integrated steering in the sense of a 'whole-of-government' approach.

The reform developments of agencification can be summarized in terms of the following country groupings (Figure 4.17).

Local-level administration: one-stop agencies and bundling of tasks

On the subnational and local levels, the agency idea has gained currency in particular in connection with the establishment of one-stop agencies (*Bürgerämter*), although these have been implemented very differently in the individual countries (cf. Askim et al., 2011). Many countries have aimed at providing a wide range of bundled local administrative services 'under one roof' so that citizens would not have to travel far, thus providing a more

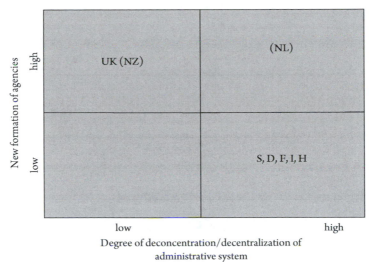

Source: Authors' own diagram.

Figure 4.17 Reform developments of agencification by comparison

customer-oriented administration. The establishment of a 'single point of contact' has been prescribed to all member states by the 2006 EU services directive. In the debate surrounding such a point of contact, which was in particular geared towards facilitating the interaction between foreign investors and companies and the respective national administrations, this long-pursued reform idea has been taken up by many countries and enshrined into EU law. Thus in Germany, so-called 'citizen shops' (*Bürgerämter*) have been introduced in 58 per cent of all local governments as well as in more than 80 per cent of cities with over 50000 residents.[74] The more localized provision of services by way of spatial decentralization has also been implemented in many German municipalities (40 per cent). The one-stop shops have proven to be one of the most successful reform concepts in Germany, based on their dissemination rates across local governments and to the related service improvements (see Figure 4.18).

There have been similar attempts in France where so-called 'service centres' (*maisons des services publics* – MSPs) have been put into place and whose numbers have multiplied since the early 1990s.[75] However, within the fragmented French administrative system, primary function of these centres is the bundling of services of various levels and institutions (local government, *département*, state, associations, public and private companies). In the meantime, though, many larger cities are beginning to tackle the internal reorganization of services (cf. Kuhlmann, 2009a, p. 214 et seq.) and 'multi-service

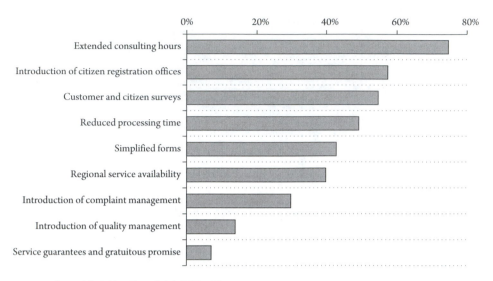

Source: Adapted from Bogumil et al. (2007, p. 68).

Figure 4.18 Expansion of customer orientation in German local governments

counters' (*guichet unique multiservice*) have been introduced that provide administrative services under one roof (*d'accueil polyvalent*).

In Italy, the establishment of 'offices for relations with the public'[76] – as the Italian variant of one-stop agencies – has been legally stipulated. However, in the implementation of this new scheme, these offices have not only been used for various local services, but also for the implementation of the new freedom of information rights and are intended to ensure citizens' access to administrative acts (Promberger et al., 2000, p. 83 et seq.). Moreover, the installation of 'all-in-one-counters' (*sportello unico*) has also been made legally binding to support the establishment of companies and to provide advice to investors.[77] According to estimates the new 'all-in-one-counters' bundle up to 60 (previously organizationally fragmented) administrative procedures (ibid., p. 85).

In Sweden – as in the Scandinavian countries overall – many citizen-related administration services have been organizationally decentralized and transferred to 'territorialized' units to reduce the spatial distance particularly for those who live in sparsely populated areas. For this, 'centre concepts' have been adopted (cf. Oppen, 1997, p. 240) and these are being increasingly characterized by a variety of service offers and provisions. Examples of such one-stop shops can be found in the municipalities of Sundvalls, Upplands Väsby and Tierps, which are also considered pioneers in other reform areas.

However, this trend has not extended throughout the country, according to the Swedish regional association.[78] Instead, the transition to a purchaser–provider split represents the predominant reform pattern (see also Section 4.4.3). Internally, within municipal administration, this is intended to create organizational flexibility by introducing NPM-inspired client/contractor relations, while, externally, it is meant to give choice options for citizens/'customers' (for instance, via vouchers) and to enhance provider diversity (Wollmann, 2008, p. 227).

In the United Kingdom, the organizational restructuring of the local administration is characterized less by task bundling and by installing citizens' one-stop shops than by implementing the NPM-derived concept of the purchaser–provider split and by practising competitive tendering, which has led to a pronounced diversification and pluralization of providers (see Section 4.4.3; Wollmann, 2008, p. 225). In contrast to Sweden and also Germany, the administrative reforms have been imposed top-down by central government and have, in the meantime, resulted in a mono-functional fragmentation of local-level actors and by no means in a (citizen-oriented) bundling of administrative services. Furthermore, the concept of one-stop shops has found less attraction in the United Kingdom than in Continental Europe, because the classic registration functions that account for a large part of the task spectrum of the 'citizen one-stop offices', for instance in Germany, exist only in a truncated form in the UK and many citizen-related functions, such as registering births/deaths and so on are carried out by state agencies; thus the organizational bundling of functions takes place, if at all, beyond and outside the local authorities proper. This is exemplified by the Job Centres Plus, which have been introduced in 2001 (with the exception of Northern Ireland) and serve as standard points of contact for unemployment as well as for social security (Askim et al., 2011, p. 1460 et seq.).

In Hungary, there are still many deconcentrated state administration units that operate on the subnational levels. These subnational state offices have been in the focus of modernization measures. Thus, the government programme of 1999 placed great emphasis on improving governmental performance by recasting these administrative units. As a result, several deconcentrated administrative offices have been merged and integrated into the general state administration (cf. Varga, 2006, p. 710). The role model for this was the concept of a single counter access as the administrative restructuring aimed at providing better information for citizens and simplifying access to administration for small and medium-sized companies (cf. OECD, 2000, p. 153). By contrast, one-stop shops have so far hardly progressed on the local level.

Table 4.21 Variants of one-stop shops by comparison

Country	National Models of One-stop Shops/Functions	Prevalence Rate
G	*Bürgeramt*: bundling of local government services	High
F	*Guichet unique multiservice*: bundling of local government services	Medium
	Maisons des services publics: bundling of various state- and local-level services (rural areas)	Medium
I	*Sportello unico*: investment consulting	Low
S	One-stop shop: bundling of local government services	Medium/increasing
UK	Job Centre Plus: bundling of social security services (implementation wing of state agencies)	High (except Northern Ireland)
H	State administrative offices: single window access for entrepreneurs (general state administration)	Low

Source: Author's own compilation.

In summary, as a voluntary local government reform movement, it can be said that the citizens' one-stop shops in the form of single counter access has spread furthest in Germany. By contrast, there is little evidence for such a development in Italy, despite pertinent state legislation. The situation is similar in Hungary where the concept of an integrated provision of services has triggered reform measures predominantly in the state administration. This can also be observed in the United Kingdom, where the one-stop shop approach has been largely limited to state administration (agencies) and is applied particularly in the Job Centres Plus. Both France and Sweden fall somewhere in between, as citizens' one-stop shops are implemented somewhat experimentally; although they are not yet widespread, their use appears to be mounting. Besides the larger cities that are testing out citizens' one-stop shops, multi-functional service points have also become quite popular 'in the countryside' (in France, the *maisons des services publics* – MSPs; see Table 4.21).

4.5.3 Procedures and steering instruments

During the previous decades, the modernization of procedures and management tools in administration was also strongly shaped by NPM concepts, in particular by the concept of performance measurement/performance management (Pollitt and Bouckaert, 2004, p. 87; Wollmann, 2003b, 2003c; Kuhlmann, 2004, 2007b, 2010d; Proeller and Siegel, 2009). This refers to the identification of the performance of public administration via performance indicators (PIs). Performance management also includes steering, that is, the targeted influence on institutional action by means of performance information. Although these reform approaches have been boosted by commercial managerialism (see above), the fundamental strategic idea of performance measurement and evaluation can also be found in earlier (pre-NPM) reforms. Thus, indicator-based performance and effects measurement experienced a remarkable initial boost internationally as early as the 1960s and 1970s (Derlien, 1997, p. 6 et seq.; Wollmann, 2003a). Aimed at enhancing the efficiency of public activities by steering through results/outputs (output steering, management by results), the New Public Management movement has revived the demand for outputs and effects transparency, which was crucial in the planning discussion and in the programme evaluation of the 1960s/1970s.

Moreover, the expansion of common quality assessment systems (e.g., Common Assessment Framework – CAF; see Saatweber, 2004), performance comparisons and benchmarking within and between European public administrations have been intensified as a result of European integration (Wallace, 2005, p. 85; Goetz, 2006, p. 483) in the context of which the horizontal cooperation of member states has developed as an independent mode of EU policy (Speer, 2002). Moreover, the requirement that was introduced by the EU of having its structural funding programmes evaluated in a textbook-type sequence of ex ante, on-going and ex post evaluation has ushered in a distinct upgrading of performance and effects monitoring in the public administrations of EU member states (Wollmann, 2004, p. 25; on Italy, cf. Lippi, 2003).

In the attempt to introduce and implement the tools of performance measurement, performance comparison and benchmarking, a striking convergence in the administrative modernization of the European countries can be stated (cf. Bouckaert and Halligan, 2008; Van Dooren and van de Walle 2008; De Lancer, 2009; Kuhlmann, 2010d). In view of the rapid concept diffusion in the international context, it appears to some observers that a comprehensive convergence towards a managerial state has taken shape.

Irrespective of this discourse and concept convergence, however, conspicuous differences among European countries can be noticed in the implementation, use and effect of performance measurement and performance management. This pertains in particular to the following aspects (cf. Bouckaert and Halligan, 2008; Van Dooren and van de Walle, 2008; de Lancer, 2009; Kuhlmann 2010d):

- instrumental arrangement, that is, type and content of performance indicators[79] ('what is measured');

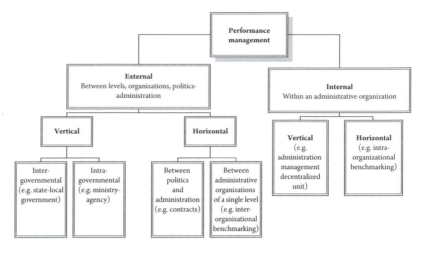

Source: Authors' own diagram.

Figure 4.19 Variants of performance management in administration

- institutionalization of performance management in the politico-administrative multi-level system ('who measures');
- steering of performance measurement (top-down versus bottom-up);
- external transparency of performance data and sanction effects (rewards/penalties for good/poor performance);
- use of performance information for decision-making and steering processes.

From viewing the different variants in which performance management can occur within administrations and between administrative bodies/levels, a picture emerges as illustrated in Figure 4.19. The individual variants of performance management can be considered typical of particular European countries, for example, the vertical-hierarchical performance management for England and the horizontal-voluntary variant of local self-managed performance comparison for Germany and Sweden (see further below).

Performance management as extensive state control: United Kingdom/England

The performance management approaches developed early on in England[80] are the best known in the European context, not least due to the linguistic accessibility. They can be considered prototypical of a variant of performance management that is central state-directed, mandatory, installed nationwide, and subject to sanctions. Hereby, the administrative units (executive agencies or local authorities) that are responsible for providing the services are required to fulfil the objectives specified in target agreements and contracts. The achievement of targets and the compliance with performance standards are observed and monitored generally by external institutions. Thus, so-called Public Service Agreements (PSAs) have been introduced on the central state level where the targets of the individual ministries over a three-year period are specified. These PSAs each contain details on how, by whom and until when the performance targets[81] must be reached and how target achievement is measured. Furthermore, the Comprehensive Spending Review (CSR) introduced in 1998 links the content of performance objectives of the PSAs to pre-defined budget targets and from 2000 onwards, includes further effects indicators added to the already defined input and output indicators (Bouckaert and Halligan, 2008, p. 346 et seq.).

During the 1980s, an increasingly sophisticated system of performance indicators and performance rankings was also established at the local government level (Wegener, 2004, p. 257), which, based on the Audit Commission established in 1982, developed into a tool of all-encompassing control and intervention by central government. Since the installation of the Best Value (BV) regime in 1999, the Comprehensive Performance Assessment (CPA) in 2002 and since 2009 the even more extensive Comprehensive Area Assessment (CAA), performance measurement and comparisons have been made mandatory for all local councils (cf. Stewart, 2003, p. 121 et seq.). In addition, local Public Service Agreements that are concluded between local councils and central government have been applied. The underlying strategy of the central government is to centrally steer and control the performance efficiency of the local authorities in providing services by constantly evaluating their achievement and their compliance with performance indicators. The latter are fixed in part by central government and in part by the local authorities themselves. For this, a four-point scale is used (outstanding/ excellent, good, adequate, inadequate; see Table 4.22).

Poor performance of the local authority concerned can be penalized – in the worst case – by ordering the dismissal of the elected local government leadership and replacing them with external experts, while (putatively) good performance is rewarded by central government, for example, by exemption from legal requirements, by handing out additional funding, and so on (cf. Kuhlmann and Wollmann, 2006, p. 385 et seq.; Kuhlmann, 2011). One major problem lies in the huge transaction costs associated with the continuous and comprehensive performance inspections and the institutional and personnel density of state audit and inspection authorities (Davis et al., 2001, p. 14). Moreover, widespread antipathy and growing resistance against the permanent performance control by central auditors have been evoked by the local authorities concerned, thus sometimes leading to subversive strategies.

Table 4.22 Extract from the Annual Performance Assessment of the city of Liverpool (Child and Youth Welfare, 2008)

Assessment Judgement Area	Annual Performance Assessment Grade
Overall effectiveness of children's services	3
Being healthy	3
Staying safe	3
Enjoying and achieving	3
Making a positive contribution	3
Achieving economic well-being	3
Capacity to improve, including the management of services for children and young people	3

Note: Inspectors make judgements based on the following scale: 4: outstanding/excellent; 3: good; 2: adequate; 1: inadequate.

Source: See http://liverpool.gov.uk/site-search?q=annual+performance+assessment; last accessed 10 March 2010.

Last but not least, the inspections often appear to generate anything but valid and reliable performance information because the process is artificial and the local actors concerned show remarkable creativity in conveying the desired Best Value climate and convenient results, as it is more about style than substance (ibid., p. 20).[82]

In the most recent development since the parliamentary elections in 2010 resulting in the formation of the Conservative–Liberal coalition government, a distinct shift in administrative policy has been embarked on by the new government (cf. Kuhlmann, 2011). For example, the decision to disband the Audit Commission that was installed under the Thatcher government and to transfer its tasks to private companies (Grant Thornton, KPMG LLP, Ernst & Young, DA Partnership) as well as the abolition of the CAA can be considered as milestones. After more than 20 years of public performance policy, the central government then withdraws and justifies this conspicuous move specifically on the grounds of the expenditure and bureaucratization that developed in administration by target control, inspection, auditing and performance comparison.[83] It remains to be seen as to whether this policy change will last.

Performance management through law and implementation gap: Italy

In Italy, the introduction of performance management in public administration has also followed a dominant, top-down pattern and has been distinctly guided by central state and, in some cases, regional legislation (Kuhlmann and Fedele, 2010). The trigger and driving force of NPM modernization in Italy were primarily the political upheaval during the 1990s and the subsequent comprehensive decentralization of the political and administrative system (see Section 4.2.3),[84] to which demands for corresponding reforms of the public sector were linked (for a detailed discussion, see Ongaro, 2009). A plethora of laws, decrees, ordinances and so forth were passed to regulate individual reform instruments in detail and make them legally binding. To begin with, the budget reforms of 1995 (Decree No. 77/1995) and 1997 (Bassanini II) and the Acts 142/1990 and 29/1993 should be mentioned. The latter stipulated a new form of output-oriented management control for local governments (supplementary to existing legality control). A core element of the 1995 reform (Decree 77/1995) was the introduction of the so-called Management Plan (Piano Esecutivo di Gestione – PEG) that intended to make controlling procedures (*controllo di gestione*) mandatory and to oblige the administrations to introduce target agreements, performance and impact indicators, and performance measurement procedures (*misurazione dei servizi*) (Garlatti and Pezzani, 2000). Moreover, the PEG was meant to bring about a clear separation of political executive (*giunta*) and administration management (*dirigenti*) on the local government level based on performance contracts (Longo and Plamper, 2004, p. 327 et seq.). Further legally stipulated and binding NPM tools included accrual accounting (Decree 77/1995), output-oriented global budgeting (1997) and the introduction of a performance indicator-based citizens' charter (*carta dei servizi*), with which the measurement of quality indicators and customer satisfaction was regulated (Acts No. 241/1990 and 59/1997).

In practice, this strategy of 'NPM through law' has only been partly successful (Capano, 2003, p. 787; Lippi, 2003, pp. 159–60), as the implementation of the legal provisions has either been very inconsistent or incomplete with a noticeable variance between the individual regions (Magnier, 2003, p. 189 et seq.). Thus, on the one hand, a distinctly clear reform progress can be observed in one section of Italian administration. For example, the budget reforms on the local level have since been largely realized and the municipalities allotted up to 60 per cent of their budgetary funds in 1993 (Lippi, 2003, p. 152). In virtually all local administrations, new systems of management control have been introduced and financial targets formally defined, for whose compliance the respective area directors (*dirigenti*) are responsible (Ongaro and Valotti, 2008). By 2001, 93 per cent of Italian local governments had installed controlling departments and 50 per cent had introduced new cost accounting procedures (Capano, 2003, p. 794, with further references; Grossi and Mussari, 2008, p. 31).

On the other hand, the practical effects of this formal institutional change are limited. The preferred budgeting method as part of the above-mentioned PEG is still input oriented, whereas outcome or even impact indicators are hardly ever used for budget preparation (Longo and Plamper, 2004, p. 328; Ongaro and Valotti, 2008, p. 184). According to a 1999 survey (Promberger et al., 2000, p. 96 et seq.), only about one-quarter of all Italian local authorities at the time had defined performance indicators within the framework of the PEG and only a few had introduced non-fiscal performance indicators. Although there is no doubt that the NPM measures in Italy have since contributed to a rise in transparency and output orientation (Bobbio, 2005, p. 42), there is still a clear gap with regard to the performance-oriented steering tools and a heterogeneous implementation status overall in the administration and that has been termed as an implementation gap (Capano, 2003, p. 794; Ongaro and Valotti, 2008). This shows that – as in the case of Britain – the central state top-down steering of performance management has had only a limited effect.

Performance management as self-development from below: Sweden, Germany, France

Sweden

Against the backdrop of the historically grown evaluation and freedom of information culture, forms of performance management and self-evaluation in the Swedish administrative system have always been widespread and widely accepted, a situation that is also due to the consensual-democratic orientation of the political system overall. Thus, contrasting starkly with the British approach, there is no central government-imposed obligation of the local authorities to undertake performance measurement and quality control; instead, these initiatives have evolved in a bottom-up manner, voluntarily. Yet, by virtue of the high degree of external transparency of performance data, this approach is very effective. Moreover, Scandinavian administration modernization is generally characterized more by its experimental-learning than ideological-dogmatic orientation (Riegler and Naschold, 1997, p. 18). Furthermore, from the outset, the dual approach of output-oriented (NPM) measures and user participation has been typical (Oppen, 1997, p. 239). Hence, performance measurement and comparison have always included an externally effective, citizen-related component.

For the local authorities as the most important performance and implementation level in Sweden, in addition to the procedures of output-oriented steering that had been already installed in the early 1990s (ibid.), two reform approaches in particular should be highlighted. The first, which has been in place since 1987, consists of the collection, compilation and publication of local performance information in a database jointly operated by the Swedish municipal association and the state statistical office. This exemplary inter-municipal benchmarking system is distinguished by the annual documentation of the costs of local government activities in a wide range of services, detailed in terms of municipality and task, and accessible online to the general public ('*Vad kostar versamheten i Din kommun?*', 'What do the activities in your local government cost?'; Wollmann, 2008, p. 228, with further references). The second approach concerns inter-municipal quality comparisons in 'comparative municipal quality networks', which have been in place since the late 1990s, and also initiated by the Swedish municipal association (see Strid, 2004). These are geared towards defining quality indicators of local performance and providing inter-municipal comparisons. In 2012, a total of 51 of about 290 Swedish municipalities took part in the quality comparisons whereby a network comprises five to ten participants and the key issues include – inter alia – preschools and local employment policy.

On the central state level, performance management has been established in the independent authorities (*ämbetsverk*), in particular in the form of a management-by-results system that obliges the authorities, via performance indicator-based contracts, to provide annual results-specific reports (cf. Tiessen, 2007, p. 150 et seq.). It should be recalled here as well that these approaches of 'output steering' (see above; Sundström, 2004) had already been an inherent part of Swedish administrative practice even before the NPM debate put performance management on the modernization agenda (Wollmann, 2008, p. 227). Hence, the performance indicator-based reports that were introduced by the Swedish finance ministry in the late 1980s regarding the productivity of the public sector have a fairly long-standing (pre-NPM) tradition. Reflecting the political culture unique to the Scandinavian countries, these performance measurement and self-evaluation procedures are intended less to be control tools 'from above' over the compliance with performance agreements (contracts) but rather embedded within the interaction and learning processes between the relevant local actors. One example of target hierarchies in the Swedish state administration is that of the Nature Conservation Authority (Box 4.3)

Germany

In Germany, the instruments of performance management and performance comparison have been introduced into public administration essentially since

---

BOX 4.3

TARGET HIERARCHIES – THE SWEDISH NATURE CONSERVATION AUTHORITY

Politikområde 'Environmental policy'
Target: 'To leave the next generation a society in which all major environmental problems in Sweden have been solved'.

Verksamhets område 'Active and preventative environmental work'
Target: 'National and international development and application of steering instruments with regard to the five fundamental environmental goals and the influence on attitudes and behaviour of individuals and organizations, in order to ensure that these fulfil their environmental responsibilities'.

Verksamhetsgren 'Supervision and regulation'
Target 2: 'By 2006 at the latest, there will be a plan for the supervisory activities of the *Naturvårdsverket* for 2007–2009, in order to improve the application of the environmental code in local governments and regions'.

Verksamhetsgren 'Information'
Target 1: 'Key actors have received information on how to contribute to achieving environmental goals'.

Source: Tiessen (2007, p. 157, with further references).

---

the arrival of the New Steering Model (NSM)-inspired reform movement. As in Sweden, the reform concepts have made their entry typically in a bottom-up manner, starting at the local level, then taken up by the *Länder* and finally, to a lesser degree, by the federal level. In passing from the traditional rule- and procedure-based to output and performance-based steering, the local governments have begun to define 'products', to write up product catalogues and to fill these in with indicators and performance data. According to the above-mentioned NSM evaluation (cf. Bogumil et al., 2007), 29 per cent of German local authorities have defined products entirely or at least in part (9.9 per cent), or are still in the process of composing product catalogues (22.9 per cent). Furthermore, the efforts of exactly specifying the costs of administrative activities have continually increased. Thus, accrual accounting has been implemented wholesale in 12.7 per cent of local governments, in part in 33 per cent and in the remaining 27.1 per cent this is still a work in progress. However, the elaborately composed product catalogues have rarely been used for steering purposes. In 14.2 per cent of the local authorities that work with product definitions, no link has been established or used between the products and the key instruments of the NSM. This raises the crucial question of whether the sizeable (personnel, financial, etc.) efforts that have been invested in creating the product catalogues are justified and pay off in the long run.

As another field of performance management in German public administration, mention should also be made of performance comparison and benchmarking. Again starting at the local level, comparison cycles have been initiated that aim at the intra-organizational comparison of administrative processes, structures and performance. What temporarily almost exploded into a comparison euphoria was triggered in 1990 by the Bertelsmann Foundation and its project 'Fundamentals of an Efficient Local Government' (cf. Schuster, 2003). This was followed up by the Municipal Association for Administration Management (Kommunale Gemeinschaft für Verwaltungsmanagement – KGSt) which, by founding the IKO network in 1996, created an 'internal information system of local governments' (see Kuhlmann, 2004). Up to 43.3 per cent of the local authorities participate at least occasionally in these inter-municipal performance comparisons, comparison cycles and competitions, while less than a quarter of them (23.3 per cent) do not take part in such measures (Bogumil et al., 2007, p. 72 et seq.; see Figure 4.20).

There are indications, however, that the municipalities have been withdrawing from the benchmarking project at a significant rate (Kuhlmann, 2004) and that, in addition, the considerable time and effort that the participating municipalities have to put into this project exceed its benefits, as performance information is not used for steering purposes. But even if and where performance comparisons have been accepted as a tool of local reform policy, they

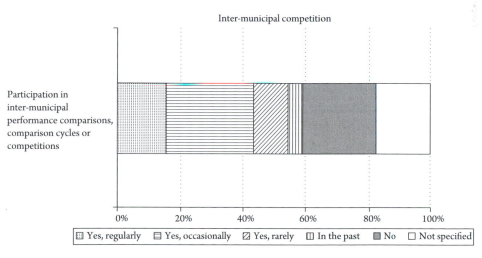

Source: Kuhlmann (2011, p. 9, with further references).

Figure 4.20 Inter-municipal competition and performance comparison in German local governments

still suffer from a serious weakness because their results are made available to local parliaments and the local public only in limited form, if at all, and are by no means binding.

In the meantime, similar comparison projects have also been introduced in the federal administration and the *Länder* authorities (e.g., tax office, police and others).[85] Furthermore, performance comparisons in Germany have moved away from the purely voluntary principle as, first, the audit offices have become involved in the steering and conduct of comparisons, in particular with regard to costs and efficiency (such as in Mecklenburg-Western Pomerania and Baden-Württemberg). Second, some *Land* authorities in charge of supervising the local authorities also use this instrument, as evinced in the example of the municipal audit agency in North Rhine-Westphalia (Banner, 2007; Bogumil and Ebinger, 2012).

In the meantime, performance comparisons/benchmarking have even been anchored in the Federal Constitution (Grundgesetz), specifically in Article 91d GG, which was inserted as part of the so-called Federal Reform II (Act of 29 July 2009, BGBI 2248). Besides reflecting and promoting the general NPM-inspired ideas of enhancing performance transparency and of increasing effectiveness and efficiency, this amendment was geared to strengthening the parliamentary control by means of performance information, which was understood as the goal of administrative modernization (BT-Drs. 16/12410, p. 8). At the same time, federal competition for the best solution is to be stimulated (cf. the statement of the expert hearing committee on legal affairs of the Bundestag of 4 May 2009, p. 3; BT-Drs 16/12410, p. 8). To what extent the new constitutional rule, which is phrased as a discretionary (as opposed to mandatory) provision, will actually lead to more federal competition and performance comparison remains to be seen, even if the Bertelsmann Foundation has already presented an 'Action Plan' for the implementation of Article 91d GG (cf. Bertelsmann Stiftung, 2010).

France
Contrary to the expectation that in France, originating from the Napoleonic centralized administration model, administrative reforms are bound to be conducted in a top-down pattern, the practice of performance management actually shows a strikingly different picture. Thus, since the 1980s, some remarkable local-level initiatives have already been established to introduce performance management. On the central state level, though, corresponding initiatives were taken up quite belatedly (as exemplified by LOLF, which was passed only in 2001; see below). A survey conducted in 1991 in 82 municipalities showed[86] that at that time already around 30 per cent of the

Table 4.23 Extract from the tableau de bord of the city of Le Havre registry office (2004)

Performance Indicator	Defined Performance Target	Result in 2004
Average waiting time at the counter	Max. 10 mins	< 6 mins
Proportion of applications processed in less than five days	Min. 90%	96%
Proportion of telephone calls answered (*appels non perdus*)	Min. 92%	99%
Proportion of calls answered after a maximum of three rings	Min. 90%	92%

Source: Kuhlmann (2009a, p. 208, with further references).

respondents had disposed of indicator-based performance reports (*tableaux de bord*) and 55 per cent had worked with different variants of cost accounting (*comptabilité analytique*). In 15 per cent of the responses at least one controller (*conseiller/analyste de gestion*) was put into place. An example extract from a *tableau de bord* for the registry office (*Etat Civil*) in the city of Le Havre is shown in Table 4.23.

Interestingly, the French central state did not initially play a leading role as a reform actor – in stark contrast to the United Kingdom. In 2002, already 85 per cent of cities with over 50000 inhabitants were familiar with self-evaluation procedures; 60 per cent had even already introduced them, 30 per cent of which had done so more than five years previously.[87] However, due to the heterogeneous territorial structure, the reform activities are very unevenly distributed locally (see Section 4.3.3). In addition, performance information is outside the respective municipality scarcely available. Thus, the general public has hardly any access to such information. Systematic inter-municipal performance comparisons have not yet been employed and the sanction effects of performance measurement are limited.

The concept of performance management has also been picked up in national legislation and has thus triggered an additional mobilization in the French administration (Naulleau, 2003, p. 136). The stage for this was set by the (previously mentioned) LOLF of 2001, which laid down a new framework for public finances, resources management and budgeting in the state administration, providing for new forms of global budgeting based on programme and performance targets (*finalités*), contract management and performance evaluation. The implementation is to be steered by programme directors through annual performance agreements (*projets annuels de performance* – PAP) and obligatory reports (*rapports annuels de performance* – RAP) (Fievet and Laurent, 2006, p. 142). According to LOLF, the parliament will restrict itself to making the strategic decisions in terms of fundamental *missions* programmes and budget targets, but leave their implementation to the ministries. The ministries receive programme budgets that are transferrable and are essentially linked to a 'cascade of effects' of 47 'strategic missions', 158 department-related programmes, 580 measures, 630 performance targets and 1300 performance indicators.

The first LOLF budget was adopted in 2006. At that stage several problems had already surfaced. Thus, in the view of some observers the (already weak) position of the Assemblée Nationale would be further degraded by being restricted to making just general decisions regarding *missions* (cf. Kempf, 2003, p. 312 et seq.). Moreover, there has been apprehension of control and steering losses on the part of the ministries vis-à-vis the deconcentrated state administration, which has been upgraded as a result of global budgeting and of being given an additional scope of action. The same applies to the relationship between state administration and the local authorities, as the latter have become more dependent on the budget allocations from the state administration, counteracting the political decentralization in France. In addition, a downright 'indicator frenzy' has emerged in the state administration since the LOLF came into force, so that signs of a new bureaucratization via performance indicators have become apparent. Notwithstanding this, debates have already set in as to whether a LOLF-type legal regime would be advisable at the local government level. However, some observers have been cautioning against this, as such a general obligation would completely fail to take into account the reality of local government activity (Fievet and Laurent, 2006, p. 145).

Performance management between transformation process and NPM discourse

At the beginning of the transformation process in the early 1990s, the reconstruction of a constitutional (rule-of-law type) and administratively decentralized state took centre stage in the Central and Eastern European (CEE) countries. Afterwards, NPM-inspired performance measurement approaches and related administrative reform strategies made their entry only towards the end of the decade (cf. Hajnal, 2008, p. 140). Moreover, the introduction of performance comparison tools were initially viewed sceptically by some, as this was reminiscent of centralist planning and control, whereas other (as it were, traditional) administrative reform approaches and action areas were still considered to be more important (Mark and Nayyar-Stone, 2002, p. 2). Because during the socialist era the citizens could neither question nor challenge the quality of administrative activity, there was also a complete lack of experience with quality requirements (cf. Varga, 2006, p. 722). Nevertheless, performance measurement systems evolved in the CEE countries especially during the pre-EU accession phase. Thus, a growing number of Hungarian local governments established performance indicators with regard to the budget, thereby forming the basis for subsequent, more extensive approaches of performance management. As this process was voluntary however, the expansion and intensity of such approaches has remained irregular (cf. Hajnal, 2008, p. 143). Also on the central state level of the CEE countries, performance management systems have been developed. Lithuania and Latvia are considered forerunners in the CEE area, with their introduction of comprehensive initiatives for the impact assessment of laws (cf. Nemec, 2008a, p. 367). In other CEE countries, the introduction of performance management at the central state level has been somewhat uncoordinated. Individual ministries have implemented various measures within the scope of their area of responsibilities, a prime example of which is Slovakia (cf. Nemec, 2008b, p. 302). There, the education ministry has installed evaluation systems in the school and higher education areas based on the British model, thereby importing both the strengths and the weaknesses of the British system (see above; ibid.). In Hungary, the application of quality assurance tools on the state level has also been at the discretion of the respective authority heads; however, ISO models (9000, 9001) and later from the 1990s the Common Assessment Framework (CAF) have been used by the administrative authorities (cf. Varga, 2006, p. 723). Because of the differences in use between authorities, in 2003 the Ministry of the Interior soon developed a Hungarian version of the CAF and has taken over more of the coordinating functions (cf. ibid.). Typical problems in performance measurement, such as the insufficient use of performance information for management and steering purposes, have nevertheless also been observed in other CEE countries (Jenei, 2009, p. 10 et seq.). Overall, there has been no consistent, cross-level introduction of performance management in the administration in Hungary as in other Eastern and Central European countries, but instead ad hoc approaches have been pursued in individual ministries or local authorities, resulting in a strong institutional variance in this reform area (cf. also Wilcox and Bugai, 2004, p. 12; Jenei, 2009, p. 11 et seq.).

On the basis of the features of 'state steering' and 'distribution rate', the introduction and employment of performance management on the local government level can be summarized for the countries under consideration as follows in Figure 4.21.

4.5.4 Administrative personnel

In the NPM-oriented administrative modernization drive, the management of human resources was initially and to a large extent a matter of rhetoric

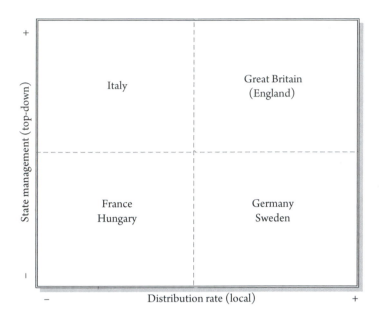

Source: Authors' own diagram.

Figure 4.21 State steering and distribution of performance management on the local level by comparison

rather than of reality and action (Demmke, 2006, p. 384). In hindsight, some observers – including even the NPM-friendly OECD – have criticized the lack of an 'investment in the people' in the theory and practice of administration modernization (OECD, 2005; Demmke, 2006; Bogumil et al., 2007, p. 61 et seq.; Demmke and Moilanen, 2013). Instead, the focus was on issues of budget management, financial management, process re-engineering, and so on, which were concerned with classic scientific management rather than with modern human resources management. This appears even more problematic as many European administrative systems are experiencing a drastic shrinking of personnel (see Chapter 3, Section 3.6).

The following listed trends in personnel reform have become widespread across Europe and internationally (cf. Naschold et al., 1999, p. 37; Selden, 2007, p. 40 et seq.), although the concrete measures and implementation strategies vary, and generally little (and rather sobering) data on effects and impact are available (Demmke, 2007; Demmke and Moilanen, 2013):

- downsizing;
- normalizing of labour/employment relations;
- testing of new personnel selection procedures and reform of the educational system;

Table 4.24 Performance-related pay in EU member states (2006)

EU Member States with Performance-related Pay	EU Member States Without Performance-related Pay	Comments
Sweden, Great Britain, Denmark, Finland, Germany, Lithuania, Estonia, Italy, Slovakia, Hungary, Malta, Spain, France, Belgium, Bulgaria	Greece, Luxembourg, Portugal, Slovenia, Netherlands, Czech Republic, Cyprus, Ireland, Poland, Romania	Austria and Slovenia are planning the introduction; in the Netherlands, performance-related pay insignificant in overall payment; there were no data available for Latvia and Poland; in Poland, performance-related pay is only given to nominated civil servants (approx. 3% of employees); in France, there is primarily a bonus system (*primes*); Portugal is currently undergoing a comprehensive reform process

Source: Demmke et al. (2007, p. 18, with further references).

- decentralizing of personnel-related powers/responsibilities;
- developing performance-related pay schemes.

The following explanations deal in particular with the last two aspects of personnel modernization, as these have gained great importance in the current reform movement of European administrative systems.

The introduction of performance-related elements in the public remuneration and payment systems reflects a common trend throughout all European administrative systems (Demmke, 2007). A study conducted in 24 EU member states[88] (plus Norway) showed that half the countries[89] have adopted measures to create a stronger link between performance and pay in the public service, including the countries under consideration here, that is, Germany, United Kingdom, France, Italy, Sweden and Hungary (see Table 4.24). Reform proposals for public service, which aim at promoting and evaluating individual performances, have been adopted in all countries and new performance evaluation systems are being increasingly introduced when target agreements have been concluded. Performance assessments are now more strongly linked with employment-related consequences and have an effect on performance agreement, performance-related pay, career development, promotion decisions and in some instances, even job security (Demmke, 2007, p. 5).

Despite these underlying trends, there are still major differences among the individual countries when considering the concrete arrangement of performance-related pay, implementation strategies, and their effects on administrative practice. These differences can also be explained with reference to the previous public service system, whereby the career-based, classic career development model and the position-based recruitment/ function model are of primary importance (see Chapter 2, Section 2.1.4). Furthermore, available studies (OECD, 2005; Demmke et al., 2007) have identified a connection between the degree of delegation of personnel-related powers/responsibilities in the administration and the significance of performance-related pay. Thus, there are only few EU countries to date (as a rule in position-based systems), such as the United Kingdom (also Finland and Denmark), in which performance-related pay is actually a key component in administrative practice. By contrast, countries with a lower delegation of personnel-related responsibility (mostly career-based systems) have hitherto relied on more traditional forms of personnel motivation such as (further) vocational training and promotion, although also in this regard a change appears to be emerging as evidenced in countries such as France, Hungary, Italy and Germany. Finally, it should be noted that numerous empirical studies have shed strong doubt on the actual motivational effects of monetary performance incentives and so the incentive-oriented payment systems are facing mounting criticism (cf. Demmke, 2009; Mühlenkamp, 2010).

Continental European systems: Germany, France and Italy

Germany – continued 'dual track' system in the public service and moderately performance-related remuneration

In Germany, due to the persistence of the duality of status (civil servants – *Beamte*/employees – *Angestellte*), the public service reform of 1997, under which performance-related pay was introduced for civil servants, needs to be distinguished from the tariff reform (2005–06) that provided for performance-related pay of employees (TVöD on the federal and local government levels and TV-L on the *Länder* level). Subsequent to the failure of the previous attempt to reform the public service law in the 1970s, the act on public service reform of 1997, which came into effect as a federal framework law,[90] has taken initial and somewhat moderate steps towards a more performance-oriented pay scheme for the status group of civil servants. The traditional principle of seniority (i.e., automatic promotion according to length of service) has been supplemented by performance-related elements. Accordingly, when determining promotion to the next salary step, individual performance of a civil servant is to be taken into account alongside the length of service. Moreover, the possibility of receiving performance bonuses as one-off payments in addition to incentive payments has also been introduced (cf. Kuhlmann, 2006b).

The basis for performance-related pay was also laid down for the federal and local government tariff employees at the conclusion of the TVöD (collective agreement for public service employees) on 13 September 2005. This pay scheme went into effect on 1 January 2007 (§ 18 Sec. 1 TVöD). Consequently, performance-related pay represents a variable and performance-oriented payment in addition to the basic salary and includes a payment amount of 1 per cent of the fixed monthly salary of the previous year, with a target amount of 8 per cent (§ 18 Sec. 2 TVöD). Practice has shown that a considerable number of administrative authorities on the federal and local government levels have made use of this instrument of performance bonuses[91] and have in some cases incorporated civil servants into this scheme (cf. Tondorf, 2006; PwC, 2008; Stellermann et al., 2009). However, this principle of indiscriminate distribution of such bonuses means that many employees (on average, 77 per cent of them in local authorities and between 93 and 100 per cent on the federal level) only receive a minimal extra, thus casting doubt on any incentive effects. In addition, the management of incentive payments appears to hinge not so much on actual performance (measurement), as the evaluation systems are generally very approximate and do not allow for much differentiation (90 per cent of federal authorities only provide for three to four performance levels). A link to previously defined targets is only rarely made. For example, only 5 per cent of federal offices associate performance incentives with target agreements (Stellermann et al., 2009, p. 23). Local governments also only scarcely use target agreements – albeit more often than on the federal level (PwC, 2008, p. 13). For the federal authorities, the range of performance-related payments is between €4 and €2415 (Stellermann et al., 2009, p. 24; see Table 4.25).

For personnel management and personnel development in Germany, in practice, there have only been limited improvements, despite the frequently

Table 4.25 Amount of performance-related pay in German Federal authorities

Category	Amount
Lowest payment (range)	€4 to €764
Highest payment (range)	€270 to €2415

Source: Stellermann et al. (2009, p. 22, with further references).

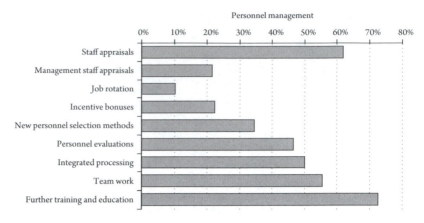

Note: n = 870 mayors.

Source: Bogumil et al. (2007, p. 61).

Figure 4.22 Personnel management in German local governments

articulated emphasis of the importance of the human resources dimension in administrative modernization. Although many administrations have employed commercially trained staff (e.g., in 36 per cent of local governments; cf. Bogumil et al., 2007, p. 61) and there has been an increase in staff appraisals, the activities have been limited to rather unsophisticated procedures in relation to the objectives, or have been relegated to the classic modality of further vocational training and education (Figure 4.22).

The limited range of personnel reforms in the German context is largely associated with the huge personnel cut-back process (by 25 per cent in local governments since 1990) and the budget crisis. As a result, there has been little scope for the application of sophisticated human resource management methods, and moderate performance-related pay cannot fundamentally remedy the decline in motivation on the part of the remaining employees caused by the related additional workload.

France – traditional bonus systems and new performance orientation

In France also the introduction of performance-related pay in previous years was hotly debated. It should be recalled that France was the first country to incorporate performance-related pay into the payment system of its public employees in the form of so-called *primes* (Demmke, 2006, p. 388). The 2006 committee report *'sur le coût et le rendement des services publics'* (on the costs and benefits of public services) expressly recommended the enhanced use of target agreements (*contrats d'objectifs*) in the public service. Essentially, the report called for a three-tier remuneration system that provided for a uniform basic salary (*traitement de base*) for all employees in a specific salary group, a function-/position-related supplement (*complément lié à l'emploi occupé*) and a supplement that took account of the individual civil servants' performance (*complément indemnitaire de rendement/prime de service*). The employees' performance was to be assessed by the respective superior to determine the basis for the incentive bonus, something that should take place as part of employee–superior appraisals (Sadran, 2006). Moreover, the LOLF of 2001 (see above) has considerably impacted the public human resources, as those responsible for the respective budgets in the ministries and deconcentrated state authorities were now able to convert superfluous personnel resources into performance incentives (cf. Forest, 2008, p. 327). In addition, under a decree in 2002, a system of systematic performance evaluation was introduced for the state administration. This linked individual performance with promotion decisions. For example, in the Economic and Finance Ministry 180 000 civil servants were affected by this in 2005 alone (ibid.). In the state administration, the performance budget may comprise up to 20 per cent of the annual payment volume – significantly more than in Germany. However, to date, this has been primarily paid out to managers. As a result, a clear 'individualization' of payment can be seen in the French civil service, in particular at the leadership level. This places great importance on performance, but has also been frequently criticized – and not just by trade unions – on the grounds of its questionable effects (Forest, 2008).

Many experiments with performance-related pay schemes (*régimes indemnitaires/primes de services*) have been embarked upon also on the local government level (cf. Crozet and Desmarais, 2004). As early as the mid-1990s, around half of the medium-sized French cities (i.e., those of more than 100000 inhabitants) had tackled personnel management reform (*gestion des ressources humaines*; cf. Crozet and Desmarais, 2004). A prime example of this is the city of Rouen where a part of the human resources, which had been previously administered centrally in the personnel department, was assigned to the heads of administrative units (*chefs de services, directeurs*) as decentralized 'bonus budgets' to be managed by them independently (cf. Kuhlmann, 2009a, p. 212 et seq.). In accordance with prescribed guidelines, the *directeurs* are to distribute the annual bonuses (*primes de service*) allocated to them among the employees in their respective remit and thereby evaluate the performance of individual members of staff. The amount of bonuses depends on an employee's position and administrative tasks. For example, a senior manager such as a DGA (*administrateur hors classe*) may receive a higher maximum bonus than a middle manager (e.g., *attaché principal*). The bonus level is thus clearly hierarchical as it provides for higher performance bonuses

Table 4.26 Performance bonuses in the non-technical administration in the city of Rouen (2005)

Bonus Group/ Hierarchy Level	Level of Bonus/Annual Performance Bonus in Euros									
	1	2	3	4	5	6	7	8	9	10
1 *Administrateur hors classe*	250	350	1160	1220	1280	1400	1420	1450	1470	1490
2 *Administrateur*	200	300	990	1060	1120	1160	1200	1220	1240	1260
3 *Directeur*	100	200	500	560	610	630	650	680	700	730
4 *Attaché principal 1er et 2ème classe*	80	130	370	410	440	470	490	530	540	610
5 *Attaché à compter du 9ème échelon*	80	130	320	380	410	440	460	500	520	590
6 *Attaché en dessous du 9ème échelon*	80	130	290	340	370	390	410	430	450	490
6 *Rédacteur chef*	80	130	290	340	370	390	410	430	450	490
6 *Rédacteur principal*	80	130	290	340	370	390	410	430	450	490
7 *Rédacteur*	30	70	200	260	300	320	340	370	390	440
8 *Adjoint administratif principal 1er et 2ème classe*	300	600	1140	1260	1380	1500	1560	1680	1800	1920
8 *Adjoint administratif*	300	600	1140	1260	1380	1500	1560	1680	1800	1920
8 *Agent administratif qualifié*	300	600	1140	1260	1380	1500	1560	1680	1800	1920
8 *Agent administratif*	300	600	1140	1260	1380	1500	1560	1680	1800	1920

Source: Kuhlmann (2009a, p. 213, with further references).

for the highest-ranking positions (e.g., *administrateur hors classe*: €250 to €1490), but lower ones for the lower ranking positions (e.g., *rédacteur*: €30 to €440). In practice, as in Germany, all employees are included in the bonus budget, albeit in different amounts. Hence, performance-related bonuses tend to represent a generalized salary supplement that has little to do with real performance evaluation. The bonus system shown below provides an example in the area of non-technical administration (*filière administrative*; Table 4.26).

Italy – transformation of the career system and privatization of employment relations

In Italy, as in France and Germany, the debate emerging from NPM on greater performance orientation in the public service comes face to face with a legalistic administrative culture characterized by the lifetime appointment of civil servants under the public service law and a promotion system developed according the principles of seniority and career (see also Chapter 3, Section 3.1.2). As it generally applies to NPM reform in Italy, the (above alluded to) 'regulation frenzy' manifesting itself in a multitude of laws, decrees, regulations, and so on, rises to the fore here too, and has also been termed as 'deregulating regulation' and illustrating a typical tendency 'to innovate by law' (Meneguzzo, 1997). In contrast to the two other classic Continental European systems (Germany and France) where the basic structure of public services has been retained, Italy has experienced some radical changes since the early 1990s. Of these, the particularly incisive 'privatization' of employment relations in the public service (with only a few exceptions) is especially noteworthy. This was first initiated by the legislative decree of 1993 (D. Lgs No. 29) and Act No. 87/1994. Limited-term employment contracts (a maximum three years for senior management level and five years for middle and lower management)[92] and the general possibility for termination of lower-grade staff were introduced. In addition, the personnel-related permeability between authorities and levels was simplified and the external recruitment of lateral entrants (career changers) was made easier. Meanwhile, 10 per cent of top-level positions in the ministries and 50 per cent among city managers in the municipalities are external recruitments (cf. Promberger et al., 2000, p. 66). Thus, the general labour law in principle now applies to public employees as well and their employment relations are subject to collective bargaining rights. For this, a new agency, the Agenzia per la Rappresentanza Negoziale delle Pubbliche Amministrazioni (ARAN), was founded in 1993, which conducts all the collective bargaining. Labour disputes have also been transferred from the administration courts to the general labour courts. Under a decree of 1993, the top administrative positions in the ministries were initially excluded from this general regulation, an exclusion that led to a division of the civil service into two status classes (Promberger et al., 2000, p. 63). However, since the reform laws of 1997 (Laws No. 59/1997 and 127/1997) and the legislative decree of 1998 (D. Lgs No. 80 and 387) the alignment of employment relations of public employees to the general labour law now applies to the administration in its entirety (Lippi, 2003, p. 148ff.).[93]

In this connection, special mention should be made of the reform measures in the area of performance-related pay and individual performance evaluation, which are applied in state as well as in local government services. As such, the traditional seniority-based career model has been supplanted by a position-based system that contains performance-related elements. For senior management, only 60 per cent of the payment is salary-based (collective agreement) and 20 per cent position-based (supplementary payment); a considerable proportion of remuneration (20 per cent) comes in the form of performance-related 'productivity bonuses' (Promberger et al., 2000, p. 64). These bonuses are awarded on the basis of individual performance evaluations, which are in turn based on performance targets defined in advance (D. Lgs No. 29/1993). As part of this, the previously mentioned NPM instruments (see Chapter 2, Section 2.2.2) of management control are applied. On the local government level, for example, this takes place by means of the above-mentioned management plan (PEG) in order to thus ensure the annual identification of performance targets and their evaluation by the respective manager.

There is still little information available on the actual effects of this comprehensive reform programme in the public service. Previous experience shows, however, that radical concepts and extensive regulations do not, at least in the Italian context (and even less so in other countries), offer a guarantee for genuine change and a transformation of administrative practices (cf. Cristofoli et al., 2011, p. 267 et seq.). Thus, according to a survey conducted by the Bocconi University, almost 40 per cent of local governments have not yet implemented the legally stipulated introduction of performance-related pay for leading personnel and in 12 per cent of the municipalities the performance pay budget is lower than the mandatory minimum level. More than ten years after the reform law went into effect, only 7.4 per cent of salaries of the leading local government personnel were performance-related (ibid., p. 268). Nevertheless, compared to the other two countries in the Continental European group, Italy has ventured to make the most consistent incisions into the traditional public service system, thereby ringing in a paradigm shift in some areas. This is, however, associated with concerns, for example regarding the potential degrading and clear politicizing of the (senior) public service resulting from the abolition of the 'permanence' of employment relations in connection with the newly introduced possibility of an automatic termination of the contracts of senior ministerial civil servants following a change in government (insofar as these are not extended within a period of 90 days after the election date). This contradicts the legislatively pursued NPM doctrine in several respects: first with a view to the required management autonomy, which would become weakened as a result, and second with regard to the separation of politics and administration, which would be reinforced.

United Kingdom: performance-related pay, performance culture, fragmentation and downgrading of the public service

The fact that the United Kingdom has become well known for its human resources reforms and represents a role model for many other countries is not just due to the radical nature of change in the civil service since the

Fulton Report of 1968, but also to the NPM-related modernization measures in its public service as a whole. The country's most consistent implementation of performance-related pay (PRP) in the public service stands out as a striking feature when compared with OECD countries. However, the Senior Civil Service (SCS), which was introduced in 1996 and comprises (merely) 3800 senior civil servants in the highest positions in ministries and agencies, frequently takes the centre of attention. In contrast, the far more comprehensive and, in practical terms, more significant public service, which also encompasses the staff at lower levels, including the about 2.9 million local government employees, is given far less international attention.

On the one hand, the notion of performance related pay (PRP) in British local administration has become increasingly widespread and has prompted the modernization of traditional human resources management. Following suit to the NPM modernization triggered by central government, the local authorities have induced a range of PRP systems and target agreements and have assigned personnel responsibility to the middle and lower management levels since the 1980s (Keen and Vickerstaff, 1997). A case study conducted in B. County Council (with 45000 full-time employees) showed that almost all senior administrative managers apply performance incentives and target agreements and carry out regular competence assessments of their employees. This has suggested a 'shift towards a new extremely rigorous, performance culture' (ibid., p. 44), one that can be considered an example of overall British local administration (ibid., p. 42).

Moreover, since the late 1990s, collective bargaining law and labour/ employment relations in the local public service have become significantly more flexible. The framework agreements, traditionally negotiated on national level (national agreements), have been largely decentralized following the withdrawal of 40 local authorities – primarily under Conservative rule – in 1989, which called for a wider scope of options in personnel policy and for more flexibility in tariff regulation (Winchester and Bach, 1999, p. 48).[94]

The innovation boost in local personnel management, which went cheek by jowl with PRP and managerialization, is problematic in several respects, though. The introduction of market competition (see Section 4.4) has resulted in considerable deterioration in the quality of employment relations of local employees. In particular for manual workers, job security has been undermined and the employment relations have worsened, evidenced in declining wages and social benefits (sick and holiday pay), more fixed-term and short-term contracts, general job insecurity and multiple jobholding and growing workloads (Reimer, 1999, p. 157 et seq.). For female employees especially, who traditionally represent the majority of local employees (about three-quarters of staff; cf. Local Government Pay Commission, 2003), employment conditions have deteriorated. This is because those (poorly paid and work-intensive) areas such as school canteens and industrial cleaning in which predominantly women are employed have been particularly and often affected by privatizations (Reimer, 1999, p. 158). Meanwhile, in the public sector, a sense of job insecurity and downgrading in the area of manual workers that even exceeds the private sector has arisen. The slashing of wages and social benefits, in particular for manual workers, has also been accompanied by a growth in financial dependence of local governments on the state (see Section 4.2.3), as the local government employers frequently pass on decreasing state subsidies to cutting personnel costs. Against this backdrop, the Local Government Pay Commission concludes that 'local government is in danger of becoming the "poor relation" of the public sector' (ibid., p. 2003).

Generally speaking, the principle of performance orientation has also applied to all aspects of the reform regarding civil service, that is, the public service in the ministries and agencies. This holds true for the introduction of flexible remuneration systems, the abandonment of the principle of seniority and fixed promotion entitlements and the establishment of performance indicator-based target agreements and target hierarchies as well as the punishing of poor performance. In order to run an agency in a business-like manner (Naschold et al., 1999, p. 46), managers from private industry have frequently been recruited externally and given permanent contracts with easy exit opportunities. During the course of the reforms under Thatcher, particularly in the agencification of the 1980s (see Section 4.5.2), the personnel responsibility in the civil service largely became decentralized, affecting hiring, firing and promotion as much as did performance evaluation, disciplinary measures, personnel planning and relocation and decisions regarding bonus payments, further vocational training and working hours regulations (Demmke, 2006, p. 386).[95] In addition, bonus payments are relatively short term and also possible for an entire team, thus ensuring a prompt and flexible use by the immediate superiors. In the Cabinet Office for example, performance-related pay is based on an annual appraisal system where superiors are to evaluate their employees according to the achieving of previously agreed-upon targets (generally four to six) and to which extent they have come with specific essential competencies/skills. These are assessed according to a 'Competency Framework' (Demmke, 2007, p. 92 et seq.). On this basis, the superiors formulate a payment recommendation that is then passed on to the subsequent decision-making Pay Committee as to how high the bonus should be (see Table 4.27).

Table 4.27 Best practice guide on performance-related pay in the Cabinet Office/UK

1. Performance Planning	2. Performance Review and Assessment	3. Performance Differentiation	4. Reward
Individual and line manager set the performance objectives in line with business goals:	Individual and line manager meet in-year and end of year to review and assess:	Each individual is assessed on their relative contribution to the organization, against peers:	Assessment leads to reward decisions in respect of bonus:
↓	↓	↓	↓
Business/delivery objectives Corporate objectives Capability objectives Personal development goals focused on PSG	Delivery against business, capability and corporate objectives Leadership skills and behaviour shown Strengths and development areas	Best performers are identified and rewarded Weakest performers are identified and managed Everyone is rewarded relative to their colleagues	Bonus rewards in year performance against objectives
➜ *Objectives are moderated for quality and*	➜ *Manager recommends provisional Performance Grouping for moderation*		➜ *Base salary rewards long-term contribution*

Source: Demmke et al. (2007, p. 93, with further references).

Sweden: performance-orientation, flexibility and individualization of employment relations

At the outset, it should be borne in mind that Sweden has a head start in public sector modernization as well as in terms of the key criteria discussed here under the aspect of public service reform. For one – with the exception of judges – there are no lifelong appointments in the public services, but instead the principle of termination (with periods of notice between 2 and 12 months; Naschold et al., 1999, p. 41). The recruitment of employees is position based and not career based (see also Chapter 3, Section 3.3). Second, the employment/labour relations in the public service are almost exclusively regulated by legal provisions and regulations and they hardly differ from the (general) labour law because of a widespread alignment of employment relations between the private and public sector dating back to the 1960s (only judges have a special public-legal status; Montin, 1999, p. 40 et seq.). It is estimated that civil servants (in the narrowest sense) constitute only 1 per cent (judges) (Demmke, 2011, p. 323). Furthermore, since the 1960s, the barriers for switching between individual ranks and salary levels have been largely removed.

From the early 1990s on, the responsibilities of the personnel department have been increasingly decentralized in the state administration. Initially (1993), the directors of the quasi-autonomous agencies (see Section 4.5.2), in which 99 per cent of the approximately 220000 state employees work, were given the responsibility for recruiting people and determining qualification requirements. Since 1994 they have been accorded comprehensive personnel-related responsibilities, including the decision on classification, payment and dismissal of personnel (Naschold et al., 1999, p. 41; Tiessen, 2007, p. 144 et seq.). Within the system of management by results the personnel-related flexibility of the agencies has been further extended (Premfors, 1998; Montin, 1999). Inter alia, the general directors that previously were appointed on a permanent contract could now be dismissed and the senior management positions that previously were permanent have been made temporary. The reforms of 1994 elasticized even more collective bargaining flexibility, with the result that the collective agreements, which previously had been negotiated centrally for all state employees by the government with the trade unions (and similarly for the local government employees by the communal umbrella organizations) were replaced by agency-specific and municipality-specific tariff agreements respectively.

It has been pointed out that the introduction of performance-related pay was initially confronted with certain reservations and resistance in Sweden due to the background of the country's deeply rooted (social-democracy–inspired) legacy of equal treatment and payment in the public service. The trade unions under which 90 per cent of all Swedes are organized considered this reform as an opportunity to achieve pay hikes for public employees, so that, in the end, they supported it. In the meantime, a widespread individualization of public employment relations and remuneration regulations in the state as well as local government sectors evolved (cf. Häggroth et al., 1993, p. 94), a development that is strongly shaped by the notion of performance.

However, the legitimation argument of Swedish NPM-inspired reformers, according to which performance-related pay would lead to a growth in productivity in the public service, has been called into question – and not only in Sweden (see further below).

Hungary: public-legal career model to ensure the independence and professionalism of the public service

As in the other former socialist countries in Central and Eastern Europe, in 1990 Hungary also 'inherited' the unitary labour law from the communist system, which applied equally to both the public and private sectors. In 1992 Hungary was the first post-socialist country to pass a law under which the employees in the public sector were subject to a separate regulation (public service law). In this – similar to German law – the distinction between a public-law–based civil servant status (appointment, permanence, career, etc.) on the one hand and private-law–based employee status (contract-based appointment, etc.) on the other was introduced. The decision to adopt this public law career model was essentially guided by the political and legislative resolve to thus ensure the political independence and neutrality of public service employees as well as their professional training and competence (cf. Dexia, 2006, p. 157). Consequently, the public service in Hungary is characterized by a 'dual' structure, with 25 per cent civil servants and 75 per cent public service employees. By contrast, other CEE countries (e.g., Slovakia, Estonia and Lithuania) have focused on the public-law–based career model. Still another group of transformation countries prefers the private-law–based contractual model (Latvia, Poland, Romania; cf. Marcou and Wollmann, 2008, p. 153; Demmke, 2011, p. 323).

4.5.5 Cross-country comparison: convergence, divergence, persistence and explanatory factors

Convergence, divergence, persistence

Drawing on the distinction between discursive convergence and practice convergence that was presented earlier (see Chapter 2, Section 2.3.4) analysis suggests that the reform moves in the policy cycles in the countries under comparative consideration and interpretation here appear to be quite different in terms of convergence, whether it be in discourse or practice.

Without a doubt, there has been a clear convergence between the countries with regard to the reform discourse and, to some extent, the reform instruments since the emergence of the international NPM doctrine in the 1980s (Christensen and Laegreid, 2010). The introduction of output-oriented management, performance measurement, performance comparisons and performance-related pay, the flexibility and individualization of employment/labour relations, decentralization and organizational 'autonomization' of administrative units, that is, a whole 'toolbox' of NPM-inspired reform elements, have become a central topic of modernization in all the countries, at least on the level of *talk*. This has resulted in a discursive convergence that can be explained by the concept diffusion of NPM and by the ensuing normative receptions and adjustments in the national reform discourses (normative isomorphism). This also confirms the tenets of sociological institutionalism (see Chapter 2, Section 2.3.3), which postulates a 'logic of appropriateness' and a resulting adjustment process. Consequently, NPM has been declared the most effective route to the modernization of the welfare state (but cf. Naschold, 1995, p. 69; see Chapter 2, Section 2.2.2), a deviation from which was considered to be normatively not desirable or just plain 'inappropriate behaviour'.

However, the NPM concept diffusion and the normative pressure thus generated in the national systems have been expedited by influential international organizations such as and in particular the OECD, but also increasingly by the EU. This can be recognized especially in the EU accession countries, as in Hungary where the anticipated EU accession and the adoption of the *acquis communautaire* have led and have been additionally promoted by Western consultants, to the mounting dominance of the NPM modernization discourse. Moreover, in the individual countries specific actors have gained special influence on the diffusion of ideas, convictions and reform models. Thus, the effectiveness of institutional and individual actors in the evolution of the NPM discourse development, in the sense of actor-centred institutionalism, should also be highlighted.

Regarding economic institutionalism, it can also be argued that within the international reform discourse, an increasing consensus among the relevant actors has become apparent in understanding and executing administrative modernization as a process of economic optimization. For a long time the rationality to be measured against economic efficiency has become the decisive evaluation criterion of the reform programmes and has determined the politico-administrative debates.

As the country analyses presented here have shown, however, there has only been a limited convergence (practice/result convergence) in the area of concrete reform implementation and with regard to results and effects (cf. also Christensen and Laegreid, 2010). In the area of organizational reform, the radical British approach of agencification, which was targeted at implementing NPM concept ideas in a 'pure form' and led to a radical transformation of Whitehall, contrasts with the Scandinavian variant of agency management. This is based on a 'home-grown', historically evolved and long since established institutional setting and has been only supplemented with new elements of output and contract management. It has thus been much more strongly shaped by continuity and a cautious NPM modernization, a reform pattern that has also been termed the 'Scandinavian regime type' in contrast to the 'Anglo-Saxon regime type' of NPM (Schröter, 2001, p. 438). In Continental Europe, on the other hand, a distinction is to be made between federal and unitary countries. In the former, the administration has proved to be less 'agencifiable' – as in the example of Germany – due to the already decentralized implementation structures (Wollmann, 1996b; Döhler, 2007), so that as a result agencification has only occurred moderately. In the unitary countries, the state administration is already highly deconcentrated due to the Napoleonic administrative tradition characterized by the dualism between state and local government administration. Thus, the potential here for additional agencification is also limited. Hence, in this regard Continental European countries show limited convergence with the United Kingdom and Sweden. Even though, there are increasing attempts of NPM-inspired output and contract management undertaken by deconcentrated authorities and agencies in Continental Europe, the implementation of these instruments and their actual functioning have so far only partly been effective. This fact points less at result/practice convergence rather than at persistence.

In management instruments and process innovations, there is only a limited convergence between countries. In the UK to a wide extent, the use of performance management as a tool of state control and intervention is obligatory and tied to sanctions. This stands in contrast to the Scandinavian context where the use of performance management is embedded into a system of voluntary self-assessment and optimization. In addition, there is no convergence to be noted between countries as to whether performance results are made public (United Kingdom, Sweden) or not (Germany, France). Instead, there is an adherence (persistence) to received traditions of freedom or (contrarily) secrecy of information. Last but not least, the distribution rate of this reform instrument in the European countries is highly heterogeneous (Kuhlmann, 2010d). Thus, there is only a limited range of practical application opportunities for performance measurement in the institutionally fragmented French administrative landscape, especially at the local government level, and also because, at least in the multitude of small municipalities, the scope of administrative functions is limited. By contrast, in Sweden and the United Kingdom the distribution is almost countrywide (for further country examples see also Christensen and Laegreid, 2010). Germany, Italy and Hungary fall in the middle range. In a comparison of performance management approaches, it also becomes apparent that the regulation and procedural perfectionism attributed to classic Continental European administrative regimes is most likely to be found in British managerialism. This is geared towards procedures (rather than outcomes) and at perfecting performance indicator systems, whereas, for example, the (larger) French administrative authorities are distinctly pragmatic, adaptive and experimental (cf. similarly Ashford, 1982; Kuhlmann, 2010d).

In the area of personnel management, the examples have also made it clear that the convergent discourse on performance-related pay in the public service has resulted in considerable variance in national and local solutions. Thus, the United Kingdom and the Scandinavian countries have undertaken the most consistent steps to introduce performance-related pay in the public service. This has meant that the traditional models of seniority-based promotion and payment have in many cases become obsolete. In Continental European countries by contrast, performance-related pay has been incorporated more moderately in the existing remuneration systems to the all but symbolic extent that (almost) all employees – in accordance with the principle of equality/*égalité* – receive performance bonuses. Hungary, however, represents a completely different case where the initial concern pertained to the build up of a public service according to the rule of law and to, hence, introduce a career system for civil servants that ensured their neutrality and professionalism. Consequently, the managerializing of staff has been less of a focus of personnel reform than the reconstruction of a classic bureaucracy; this could be interpreted as a divergence when viewed along with the other analogous countries. By withdrawing from traditional career-based systems and by 'privatizing' the public employment relations, Italy has experienced a distinct convergence towards the British and Scandinavian position-based system, in which the distinction between public and private labour law is not particularly pronounced or may even be non-existent in some cases. Figure 4.23 summarizes.

Explanatory factors

One key explanation for the observed persistence and only moderate or bounded convergence in the area of reform implementation and reform results is to be found first and foremost in historical variables and thus in the concepts of historical institutionalism. The very different use and effects of the (similar) reform instruments discussed here can be traced back primarily to institutional path dependencies and to the persistence of historically

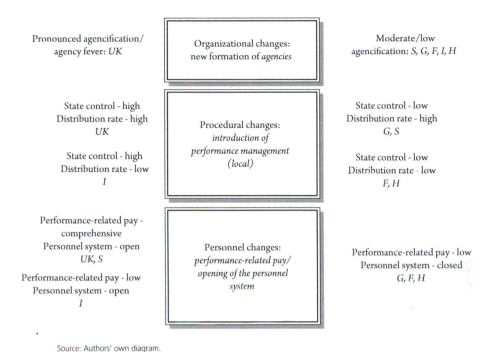

Pronounced agencification/
agency fever: *UK*

Organizational changes:
new formation of *agencies*

Moderate/low
agencification: *S, G, F, I, H*

State control - high
Distribution rate - high
UK

Procedural changes:
*introduction of
performance management
(local)*

State control - low
Distribution rate - high
G, S

State control - high
Distribution rate - low
I

State control - low
Distribution rate - low
F, H

Performance-related pay -
comprehensive
Personnel system - open
UK, S

Personnel changes:
*performance-related pay/
opening of the personnel
system*

Performance-related pay - low
Personnel system - closed
G, F, H

Performance-related pay - low
Personnel system - open
I

Source: Authors' own diagram.

Figure 4.23 Practical divergence of the internal modernization and personnel reforms by country comparison

established administrative structures and administrative-cultural traditions. Hence, the NPM doctrine can be seamlessly incorporated into the public interest culture of the United Kingdom (cf. König, 2006) because it is characterized by a pragmatic-instrumental use of the rule-of-law and the notion of the stateless society (see Section 4.3.2). Within the classic Continental European rule-of-law and administrative culture, by contrast, administrative action still remains largely a conditionally programmed (*konditional programmiert*) implementation of legal provisions, thus raising compatibility problems with managerial steering, output orientation and 'commercialization'. In the area of personnel and personnel management, it can also be seen that the majority of respective traditional public service systems have not been restructured, but instead, NPM instruments such as performance-related pay or target agreements have largely been embedded in the established systems (and thereby often diluted).

Historical institutionalism reaches its limits, however, in the question regarding the explanation of paradigmatic shifts in administrative systems, although it does provide some useful concepts, such as 'critical junctures' and 'external pressures' (cf. Steinmo et al., 1992). In this regard, actor-centred

Table 4.28 Theoretical explanation of the reform development in the area of internal modernization

Factor	Explanation	Neo-institutional Theory Approach
Exogenous explanatory factors (supra-/international)		
NPM discourse dominance	Normative pressure, logic of	Sociological institutionalism
Economic and financial crisis	appropriateness, framing	
Influence of international organizations/actors (EU, OECD)		
Endogenous explanatory factors (national/local)		
Policy preferences of actors; opinion leaders in the reform process	Actor constellations; strategic action; voter maximization	Actor-centred institutionalism
(In-) compatibility of administration and management	Administrative/legal culture; cognitive-cultural character of administration	Historical institutionalism
National policy crises; political shocks	Critical junctures	

Source: Authors' own compilation.

institutionalism is more effective because it focuses greater attention on relevant actors, their pursuit of power, their 'will and skill' and political strategies within the modernization process. This is evident for the United Kingdom, where the managerialization of Whitehall and the 'war against local governments' can be traced back essentially to neo-conservative policy and party-political strategies of the then Prime Minister Margaret Thatcher.

In Italy also, the actor variable comes into play especially regarding the explanation of politico-administrative incisions, such as in the area of the public service, and the unprecedented flood of NPM legislation. Political conflicts provide the background to this – or more precisely, the 'political shocks' (Bobbio, 2005, p. 34 et seq.) the country has experienced since the early 1990s. The profound political crisis that ensued in Italy has resulted in numerous reform attempts and the effort to bring about radical change, thus explaining the said paradigm shift in the public service, as well as the efforts to unbundle politics and administration, strengthen the local executive and to withdraw from party-political influence, and so on. Conceptually, however, this development can also be elucidated very well by the notion of 'critical juncture' proposed by historical institutionalism. This critical juncture was reached by the Italian administration as a result of the political crisis and it ushered in significant changes, promoted by significant pressure on the entire system (external pressure).

For Germany, France and Sweden, the actor constellations have been of such reform-political importance to the extent that the implementation of NPM in these countries has rather depended on a broad consensus of relevant actor groups and reform participants. Here, the existence of significant (and in some cases constitutionally anchored) veto players and the ensuing generated pressure to attain a consensus provides a (further) plausible explanation for the more cautious and moderate implementation of the reform concept. Table 4.28 summarizes.

NOTES

1 The following section is based on Wollmann (2002a).
2 Cf. also the similarly conceived difference by V. Schmidt between *multi-actor* and *single-actor countries* (V. Schmidt, 2008, p. 232 et seq.).
3 On the explanatory power of starting conditions cf. in particular Pollitt and Bouckaert (2004, p. 62 et seq.).
4 On the differentiation between 'NPM', 'traditional' and 'alternative' modernizers, cf. Wollmann (1996b, p. 15 et seq.).
5 Examples are city networks, regional conferences and metropolitan regions (in Germany, e.g., Rhine-Neckar, Hamburg, Bremen, South Bavaria, Frankfurt am Main), in which often private and social actors are also involved. Consequently, one often speaks of 'regional governance'.
6 Of the United Kingdom's 60 million inhabitants, 50 million live in England, 5 million live in Scotland, 2.9 million live in Wales and 1.7 million live in Northern Ireland.
7 Thus, Northern Ireland was governed most recently between 2002 and 2007 directly by the Northern Ireland Office in London. The reason for the suspensions of Stormont was the continuing conflict between Catholics and Protestants.
8 The overlap with the concepts and terms of political/administrative decentralization and deconcentration also used here is obvious (see below).
9 For a list of the 50 still existing and/or amalgamated and thus abolished provinces, cf. http://www.landesverf assungsgericht-mv.de/presse/aktuelle/download/LVFG9-17u.pdf; last accessed 6 March 2014.
10 The full title of the commission: Hållbar samhällsorganisation med utvecklingskraft, Ansvarskommitténs slutbetänkande (= Innovative Capability for the Sustainable Development of the Welfare State; cf. also Wollmann, 2008, p. 40 et seq.).
11 See   http://www.landesverfassungsgericht-mv.de/presse/aktuelle/download/LVFG9-17u.pdf;   last accessed 6 March 2014.
12 On this, the court ruled among other things: 'Counties must be organized in a way that provides a typical opportunity for its citizens to carry out sustainably and reasonably voluntary activities in the Kreistag [county council] and its committees. This aspect has been neglected by the legislature. It appears obvious that a voluntary activity as a member of the Kreistag or one of its committees can be, and frequently is, significantly impeded as the result of a considerable enlargement of the area of a county. Due to the increased time expenditure involved, there is a recognizable danger that the willingness of citizens to perform voluntary duties on the county level would continue to decline'.
13 The starting point was the framework law (*loi-cadre*) for decentralization, which was adopted by the then socialist government under state president François Mitterrand on 2 March 1982. This was followed by 48 laws and 269 decrees that ushered in the most comprehensive decentralization reform in French history up to that point.
14 Loi Constitutionnelle No. 2003-276 du 28 mars 2003 relative à l'organisation décentralisée de la République.

15 To enforce legal oversight-related objections, the prefect must now appeal to the administrative courts or the Court of Audit.

16 This arrangement goes back as far as 1790 and still includes the dualistic function of the French mayor as carrying out decisions taken by the municipal council, on the one hand, and as acting in a state function (*agent d'Etat*), on the other.

17 Thus, for the RMI (*revenu minimum d'insertion*), a minimum income for the long-term unemployed comparable to social security benefits, was completely transferred to the General Councils, along with the associated reintegration measures (*actions d'insertion*), suggesting an important thrust towards an integrated labour market and social policy under the auspices of the *départements*.

18 Similar 'functional reforms' have been embarked upon by the (three-tier) *Länder* of North Rhine-Westphalia, Rhineland-Palatinate, Hesse and Saxony. Different are the cases of the *Länder* of Thuringia and Saxony-Anhalt, both of which, in the absence of a meso-level administrative district authority, have a *Land* administration office (*Landesverwaltungsamt*) that assumes the functions of a meso-level administrative district authority. In the (two-tier) *Länder* of Mecklenburg-Western Pomerania, Brandenburg, Saarland, and Schleswig-Holstein) functional reforms by way of 'municipalizing' state tasks have been initiated as well.

19 After important local government tasks (National Health Service, gas, electricity, social security) had been already nationalized in the post-war period and after they were subsequently in part privatized, the grip of central government on local government was intensified as part of the Thatcherist Revolution. This had a lasting, weakening effect on England's traditionally strong local government model and led to a significant recentralization of the administrative system.

20 The most common definition (cf. Skelcher, 1998, p. 13) of quangos includes so-called NDPBs (non-departmental public bodies), which do not belong directly to a ministry, but are publically financed and perform separate tasks. Quangos operate largely outside the influence of local authorities/councils and are financially, and so on, dependent on central government (cf. Skelcher, 2000). They are directed by appointed boards (hence the common term 'appointed bodies'), represented by central government and further actors.

21 In the mid-1990s, local, central-state–funded quangos had a budget of around £40 billion, which almost corresponds to that of the local governments (Stoker, 1999, p. 42).

22 N. Morris, *The Independent*, 27 July 2010: 'Quango list shows 192 to be axed'; last accessed 6 March 2014 at http://www.bbc.co.uk/news/uk-politics-11538534.

23 In Germany, the direct election now applies to the (full-time) mayors in all *Länder* and to the heads of county (*Landräte*) in most of them. The direct election of the mayors has also been introduced in Hungary, Italy and (in exceptional) cases in England.

24 The number of elected position-holders, especially municipal mayors, who held at least one additional elected position at upper government levels, doubled between 1956 and 1985 (Mény, 1992, p. 23).

25 In the following, both levels are referred to by the umbrella term of 'local government'.

26 Toulouse and Nice.

27 'La voie pragmatique de la réforme territoriale malgré l'échec des fusions de communes'.

28 This has been aptly described with the image '*millefeuille*' (= 'cake made out of several layers of puff pastry').

29 Proposition 9: 'L'objectif à atteindre est, à terme, que les intercommunalités se transforment en communes de plein exercice, ce qui permettrait à la France de compter des communes fortes, en nombre raisonnable'.

30 Particularly the municipalities in the North are highly fragmented (referred to pointedly as 'pulverized municipalities', *comuni-polvere*), while in the South, they are much larger (cf. Dexia, 2008, p. 404).

31 Testo unico delle leggi sull'ordinamento degli enti locali – 'Tuel'.

32 The tactic of the Monti government to take resort to governmental 'decrees' (instead of constitutional legislation) was justified by claiming 'extraordinary urgency' (*casi straordinaria necessità e urgenza*). The legal provisions were to become effective by 1 January 2013 (respectively, by way of prolongation) and by 1 January 2014.

33 The local-level government structure that arose according to this pattern in Rhineland-Palatinate comprises 12 county-free municipalities, 163 *Verbandsgemeinden*, 28 non-associated municipalities (*Einheitsgemeinden*) and 2258 (or 97 per cent) municipalities (with an average of 1700 inhabitants) grouped in a *Verbandsgemeinde*.

34 Prior to German unification, the German Democratic Republic had a total of 7565 municipalities (with an average of 2100 inhabitants), 38 county-free cities (*kreisfreie Städte*) and 189 counties (with an average of 60 000 inhabitants).

35 Cf. the draft law of the (First) Land Act on local government and administrative reform of 20 April 2010, *Landtag* Rhineland-Palatinate, Drs. 15/4488.

36 This term was coined by Ernst Forsthoff (1938) and is intended to characterize the new tasks of public service administration that by necessity had to be performed collectively to serve the needs of the individual in the course of industrialization (cf. also Hösch, 2000, p. 25 et seq.). Tasks of the '*Daseinsvorsorge*' are delivered primarily in the municipality as 'local community'.

37 In his path-breaking book *The Great Transformation* (1944) Karl Polanyi, inter alia, conceptualized and coined the 'pendulum' interpretation of the socio-economic development, which moved from the early capitalist market economy of the nineteenth century to the 'Keynesian' welfare state economics, culminating in the mid-twentieth century and 'swinging back' again to a 'free market' economy since the late 1970s.

38 To the extent that it may also be viewed as a form of administrative deconcentration, agencification as a variant of organizational outsourcing has already been addressed in Section 4.2.

39 In addition, there is the 'pure' dismantling of tasks, which goes hand in hand with a partial or complete discontinuation of the respective task and applies to specific voluntary local tasks, evident, for example, in the closing of swimming pools, sports facilities, cultural institutions, and so on.

40 France Télécom transferred 37.5 billion francs to the French national budget for the assumption of a part of the pension liabilities by the government – this lowered the deficit by around 0.5 of the GDP (cf. Mayer, 2006, p. 154).

41 Article L. 1522-1 du CGCT.

42 The remaining 16 per cent of the total of 11 billion francs, which make up the capital of French SEMLs (status 2002), are state institutions and other SEMLs.

43 ENEL (Ente Nazionale per l'Energia Elettrica) is the national energy provider, which emerged from the nationalization of the energy sector in 1962. The local *municipalizzate* were exempted from the nationalization and were able to assert themselves into the Italian energy market (see further below). IRI (Istituto per la Ricostruzione Industriale) is the national holding company for industrial development. ENI is the oil and gas company.

44 For example, the so-called Andreatta van Miert agreement between the then Italian minister for industry, Paolo Savona, and the European Commissioner for competition, Karel van Miert, allowed for the recapitalization of the steel company ILVA, (which was in need of rehabilitation), on the condition of its subsequent privatization (Mayer, 2006, p. 181). The agreement further provided for the privatization of indirect public enterprises and defined a monitoring procedure so as to ensure implementation.

45 The 2005 announcement of a further 32000 redundancies and the contracting out of 50000 employees to a job placement company announced in 2007 then led to the first strike in the history of Telekom (Deckwirth, 2008, p. 72).

46 In April 2003, almost 40000 post boxes were removed overnight (Wehner, 2005, p. 24). Of the 22000 branches in 1992, only 12000 were remaining in 2005 (ibid.).

47 The data are based on a survey in 190 local governments with more than 50000 inhabitants with a response rate of 71 per cent (= 135 cities; Richter et al., 2006).

48 Pollitt and Bouckaert (2004) base their country typology on the entire NPM repertoire, while the classification submitted here refers only to privatization approaches.

49 Figures for 2003.

50 Thus, for example, the first historical mention of concession contract in France goes back as far as the *ancien régime*, when Louis XVI transferred the water purification of the Seine to the Compagnie des Eaux de Paris des Frères Perrier in 1778 (Duval, 2006, p. 6).

51 The 'optimal territorial districts' (*ambiti territoriali ottimali* – ATO) were established in Italy for the individual service sectors (water, waste, etc.; see above). These are mono-functional forms of organization, in which several local governments and their respective municipal enterprises combine to form a specific (in supply terms: 'optimal') territory. In this, they approximate German cooperation associations (*Zweckverbände*). The regulation of the ATOs is subject to regional legislation (Lippi et al., 2008).

52 In the area of childcare and in other fields of child and youth assistance, the market opening is less

advanced (see Grohs, 2010). Here, the traditional welfare organizations (West Germany) and municipal providers (East Germany) continue to prevail.

53 Mühlenkamp (2013, p. 18): 'Research does not support the conclusion that privately owned firms are more efficient than otherwise-comparable state-owned firms'. See also Bel et al. (2010), who, on the basis of numerous studies on water and waste services, summarize, that 'our analysis provides empirical evidence that private production of local services is not systematically less costly than that of public' (see also Bel and Warner, 2008, p. 1341).

54 On this see also APSE (2011, p. 11).

55 Florio (2004, p. 341): 'The main conclusion of my study is that privatization had more modest effects on efficiency than the theory or property rights and other orthodox privatization theories may have expected. On the other hand, privatization did have substantive regressive effects on the distribution of incomes and wealth in the United Kingdom'.

56 See http://www.attac.org/node/3727; last accessed 10 March 2014.

57 Rule 201 of the Rules of Procedure of the European Parliament, accessed 10 march 2014 at http://www.europarl.europa.eu/sides/getLastRules.do?reference=RULE-201&language=EN.

58 See http://www.right2water.eu/; last accessed 10 March 2014.

59 The survey addressed 699 German local governments with more than 20000 inhabitants (response rate: 159 municipalities from all 13 *Länder*; 22.7 per cent; cf. Institut für den öffentlichen Sektor, 2011. p. 6).

60 In 2001 the Federal Cartel Office stipulated that minority shares held by external investors in *Stadtwerke* must not exceed 10 per cent.

61 *Süddeutsche Zeitung*, 13 August 2009.

62 *Frankfurter Allgemeine Zeitung*, 11 April 2009.

63 On 28 August 2010, Chris Huhne, Secretary of State for Energy and Climate Change, wrote an official letter to all local authorities, in which he argued, inter alia, that 'for too long, Whitehall's dogmatic reliance on "big" energy has stood in the way of the vast potential role of local authorities in the UK's green energy revolution' (see https://www.gov.uk/government/news/huhne-ends-local-authority-power; last accessed 10 March 2014).

64 Cf. the league table of the local governments that are active in energy policy at: http://www.aeat.com/cms/assets/MediaRelease/2011-press-releases/Microgeneration-Index-Press-Release-11th-March-2011.pdf; last accessed 10 March 2014.

65 See APSE's website www.apse.org.uk.

66 See http://www.acquabenecomune.org/raccoltafirme/; last accessed 10 March 2014.

67 See http://www.wasser-in-buergerhand.de/nachrichten/2010/stgt_fuer_rekommunalisierung_wasser.htm; accessed 10 March 2014.

68 See *Berliner Morgenpost* dated 9 August 2012.

69 Thus, many German local governments sold their enterprises, facilities and infrastructure with the primary goal of unburdening the administration budget and getting away from budgetary state supervision (cf. Bogumil and Holtkamp, 2002, p. 81).

70 However – as with procurement law – there are general and sector-specific exceptions (see Inhouse-Lagen; Altmark Trans Judgement of the ECJ, etc.).

71 At their summit, held in March 2007, the European heads of state agreed on an Energy Policy for Europe, which called for a 20 per cent increase in energy efficiency, a 20 per cent reduction of greenhouse gas (GHG) emissions and a 20 per cent share of renewable energy sources in overall EU energy consumption by 2020 (see Praetorius and Bolay, 2009).

72 It would be more accurate to speak of deconcentration here, as implementation responsibilities (such as the responsibility for personnel, budget, etc.) are delegated 'downwards' within the administration. This is not linked whatsoever to changes in political decision-making powers or shifts in power between levels of the politico-administrative system – in the sense of political decentralization/regionalization (see Section 4.2). Thus, when the term 'decentralization' (which is common in the literature) is used in this chapter, it refers to the 'layering' and delegation of administrative responsibilities within an administrative organization (e.g., ministry, local administration), which are more similar in concept to the 'administrative deconcentration' dealt with in Section 4.2.3.

73 In 1720, King Vittorio Amendo initiated the restructuring of ministries and the founding of three agencies: the Fiscal Agency, the Tax Agency and the Agency of the Royal Household (cf. Fedele et al., 2007).

74 This refers to the results of the evaluation of the 'New Steering Model' (NSM), which represents the most exhaustive empirical study yet on the topic in Germany (for details and methods, see Bogumil et al., 2007; Kuhlmann et al., 2008). In the following, it will be termed 'NSM evaluation'.

75 Overall, there are now 352 MSPs in France (status 2002), whereby the list is topped by the region of Rhône-Alpes with 39 MSPs, while the region of Limousin is at the bottom of the list nation-wide with five MSPs (not including Corsica with two MSPs). On average, each French *région* has about 15 MSPs (Kuhlmann, 2009a).

76 Act No. 241/90; Legislative Decree No. 29/1993; directive of the Council of Ministers of October 1994 and January 1995.

77 Legislative Decree No. 112 of March 1998 in connection with Bassanini I (Act No. 59 of March 1997).

78 Announcement of 3 April 2012 (Sveriges Kommuner och Landsting).

79 In general, the distinction is made between input, output, outcome and process indicators, each relating to specific aspects of performance (cf. Jann and Jantz, 2008; Van Dooren and van de Walle, 2008). Frequently, the relatively easily measurable input and output indicators predominate for the measurement where simply data on expenditure, personnel costs, unit numbers, and so on can be used. By contrast impact and outcome indicators that are more difficult to quantify (as their causal structures are more complex and they also include relational dimensions, such as effectiveness, etc.) are less frequently employed.

80 In Britain, the first attempts to measure and evaluate the provision of public services reaches back more than 100 years. Even as late as the late nineteenth century, performance indicators were used to measure the performance of teachers in state schools (Pollitt and Bouckaert, 2004, p. 87).

81 The PSA of the Cabinet Office contains – inter alia – the following objectives: 'Support the Prime Minister in leading the Government'; 'Achieve co-ordination of policy and operations across government'.

82 'Authorities that are good at producing strategies and plans, collecting performance data and establishing audit trails may be able to "paper over" problems with service delivery' (Davis et al., 2001, p. 20). 'We're sceptical of the value of audit and inspection. . . There's a danger that the inspectors will lose touch with reality' (senior officer, local authority, quoted in the same place).

83 'Through a load of targets and inspections and performance indicators, our public service professionals have been forced to answer to Ministers in Whitehall. And that's why things haven't improved enough. . . We're turning that system on its head. We're going to get rid of the bureaucracy that wastes so much money and saps so much staff morale' (D. Cameron, news story, 'Public Services – you call the shots', 19 January 2011; last accessed 12 March 2014 at https://www.gov.uk/government/news/public-services-you-call-the-shots).

84 The Bassanini reforms (Bassanini I–IV; see Section 4.2.3) that were adopted between 1997 and 2001 (Acts 59/1997, 127/1997; 191/1998; 50/1999; 3/2001) constitute the regulatory core of Italian NPM reforms (as also of decentralization policy; cf. Promberger et al., 2000, pp. 30–37; Longo and Plamper, 2004, p. 330).

85 Cf. the articles in the journal *Behördenspiegel*, Executive Letter 'Grundgesetz Art. 91d: Leistungsvergleich in der öffentlichen Verwaltung' ('Basic Law Article 91d: Performance comparison in public administration'), September 2010.

86 The data are based on a survey conducted in 1991 by Meyssonnier in 82 municipalities (*communes*) and governments with over 5000 inhabitants (Meyssonnier, 1993).

87 The data are based on a survey conducted by Basle on behalf of the Institut des Villes in a total of 118 cities with more than 50000 inhabitants. Forty-eight of the cities responded (cf. Basle, 2003).

88 Belgium, Bulgaria, Denmark, Germany, Estonia, Finland, France, Greece, United Kingdom, Ireland, Italy, Lithuania, Luxembourg, Malta, Netherlands, Poland, Portugal, Romania, Sweden, Slovakia, Slovenia, Spain, Czech Republic, Hungary, Cyprus (for details and methods, see Demmke, 2007).

89 Also: Denmark, Finland, Lithuania, Estonia, Slovakia, Malta, Spain, Belgium, Bulgaria (Demmke, 2007, p. 18).

90 Through the so-called Federal Reform I of 2006, the legislative power of the federal level (Federation, *Bund*) to pass framework legislation (*Rahmengesetze*) was abolished and the 'concurrent' (*konkurrierende*) federal legislation (Art. 74 Basic Law), which requires approval by the Federal Council, was limited to fundamental status matters. The federal level made use of this power by passing the new Civil Servant Status Law (Beamtenstatusgesetz), which came into force on 1 April 2009 and replaced the existing

BRRG (Beamtenrechtsrahmengesetz). The *Länder* now have exclusive legislative power on matters of civil servant remuneration, pensions and public service law for their *Länder* and local government civil servants.

91 According to a study by PricewaterhouseCoopers (PwC) based on a survey of 136 German local authorities (see PWC, 2008), 46 per cent of them had made service/employment agreements for the introduction of performance-related pay in 2007 and paid incentive bonuses to their employees at the end of 2007. On the federal level, this held true for 176 authorities (out of 183 participating in the survey) in mid-2009, which corresponded to a proportion of 96 per cent of authorities surveyed or 94 per cent of employees. Hence, service agreements for performance-related pay have been introduced extensively in the federal administration (see Stellermann et al., 2009, p. 19 et seq.).

92 However, limited-term contracts in management apply only to the actual position in which the civil servant is employed, and not to the employment as such. As in the private sector, the employment contract comprises two components, whereby in the public service, two contracts are usually signed: a permanent contract with the respective ministry/local government on which the tariff law is based, and an individual limited-term contract with the respective head of department, in which the individual payment regulations are also stipulated.

93 There are, however, still some exceptions from the 'privatization' of employment relations, for example, for university professors, researchers and diplomats.

94 Teachers are an important exception from the general regulation system for local employees. In the United Kingdom, the majority of teachers are – as mentioned – still local government employees and alone constitute around a quarter of local staff. The negotiation and regulation power for employment relations with teachers, traditionally in the remit of local government collective agreement partners, was withdrawn from them in 1991 and transferred to a new quango, the School Teachers' Review Body (STRB). Hence, the entire teaching staff was excluded from the decentralization attempts of employment relations in local services and is subject (to this extent similar to Continental Europe) to national – state fixed – framework regulation (Winchester and Bach, 1999, p. 49).

95 Interestingly, the decision regarding the salaries of senior civil servants (SCS) is still centrally located with the Minister for the civil service.

5

Comparative summary

LEARNING OBJECTIVES

At the end of this chapter, you should:

- be aware of the commonalities and differences in the administrative reform discourses of the European countries;

- know how the countries differ in terms of the practical reform implementation and how they can be classified from a comparative perspective;

- be able to explain the reform trajectories of convergence, divergence and persistence by means of neo-institutionalist theory.

5.1 Administrative reform discourses

The comparative analysis of administrative systems and reforms in Europe has shown that the question of convergence, divergence and persistence must be addressed differently according to the reform area (decentralization/ federalization, territorial reform, privatization, internal modernization) and the reform phase (discourse, decision-making, implementation, effect). The various administrative levels and sectors also play an important role as (intervening) variables, so that an obvious convergence on the central state/ national level cannot automatically be associated with convergence on the subnational/local level. The same applies to different task areas of public administration. It thus becomes clear that there is an EU-contingent convergence of administrative profiles in the area of infrastructure administration and network service provision as traditionally public areas of activity (such as in the energy sector). However, the social services and public-order–related administration exhibit strongly, persistent and partly divergent institutionalizing patterns. In general, convergent patterns become more visible in the area of reform discourses, concepts and ideas, and they may fade away while on the way to concrete administrative decisions, material institutionalization and practical implementation measures.

This becomes particularly apparent in the example of the international New Public Management (NPM) doctrine that developed to become the predominant reform principle of the 1980s (in the Anglo-Saxon and, to a lesser degree, in Scandinavian countries) and during the 1990s (in Continental Europe). This NPM message was taken up in all countries examined here and led to an obvious convergence in the administrative reform discourse. However, the concrete implementation and effects of NPM in the various countries shows very different (and in some cases diverging) profiles. Furthermore, on the discourse level itself, individual components of the NPM reform model differ, in part and pronouncedly between countries and country groups. Thus, the retreat of the state, its limitation to an enabling and regulatory function and the withdrawal of public providers from the direct provision of services represent significant elements of the political discourse. However, the debatable variants of possible privatization steps (formal/asset/functional), the envisaged scope of privatization measures and the resulting intensity of the privatization discourse vary. Whereas in the United Kingdom a radical marketization-accentuated reform discourse was dominant and driven by the slogan 'private is better than public', such extreme privatization discourses were not able to gain a foothold in countries such as Sweden and France, which are characterized by a public sector tradition that is strongly rooted in politics and society and the politico-culturally anchored notion of the 'strong (reformist) state'. In Germany by contrast, the discourse intensity in the area of national privatization policy can be considered fairly weak. This can be explained by the broad privatization consensus among the relevant political, economic and social elites. However, in real terms the scope of actually carried out (asset) privatizations (such as Telekom, the postal system) has been considerable.

Furthermore, the administrative reform discourse in Europe has been shaped by the concepts of micro-economics–oriented internal modernization and managerialism, both of which aim at a private-sector–inspired commercially oriented modernization of the internal administrative structures and procedures and an economization of human resources. As to administrative procedures, in all the countries notions of performance management, measurement and comparison have gained wide currency. In the administrative modernization of organizational structure, the emphasis has been on the deconcentration and autonomy of administrative units, the dismantling of hierarchies and the creation of customer-oriented service centres ('one stop agencies'). With regard to personnel and human resources – besides the slashing of administrative staffs and personnel – the debate has focused on introducing performance-related pay and on the flexibility and individualization of employment/labour relations. Despite this obvious convergence in the Europe-wide debate on administrative reform policy, there are also striking differences and divergence that stand out. Thus, the rampant rise of managerialism in the United Kingdom can be plausibly accounted for by the traditional efficiency orientation that has long since been peculiar of territorial and institutional reform policies in the UK and that has been further accentuated by neo-liberal policy preference, with the private sector looked at as the archetypal reference model. In Sweden by contrast, the performance-oriented modernization discourse, which was debated primarily in terms of 'output-/result-based management', is inherent in the country's 'rationalist' evaluation culture. In France, Germany and Italy the internal administrative managerialism – alongside the enduring influence of the traditional rule-of-law–guided bureaucracy model – has also been taken up in particular in variants of 'output' and performance management.

Moreover, the issues of decentralization and deconcentration of the politico-administrative macro-structures have been a dominant theme in the administrative reform discourse. This applies particularly to the traditionally centralized countries such as France, the United Kingdom and Italy. For this reason, two distinctly different basic patterns can be identified. In the United Kingdom (and similarly New Zealand), also guided by neo-liberal policy concepts, the modernization drive aimed at administrative deconcentration. Many tasks hitherto performed at central government level were transferred to mono-functional organizationally autonomous administrative units (executive agencies). These single-purpose agencies were intentionally located outside the elected (multi-purpose) local self-government. On the other hand, France (after 1982) and Italy (following the 1990s) have pursued a (political) decentralization by transferring public tasks from state authorities to local self-government levels; in doing so the explicit reform policy goal was to expand the multi-functional task model of the local government levels and to strengthen their local autonomy. The fact that in Germany and Sweden, which are already significantly decentralized, further decentralization measures have been embarked on (by means of 'municipalizing' state tasks) mirrors and underscores the long-term and long-lasting effects of this traditional reform discourse.

In the conceptual guidance of the territorial reform policy targeted at 'rescaling' the local government levels, two related discourses – each relevant in different phases – can be recognized. The first phase of territorial reform, especially during the 1960s and 1970s, was characterized by the guiding concept of a radical territorial and demographic enlargement of the existing local territorial structure. In the UK/England and Sweden in particular, the reform intention was, in line with the 'rationalist' *zeitgeist* of those decades, to

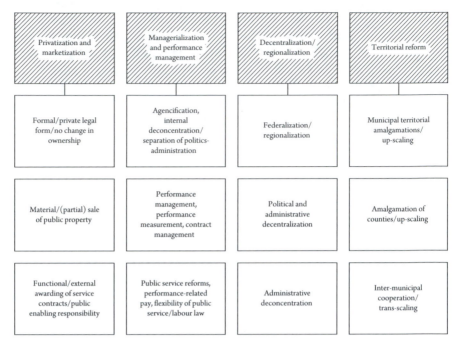

Source: Authors' own diagram.

Figure 5.1 Themes and contents of administrative reform discourses

strengthen the operative capacity of the local authorities by achieving 'economies of scale'. In the more recent phase (i.e., since the 1990s), the reform
discourse, for one, has fallen under the spell of Europeanization and has been
propelled by the aim of improving the ability of the subnational administrative units (regions, local governments) of coping with the new challenges
(namely, European and international competition for locations and for EU
funding). Second, the reform discourse addresses the serious demographic,
socio-economic, budgetary and coordination problems that have increasingly beset the subnational self-government levels. Figure 5.1 summarizes.

5.2   Reform implementation

While the administrative reform discourse thus shows a noticeable degree of
convergence and similarities between countries, albeit with some variance in
details, a closer look at the actual implementation of measures and the reform
practice in those countries under consideration here reveals a more strongly
differentiated picture. Although some convergent lines of development can
still be identified, the features of institutional divergence and persistence of
these countries stand out more clearly, thereby pointing out lasting country-
specific or country-group–specific peculiarities and path dependencies.

In the (vertical) administrative reforms of the multi-level system, the underlying decentralizing tendency in the state modernization and administrative reform policies undoubtedly represents a general mega-trend in the European countries, a trend from which only a few deviate. These deviant cases, which diverge from the main administrative reform trend, include the United Kingdom, where different from most European countries, the decentralized local level has not been strengthened, but, on the contrary, has been hollowed out. Alongside this, in Hungary, earlier decentralization measures have also been reversed so that it has recently moved away from the rest of European countries (except the UK). Within the Napoleonic country group, France represents a somewhat aberrant case, insofar as merely 'simple' regions have been put into place on the country's meso-level – and not (quasi-) federal regions such as Italy, Spain or Belgium. Divergence and persistence can further be noted with regard to the 'municipalization' strategies pursued by the countries, that is, the transfer of tasks to the local government level. In Sweden, state tasks have been transferred (politically decentralized) to the local government levels through 'genuine municipalization' (i.e., once public tasks are assigned to the local authorities, they become fully-fledged local self-government tasks with the elected local council exercising full responsibility). By contrast, in the German *Länder* such a transfer of public tasks to the local government levels is often effected by way of 'delegating' the tasks, meaning that they are carried out by the local executive (that is, the mayor in the municipalities) while the elected local council has no formal influence on the conduct of such 'delegated' tasks. So one can speak of a 'false municipalization' that tends to 'integrate' local administration into state administration (see above).

The pattern of local-level territorial reforms by which three country groups can be distinguished (Northern, Southern European, hybrid), is, by and large, still visible. Thus, in the Northern European group of countries, where during the 1960s and 1970s, large-scale (up-scaling) territorial reforms of the local levels were effected (ultimately by means of binding parliamentary decisions), these large-scale territorial structures still prevail. By contrast, in the Southern European group where territorial reform hinges on the voluntary principle and which is exemplified by France, territorial amalgamations have not occurred. In these countries, typically inter-municipal bodies (in France: *syndicats, intercommunalité*) have been established for the operative support of the existing smaller and smallest municipalities (trans-scaling). More recently, a new wave of territorial reforms can be observed, as some countries (such as Denmark, but also Greece and Portugal, the latter belonging previously to the Southern European territorial pattern) have embarked on large-scale territorial reforms through amalgamation. A convergence of the two territorial reform patterns can be recognized in the increasing replacement of inter-municipal structures by territorially amalgamated municipalities (such as in the East German *Länder*). Furthermore, the creation of functionally and financially more integrated local government structures (such as in France), points to an increasing convergence towards the Northern European type of viable municipal entities.

In the European and international context, the privatization, marketization and commercialization of public services also represent important mega-trends in administrative reform. Convergence within the administrative systems is evinced in the privatization of nationalized industries and municipalized companies through the growing involvement of private-sector/commercial service providers and the limitation of public/municipal institutions to an 'enabling function'. The formal and (partial) asset privatization of state-owned enterprises, the outsourcing (functional privatization) of public/municipal services by way of establishing private-law municipal companies (corporatization) and the involvement of private-sector service providers via service contracts, concessions, and so on (purchaser–provider split) have been taken up as administrative reform instruments by public/municipal authorities and actors throughout Europe. As a result, the actor landscape in the conduct and delivery of public tasks has become extremely diversified in what has been termed as a 'shift from a system of local government to a system of local governance' (Stoker, 1999, p. 41). Hence, a 'satellite model' has developed in which the institutionally shrinking core administration has come to be surrounded by an expanding circle of mono-functional private, public, semi-public and non-profit 'vicarious agents' with the result that the establishment of a comprehensive territory-related steering and management is becoming more and more difficult.

However, 'divergence within convergence' *does* exist, as the countries can be assigned to different reform types and a differentiation within the countries according to administrative levels and/or sectors can also be made. Following its pointedly neo-liberal policy discourse, the United Kingdom, with the greatest extensive changes in ownership from public to private, has pursued the most market-radical privatization programme with the most dramatic effects when compared to other European countries. Thus, the UK can be considered an exemplar of what has been typified as the 'marketizer' and 'minimizer' model (cf. Pollitt and Bouckaert, 2004). Germany and Italy, too, have converged close enough to pass as 'marketizers' and 'minimizers', at least if the corresponding development at the national level and in the national context is taken into account. For one, this is evidenced in the public employment quota, which in Germany has declined significantly. With regard to this indicator both Germany and Italy lie below even the United Kingdom. Second, a forced privatization policy concerning state-owned infrastructural enterprises was pursued in both countries during the 1990s, irrespective of the political composition and 'colour' of their governments. In Germany, which has proved to be an 'assiduous outperformer' of European liberalization requirements, out of the initially large stock of state-owned infrastructure enterprises only the railways remained under state control. By the same token, during that period Italy embarked on the most comprehensive privatization programme of all the European countries under consideration here.

Contrasting with the national level, on the local level the municipal economy (as institutionalized in Germany in the *Stadtwerke* and in Italy in the *municipalizzate*) has manifested itself with both remarkable persistence and inertia. While in Germany the local authorities have initiated and effected numerous formal privatizations ('corporatization') and functional privatization ('outsourcing'), the (asset) privatization of municipal assets has so far remained limited, thereby making Germany's local level a 'modernizer' (in Pollitt and Bouckaert, 2004 typology).

Sweden and France can be classified (drawing on Pollitt and Bouckaert, 2004 again) as 'modernizers'. Their reform trajectories can be seen convergent insofar as (asset) privatization has been moderate and in some cases even stunted, and has been embedded in the respective existing administrative culture and welfare state tradition. In Sweden, this reform course has been described as 'modernization of the welfare state by way of competition', and characterized by diversification of providers, social re-regulation and user democracy, while asset privatization has occurred only limitedly. In France, attempts have also been made to retain and defend the French tradition of *service public*, which was probably one of the reasons why the national level was opened up to market competition only belatedly. By contrast, on the local level the provision of public services/public utilities has long since (historically) been outsourced to private providers by way of *délégation* (whose underlying logic is a forerunner of the purchaser–provider split). In sum, France's local level can be typified as one that is 'maintaining'. In the case of Hungary's transformation, the dissolution of the communist state economy and the asset privatization of numerous economic sectors after 1990 marked a decidedly radical break. However, the privatization of the centralized state economy has gone hand in hand with an almost complete municipalization of public services and the attempt to 'revive' pre-communist rule-of-law administrative traditions with the modernization of the state. Nonetheless, despite its particularities as a transformation country, Hungary can be assigned to the 'modernizer' type, along with Sweden and France.

Concerning the internal modernization of administration, convergence has occurred insofar as the concepts of performance management and agency have been taken up in all the countries under consideration here. However, Sweden, Germany, France, Italy and Hungary show in applying the agency concept markedly more institutional persistence than the United Kingdom, where in the context of its radical agencification, the entire Whitehall bureaucracy was transformed. Sweden's version of agencification is based on the historically founded *ämbetsverk*, which has been rather moderately managerialized through the introduction of output and contract management. Germany is even less agencifiable from the outset due to the federalism-typical decentralization and layering of administrative implementation to the *Länder* (Döhler, 2007), so that also in this case practice convergence can hardly be noticed. For the countries shaped by a Napoleonic legacy, the administrative deconcentration and presence of the state in the subnational space is characteristic and the agency fever of Anglo-Saxon provenance is thus largely unknown.

As to the implementation and use of new output-oriented management tools in public administration, convergence has been limited. Although corresponding reform approaches and measures exist everywhere, a brief look at the distribution rate of performance management shows significant variance. While France lags behind, which not least of all is due to the scant administrative capacity of the multitude of small municipalities for which an elaborate performance management system would not make sense, the latter has been put in place in Sweden and the United Kingdom throughout the local government levels. Germany and Italy have a medium distribution. Whereas in the United Kingdom performance management is obligatory for the local authorities and serves largely as a control instrument for central government, Sweden adheres to the principle of voluntary self-assessment and optimization by local governments. The same applies to the obligation of disclosure of performance data of administrations, an obligation that exists in the United Kingdom and Sweden, but not in Germany, France and Italy. This indicates persistent patterns in the respective freedom of information or secrecy of information culture and practice. For the Continental European country group, the embedding of performance management in the traditional system of legal and regulatory guidance is also still characteristic and constitutes an important and steadfastly distinctive feature, especially in comparison with the Anglo-Saxon administration context. The discursive and instrumental convergence in administrative policy is thus obviously not linked to 'practice/result convergence' to the same extent.

The cross-country debate on performance-related pay in the public service has also entailed variance, and in part divergence in, national and local implementation. The seniority-based promotion and payment system has now become obsolete in the United Kingdom and the Scandinavian countries where performance-related pay has been introduced most consistently. By contrast, in Continental European countries this reform approach has in part been perverted, as in some cases, the entire administrative staff – in line with the principle of equal treatment – are 'rewarded' with performance bonuses. Overall, the concept of performance-related pay has been implemented with restraint in the administrative systems in Continental European countries and inserted somewhat reluctantly in the existing payment schemes. Italy, however, deviates from the Continental European pattern of persistence as – in contrast to France and Germany – it has experienced a downright 'system change' in the civil service by abandoning the traditional career-based system and by 'privatizing' public employment relations. This can be interpreted as a convergence towards the British and Scandinavian models where the position-based system also predominates and the boundaries between public and private labour law either do not exist or are minimal at best.

The following (approximate) rating results from the analyses of the administrative reform practice in the countries examined in Table 5.1.

5.3 Explaining convergence, divergence and persistence

In this section, the institutional developments in the administrative systems of the countries under consideration here will be explained from the perspective of different neo-institutionalist approaches. Throughout, it is assumed that the complex processes of change and continuity of politico-administrative institutions cannot be sufficiently captured and explained by a single theoretical model. Because of the multiple causes of institution genesis, development and persistence, it would appear appropriate to fall back on socio-cognitive, economic-rational and historical time-related factors and to use the corresponding institutionalisms as (mutually) complementary explanatory models.

Sociological institutionalism – adaptation through coercion, normative pressure and mimicry

Various approaches of New Institutionalism have been enlisted for a causal explanation of the converging development patterns in the reform areas examined here. The convergence within the administrative reform discourse is generally apparent in decentralization (with the exception of the United Kingdom) and NPM – albeit with country-specific nuances and

Table 5.1 Administrative reform practice by comparison – country rating

	Germany	France	Italy	Great Britain	Sweden	Hungary
Administrative reform between state and market/privatization/marketization						
Formal privatization	1	1	1	0	2	1
Asset privatization	2	0	2	2	0	1
Functional privatization	1	1	1	2	1	1
Internal modernization/managerializing/performance management						
Agencification	0	0	0	2	1	0
Performance management	1	1	1	2	2	1
PRP in the public service	0	0	1	2	2	0
Flexibility of public employment relations	0	0	2	1	1	0
Inter-governmental reforms/decentralization						
Regionalization/federalization	0	0	2	1	0	0
Municipalization	2	2	1	0	2	1
Territorial reforms						
Territorial amalgamation	1	0	0	0	0	0
Inter-municipal cooperation	1	2	1	0	0	1

Note: With reference to the degree of implementation of the respective reform element, the following coding system has been used: 0 = low; 1 = medium; 2 = high (comparative estimation by the authors on the basis of the qualitative country analyses).

Source: Authors' own compilation.

accentuations. With regard to sociological institutionalism, convergence can be explained on the one hand by reforms being 'mimicked' ('mimetic isomorphism'), either because they have proven successful elsewhere or because a deviation from others has been deemed as inappropriate behaviour. The national actors have thus felt under normative pressure to 'emulate' other reforms (normative pressure), as this conforms to the logic of appropriateness. Normative pressure has been generated by the European Commission in the context of the European integration process, particularly pronounced in those areas in which it lacks regulation powers itself. Normative concepts regarding the preferred ways of performance and specific related techniques (OMC [open method of coordination], benchmarking, peer review) have been suggested to the public actors of the member states for mutual learning (policy learning), and for promoting mimetic practices such as privatization and competition-centred management. This is also known as 'framing'.

According to the sociological institutionalism, exogenous pressure represents a further rationale for explaining converging developments ('coercive isomorphism'). Such pressure has been applied particularly effectively by EU politics that induced isomorphic adaptations through legal obligations. This has become particularly evident in the reform area of privatization policy, in which the EU has generated both direct and indirect legal adaptation pressure in the public service sector systems of the member states by way of directives, sector-specific regulations, subsidies and internal market policy, competition and public procurement laws as well as through the case law of the ECJ and convergence criteria of the economic and currency union, albeit to varying degrees depending on initial situations and political context. In the national multi-level systems, the EU structural subsidies have further engendered coercive pressure, at least indirectly, to the extent that the hitherto centralized states have felt compelled to install decentralized/ regional institutions; otherwise, direct or indirect sanctions would have been expected. Thus, the formation of EU-adequate NUTS regions are seen in Hungary and Poland as a precondition for improving the chances for the application and approval of EU funding. Hence, convergence in the administrative reform debate and practice of EU member states has been largely initiated and accelerated exogenously and top-down by EU institutions. In the research on Europeanization, this has been referred to as 'downloading', that is, the adoption of EU requirements into the national systems and the corresponding (top-down) adjustments.

Rational choice or actor-centred institutionalism: functional adaptation, veto player configurations and vote maximization

From the perspective of rational choice or actor-centred as well as economic institutionalism, convergence in the administrative reform discourse and action can be explained by the national actors in Europe being faced with similar challenges and by their reacting with similar solution strategies. According to the economic approach, this is justified by the maximization of personal advantage and the approximation to an (economic) optimum. For instance, the regionalization trend in Europe can be explained by functional necessities, in particular by the growing (urbanization-, industrialization- and welfare-state–related) coordination, planning and management needs, which have compelled the European countries to establish a new administrative action and planning level on the meso-level.

The territorial consolidation of the local government level has also been propelled by the quest for functional optimization and institutional 'rationalization'. For one, the capacity of the meso-level (counties, *Kreise, landsting kommuner*, etc.) was to be strengthened in the face of the international economic location competition – in pursuit of the 'Lisbon Strategy' proclaimed by the European Council in 2000. Hereby, the adaptation to the regional NUTS 2 territorial categories of the EU appears as a rational institution political strategy to boost the chances of accessing EU funding programmes. Second, the achievement of economies of scale by means of radical territorial up-scaling at the lower local government level has represented a central intention of the national actors in the countries of the Northern European reform path. Since the 1990s, the demographic and economic erosion of rural areas and the functional deficits exhibited in the countries of the Southern European reform pattern with regard to their inter-municipal structures have also triggered strategies of institutional optimization there. From the perspective of economic institutionalism, the resulting convergence to the Northern European country group represents an appropriate response of the national actors to similar external challenges and functional necessities.

This finding is also confirmed with a view to commercial reform ideas and privatization and market opening policy. As all the countries examined here have been confronted with signs of economic crisis and financial problems of the welfare state, from the perspective of the actors the retreat of the state and opening up of competition have been considered administrative reform concepts that promise benefit maximization and drawback minimization. The rationality measured against economic efficiency has become the key criterion in the design of politico-administrative institutions and thus entails converging reform discourses and (in some cases) practices marked by commercial-managerial aspects.

Moreover, the administrative reform strategy choices by actors and veto player configurations in the individual reform areas have proved to be significant explanatory variables for concrete institutionalization decisions and trajectories. For EU policy, especially in the areas of competition opening and market liberalization, it has been shown that the national governments have used 'Europe' strategically to better enforce specific policy preferences in their own country from an actor-centred perspective (cf. Goetz, 2006). This has been termed as the 'usage of Europe'. For example, EU policy only provided additional legitimacy to Germany's privatization plans (except for the energy sector) and gave these a further boost towards the 'assiduous outperformance' of European requirements. Germany has become one of the promoters of the European liberalization movement, and this has in turn radiated to other countries and generated convergence pressure there. But also the example of the United Kingdom shows how strongly the administrative reform strategy choices of individual national actors (in particular the Thatcher government) have impacted the EU agenda and thereby influenced the member states. Thus, convergence can also be explained by bottom-up processes that were rooted endogenously in the administrative reform action choices of national actors, taken up on EU level ('uploading') and then had (exogenously) a 'Europeanizing' effect.

Furthermore, the development of national and local reform coalitions provides an explanation for the diffusion and convergence of specific administrative policy patterns. Thus, many countries have experienced broad 'privatization coalitions' (in some cases permanent, in some temporary), which have encouraged the ideological opening towards a market model and liberalization policy.

The ideological turnaround of the major parties and the overall low level of mobilization on the part of the trade unions has turned out, for example in Germany, to be 'privatization-friendly' veto player configurations that have fed into a broad privatization consensus. There has been similar cross-party unity in Italy with respect to privatization, where this was pursued as a successful vote-seeking strategy to consolidate the state budget during the political and economic crisis and to dissolve the publicly discredited close relationships between the management of state-owned enterprises and the political class. The determining power of actors and their political strategies is strikingly noticeable in the case of the United Kingdom, where privatization and agencification have been used – locally, for instance – to weaken the opposition and fragment the (Labour-dominated) public service unions.

The converging decentralization and regionalization processes in Europe also have endogenous determining factors in the individual countries and can be considered as the result of politico-strategic action choices of the national/ local actors. Thus, attempts on the part of national policy actors to restrain political conflicts, which have resulted from a lack of self-determination of regional actors and in some cases ended in deep political crises (Italy, Belgium), were decisive factors for the federalization and regionalization in the unitary countries. These attempts to mediate conflicts in their own country compelled the central governments to grant the regions (in some instances, very extensive) autonomy and scope for politico-democratic and cultural self-determination. The subnational and local actors themselves have also proved to be initiators and promoters of national decentralization policies. This is especially evident in France, where decentralization has been strongly driven and determined by the local notables, as these accumulate national and local political mandates and are thus able to influence the entire state-related political and legislative process.

However, the acting political and administrative actors also represent a crucial explanatory variable for the persistence, inertia and in some cases divergence (divergence within convergence) in the development of administration. Thus, the different NPM paths and the specificity of various NPM reform types (minimizers/modernizers) can essentially be traced back to the significant freedom of choice possessed and exercised by relevant administrative reform actors. This is true too not only for the initiation but also for the prevention of administrative reform measures as well as for the implementation or outperformance or non-fulfilment of European directives. Thus, the classification of the United Kingdom as a minimizer/marketizer can essentially be explained by the market-liberal political ideology of the Thatcher government in interaction with the British policy style of 'elective dictatorship' (Rose, 1982). From the actor-centred standpoint, the virtual absence of veto players within the competitive democratic government system is a key reason why the Thatcher government was able to bring about an unprecedented restructuring of the traditional administrative model.

By contrast, other countries have actor coalitions that have prevented such radical reform measures. This is true in Germany, for example, in the area of internal modernization and in some aspects of privatization. The German federal constitutional context contains numerous veto positions that make the abrupt and radical administrative reform change of the British type difficult. In addition, the liberalization policy on the local government level has been cushioned slightly due to the formation of a supporting coalition that is made up of the federal government, the EU Commission, and local governments and is targeted at protecting the municipal utilities/city works (*Stadtwerke*) from overly competitive pressure. Moreover, electoral considerations of the local political actors (vote-seeking) have fostered municipalization or withdrawal of privatization plans, a fact that has also been encouraged by the new direct-democratic context (local referenda against privatization). Privatization-adverse veto player configurations have also been able to establish themselves in France and Sweden, so that asset privatizations have been implemented either as a compromise and thus delayed or weakened (France) or put on the agenda only in exceptional cases (Sweden).

Historical institutionalism: temporality, path dependence and persistence of administrative culture

As discussed above, the concept of historical institutionalism addresses determining factors whose origins lie in the past and which have a formative effect on the further path and course of administrative reforms. For this reason, micro-developments that can be observed in the administrative systems of the individual countries beneath the convergent macro-trends, evince considerable country-specific differences and divergence. These are deeply entrenched in the historical, path-dependently, lasting particularities of each of the administrative systems and cultures. This is illustrated in the differing degrees of penetration and realization of the modernization message of New Public Management. Thus the private-sector–derived NPM doctrine in the private sector could find relatively easy and rapid entry into the Anglo-Saxon administrative context because of its historically rooted legal and cultural fundamentals. The transfer of private-sector managerial principles to the public sector proved to be smooth within the British public interest culture and common law tradition where the legal and conceptual differentiation between the public and private sector is unknown. In contrast, the acceptance of these principles did not only come later, but also to a considerably lesser degree in Roman-law–based Continental European countries with a legalist administrative tradition. In these countries, the conditionally programmed execution of law is still the predominant administrative activity. Therefore, they are not easily accessible to managerial instruments and output orientation. Similar considerations apply to the classic Continental public service systems, which for the most part were not drastically revamped, but in which economic incentive measures (performance-related pay, target agreements, etc.) instead were often put in place, if only somewhat symbolically.

Institutional path dependencies and legacies are also evident in the vertical relationship between state and local government. Whereas the decentralizing principle of institutional development continued to guide the Swedish administrative reform policy, the historic legacy of the late-authoritarian state of the nineteenth century in Germany appears in the still existing duality of the local government task model, which, being rooted in German-Austrian administrative history, ensures continuous state control over tasks 'delegated' to the local authorities (cf. Wollmann, 1999a, p. 51 et seq., 2010a). Finally, the observed variance of privatization among the countries can be accounted for by their respective administrative and public sector traditions. Despite the (similar) European and international privatization pressure, some countries have embarked on a market-radical course, while others have chosen to set more moderate steps and to pursue rather more conservative strategies. In the consensus-based state tradition of the Swedish 'home of the people', the radical privatizations are difficult to enforce; this is similarly true for the French administrative culture with its socially integrating *service public*. The German administrative tradition of the municipal utilities/city works (*Stadtwerke*) appears to be comparatively resistant and 'fit to survive', as is that of the Italian *municipalizzate*. This confirms the hypothesis of historical institutionalism where the given institutional structures and administrative cultures significantly pre-shape subsequent institutionalization decisions and trajectories.

In summary, it can be argued that institutional arrangements, once emerged and consolidated, display considerable persistence (inertia). This is due to the conflicts and conflict decisions on which, as a rule, institution-building and institution-choice are historically based and whose change requires the renewed efforts of conflict mediation and resolution between the stakeholders. Hence, path dependence frequently has a restrictive and conserving effect, entailing the prolongation, if not the perpetuation of existing institutional trajectories. It thus becomes clear that time is a variable that makes a significant difference in the further course of institutional development. The longer an institution exists, the more difficult it becomes to effect radical change and the more likely that there will be only incremental adjustments or the maintaining of the status quo (Pierson, 2004, p. 147). Institutions that originate later in time and thus are less basic – one might also speak of 'secondary order institutions' (or 'less foundational institutional arrangements'; ibid., p. 150) – build on those developed earlier, so that the former institutions are further cemented.

Leaving a historically staked-out developmental corridor requires from the relevant actors the firm decision to abandon and break out of existing institutional paths, as conceptually highlighted by actor-centred institutionalism. In addition, if and when the external pressure also increases and the actors pick up on this in their agenda setting, the institutional balance starts to become unstable (punctuated equilibrium) and policy windows/windows of opportunity are opened (Kingdon, 1995), which may lead to new critical junctures. The politico-ideological, conceptual and institutional 'revolution', which was effected by the conservative government under Thatcher after 1979, is the internationally most spectacular example in recent history for such a power-politically enforced rupture with path dependency.

6

Future prospects of comparative public administration

LEARNING OBJECTIVES

At the end of this chapter, you should:

- know how to criticize comparative public administration in conceptual, methodological and substantial terms;

- have gained insight into future challenges and tasks of comparative public administration;

- be aware of initial solutions to address the critical points and research gaps.

At the beginning of this book, we argued that comparative public administration encounters a number of problems that account for the limitations in theory and concept formation and the observed lack of 'true' comparisons in public administration. In conclusion, against this backdrop, we wish to address the challenges and perspectives of future comparative public administration and research. For this, the following four aspects appear to be most urgent:

Comparative knowledge about administration

Expanding and enriching the substantial knowledge of the structures, functions and cultural features of different European administrative systems – let alone those outside Europe – is still needed. Conducting comparisons in administrative science still requires 'substantially greater contextual and institutional knowledge' (Peters, 1996, p. 18). In order to explain structures and functions of administrative institutions, highly differentiated knowledge is essential, as subtle differences are of great importance in order to understand administrative systems. However, the attempt to generate such knowledge of contexts, institutions and administrative cultures is not just an empirically elaborate and time-consuming undertaking, but also requires access to the field of investigation – not least in overcoming linguistic and cultural barriers. This may be a prime (research-pragmatic) reason for the lack of 'true' comparisons of public administration which, hence, is the point from which a further expansion of the research field should start. Moreover, the well-known 'travelling problem' has also been mentioned, highlighting the intrinsic problems involved in transferring concepts and terms between different linguistic and cultural contexts. Nonetheless, every comparison requires a venturing of some abstractions because otherwise no comparative statements could meaningfully and fruitfully be made. In this dispute between 'country specialists' on the one hand and 'comparatists' on the other, comparative public administration is called upon to link sufficiently specific contextual and institutional knowledge with the necessary amount of generalization, something that admittedly requires a difficult balancing act. For this, on the one hand, abstractions need to be deduced from the mass of specific empirical data on the countries and cases under investigation in order to be able to generate theory. On the other hand, it is only on the basis of appropriate specific knowledge of these countries that the researchers can meaningfully decide which details can be ignored for purposes of comparison and which particularities and specificities are indispensable for an understanding of the subject matter.

Theory and concept building

What has been claimed for political science research on public administration in general (Benz, 2003; Bogumil and Jann, 2009, p. 302) is all the more true for comparative public administration: a stronger theoretical foundation and concept formation are both desirable and needed for further sharpening the profile of this research direction and for enhancing its recognition in political science. However, because of its trans- and inter-disciplinary orientation and of its international perspective, comparative public administration is faced with even higher barriers than in other comparative sub-disciplines in political science. It was mentioned at the outset that 'administration' as an object of research entails recourse to several scientific sub-disciplines (political science, law, economics, history, sociology and psychology) and thus demands the integration of these various disciplinary approaches. This in turn makes concept formation and theory building more difficult and can impede the attempt to find the demarcation between and consolidation of knowledge and theory. In Chapter 2, Section 2.3, we showed that neo-institutionalism has proved to be a useful starting point for honing the theoretical profile of comparative public administration. 'Institutions' offer a trans-disciplinary bridge between the different administrative science-oriented sub-disciplines and can serve as a type of unifying bracket. Moreover, linking policy research and institutional research (cf. Jann, 2001) holds a conceptual and empirical potential that can be used for further theory formation in comparative public administration. For this, however, the call would have to be heeded to pursue a stronger policy orientation and to expand the hitherto prevalent more general view on administrative reforms by shifting the analytical attention to concrete task areas and specific sectors of public administration. Finally, the various comparative research strands in administrative science (see Chapter 2, Section 2.1) should be linked in order to generate mutual synergy effects for further theory formation (cf. Jann, 2009). So far, the researchers in the different fields, for example in comparative local government, in civil service and in administrative elites or Europeanization research, still take too little notice of each other. However, as their empirical perceptions are focused on and restricted to their respective specific levels or areas of the administrative system (EU, ministerial administration, local government), the scope of their conclusions and theories is bound to remain limited. In light of this, it has been rightly criticized that comparative administration research is too fragmented in terms of content and geographical coverage (for instance between 'Western comparative public administration' and 'non-Western/development CPA'; cf. Raadschelders, 2011, p. 832) as well as in terms of methods. Thus, for the further conceptual and theoretical development in comparative public administration a stronger exchange between the different research fields and researchers is urgently needed. For this reason, the dialogue and exchange between researchers and practitioners in public administration should be intensified.

Raising the methodological profile

Another significant task of comparative public administration lies in the development of methods. Thus, it is crucial to conceptualize and to empirically test robust indicators for comparative analyses. Despite the broad discussion that has been triggered by the New Public Management (NPM)-inspired reforms on output-based performance indicators and output there are still not enough indicators that can lend themselves to cross-country, cross-policy and cross-sector comparisons. The conceptual formation and empirical validation of indicators, the collection of empirical data and the set-up of databases that are reliable, internationally comparable and accessible needs to become a stronger focus of comparative public administration.

However, this should not be misunderstood as an unqualified plea for a primarily quantitative approach of comparative public administration (CPA).

Quite the contrary, because of its very subject matter, CPA should, in our view, stand out from the mainstream of increasingly quantifying empirical social science and political science research. Administrative comparisons depend on a proximity to the object of investigation, as they are not just concerned with, as it were, static system descriptions (such as in 'classic' comparative government) or with statistically significant statements about particular behavioural dispositions (such as in political culture research), but rather with concrete institutional changes, complex transformations and transition processes and 'real acts' within organizations. The questions asked by empirical administration research are therefore regularly confronted by an investigative situation that can be described by the rule-of-thumb of 'many variables, few cases'. Research designs that are contingent on quantitative data based on many cases and few variables (large-n design, that is, statistical procedures, but also quasi-experiments) are often only of limited use for comparisons in public administration and, hence, as a rule, case studies are the preferred method. The well-known methodological limits of single-case studies (in particular their restricted generalizability) can, however, be overcome by conducting, when and where possible, multiple comparative case studies. In doing so, a methodologically sound and analytically productive approximation to a 'quasi-experimental' research design can be achieved. The potential of such an approach for contributing to the validation of causal statements can be therefore deemed the more promising as the more strongly it is supported by hypotheses that are theoretically derived and empirically informed (on the basis of secondary studies).

Following this road, the methodological dialectic could be reached and met, which, in our view and conviction, should be key to comparative public administration, and which Fritz Morstein-Marx, the venerable pace-setter of CPA, years ago admirably formulated as the methodological imperative that the researcher 'is held to return, time and again, from the thin air of generalizations to the reinvigorating proximity of the individual circumstances in the life of administration because only by finding out what really is one can take a trustworthy path back to generalization' (Morstein-Marx, 1965, p. 117). Or, to turn it into a research-practical call and advice: 'scholars should use multi-method approaches instead of only talking about them' (Raadschelders, 2011, p. 833).

Administrative performance and effects of reforms

The comparative analysis of different administrative models and the effects of administrative reforms, hence evaluative administrative research, are still conceptually, methodologically and empirically underdeveloped, although attempts are still being made to redress this problem (Jreisat, 2011, p. 834). Nonetheless, in the national and international context, systematic impact analyses regarding development and outcome of administrative reforms and performance comparisons of various administrative reforms remain a rarity. This deficiency is all the more surprising as the creation of transparency of effects, costs and benefits of administrative actions is a core message of administrative modernization. Therefore, the question of how different administrative configurations and institutionalization solutions affect administrative performance, in other words, the evaluation focus, rates high on the agenda of future research in comparative public administration. For this reason, the task of CPA should be to initiate and conduct an empirically informed discourse about the performance of administration and the effectiveness of administrative policy from a country-comparative perspective, including evaluative analyses of the success and failure of administrative reforms (ibid.). Hereby, the plurality of evaluation criteria of administrative action (legality, efficiency, democratic legitimacy, professional quality, etc.) should be taken into account. These, unfortunately, are often weighted differently in the individual national and local administrative contexts and often cannot be simultaneously optimized (trade off). Moreover, such evaluative analyses should also consider the transaction costs of changes in order to reach a realistic cost–benefit balance of administrative reforms (Kuhlmann and Wollmann, 2006). In sum, extending the focus of CPA on the evaluation of administrative reforms will be of great importance as this will, for one, add a hitherto largely ignored dimension to the research agenda. Second, it will generate information that is empirically grounded on the strengths and weaknesses of different administrative models, reform approaches and measures, thus providing knowledge that can be used by political and administrative actors in the European, national and subnational contexts in their decision-making on administrative reforms.

Recommended reading

Baldersheim, H. and L.E. Rose (eds) (2010), *Territorial Choice. The Politics of Boundaries and Borders,* **Basingstoke: Palgrave Macmillan**
This anthology gives an overview of the territorial organization of the local levels in Europe. Based on 11 country studies, the differences regarding the number and size of local territorial bodies in the individual countries are shown. The focus of the book is not so much to show the advantages and disadvantages of large or small territorial units, but rather to indicate the territorial policies themselves, that is, the various strategies and their outcomes in the individual countries as well as the search for explanations for implemented or failed territorial reforms. At the end of the volume, the editors summarize the results in a typology comprising five cases.

Chandler, J.A. (ed.) (2000), *Comparative Public Administration,* **New York/London: Routledge**
This anthology offers the reader an introduction to the public administration and management systems of a range of democratic countries. This includes a look at Western European countries, the United States of America and Japan and their administrative systems in separate country chapters with a largely uniform analysis pattern. In this way, the authors carve out commonalities and differences between the individual systems, whereby particular emphasis is placed on treatises of the administration-shaping effects of globalization processes and international developments. In addition, the influence of political actors and public opinion on the structures and actions of public administration in the examined countries is analysed.

Christensen, T. and P. Laegreid (eds) (2011), *The Ashgate Research Companion to New Public Management,* **Farnham: Ashgate**
This book provides an up-to-date and comprehensive overview of the dominant reform trend of New Public Management (NPM). To begin with, the concept of NPM is illustrated and discussed. Further, there is an analysis of the convergence and divergence in the reform process between various countries as well as individual contributions that provide a closer examination of individual policy areas and NPM components. Finally, the difficult question of the effects and implications of NPM is explored in depth and building on this, an outlook of future developments in public administration.

Derlien, H.-U. and B.G. Peters (eds) (2009), *The State at Work,* **volume 1, Cheltenham, UK and Northampton, MA, USA: Edward Elgar Publishing**

This anthology by Derlien and Peters addresses the public service in ten countries, whereby Anglo-American as well as European countries are represented. The topic of the individual country chapters is the development of employment in the public service, the distribution of employees to the individual administration levels, but also the composition and recruitment of administrative personnel. At the same time, the share of personnel in the individual policy areas is analysed and the influences of reform trends, such as New Public Management, are looked at in detail. By means of the analysis of public employment, individual reform trends, such as decentralization and privatization, are made visible by means of relevant personnel development tendencies in the administration.

Dyson, K.H.F. (1980), *The State Tradition in Western Europe,* **Oxford: Robertson, new (paperback) edition 2010, European Consortium for Political Research (ECPR) Press**

In this volume, the conceptions of state and aetiological relationships of various administrative traditions in Western Europe are analysed. In this, the focus is first on the British and Continental European conception of state. Second, the author addressed the differences between the German and French conceptions of statehood. In this, the individual chapters chart the historical development, different theoretical explanations as well as normative and analytic approaches to state tradition. The final chapter is dedicated to the preconditions for democratic order and statehood. The book by Dyson remains indispensable for a state-theoretic access to administrative traditions in Western Europe.

Goldsmith, M.J. and E.C. Page (2010), *Changing Government Relations in Europe. From Localism to Intergovernmentalism,* **London/New York: Routledge**

European integration entailed significant changes for the administrative systems of the various European countries. This anthology offers a comparative investigation of the most recent developments in different Eastern and Western European countries from Belgium to Hungary. A particular focus is on the meaning of these changes for the relations between local, national and supranational levels. The publication is based on the 1987 volume by the same editors *Central and Local Government Relations* in Western European nations, which can be considered a trailblazer for comparative research on intergovernmental relations between state and subnational territorial bodies.

Heady, F. (2001), *Public Administration. A Comparative Perspective,* **Boca Raton, FL: CRC Press**
Already in its sixth edition, this important reference work of comparative public administration compares national administrative systems, whereby the current edition from 2001 contains an update with regard to the administrative development in the former Soviet Union, Eastern European countries and other nascent democracies. The author's intention is to initially describe as many facets as possible of the highly disparate national administrative systems. Subsequently, country-specific particularities of the bureaucracies are examined in more detail and finally, the relationship between national bureaucracy and the type of political regime is analysed, in order to explain the crucial differences between the countries. The book's strength is not least in the examination of administrative and political systems on all continents, and in the laying down of conceptional foundations for comparative public administration.

John, P. (2001), *Local Government in Western Europe,* **London: Sage**
This work is still of major relevance for comparative local research. Beginning with a classic typology of local research, the monograph focuses on development trends, such as New Public Management, Europeanization, regionalization and democracy reform, on the local level. The book's central hypothesis is that these reform trends lead to a transition from local government to local governance. By structuring according to topic areas, the book manages to thematically compare the individual Western European countries and to carve out their commonalities and differences. This work is very suitable as an introduction to local government systems of Western European countries and their comparative discussion.

Kuhlmann, S. (2009), *Politik- und Verwaltungsreform in Kontinentaleuropa. Subnationaler Institutionenwandel im deutsch-französischen Vergleich* **[Policy and Public Administration Reform in Continental Europe. Subnational Institutional Change in Franco-German Comparison], Baden-Baden: Nomos**
This monograph examines the subnational administration as well as political and administrative reform in Germany and France. It thus places the classic Continental European nations, which are often neglected in comparative administration research, in the focus of the analysis. The study is dedicated to four fields of subnational institutional policy: decentralization and territorial reform, privatization, management reform as well as policy and democracy reform. It should be emphasized that not only institutional change, but also the reform effects and further-reaching effects are comparatively considered. As a result, the book provides a comprehensive treatise of the commonalities

and differences of the most recent administrative and political reforms in a German-French comparison.

Loughlin, J., F. Hendriks and A. Lidström (eds) (2010), *The Oxford Handbook of Local and Regional Democracy in Europe,* **Oxford: Oxford University Press**
This anthology, which is issued as part of the renowned Oxford Handbook Series, provides an important contribution for the documentation of local and regional democracy in Europe. The strengths of the volume lie in the comprehensive selection of countries, which includes all 27 member states of the European Union as well as Norway and Switzerland. The presentation of local democracy and direct-democratic reforms is embedded within the individual country chapters into the description of the subnational administration structure, offering the reader a good overview of the position of the local level in the inter-governmental system of the respective country. In addition, the final chapter summarizes the results transnationally in a systematic fashion.

Norton, A. (1994), *International Handbook of Local and Regional Government. A Comparative Analysis of Advanced Democracies,* **Aldershot, UK and Brookfield, VT, USA: Edward Elgar Publishing**
The work published by Alan Norton in 1994 has long since become a 'classic' and is still indispensable for comparative studies and research on local government systems. The book contains ten country chapters, which (following a uniform structure) focus on a remarkably 'global' consideration of the USA, Canada and Japan in addition to important European countries. Within the country chapters, the knowledgeable and insightful sections on 'history and traditions' as well as 'concepts and values' should not least of all be emphasized. The detailed introductory as well as the summarizing chapter is permeated by the author's impressive comparative knowledge of the ten countries examined; this makes the book an indispensable reference work.

Painter, M. and B.G. Peters (eds) (2010), *Tradition and Public Administration,* **Basingstoke: Palgrave Macmillan**
Administrative systems are permanently subject to, in some instances, massive change. The international developments of the last few years up to globalization, Europeanization or also New Public Management are potential factors for the rapid alignment or at least convergence of individual countries' public administration systems. In this volume on administrative traditions, the authors pursue this conjecture and ask the question whether particular administrative models, traditions and particularities will be retained despite the standardization pressure or how they will adapt to external changes. In

this, a range of groups of administrative traditions is introduced in the beginning. Then, a detailed analysis of administrative traditions is made by means of case studies. Finally, the effects of existing administrative traditions on current reform attempts are discussed in detail.

Peters, B.G. and J. Pierre (eds) (2004), *Politicization of the Civil Service in Comparative Perspective. The Quest for Control,* **London: Routledge**
In this volume, the public service systems and the various degrees of politicization of civil service bureaucracy are presented in 12 country cases. In their analyses, the authors show the effects of varying forms and degrees of politicization on the function and organization of ministerial administrations. The type and scope of politicization of the public administration are used to explain the processes and structures in the ministerial authorities of the individual countries. It is shown how political and administrative actors interact and how this impacts the different states of development, such as intensity of administrative reforms (e.g., NPM).

Peters, B.G. (2009), *The Politics of Bureaucracy. An Introduction to Comparative Public Administration,* **6th edition, London: Routledge**
This book by Peters has already run into its sixth edition at Routledge, illustrating its outstanding importance for comparative administration research. The publication deals with all key aspects of comparative administration research; beginning with the various administrative cultures, the personnel and organization of administration as well as the role and status of bureaucracy in the political process. Moreover, the crucial reform trends in the public sector are described. With its informative and never overladen presentation of different administration aspects from a comparative perspective, this book is to be recommended as an English-language introduction to comparative administration research.

Pollitt, C. and G. Bouckaert (2011), *Public Management Reform. A Comparative Analysis – New Public Management, Governance, and the Neo-Weberian State,* **3rd edition, Oxford: Oxford University Press**
This publication, which is now into its third edition, is already a 'classic' of comparative administration science. Its status as such is due to the comprehensive and systematic examination of (New) Public Management reforms from a country comparative perspective. The book deals with the dominant reform concepts and their dissemination during the last three decades, develops a model to explain public management reforms and draws attention to the importance of different administrative-cultural traditions in the introduction, implementation and effects of management reforms. In addition, the limits, paradoxes and contradictions of such reform approaches are

addressed. The book concludes in the appendix with a summary of the individual country profiles.

Raadschelders, J.C.N., T.A.J. Toonen and F.M. van der Meer (eds) (2007), *Comparative Civil Service Systems in the 21st Century*, Basingstoke: Palgrave Macmillan

This volume introduces further results from the comparative project initiated in 1990 by an international team of researchers and authors, who deal with comparative civil service systems in Africa, Asia, Europe and North America as well as Australasia. The contributions compiled in the volume are concerned with the development of the public service from a country-comparative perspective with a special focus on aspects of globalization, performance and legitimacy. Further, the influence of subnational levels on the public service and varying degrees of legal regulation are used to illuminate the differences between national public service systems.

Schnapp, K.-U. (2004), *Ministerialbürokratien in westlichen Demokratien. Eine vergleichende Analyse* [Ministerial Bureaucracies in Western Democracies: A Comparative Analysis], Opladen: Leske + Budrich

Civil service bureaucracies are indispensable functional components of democratic government systems and are directly involved in political formation processes. In his study, the author is concerned with the question of how and to what degree civil service bureaucracies can influence political decision-making processes. With a view to structural features of 21 Western countries, the impact potential of civil service bureaucracies is illuminated in the pre-political, political and implementation phase. In his work, he carves out three models of potential political influence of bureaucracies in interaction with political actors, which take place in the different phases of political processes.

Van der Meer, F.M. (ed.) (2011), *Civil Service Systems in Western Europe*, Cheltenham, UK and Northampton, MA, USA: Edward Elgar Publishing

The Dutch author Frits M. van der Meer provides a compilation of contributions by distinguished Western European authors who report on the structure and development of the public service in their country of origin. The individual contributions deal with the history of the public service, its structure and integration into the politico-social environment as well as with the reform and change of the respective civil service systems. The treatment of various Western European countries enables the identification of commonalities as well as differences among the civil services in Western Europe, which can be traced back to joint roots on the one hand and diverging administrative traditions and national particularities on the other.

Wollmann, H. (2008), *Reformen in Kommunalpolitik und -verwaltung. England, Schweden, Deutschland und Frankreich im Vergleich* [**Reforms in Local Politics and Administration: England, Sweden, France and Germany Compared**], **Wiesbaden: VS Verlag für Sozialwissenschaften**
This book provides a comparative presentation of the political and administrative structures of local governments and their reforms in England, Sweden, France and Germany. In this, the key institutional structures (inter alia, territorial structure, local democracy, politico-administrative leadership, administration and personnel, finances) are pared out and dealt with in detail using the example of two central local government task areas (local social policy and planning). A comparative ranking of the functional strength and ability of four selected local government systems is provided as a summary. The book is suitable as an up-to-date comparative introduction in local government systems of the four countries examined.

Wollmann, H. and G. Marcou (eds) (2010), *The Provision of Public Services in Europe. Between State, Local Government and Market,* **Cheltenham, UK and Northampton, MA, USA: Edward Elgar Publishing**
This anthology is aimed at providing a comparative analysis of the provision of social/public services in a wide range of relevant service areas (youth welfare, care of the elderly, health, waste removal, energy and water supply) in the United Kingdom, France, Italy, Germany and Norway. The contributions, which have been compiled and written by experts from the respective countries, are guided by the question of the changes experienced by organizational forms of service provision (from state/local government to the private sector and 'back'?) during the course of the historical development and whether this has resulted in a convergence or divergence between the countries (and service sectors). The anthology provides an up-to-date comparative insight into the development of the areas of policy and action discussed.

References

Aberbach, J.D., R.D. Putnam and B.A. Rockman (1981), *Bureaucrats and Politicians in Western Democracies*, Cambridge, MA: Harvard University Press.

Adler, E. and P.M. Haas (1992), 'Conclusion. Epistemic communities, world order, and the creation of a reflective research program', *International Organization*, **46**(1), 367–90.

Alam, M.M. (1998), *Public Personnel Policy in Europe. A Comparative Analysis of Seven European Countries*, Helsinki: Ministry of Finance.

Alba, A. (1998), 'Re-employment probabilities of young workers in Spain', *Investigaciones Económicas*, **22**(2), 201–24.

Alba, C. and C. Navarro (2003), 'Twenty-five years of democratic government in Spain', in N. Kersting and A. Vetter (eds), *Reforming Local Government in Europe*, Opladen: Leske + Budrich, pp. 197–21.

Alesina, A. and E. Spolarole (2003), *The Size of Nations*, Cambridge, MA: MIT Press.

Andrews, C. and M. De Vries (2007), 'High expectations, varying outcomes. Decentralization and participation in Brazil, Japan, Russia and Sweden', *International Review of Administrative Sciences*, **73**(3), 424–51.

Archambault, E. (1997), *The Nonprofit Sector in France*, Manchester and New York: Manchester University Press.

Arndt, C. (2008), 'The politics of governance ratings', *International Public Management Journal*, **11**(3), 1–23.

Ashford, D.E. (1982), *British Dogmatism and French Pragmatism. Central–Local Policymaking in the Welfare State*, London: George Allen & Unwin.

Askim, J., A.L. Fimreite, A. Mosley and L.H. Pedersen (2011), 'One stop shop for social welfare. The adaption of an organizational form in three countries', *Public Administration*, **89**(4) 1451–68.

Association of Public Service Excellence (APSE) (2011), 'UNISON insourcing update. The value of returning local authority services in-house in an era of budget constraints', last accessed 9 March 2014 at https://www.unison.org.uk/upload/sharepoint/On%20line%20 Catalogue/20122.pdf.

Auer, A., C. Demmke and R. Polet (1996), *Civil Service in the Europe of Fifteen. Current Situation and Prospects*, Maastricht: EIPA.

Baar, K.K. (2001), 'Open competition, transparency, and impartiality in local government contracting out of public services', in T.M. Horvath and G. Peteri (eds), *Navigation to the Market. Regulation and Competition in Local Utilities in Central and Eastern Europe*, Budapest: Open Society Institute, pp. 99–140.

Bach, S. and D. Winchester (2003), 'Industrial relations in the public sector', in P. Edwards (ed.), *Industrial Relations. Theory and Practice*, 2nd edition, Oxford, UK: Blackwell, pp. 285–312.

Bach, T. and W. Jann (2010), 'Animals in the administrative zoo. Organizational change and agency autonomy in Germany', *International Review of Administrative Sciences*, **76**(3), 443–68.

Bach, T., J. Fleischer and T. Hustedt (2010), *Organisation und Steuerung zentralstaatlicher Behörden. Agenturen im westeuropäischen Vergleich* [Organization and Control of the Central Government Agencies in Western European Comparison], Berlin: Edition Sigma.

Bäck, H., H. Heinelt and A. Magnier (eds) (2006), *The European Mayor*, Wiesbaden: Springer.

Baldersheim, H. and L.E. Rose (2010a), 'Territorial choice. Rescaling governance in European states', in H. Baldersheim and L.E. Rose (eds), *Territorial Choice*, Basingstoke: Palgrave Macmillan, pp. 1–20.

Baldersheim, H. and L.E. Rose (2010b), 'A comparative analysis of territorial choice in Europe – conclusions', in H. Baldersheim and L.E. Rose (eds), *Territorial Choice*, Basingstoke: Palgrave Macmillan, pp. 234–59.

Baldersheim, H. and L.E. Rose (eds) (2010c), *Territorial Choice*, Basingstoke: Palgrave Macmillan.

Baldersheim, H., M. Illner, A. Offerdal, L.E. Rose and P. Swianiewicz (eds) (1996), *Local Democracy and the Processes of Transformation in East-Central Europe*, Boulder, CO: Westview Press.

Banner, G. (2007), 'Leistungstransparenz durch interkommunalen Haushaltsvergleich. Der Kommunalindex für Wirtschaftlichkeit (KIWI)' [Performance transparency through inter-municipal budget comparison. The local index for efficiency (KIWI)], in M. Brüggemeier, R. Schauer and K. Schedler (eds), *Controlling und Performance Management im öffentlichen Sektor* [Controlling and Performance Management in the Public Sector], Bern: Haupt, pp. 101–9.

Bardhan, P. and D. Mookherjee (2006), 'Decentralization, corruption and government account-ability. An overview', in S. Rose-Ackerman (ed.), *International Handbook on the Economics of Corruption*, Cheltenham, UK and Northampton, MA, USA: Edward Elgar Publishing, pp. 161–88.

Basle, M. (2003), 'Les pratiques évaluatives des villes de plus de 50 000 habitants' [Evaluation practices of cities of over 50 000 inhabitants], *Pouvoirs Locaux*, **57**(2), 42–4.

Bastida, B. and B. Benito (2007), 'Central government budget practices and transparency. An international comparison', *Public Administration*, **85**(3), 667–716.

Batt, J. (1991), *East Central Europe From Reform to Transformation*, London: Royal Institute of International Affairs.

Bauer, M., J. Bogumil, C. Knill, F. Ebinger, S. Krapf and K. Reißig (2007), *Modernisierung der Umweltverwaltung. Reformstrategien und Effekte in den Bundesländern* [Modernization of Environmental Management. Reform Strategies and Effects in the federal states/Länder], Berlin: Edition Sigma.

Beckmann, J. (2008), 'Die Entkernung des Service Public in Frankreich' [The gutting of the public service in France], in H.-J. Bieling, C. Deckwirth and S. Schmalz (eds) (2008), *Liberalisierung und Privatisierung in Europa. Die Reorganisation der öffentlichen Infrastruktur in der Europäischen Union* [Liberalization and Privatization in Europe. The Reorganization of the Public Infrastructure in the EU]. Münster: Westfälisches.

Behnke, N. (2010), 'Politische Dezentralisierung und administrative Dekonzentration in Italien' [Political decentralization and administrative deconcentration in Italy], in J. Bogumil and S. Kuhlmann (eds), *Kommunale Aufgabenwahrnehmung im Wandel. Kommunalisierung, Regionalisierung und Territorialreform in Deutschland und Europa* [Local Government Task Performance in Transition: Municipalization, Regionalization and Territorial Reform in Germany and Europe], Wiesbaden: VS Verlag für Sozialwissenschaften, pp. 301–24.

Bekke, H.A.G.M. and F.M. Van der Meer (eds) (2000), *Civil Service Systems in Western Europe*, Cheltenham, UK and Northampton, MA, USA: Edward Elgar Publishing.

Bekke, H.A.G.M., J.L. Perry and T.A.J. Toonen (eds) (1996), *Civil Service Systems in Comparative Perspective*, Bloomington, IN: Indiana University Press.

Beksta, A. and A. Petkevicius (2000), 'Local government in Lithuania', in T.M. Horváth (ed.), *Decentralization. Experiments and Reforms*, Budapest: Open Society Institute, pp. 165–217.

Bel, G. and M. Warner (2008), 'Does privatization of solid waste and water services reduce costs?', *Resources, Conservation and Recycling*, **52**, 1337–48.

Bel, G., X. Fegeda and M.E. Warner (2010), 'Is private production of public services cheaper than public production? A meta-regression analysis of solid waste and water services', *Journal of Policy Analysis and Management*, **29**(3), 553–77.

Benedetti, A. (1996), 'Le privatizzazioni in Italia' [Privatization in Italy]. *Quaderni del pluralismo*, **1**, 29–78.

Bennett, R. (ed.) (1989), *Territory and Administration in Europe*, London and New York: Pinter.

Benz, A. (2002), 'Die territoriale Dimension von Verwaltung' [The territorial dimension of administration], in K. König (ed.), *Deutsche Verwaltung an der Wende zum 21. Jahrhundert* [German Administration at the Turn of the 21st Century], Baden-Baden: Nomos, pp. 207–28.

Benz, A. (2003), 'Status und Perspektiven der politikwissenschaftlichen Verwaltungsforschung' [Status and perspectives of political science-guided adminstration research], *Die Verwaltung*, **36**(3), 361–88.

Benz, A. (2004a), 'Path-dependent institutions and strategic veto players: national parliaments in the European Union', *West European Politics*, **27**(5), 875–900.

Benz, A. (2004b), 'Institutionentheorie und Institutionenpolitik' [Institutional theory and institution policy], in A. Benz, H. Siedentopf and K.-P. Sommermann (eds), *Institutionenwandel in Regierung und Verwaltung. Festschrift für Klaus König zum 70. Geburtstag* [Institutional Change in Government and Administration. In Honour of Klaus König's 70th Birthday], Berlin: Duncker & Humblot, pp. 19–31.

Benz, A., F.W. Scharpf and R. Zintl (1992), *Horizontale Politikverflechtung. Zur Theorie von Verhandlungssystemen* [Horizontal Policy Interweaving. On the Theory of Negotiation Systems], Frankfurt a.M. and New York: Campus Verlag.

Bertelsmann Stiftung (2010), 'Leistungsvergleiche in der öffentlichen Verwaltung. Aktionsplan zur Umsetzung von Art. 91d' [Benchmarking in public administration. Action plan for the implementation of Article 91d of the Basic Law], unpublished.

Berti, L. (1998), *Affari di fine secolo. Le privatizzazioni in Italia* [Business at the End of the Century: Privatization in Italy], Rome: Ediesse.

Bieling, H.-J., C. Deckwirth and S. Schmalz (eds) (2008), *Liberalisierung und Privatisierung in Europa. Die Reorganisation der öffentlichen Infrastruktur in der Europäischen Union* [Liberalization and Privatization in Europe. The Reorganization of the Public Infrastructure in the EU], Münster: Westfälisches.

Blauberger, M. and A.E. Töller (2011), 'Competition policy', in M. Knodt and H. Heinelt (eds), *Policy Fields in the European Multi-level System. Instruments and Strategies of European Governance*, Baden-Baden: Nomos, pp. 123–52.

Bobbio, L. (2005), 'Italy. "After the storm"', in B. Denters and L.E. Rose (eds), *Comparing Local Governance. Trends and Developments*, Basingstoke: Palgrave Macmillan, pp. 29–46.

Bogumil, J. (2001), *Modernisierung lokaler Politik. Kommunale Entscheidungsprozesse im Spannungsfeld zwischen Parteienwettbewerb, Verhandlungszwängen und Ökonomisierung* [Modernization of Local Politics. Municipal Decision-making Processes in the Tension Between Party Competition, Negotiation Constraints and Economization], Baden-Baden: Nomos.

Bogumil, J. and F. Ebinger (2005), *Die Große Verwaltungsstrukturreform in Baden-Württemberg* [The Big Reform of Administrative Structures in Baden-Württemberg], Ibbenbüren: ICD.

Bogumil, J. and S. Grohs (2010), 'Möglichkeiten und Grenzen von Regionalverwaltungen' [Possibilities and limits of regional governments], in J. Bogumil and S. Kuhlmann (eds), *Kommunale Aufgabenwahrnehmung im Wandel. Kommunalisierung, Regionalisierung und Territorialreform in Deutschland und Europa* [Local Government Task Performance in

Transition: Municipalization, Regionalization and Territorial Reform in Germany and Europe], Wiesbaden: VS Verlag für Sozialwissenschaften, pp. 89–110.

Bogumil, J. and L. Holtkamp (2002), 'Liberalisierung und Privatisierung kommunaler Aufgaben – Auswirkungen auf das kommunale Entscheidungssystem' [Liberalization and privatization of municipal tasks – impact on the municipal decision-making] in J. Libbe, S. Tomerius and J.-H. Trapp (eds), *Liberalisierung und Privatisierung kommunaler Aufgabenerfüllung. Soziale und umweltpolitische Perspektiven im Zeichen des Wettbewerbs* [Liberalization and Privatization of the Provision of Municipal Services. Social and Environmental Perspectives in the Light of Competition], Berlin: German Institute of Urban Affairs, pp. 71–87.

Bogumil, J. and L. Holtkamp (2013), *Kommunalpolitik und Kommunalverwaltung. Eine praxisorientierte Einführung* [Local Politics and Local Government. A Practice-oriented Introduction], Bonn: Bpb.

Bogumil, J. and W. Jann (2009), *Verwaltung und Verwaltungswissenschaft in Deutschland. Einführung in die Verwaltungswissenschaft* [Public Administration and Adminstrative Science in Germany: Introduction to Administrative Science], 2nd revised edition, Wiesbaden: VS Verlag für Sozialwissenschaften.

Bogumil, J. and S. Kottmann (2006) 'Verwaltungsstrukturreform – die Abschaffung der Bezirksregierungen in Niedersachsen' [Administrative structure reform – the abolition of district governments in Lower Saxony], *Schriftenreihe der Stiftung Westfalen-Initiative*, **11**, Ibbenbüren: IVD.

Bogumil, J. and S. Kuhlmann (2007), 'Public servants at sub-national and local levels of government. A British-German-French comparison', in J.C.N. Raadschelders, T.A.J. Toonen and F.M. van der Meer (eds), *Comparative Civil Service Systems in the 21st Century*, Basingstoke: Palgrave Macmillan, pp. 137–51.

Bogumil, J. and J. Schmid (2001), *Politik in Organisationen. Organisationstheoretische Ansätze und praxisbezogene Anwendungsbeispiel* [Politics in Organizations. Organization Theoretical Approaches and Practice-oriented Application Examples], Opladen: Leske + Budrich.

Bogumil, J., S. Grohs, S. Kuhlmann and A. Ohm (2007), *Zehn Jahre Neues Steuerungsmodell. Eine Bilanz kommunaler Verwaltungsmodernisierung* [Ten Years of the New Steering Model. An Assessment of Local Government Modernization], Berlin: Edition Sigma.

Bönker, F., M. Hill and A. Marzanati (2010), 'Towards marketization and centralization? The changing role of local government in long-term care in England, France, Germany and Italy', in H. Wollmann and G. Marcou (eds), *The Provision of Public Services in Europe. State, Local Government and Market*, Cheltenham, UK and Northampton, MA, USA: Edward Elgar Publishing, pp. 97–119.

Bordonneau, M.-A., G. Canneva, G. Orange and D. Gambier (2010), 'Le changement de mode de gestion des services d'eau' [The change of management mode for water services], in *Droit et Gestion des Collectivités Territoriales. Annuaire 2010* [Law and Management of Local Authorities. Yearbook 2010], Paris: GRALE, pp. 131–47.

Borraz, O. and P. Le Galès (2005), 'France. The inter-municipal revolution', in B. Denters and L.E. Rose (eds), *Comparing Local Governance. Trends and Developments*, Basingstoke: Palgrave Macmillan, pp. 12–28.

Bossaert, D. and C. Demmke (2002), *Der öffentliche Dienst in den Beitrittsstaaten* [The Civil Service in the Accession Countries], Maastricht: EIPA.

Bouckaert, G. (2006), 'Auf dem Weg zu einer Neo-Weberianischen Verwaltung. New Public Management im internationalen Vergleich' [Towards a Neo-Weberian administration. New Public Management in international comparison], in J. Bogumil, W. Jann and F. Nullmeier (eds), *Politik und Verwaltung. PVS-Sonderheft* [Politics and Administration. PVS Special Issue], **37**, Wiesbaden: VS Verlag für Sozialwissenschaften, pp. 354–72.

Bouckaert, G. and J. Halligan (2008) *Managing Performance. International Comparisons*, New York: Routledge.

Bouckaert, G. and W. van de Donk (eds) (2010), *The European Group for Public Administration (1975–2010). Perspectives for the Future*, Brussels: Bruylant.

Bouckaert, G., B.G. Peters and K. Verhoest (2010), *The Coordination of Public Sector Organizations. Shifting Patterns of Public Management*, Basingstoke: Palgrave Macmillan.

Boyne, C.A., C. Farrell, J. Law, M. Powell and R. Walker (2003), *Evaluating Public Management Reform: Principles and Practice*, Buckingham: Open University Press.

Brändli-Traffelet, S. (2004), 'Verwaltung des Sonderfalles. Plädoyer für eine Verwaltungskulturgeschichte der Schweiz' [Administration in the special case. Plea for a history of the administrative culture of Switzerland], *Revue Suisse d'histoire*, **54**(1), 79–89.

Briški, A. (2003), 'Public services on the local and regional level. Workshop summary: 'Reforms of Public Services Experiences of Municipalities and Regions in South-East Europe', Zagreb, pp. 93–8.

Brunsson, N. (1989), *The Organization of Hypocrisy. Talk, Decision and Actions in Organizations*, Chichester: Wiley.

Brunazzo, M. (2010), 'Italian regionalism. A semi-federation is taking shape – or is it?', in H. Baldersheim and L.E. Rose (eds), *Territorial Choice*, Basingstoke: Palgrave Macmillan, pp. 180–96.

Brusis, M. (2010), 'Regionalisierung in Mittel- und Osteuropa. Ursachen, Formen und Effekte' [Regionalization in Central and Eastern Europe. Causes, forms and effects], in J. Bogumil and S. Kuhlmann (eds), *Kommunale Aufgabenwahrnehmung im Wandel. Kommunalisierung, Regionalisierung und Territorialreform in Deutschland und Europa* [Local Government Task Performance in Transition: Municipalization, Regionalization and Territorial Reform in Germany and Europe], Wiesbaden: VS Verlag für Sozialwissenschaften, pp. 325–49.

Bull, H.P. (2008), 'Kommunale Gebiets- und Funktionalreform – aktuelle Entwicklung und grundsätzliche Bedeutung' [Local level territorial and functional reform – current development and importance], *der moderne staat* (dms), **1**(3), 285–302.

Bull, M. (2007), 'The constitutional referendum of June 2006. End of the "Great Reform" but not of reform itself', in J.-L. Briquet and A. Mastropaolo (eds), *Italian Politics. The Centre-Left's Poisoned Victory*, Vol. 22, New York and Oxford, UK: Berghahn Books, pp. 99–118.

Bulpitt, J. (1983), *Territory and Power in the United Kingdom. An Interpretation*, Manchester: Manchester University Press.

Bundesverband der deutschen Gas- und Wasserwirtschaft (BGW) 2005, *Branchenbild der deutschen Wasserwirtschaft 2005* [Profile of the German Water Sector 2005], last accessed 10 March 2010 at http://www.wasserverbandstag.de/main/pdfs/Branchenbild_2005_Bildschirmdarstellung_endg.pdf.

Burgi, M. (2009), 'Kommunalisierung als gestaltungsbedürftiger Wandel von Staatlichkeit und von Selbstverwaltung' [Municipalization as a design requiring transformation of the state and of local self-government], *Die Verwaltung*, **42**(2), 155–77.

Burgi, M. (2010), 'Kommunalisierung staatlicher Aufgaben – Möglichkeiten, Grenzen und Folgefragen aus rechtlicher Sicht' [Municipalization of State functions – possibilities, limitations and follow-up issues from a legal perspective], in J. Bogumil and S. Kuhlmann (eds), *Kommunale Aufgabenwahrnehmung im Wandel. Kommunalisierung, Regionalisierung und Territorialreform in Deutschland und Europa* [Local Government Task Performance in Transition: Municipalization, Regionalization and Territorial Reform in Germany and Europe], Wiesbaden: VS Verlag für Sozialwissenschaften, pp. 23–46.

Burns, T., T. Baumgartner and P. Deville (1985), *Man, Decisions, Society*, London and New York: Gordon and Breach/Wiley.

Campbell, C. (1983), *Governments Under Stress: Political Executives and Key Bureaucrats in Washington*, London, Ottawa and Toronto: University of Toronto Press.

Capano, G. (2003), 'Administrative traditions and policy change. When policy paradigms matter. The case of Italian administrative reform during the 1990s', *Public Administration*, **81**(4), 781–801.

Cassese, S. (2002), 'Is there really a democratic deficit?', in S. Cassese and G.D. Cananea (eds), *Institutional Reforms in the European Union – Memorandum for the Convention*, Rome: EuropeEos, pp. 19–30.

Chandler, J.A. (eds) (2000), *Comparative Public Administration*, New York/London: Routledge.

Chardon, M. (2009), 'Wahlen im Auge des Hurrikans. Die Positionierung der flämischen Parteien vor den Regionalwahlen im Juni 2009' [Elections in the eye of the hurricane. The positioning of the Flemish parties before the regional elections in June 2009] in Europäisches Zentrum für Föderalismus-Forschung Tübingen (eds), *Jahrbuch des Föderalismus 2009. Föderalismus, Subsidiarität und Regionen in Europa* [Yearbook on Federalism 2009. Federalism, Subsidiarity and Regions in Europe], Baden-Baden: Nomos, pp. 251–63.

Christensen, T. and P. Laegreid (2001a), 'A transformative perspective on administrative reforms', in T. Christensen and P. Laegreid (eds), *New Public Management. The Transformation of Ideas and Practice*, Aldershot: Ashgate, pp. 13–43.

Christensen, T. and P. Laegreid (2001b), 'New Public Management – undermining political control?', in T. Christensen and P. Laegreid (eds): *New Public Management. The Transformation of Ideas and Practice*, Aldershot: Ashgate, pp. 93–120.

Christensen, T. and P. Laegreid (2005), 'Autonomization and policy capacity – the dilemmas and challenges facing political executives', in M. Painter and J. Pierre (eds), *Challenges to State Policy Capacity*, London: Macmillan, pp. 137–63.

Christensen, T. and P. Laegreid (eds) (2010), *New Public Management*, London: Routledge.

Christensen, T. and P. Laegreid (eds) (2011), *The Ashgate Research Companion to New Public Management*, Farnham: Ashgate.

Christmann, C. (2004), *Liberalisierung von Monopolmärkten* [Liberalization of Monopoly Markets], Frankfurt a.M: Lang.

Citroni, G. (2010), 'Neither state nor market. Municipalities, corporations and municipal corporatization in water services – Germany, France and Italy compared', in H. Wollmann and G. Marcou (eds), *The Provision of Public Services in Europe. Between State, Local Government and Market*, Cheltenham, UK and Northampton, MA, USA: Edward Elgar Publishing, pp. 191–216.

Clifton, J., P. Lanthier and H. Schröter (2011), 'Regulating and deregulating the public utilities, 1830–2010', *Business History*, **53**(5), 659–72.

Colino, C. (2009), 'Keine Ruhe nach dem Sturm? Neuere Entwicklungen im spanischen Föderalismus' [No calm after the storm? Recent developments in Spanish federalism], in Europäisches Zentrum für Föderalismus-Forschung Tübingen (eds), *Jahrbuch des Föderalismus 2009. Föderalismus, Subsidiarität und Regionen in Europa* [Yearbook of Federalism 2009. Federalism, Subsidiarity and Regions in Europe], Baden-Baden: Nomos, pp. 312–25.

Comité Balladur (2009), 'Comité pour la réforme des collectivités locales', last accessed 14 March 2014 at http://www.reformedescollectiviteslocales.fr/home/index.php.

Confservizi (2006), *Annuario associate 2006. Le gestioni del sistema Confservizi* [Associated Yearbook 2006. The Management System], Rome: Confservizi.

Connolly, T., E.J. Conlon and S.J. Deutsch (1980), 'Organizational effectiveness. A multiple-constituency approach', *Academy of Management Review*, **5**(2), 211–17.

Cristofoli, D., L. Macciò and L. Pedrazzi (2011), 'Managing successful networks. A "managerial style" for each season? The case of inter-municipal collaboration in Switzerland', paper presented at the 2011 IRSPM Conference.

Crozet, P. and C. Desmarais (2004), 'Les habits neufs de la gestion des ressources humaines dans les villes depuis les lois de décentralisation' [New forms for the management of human resources in the cities since the decentralization laws], *Revue Politiques et Management Public*, **22**(2), 55–75.

Crozier, M. (1964), *The Bureaucratic Phenomenon*, Chicago: University of Chicago Press.

Dahl, R.A. and E.R. Tufte (1973), *Size and Democracy*, Stanford, CA: Stanford University Press.

Dansbo, E. and O. Wallner (2008), 'Sweden's privatization program', *The PB Report: A Publication of Privatization Barometer*, last accessed 10 March 2014 at http://www.privatizationbarometer. net.

Davies, K. (1995), 'Local government in Hungary', in A. Coulson (eds), *Local Government in Eastern Europe. Establishing Democracy at the Grassroots*, Aldershot, UK and Brookfield, VT, USA: Edward Elgar Publishing, pp. 57–74.

Davis, G., P. Weller, E. Craswell and S. Eggins (1999), 'What drives machinery of government change? Australia, Canada and the United Kingdom', *Public Administration*, **77**(1), 7–50.

Davis, H., J. Downe and S. Martin (2001), *External Inspection of Local Government. Driving Improvement or Drowning in Detail*, York: York Publishing Services.

Deckwirth, C. (2008), 'Der Erfolg der Global Player. Liberalisierung und Privatisierung in der Bundesrepublik Deutschland' [The success of the global players. Liberalization and privatization in the Federal Republic of Germany], in H.-J. Bieling, C. Deckwirth and S. Schmalz (eds) (2008), *Liberalisierung und Privatisierung in Europa. Die Reorganisation der öffentlichen Infrastruktur in der Europäischen Union* [Liberalization and Privatization in Europe. The Reorganization of the Public Infrastructure in the EU], Münster: Westfälisches, pp. 64–95.

De Lancer, J.P. (2009), *Performance-based Management Systems: Effective Implementation and Maintenance*, Boca Raton, FL: CRC Press.

Demmke, C. (2006), 'Europäisierung der Personalpolitiken in Europa' [Europeanization of personnel policies in Europe], in J. Bogumil, W. Jann and F. Nullmeier (eds), *Politik und Verwaltung. PVS-Sonderheft* [Politics and Public Administration, PVS Special Issue], **37**, Wiesbaden: VS Verlag für Sozialwissenschaften, pp. 373–96.

Demmke, C. (2007), *Leistungsbewertung im öffentlichen Dienst in den Mitgliedsstaaten der EU* [Performance Assessment in the Public Sector in the Member States of the EU], Maastricht: EIPA.

Demmke, C. (2009), 'Leistungsbezahlung in den öffentlichen Diensten der EU-Mitgliedstaaten' [Performance-related pay in the public services of the EU member states], *der moderne staat* (dms), **2**(1), 53–71.

Demmke, C. (2011), 'Öffentliche Dienste im Vergleich' [Public services in comparison], in B. Blanke, F. Nullmeier, C. Reichard and G. Wewer (eds), *Handbuch zur Verwaltungsreform* [Handbook of Administrative Reform], 4th edition, Wiesbaden: Springer, pp. 321–9.

Demmke, C. and T. Moilanen (2013), *Transformation and the Future of Public Employment: The Impact of Restructuring on Status Development in the Central Administration of the EU-27*, Frankfurt a.M.: Peter Lang.

Demmke, C., G. Hammerschmid and R.E. Meyer (2007), *Dezentralisierung und Verantwortlichkeit als Schwerpunkte der Modernisierung der öffentlichen Verwaltung: Herausforderungen und Folgen für das Personal-Management* [Decentralization and Accountability as the Focus of the Modernization of Public Administration: Challenges and Consequences for Human Resource Management], Maastricht and Brussels: EIPA.

Deporcq, D., P. Géraud, J. Paisley and M. Poignet (2003), *Code pratique des sociétés d'économie mixte locales* [Code of Practice in Public–Private Companies] Paris: Berger-Levrault.

Derlien, H.-U. (1988), *Innere Struktur der Landesministerien in Baden-Württemberg* [Internal Structure of the Land Ministries in Baden-Württemberg], Baden-Baden: Nomos.

Derlien, H.-U. (1992), 'Observations on the state of comparative administrative research in Europe – rather comparable than comparative', *Governance*, **5**(3), 279–311.

Derlien, H.-U. (1994), 'Karrieren, Tätigkeitsprofil und Rollenverständnis der Spitzenbeamten des Bundes – Konstanz und Wandel' [Careers, job profiles and role perception of the top officials of the federal government – stability and change], *Verwaltung und Fortbildung*, **22**, 255–74.

Derlien, H.-U. (1996), 'Zur Logik und Politik des Ressortzuschnitts' [On the logic and policy of tailoring ministerial departments], *Verwaltungsarchiv*, **36**(4), 548–80.

Derlien, H.-U. (1997), 'Die Entwicklung von Evaluation im internationalen Kontext' [The development of evaluation in the international context], in W. Bussmann, U. Klöti and P. Knoepfel (eds), *Einführung in die Politikevaluation* [Introduction to the Policy Evaluation], Basel and Frankfurt a.M.: Helbing & Lichtenhahn, pp. 4–12.

Derlien, H.-U. (2002), 'Öffentlicher Dienst im Wandel' [Public service in transition], in K. König (eds), *Deutsche Verwaltung an der Wende zum 21. Jahrhundert* [German Administration at the Turn of the 21st Century], Baden-Baden: Nomos, pp. 229–54.

Derlien, H.-U. and G.B. Peters (eds) (2009), *The State at Work. Public Sector Employment in Ten Western Countries, Vol. 1.*, Cheltenham, UK and Northampton, MA, USA: Edward Elgar Publishing.

Deutsches Institut für Urbanistik – DIfU/Bundesministerium für Verkehr, Bau- und Wohnungswesen – BMVBW (2005), 'Public Private Partnership. Eine aktuelle Bestandsaufnahme in Bund, Ländern und Kommunen. Im Auftrag der PPP Task Force im BMVBW. Kurzfassung' [Public–Private Partnership. A Recent Survey in Federal, State and Local Governments. On Behalf of the PPP Task Force in BMVBW. Summary], Berlin: DIfU/BMVBW.

De Vries, M. (2000), 'The rise and fall of decentralization. A comparative analysis of arguments and practices in European countries', *European Journal of Political Research*, **38**(2), 193–224.

Dexia (2006), *Les fonctions publiques locales dans les 25 pays de l'Union Européenne* [Local Public Services in the 25 Countries of the European Union], Paris: Dexia Editions.

Dexia (2008), *Sub-national Governments in the European Union. Organisation, Responsibilities and Finance*, Paris: Dexia Editions.

Dexia Crédit Local/AMGVF (2004), 'Les services publics locaux' [Local public services], accessed 10 March 2014 at http://www.grandesvilles.org/sites/default/files/publications/etude-sondage/les_services_publics_locaux_20748.pdf.

Dickhaus, B. and K. Dietz (2004), *Private Gain – Public Loss? Folgen der Privatisierung und Liberalisierung öffentlicher Dienstleistungen in Europa* [Private Gain – Public Loss? Consequences of Privatization and Liberalization of Public Services in Europe], Berlin: Rosa-Luxemburg-Stiftung.

DiMaggio, P.J. and W.W. Powell (1991), *The New Institutionalism in Organizational Analysis*, Chicago: University of Chicago Press.

Dimitrov, V., K.H. Goetz and H. Wollmann (2006), *Governing After Communism. Institutions and Policymaking*, Lanham: Rowman & Littlefield.

Dipartimento della Funzione Pubblica (2006), *L'esternalizzazione strategica nelle amministrazioni pubbliche* [Strategic Outsourcing in Public Administration], Catanzaro: Rubettino.

Döhler, M. (2007), 'Vom Amt zur Agentur? Organisationsvielfalt, institutioneller Anpassungsdruck und Wandlungsprozesse im deutschen Verwaltungsmodell' [From the office to the agency? Organizational diversity, institutional adjustment pressures and processes of change in the German administrative model], in W. Jann and M. Döhler (eds), *Agencies in Westeuropa* [Agencies in Western Europe], Wiesbaden: VS Verlag für Sozialwissenschaften, pp. 12–47.

Döhler, M. (2008), 'Regieren mit Agenturen – Strategien und Interessen im exekutiven

Binnenverhältnis' [Governance by agencies – strategies and interests in the internal relations of the executive], in W. Jann and K. König (eds), *Regieren zu Beginn des 21. Jahrhunderts* [Governance at the Beginning of the 21st Century], Tübingen: Mohr Siebeck, pp. 259–89.

Döhler, M. and W. Jann (2007), 'Foreword', in W. Jann and M. Döhler (eds), *Agencies in Westeuropa*, Wiesbaden: VS Verlag für Sozialwissenschaften, pp. 7–11.

Dowding, K. (1995), 'Interpreting formal coalition theory', in K. Dowding and D.S. King (eds), *Preferences, Institutions, and Rational Choice*, Oxford, UK: Oxford University Press, pp. 43–59.

Dowding, K. and D. King (eds) (1995), *Preferences, Institutions and Rational Choice*, Oxford, UK: Oxford University Press.

Downs, A. (1957), *An Economic Theory of Democracy*, New York: Harper Collins.

Drews, K. (2008), 'Großbritannien. "TINA" oder Paradigma einer gescheiterten Reorganisation?' [United Kingdom. 'TINA' or paradigm of a failed reorganization?] in H.-J. Bieling, C. Deckwirth and S. Schmalz (eds), *Liberalisierung und Privatisierung in Europa. Die Reorganisation der öffentlichen Infrastruktur in der Europäischen Union* [Liberalization and Privatization in Europe. The Reorganization of the Public Infrastructure in the EU], Münster: Westfälisches, pp. 34–63.

Dreyfus, M., J. McEldowney, C. Ianello and A.E. Töller (2010), 'Comparative study of local services. Waste management in France, Germany, Italy and UK', in H. Wollmann and G. Marcou (eds), *The Provision of Public Services in Europe. Between State, Local Government and Market*, Cheltenham, UK and Northampton, MA, USA: Edward Elgar Publishing, pp. 146–65.

Dunleavy, P. (1991), *Democracy, Bureaucracy and Public Choice*, London: Pearson.

Dunleavy, P., H. Magretts, S. Bastow and J. Tinkler (2006), *Digital Era Governance. IT Corporations, the State and e-Government*, Oxford, UK: Oxford University Press.

Duval, C. (2006), 'L'Offre communale de services publics. L'Exemple Français de l'eau' [The local provision of public services. The French example of water], unpublished discussion paper presented to the Conference on Public Service Delivery in Cross-Country Comparison, 3–4 March, Menaggio.

Dwivedi, O.P. and K.M. Henderson (eds) (1990), *Public Administration in World Perspective*, Ames/Iowa: Iowa State University Press.

Dyson, K. (1980), *The State Tradition in Western Europe*, Oxford, UK: Robertson.

Dyson, K. and K.H. Goetz (2003), 'Living with Europe. Power, constraint and contestation', in K. Dyson and K.H. Goetz (eds), *Germany, Europe and the Politics of Constraint*, Oxford, UK: Oxford University Press, pp. 3–36.

Easton, D.A. (1965), *A Framework for Political Analysis*, Englewood Cliffs, NJ: Prentice Hall.

Ebinger, F. (2010), 'Aufgabenkommunalisierungen in den Ländern. Legitim – Erfolgreich – Gescheitert?' [Municipalization of tasks in the German *Länder*. Legitimate – successful – failed?] in J. Bogumil and S. Kuhlmann (eds), *Kommunale Aufgabenwahrnehmung im Wandel. Kommunalisierung, Regionalisierung und Territorial Reform in Deutschland und Europa* [Local Government Task Performance in Transition: Municipalization, Regionalization and Territorial Reform in Germany and Europe], Wiesbaden: VS Verlag für Sozialwissenschaften, pp. 47–66.

Edeling, T. (1999), 'Einführung. Der Neue Institutionalismus in Ökonomie und Soziologie' [Introduction. The New Institutionalism in economics and sociology], in T. Edeling, W. Jann and D. Wagner (eds), *Institutionenökonomie und Neuer Institutionalismus. Überlegungen zur Organisationstheorie* [Institutional Economics and New Institutionalism. Reflections on Organizational Theory], Opladen: Leske + Budrich, pp. 7–15.

Eisen, A. (1996a), *Institutionenbildung im Transformationsprozess. Der Aufbau der Umweltverwaltung in Sachsen und Brandenburg* [Institution Building in the Transformation Process. The build-up of Environmental Management in Saxony and Brandenburg], Baden-Baden: Nomos.

Eisen, A. (1996b), 'Institutionenbildung und institutioneller Wandel im Transformationsprozess.

Theoretische Notwendigkeiten und methodologische Konsequenzen einer Verknüpfung struktureller und kultureller Aspekte des institutionellen Wandels' [Institution building and institutional change in the transformation process. Theoretical necessities and methodological consequences of linking structural and cultural aspects of institutional change] in A. Eisen and H. Wollmann (eds), *Institutionenbildung in Ostdeutschland. Zwischen externer Steuerung und Eigendynamik* [Institution Building in East Germany. Between Guidance from outside and Dynamics from inside), Opladen: Leske + Budrich, pp. 33–61.

Ellwein, T. (1982), 'Verwaltungswissenschaft: Die Herausbildung der Disziplin' [Administrative science: the development of the discipline] in J.J. Hesse (ed.), *Politikwissenschaft und Verwaltungswissenschaft*, Political Quarterly, **13**, 34–54.

Ellwein, T. (1997), 'Verwaltung und Verwaltungswissenschaft' [Administration and administrative science], *Staatswissenschaft und Staatspraxis*, **8**, 5–18.

Engartner, T. (2009), 'Kehrt der Staat zurück? Rekommunalisierung in den Aufgabenbereichen Entsorgung und Gebäudereinigung' [Return of the state? Remunicipalization of tasks relating to waste disposal and cleaning of buildings], *Zeitschrift für öffentliche und gemeinnützige Unternehmen*, **32**(4), 339–55.

Enticott, G. (2004), 'Multiple voices of modernization. Some methodological implications', *Public Administration*, **82**(3), 743–56.

Ernst & Young (2007), *Privatisierungen und ÖPP als Ausweg? Kommunalfinanzen unter Druck – Handlungsoptionen für Kommunen* [Privatization and PPPs as a Way Out? Local Government Finances Under Pressure – Strategies for Municipalities], Stuttgart: Ernst & Young.

Esping-Andersen, G. (1990), *The Three Worlds of Welfare Capitalism*, Cambridge, UK: Polity Press.

Falkner, G., O. Treib, M. Hartlapp and S. Leiber (2005), *Complying with Europe. EU Harmonisation and Soft Law in the Member States*, Cambridge, UK: Cambridge University Press.

Färber, G. (2006), 'Finanzkontrolle' [Financial control] in R. Voigt and R. Walkenhaus (eds), *Handwörterbuch zur Verwaltungsreform* [Concise Dictionary of Administrative Reform], Wiesbaden: VS Verlag für Sozialwissenschaften, pp. 112–17.

Fargion, V. (1997), 'Social assistance and the North–South cleavage in Italy', in M. Rhodes (ed.), *Southern European Welfare States. Between Crisis and Reform*, London: Frank Cass, pp. 135–54.

Fedele, P., D. Galli and E. Ongaro (2007), 'Disaggregation, autonomy, contractualisation. A clear trend or a blurred mix? The agencification of the Italian public sector', *Public Management Review*, **9**(4), 557–85.

Fievet, F. and P. Laurent (2006), 'Faut-il une LOLF pour les collectivités locales?' [Should there be a LOLF for the local authorities?] *Revue Française de Finances Publiques*, **95**(1), 129–45.

Fisch, S. (2010), '"The Speyer Conference" – some origins of EGPA/GEAP before 1975', in G. Bouckaert and W. van de Donk (eds), *The European Group for Public Administration (1975–2010). Perspectives for the Future*, Brussels: Bruylant, pp. 7–10.

Fitzpatrick, J., M. Goggin, T. Heikkila, D. Klingner, J. Machado and C. Martell (2011), 'A new look at comparative public administration. Trends in research and an agenda for the future', *Public Administration Review*, **71**(6), 821–30.

Florio, M. (2004), *The Great Divestiture – Evaluating the Welfare Impact of the British Privatization 1979–1997*, Cambridge, MA and London: MIT Press.

Flynn, N. and F. Strehl (eds) (1996), *Public Sector Management in Europe*, Hemel-Hempstead: Harvester Wheatsheaf.

Forest, V. (2008), 'Performance-related pay and work motivation. Theoretical and empirical perspectives for the French civil service', *International Review of Administrative Sciences*, **74**(2), 325–39.

Forsthoff, E. (1938), *Die Verwaltung als Leistungsträger* [Public Administration as a Service Provider], Stuttgart: Kohlhammer.

Füzesi, Z., V. Ivády, Z. Kovácsy and K. Orbán (2005), 'Hungarian healthcare reforms in the 1990s', in G. Shakarishvili (ed.), *Decentralization in Healthcare Analyses and Experiences in Central and Eastern Europe in the 1990s, Local Government and Public Service Reform Initiative*, Budapest: Open Society Institute, pp. 276–312.

Garlatti, A. and F. Pezzani (2000), *I sistemi di programmazione e controllo negli enti locali* [Programming and Control Systems in Local Government], Milan: ETAS.

Gayl, J. Baron v. (2010), 'Kreisgebietsreform in Mecklenburg-Vorpommern' [Territorial reform of the counties/districts in Mecklenburg-Vorpommern], in J. Bogumil and S. Kuhlmann (eds), *Kommunale Aufgabenwahrnehmung im Wandel. Kommunalisierung, Regionalisierung und Territorialreform in Deutschland und Europa* [Local Government Task Performance in Transition: Municipalization, Regionalization and Territorial Reform in Germany and Europe], Wiesbaden: VS Verlag für Sozialwissenschaften, pp. 125–42.

Getimis, P. and N. Hlepas (2010), 'Efficiency imperatives in a fragmented polity. Reinventing local government in Greece', in H. Baldersheim and L.E. Rose (eds), *Territorial Choice*, Basingstoke: Palgrave Macmillan, pp. 198–213.

Goetz, K.H. (1995), 'Ein neuer Verwaltungstyp in Mittel- und Osteuropa? Zur Entwicklung der post-kommunistischen öffentlichen Verwaltung' [A new type of administration Central and Eastern Europe? On the development of post-communist public administration], in H. Wollmann, H. Wiesenthal and F. Bönker (eds), *Transformation sozialistischer Gesellschaften. Am Ende des Anfangs* [Transformation of Socialist Societies: At the End of the Beginning], Opladen: Leviathan, pp. 538–53.

Goetz, K.H. (2003), 'The Federal Executive. Bureaucratic fusion versus governmental bifurcation', in K.H.F. Dyson and K.H. Goetz (eds), *Germany, Europe and the Politics of Constraint*, Oxford, UK: Oxford University Press, pp. 55–72.

Goetz, K.H. (2006), 'Europäisierung der öffentlichen Verwaltung – oder europäische Verwaltung?' [Europeanization of public administration – or European administration?], in J. Bogumil, W. Jann and F. Nullmeier (eds), *Politik und Verwaltung. PVS-Sonderheft* [Politics and Public Administration, PVS Special Issue], **37**, Wiesbaden: VS Verlag für Sozialwissenschaften, pp. 472–90.

Goetz, K.H. and H. Wollmann (2001), 'Governmentalizing central executives in post-communist Europe. A four-country comparison', *Executive Government in Central and Eastern Europe. Special Issue of Journal of European Public Policy*, **8**(6), 864–87.

Göhler, G. (1987), 'Institutionenlehre und Institutionentheorie in der deutschen Politikwissenschaft nach 1945' [Institutional theory in German political science], in G. Göhler (ed.), *Grundfragen der Theorie politischer Institutionen. Forschungsstand – Probleme – Perspektiven* [Fundamental Questions of the Theory of Political Institutions. State of Research – Problems – Perspectives], Opladen: Westdeutscher Verlag, pp. 15–47.

Goldsmith, M.J. and E.C. Page (2010), *Changing Government Relations in Europe. From Localism to Intergovernmentalism*, London and New York: Routledge.

Goodin, R.E. (1996), *The Theory of Institutional Design*, Cambridge, UK: Cambridge University Press.

Gray, A., B. Jenkins and B. Segsworth (eds) (1993), *Budgeting, Auditing and Evaluation. Functions and Integration in Seven Governments*, London: Transaction Publishers.

Grémion, P. (1976), *Le pouvoir périphérique. Bureaucrates et notables dans le système politique français* [Peripheral Power. Bureaucrats and notables in the French Political System], Paris: Seuil.

Grohs, S. (2010), *Modernisierung kommunaler Sozialpolitik. Anpassungsstrategien im Wohlfahrtskorporatismus* [Modernizing Local Social Policy. Adaptation Strategies in Welfare Organizations], Wiesbaden: VS Verlag für Sozialwissenschaften.

Grohs, S., J. Bogumil and S. Kuhlmann (2012), 'Überforderung, Erosion oder Aufwertung der

Kommunen in Europa? Eine Leistungsbilanz im westeuropäischen Vergleich' [Excessive demand, erosion or upgrading of local authorities in Europe? A performance balance in Western European comparison], *der moderne staat* (dms), **5**(1), Special Issue 'Die ärmen Städte', 125–48.

Grossi, G. (1999), 'The group phenomenon in the Italian municipalities. The experience of Rome', seminar at the Institute of Local Government Studies, 28 February, Stockholm.

Grossi, G. and R. Mussari (2008), 'Effects of outsourcing on performance measurement and reporting. The experience of Italian local governments', *Public Budgeting & Finance*, **28**(1), 22–38.

Grossi, G. and C. Reichard (2008), 'Municipal corporatization in Germany and Italy', *Public Management Review*, **10**(5), 597–618.

Grossi, G., G. Marcou and C. Reichard (2010), 'Comparative aspects of institutional variants for local public service provision', in H. Wollmann and G. Marcou (eds), *The Provision of Public Services in Europe. Between State, Local Government and Market*, Cheltenham, UK and Northampton, MA, USA: Edward Elgar Publishing, pp. 217–39.

Gruner, R., B. Klippel and F. Wißkirchen (2009), 'Das Pendel schwingt zurück' [The pendulum swings back], *Recycling Magazine*, **5**(7), 34–5.

Grunow, D. (2006), 'Auswirkungen der europäischen Integration auf die Rolle der Kommunen im politischen Mehrebenensystem' [Impact of European integration on the role of the local authorities in the multi-level political system], in DIfU (ed.), *Brennpunkt Stadt. Lebens- und Wirtschaftsraum, gebaute Umwelt, politische Einheit. Festschrift für Heinrich Mäding zum 65. Geburtstag* [City Focus. Living and Economic Space, Built Environment, Political Unity. In Honour of Heinrich Mäding's 65th Birthday] Berlin: DIfU, pp. 137–53.

Guérin-Schneider, L. and D. Lorrain (2003), 'Note de recherché sur une question sensible. Les relations puissance publique – firmes dans le secteur de l'eau et de l'assainissement' [Research note on a touchy question. The relations between public authorities and private sector firms in the sectors of water and sanitation], *Flux*, **52/53**, 35–54.

Häggroth, S., K. Kronvall, C. Riberdahl and K. Rudebeck (1993), *Swedish Local Government. Traditions and Reform*, Stockholm: The Swedish Institute.

Hailsham, Lord (1978), *The Dilemma of Democracy. Diagnosis and Prescription*, London: Collins.

Hajnal, G. (2008), 'Public management reforms. Hungary', in G. Bouckaert, J. Nemec, V. Nakrošis, G. Hajnal and K. Tõnnison (eds), *Public Management Reforms in Central and Eastern Europe*, Bratislava: NISPAcee, pp. 121–50.

Hajnal, G. (2010), 'Central government organization in times of crisis. Administrative policy on non-departmental public bodies 2002–2009', Budapest: ECOSTAT/Budapest Corvinus University.

Hajnal, G. and K. Kádár (2008), *The Agency Landscape in Hungary. An Empirical Survey of Non-departmental Public Bodies 2002–2006*, Budapest: Institute for Economic Analysis and Informatics.

Hall, D., E. Lobina and P. Terhorst (2012), Remunicipalization in Europe, last accessed 14 March 2014 at http://www.psiru.org/reports/re-municipalisation-europe.

Hall, D., E. Lobina and P. Terhorst (2013), 'Re-municipalization in the early twenty-first century: water in France and energy in Germany', *International Review of Applied Economics*, **27**(2), 193–214.

Hall, P.A. and R.C.R. Taylor (1996), 'Political science and the three new institutionalisms', *Political Studies*, **44**(5), 936–57.

Halligan, J. (2003), 'Anglo-American civil service systems: an overview', in J. Halligan (eds), *Civil Service Systems in Anglo-American Countries*, Cheltenham, UK and Northampton, MA, USA: Edward Elgar Publishing, pp. 1–10.

Hansen, W. and N. Herbke (2004), 'Länderstudie Frankreich' [Country Study on France], in W. Schönbäck, G. Oppolzer, A. Kraemer, W. Hansen and N. Herbk, *Internationaler Vergleich der Siedlungswasserwirtschaft* [International Comparison of Water Management], Vienna: Österreichischer Städtebund/Bundesarbeitskammer.

Hartmann, J. (2005), *Westliche Regierungssysteme. Parlamentarismus, präsidentielles und semi-präsidentielles Regierungssystem* [Western Government Systems. Parliamentary, Presidential and Semi-presidential Systems of Government], 2nd edition, Wiesbaden: VS Verlag für Sozialwissenschaften.

Heady, F. (1960), 'Recent literature on comparative public administration', *Administrative Science Quarterly*, **5**(1), 134–54.

Heady, F. (1996), 'Configurations of civil service systems', in H. Bekke, J. Perry and T. Toonen (eds), *Civil Service Systems in Comparative Perspective*, Bloomington, IN: Indiana University Press, pp. 207–26.

Heady, F. (2001), *Public Administration. A Comparative Perspective*, 6th edition, Boca Raton, FL: CRC Press.

Hecking, C. (2003), *Das politische System Belgiens* [The Political System of Belgium], Opladen: Leske + Budrich.

Heclo, H. and A.B. Wildawsky (1974), *The Private Government of Public Money. Community and Policy Inside British Politics*, Berkeley, CA: University of California Press.

Heinelt, H. and N.-K. Hlepas (2006), 'Typologies of local government systems', in H. Bäck, H. Heinelt and A. Magnier (eds), *The European Mayor*, Wiesbaden: Springer, pp. 21–42.

Henningsen, B. (1986), *Der Wohlfahrtsstaat Schweden* [Sweden's Welfare State], Baden-Baden: Nomos.

Héritier, A., C. Knill, D. Lehmkuhl, M. Teutsch and A.-C. Douillet (2001), *Differential Europe. The European Union Impact on National Policymaking*, Lanham, MD: Rowman & Littlefield.

Hesse, J.J. and L.J. Sharpe (1991), 'Local government in international perspective. Some comparative observations', in J.J. Hesse (ed.), *Local Government and Urban Affairs in International Perspective*, Baden-Baden: Nomos, pp. 603–21.

Hlepas, N.-K. (2003), 'Local government reforms in Greece', in N. Kersting and A. Vetter (eds), *Reforming Local Government in Europe*, Wiesbaden: VS Verlag für Sozialwissenschaften, pp. 221–41.

Hlepas, N.-K. (2010), 'Incomplete Greek consolidation', *Local Government Studies*, **36**(2), 223–51.

Hlepas, N.-K. and P. Getimis (2010), 'Impacts of local government reforms in Greece. An interim assessment', *Local Government Studies*, **37**(5), October 2011, Special Issue on Evaluating Functional and Territorial Reforms in European Countries (guest-edited by S. Kuhlmann and H. Wollmann), 517–32.

Hoffmann-Martinot, V. (2003), 'The French Republic. One yet divisible?', in N. Kersting and A. Vetter (eds), *Reforming Local Government in Europe. Closing the Gap between Democracy and Efficiency?*, Opladen: Leske + Budrich, pp. 157–82.

Hoffmann-Martinot, V. (2006), 'Reform and modernization of urban government in France', in V. Hoffmann-Martinot and H. Wollmann (eds), *State and Local Government Reforms in France and Germany. Divergence and Convergence*, Wiesbaden: Springer, pp. 231–51.

Holmes, M and D. Shand (1995), 'Management reform. Some practitioner perspectives on the past ten years', *Governance*, **8**(4), 551–78.

Holtkamp, L. (2008), 'Das Scheitern des Neuen Steuerungsmodells' [The failure of New Steering Model], *der moderne staat* (dms), **1**(2), 423–46.

Hood, C. (1991), 'A public management for all seasons?', *Public Administration*, **69**(1), 3–19.

Hood, C. and M. Lodge (2006), *The Politics of Public Service Bargains. Reward, Loyalty, Competency and Blame*, Oxford, UK: Oxford University Press.

Horn, M. (1995), *The Political Economy of Public Administration*, Cambridge, UK: Cambridge University Press.

Horváth, T.M. (eds) (2000), *Decentralization. Experiments and Reforms*, Budapest: Open Society Institute.

Horváth, T. (2008), 'Le cas de modernisation administrative dans les collectivités locales hongroises' [Administrative modernization in the Hungarian local authorities], in G. Marcou and H. Wollmann (eds), *Annuaire 2008 des Collectivités Locales* [Local Government Yearbook 2008], Paris: CNRS, pp. 225–41.

Hösch, U. (2000), *Die kommunale Wirtschaftstätigkeit. Teilnahme am wirtschaftlichen Wettbewerb oder Daseinsvorsorge. Beiträge zur Ordnungstheorie und Ordnungspolitik* [Local Economic Activities. Participation in Economic Competition or General Interest. Contributions to the Theory of Order and Governance], Tübingen: Mohr Siebeck.

Hrast, M.F., E. Somogyi and N. Teller (2009), 'The role of NGOs in the governance of homelessness in Hungary and Slovenia', Budapest: Centre for Welfare Studies, Faculty of Social Sciences, University of Ljubljana and Metropolitan Research Institute.

Hughes, J., G. Sasse and C. Gordon (2004), 'Conditionality and compliance in the EU's eastward enlargement. Regional policy and the reform of sub-national government', *Journal of Common Market Studies*, **42**(3), 523–51.

Hulst, R. and A. v. Montfort (eds) (2007), *Inter-municipal Cooperation in Europe*, Dordrecht: Springer.

Iannello, C. (2007), 'L'emergenza dei rifiuti in Campania. I paradossi delle gestioni commissariali' [The waste crisis in Campania. The paradoxes of management commissioner government], *Rassegna di Diritto Pubblico Europeo*, **2**, 137–78.

Illner, M. (2003), 'The Czech Republic 1990–2001. Successful reform at the municipal level and a difficult birth of the intermediary government', in H. Baldersheim, M. Illner and H. Wollmann (eds), *Local Democracy in Post-Communist Europe*, Opladen: Leske + Budrich, pp. 61–91.

Illner, M. (2010), 'The voluntary union of municipalities. Bottom-up consolidation of local government in the Czech Republic', in P. Swianiewicz (ed.), *Territorial Consolidation Reforms in Europe*, Budapest: Open Society Institute, pp. 219–36.

Immergut, E. (1992), *Health Care Policies. Ideas and Institutions in Western Europe*, Cambridge, UK: Cambridge University Press.

Institut für den öffentlichen Sektor (2011), 'Rekommunalisierung in der Energieversorgung' [Remunicipalization in energy supply], *Public Governance*, Spring, 6–11.

Jaedicke, W., T. Thrun and H. Wollmann (2000), *Modernisierung der Kommunalverwaltung. Evaluierungsstudie zur Verwaltungsmodernisierung im Bereich Planen, Bauen und Umwelt* [Modernization of Municipal Administration. Evaluation Study on Administrative Modernization in the Sectors of Planning, Construction and Environment], Stuttgart: IfS.

Jäkel, T. and S. Kuhlmann (2012), 'Kann man von der Schweiz lernen? Leistungsvergleiche kommunaler Finanzkennzahlen in föderalen Ländern' [Can we learn from Switzerland? Benchmarking by way of financial indicators in federal countries], *Verwaltung & Management*, **18**(3), 131–5.

Jann, W. (1983), *Politische Programme und 'Verwaltungskultur'. Bekämpfung des Drogenmissbrauchs und der Jugendarbeitslosigkeit in Schweden, Großbritannien und der Bundesrepublik Deutschland im Vergleich* [Political Programmes and 'Administrative Culture'. Combatting Drug Abuse and Youth Unemployment in Sweden, Great Britain and the Federal Republic of Germany in Comparison], Opladen: Westdeutscher Verlag.

Jann, W. (2001), 'Verwaltungsreform als Verwaltungspolitik. Verwaltungsmodernisierung und Policy-Forschung' [Administrative reform as an administrative policy. Administrative modernization and policy research], in E. Schröter, (ed.), *Empirische Policy- und Verwaltungsforschung*.

Lokale, nationale und international Perspektiven [Empirical Policy and Administration Research. Local, National and International Perspectives], Opladen: Leske + Budrich, pp. 279–303.

Jann, W. (2002), 'Der Wandel verwaltungspolitischer Leitbilder. Von Management zu Governance?' [The Change in administrative guiding principles. From management to governance?], in K. König (ed.), *Deutsche Verwaltung an der Wende zum 21. Jahrhundert* [German Administration at the Turn of the 21st Century] Baden-Baden: Nomos, pp. 279–303.

Jann, W. (2006), 'Die skandinavische Schule der Verwaltungswissenschaft. Neo-Institutionalismus und die Renaissance der Bürokratie' [The Scandinavian School of Administrative Science. Neo-institutionalism and the renaissance of bureaucracy], in J. Bogumil, W. Jann and F. Nullmeier (eds), *Politik und Verwaltung. PVS-Sonderheft* [Politics and Administration, PVS Special Issue], **37**, Wiesbaden: VS Verlag für Sozialwissenschaften, pp. 121–48.

Jann, W. (2009), 'Policy-Analyse und Verwaltungsforschung: 50 Jahre praktische Fragen und theoretische Antworten' [Policy Analysis and administrative research. 50 years of practical questions and theoretical answers], *PVS*, **50**(3), 474–503.

Jann, W. and B. Jantz (2008), 'A better performance of performance management', in KPMG (ed.), *Holy Grail or Achievable Quest? International Perspectives on Public Sector Performance Management*, Switzerland: KPMG International, pp. 11–28.

Jeffery, C. (2009), 'Devolution in the United Kingdom. Ever looser union?', *der moderne staat* (dms), **2**(1), 207–18.

Jenei, G. (2009), 'A post-accession crisis? Political developments and public sector modernization in Hungary', working paper, Bamberg University.

Jenei, G. and E. Kuti (2003), 'Duality in the third sector. The Hungarian case', *Asian Journal of Public Administration*, **25**(1), 133–57.

John, P. (2001), *Local Governance in Western Europe*, London: Sage.

John, P. (2010), 'Larger and larger? The endless search for efficiency in the U.K.', in H. Baldersheim and L.E. Rose (eds), *Territorial Choice*, Basingstoke: Palgrave Macmillan, pp. 101–17.

Jreisat, J.E. (2011), 'Commentary. Comparative public administration. A global perspective', *Public Administration Review*, **71**(6), 834–8.

Kaiser, A. (1999), 'Die politische Theorie des Neo-Institutionalismus. James March und Johan Olsen' [The political theory of neo-institutionalism. James March and Johan Olsen], in A. Brodocz and G.S. Schaal (eds), *Politische Theorien der Gegenwart* [Political Theories of the Present], Opladen: Leske + Budrich, pp. 189–211.

Kaltenbach, J. (1990), 'Die Entwicklung der kommunalen Selbstverwaltung in Ungarn' [The development of local self-government in Hungary], *Jahrbuch für Ostrecht*, **31**(1), 77–93.

Kassim, H., B.G. Peters and V. Wright (eds) (2000), *The National Co-ordination of EU Policy. The Domestic Level*, Oxford, UK: Oxford University Press.

Kastendiek, H., R. Stinshoff and R. Sturm (eds) (1999), *The Return of Labour – A Turning Point in British Politics?*, Berlin and Bodenheim: Philo.

Katzenstein, P.J. (1987), *Policy and Politics in West Germany. The Growth of a Semi-sovereign State*, Philadelphia: Temple University Press.

Keen, L. and S.A. Vickerstaff (1997), '"We're all human resource managers now". Local government middle managers', *Public Money & Management*, **17**(3), 41–6.

Kempf, U. (2003), 'Das politische System Frankreichs' [The political system of France], in W. Ismayr (ed.), *Die politischen Systeme Westeuropas* [The Political Systems of Western Europe], 2nd edition, Opladen: Leske + Budrich, pp. 301–47.

Kerrouche, E. (2010), 'France and its 36 000 communes. An impossible reform?', in H. Baldersheim and L.E. Rose (eds), *Territorial Choice*, Basingstoke: Palgrave Macmillan, pp. 160–79.

Kersting, N. and A. Vetter (ed.) (2003), *Reforming Local Government in Europe*, Opladen: Leske + Budrich.

Kickert, W.J.M. (ed.) (1997), *Public Management and Administrative Reforms in Western Europe*, Cheltenham, UK and Northampton, MA, USA: Edward Elgar Publishing.

Kickert, W.J.M. (ed.) (2008), *The Study of Public Management in Europe and the US*, London: Routledge.

Kickert, W.J.M. (2011), 'Public management reform in Continental Europe. National distinctiveness', in T. Christensen and P. Laegreid (eds), *The Ashgate Research Companion to New Public Management*, Aldershot: Ashgate, pp. 97–112.

Kingdon, J.W. (1995), *Agendas, Alternatives and Public Policies*, 2nd edition, New York: Longman.

Knill, C. (2001), *The Europeanisation of National Administrations. Patterns of Institutional Change and Persistence*, Cambridge, UK: Cambridge University Press.

Kogan, M. (ed.) (1989), *Evaluating Higher Education*, London: Jessica Kingsley.

Kollmorgen, R. (2009), 'Postsozialistische Wohlfahrtsregime in Europa. Teil der "Drei Welten" oder eigener Typus?' [Post-socialist welfare regimes in Europe. Part of the 'Three Worlds' or unique?], in B. Pfau-Effinger, S.S. Magdalenic and C. Wolf (eds), *International vergleichende Sozialforschung* [International Comparative Social Research], Wiesbaden: VS Verlag für Sozialwissenschaften, pp. 65–92.

Kommunale Gemeinschaftsstelle für Verwaltungsmanagement – KGSt (1993), *Das Neue Steuerungsmodell. Begründung, Konturen, Umsetzung. Bericht 1993*, No. 5 [The New Steering Model. Reasons, Profiles, Implementation, Report 1993], Köln: KGSt-Bericht.

König, K. (1993), 'Die Transformation der öffentlichen Verwaltung' [The transformation of public administration], in R. Pitschas (ed.), *Verwaltungsintegration in den neuen Bundesländern* [Adminstrative Integration in the New Federal States/Länder], Berlin: Duncker & Humblot, pp. 29–46.

König, K. (2002), 'Zwei Paradigmen des Verwaltungsstudiums – Vereinigte Staaten von Amerika und Kontinentaleuropa' [Two paradigms of administrative studies: United States of America and Continental Europe], in K. König (ed.), *Deutsche Verwaltung an der Wende zum 21. Jahrhundert* [German Administration at the turn of the 21st Century], Baden-Baden: Nomos, pp. 393–423.

König, K. (2006), 'Öffentliches Management in einer legalistischen Verwaltungskultur' [Public management in a legalistic administrative culture], in W. Jann, M. Röber and H. Wollmann (eds), *Public Management. Grundlagen, Wirkungen, Kritik. Festschrift für Christoph Reichard zum 65. Geburtstag* [Public Management. Basics, Effects, Critique. In Honour of Christoph Reichard's 65th Birthday, Wiesbaden: VS Verlag für Sozialwissenschaften, pp. 23–34.

König, K. (2007), 'Verwaltungskulturen und Verwaltungswissenschaften' [Administrative cultures and administrative sciences], in K. König and C. Reichard (eds), *Theoretische Aspekte einer managerialistischen Verwaltungskultur* [Theoretical Aspects of a Managerial and Administrative Culture], *Speyerer Forschungsberichte*, **254**, Speyer, 1–24.

König, K. (2008), *Moderne öffentliche Verwaltung. Studium der Verwaltungswissenschaft* [Modern Public Administration. Study of Administrative Science], Berlin: Duncker & Humblot.

König, K. and N. Füchtner (2000), *Schlanker Staat – eine Agenda der Verwaltungsmodernisierung im Bund* [Lean State – An Agenda of Federal Administrative Modernization], Baden-Baden: Nomos.

Kopányi, M., S. El Daher, D. Wetzel, M. Noel and A. Papp (2000), 'Modernizing the sub-national government system', Washington DC: World Bank.

Kopecký, P. and P. Mair (2012), 'Party patronage as an organizational resource: introduction', in P. Kopecký, P. Mair and M. Spirova (eds), *Party Government and Party Patronage. Public Appointments and Political Control in European Democracies*, Oxford, UK: Oxford University Press, pp. 3–16.

Kovács, I.P. (2012), 'Roots and consequences of local government reforms in Hungary', unpublished manuscript.

Krasner, S. (1984), 'Approaches to the state. Alternative conceptions and historical dynamics', *Comparative Politics*, **16**(2), 223–46.

Kropp, S. (2006), 'Ausbruch aus "exekutiver Führerschaft"? Ressourcen- und Machtverschiebungen im Dreieck von Regierung, Verwaltung und Parlament' [Breaking out of 'executive leadership'? Resource and power shifts in the triangle of government, administration and parliament], in J. Bogumil, W. Jann and F. Nullmeier (eds), *Politik und Verwaltung. PVS-Sonderheft* [Politics and Administration, PVS Special Issue], **37**, Wiesbaden: VS Verlag für Sozialwissenschaften, 275–98.

Kropp, S. (2010), *Kooperativer Föderalismus und Politikverflechtung* [Cooperative Federalism and Policy Interwovenness], Wiesbaden: VS Verlag für Sozialwissenschaften.

Kropp, S. and M. Ruschke (2010), 'Parlament und Verwaltung in Rollenpartnerschaft vereint? Ein Plädoyer für die Verknüpfung von Parlaments- und Verwaltungsforschung' [Parliament and administration united in a partnership role? A plea for the combination of parliamentary and administrative research], *Zeitschrift für Parlamentsfragen*, **41**(3), 654–76.

Kuhlmann, S. (2003), *Rechtsstaatliches Verwaltungshandeln in Ostdeutschland. Eine Studie zum Gesetzesvollzug in der lokalen Bauverwaltung* [Administrative Action in East Germany. A Study on Implementation in the Local Construction Administration], Opladen: Leske + Budrich.

Kuhlmann, S. (2004), 'Interkommunaler Leistungsvergleich in deutschen Kommunen. Zwischen Transparenzgebot und Politikprozess' [Inter-municipal benchmarking in German local authorities. Between transparency and the political process], in S. Kuhlmann, J. Bogumil and H. Wollmann (eds), *Leistungsmessung und -vergleich in Politik und Verwaltung* [Performance Measurement and Benchmarking in Politics and Administration], Wiesbaden: VS Verlag für Sozialwissenschaften, pp. 94–120.

Kuhlmann, S. (2006a), 'Kommunen zwischen Staat und Markt. Lokalmodelle und -reformen im internationalen Vergleich' [Local authorities between state and market. Local models and reforms in international comparison], *Deutsche Zeitschrift für Kommunalwissenschaft*, **45**(2), 84–102.

Kuhlmann, S. (2006b), 'Öffentlicher Dienst in Deutschland: Reformfähig oder -resistent?' [Public service in Germany: capable of reform or resistant to reform?], in L. Kißler, R. Lasserre and H. Pautrat (eds), *Öffentliche Beschäftigung und Verwaltungsreform in Deutschland und Frankreich* [Public Employment and Administrative Reform in Germany and France], Frankfurt a.M. and New York: Campus Verlag, pp. 71–96.

Kuhlmann, S. (2007a), 'Trajectories and driving factors of local government reforms in Paris-city. A "deviant case" of institutional development?', *Local Government Studies*, **33**(1), 7–26.

Kuhlmann, S. (2007b) 'Performance management und Leistungsmessung im internationalen Kontext. Was können die deutschen Kommunen lernen?' [Performance management and benchmarking in an international context. What can the German local authorities learn?], in J. Bogumil, L. Holtkamp, L. Kißler, S. Kuhlmann, C. Reichard, K. Schneider and H. Wollmann, *Perspektiven lokaler Verwaltungsmodernisierung* [Perspectives of Local Government Modernization], Berlin: Edition Sigma, pp. 75–84.

Kuhlmann, S. (2008), 'Dezentralisierung in Frankreich. Ende der unteilbaren Republik?' [Decentralization in France. End of the indivisible republic?], *der moderne staat* (dms), **1**(1), 201–20.

Kuhlmann, S. (2009a), 'Politik- und Verwaltungsreform in Kontinentaleuropa. Subnationaler Institutionenwandel im deutsch-französischen Vergleich. Habilitationsschrift an der Universität Potsdam' [Policy and public administration reforms in Continental Europe. Subnational institutional change in Franco-German comparison. Habilitation thesis at the University of Potsdam]. Baden-Baden: Nomos.

Kuhlmann, S. (2009b), 'Die Evaluation von Institutionenpolitik in Deutschland. Verwaltungsmodernisierung und Wirkungsanalyse im föderalen System' [The evaluation of institution policy in Germany. Administrative modernization and impact analysis in the federal system], in T. Widmer, W. Beywl and F. Carlo (eds), *Evaluation. Ein systematisches Handbuch* [Evaluation. A Systematic Handbook], Wiesbaden: VS Verlag für Sozialwissenschaften, pp. 371–80.

Kuhlmann, S. (2010a), 'Vergleichende Verwaltungswissenschaft: Verwaltungssysteme, Verwaltungskulturen und Verwaltungsreformen in internationaler Perspektive' [Comparative public administration: administrative systems, administrative cultures and administrative reforms in international perspective], in H.-J. Lauth (eds), *Vergleichende Regierungslehre* [Comparative Government], Wiesbaden: VS Verlag für Sozialwissenschaften, pp. 140–60.

Kuhlmann, S. (2010b), 'Siegeszug der Territorialität? Dezentralisierungsprofile und -wirkungen in Westeuropa' [Triumph of territoriality? Decentralization profiles and effects in Western Europe], in D. Schimanke (ed.), *Verwaltung und Raum – Zur Diskussion um Leistungsfähigkeit und Integrationsfunktion von Verwaltungseinheiten* [Administration and Space – Discussion of the Performance and Integration Function of Administrative Units] Wiesbaden: VS Verlag für Sozialwissenschaften, pp. 101–26.

Kuhlmann, S. (2010c), '"Interkommunale Revolution" in Frankreich? Reformschritte, Effekte und Schwächen territorialer Konsolidierung ohne Gebietsfusion' ['Intermunicipal revolution' in France? Reforms, effects and weaknesses of territorial consolidation without fusion], in J. Bogumil and S. Kuhlmann (eds), *Kommunale Aufgabenwahrnehmung im Wandel: Kommunalisierung, Regionalisierung und Territorialreform in Deutschland und Europa* [Local Government Task Performance in Transition: Municipalization, Regionalization and Territorial Reform in Germany and Europe], Wiesbaden: VS Verlag für Sozialwissenschaften, pp. 277–98.

Kuhlmann, S. (2010d), 'Performance measurement in European local governments. A comparative analysis of reform experiences in Great Britain, France, Sweden and Germany', *International Review of Administrative Sciences*, **76**(2), 331–45.

Kuhlmann, S. (2011), 'Messung und Vergleich von Verwaltungsleistungen. Benchmarking-Regime in Westeuropa' [Measurement and comparison of administrative performance: benchmarking regimes in Western Europe], *Die Verwaltung*, **44**(2), 155–78.

Kuhlmann, S. and J. Bogumil (2010), 'Kommunalisierung, Regionalisierung, Kooperation – die "neue Welle" subnationaler Verwaltungsreform' [Municipalization, regionalization, cooperation – the 'new wave' of subnational administrative reform], in J. Bogumil and S. Kuhlmann (eds), *Kommunale Aufgabenwahrnehmung im Wandel: Kommunalisierung, Regionalisierung und Territorialreform in Deutschland und Europa* [Local Government Task Performance in Transition: Municipalization, Regionalization and Territorial Reform in Germany and Europe], Wiesbaden: VS Verlag für Sozialwissenschaften, pp. 11–22.

Kuhlmann, S. and P. Fedele (2010), 'New Public Management in Continental Europe: Local government modernization in Germany, France and Italy from a comparative perspective', in H. Wollmann and G. Marcou (eds), *The Provision of Public Services in Europe. Between State, Local Government and Market*, Cheltenham, UK and Northampton, MA, USA: Edward Elgar Publishing, pp. 49–74.

Kuhlmann, S. and M. Röber (2006), 'Civil service in Germany. Between cutback management and modernization', in V. Hoffmann-Martinot and H. Wollmann (eds), *State and Local Government Reforms in France and Germany. Divergence and Convergence*, Wiesbaden: VS Verlag für Sozialwissenschaften, pp. 89–110.

Kuhlmann, S. and H. Wollmann (2006), 'Transaktionskosten von Verwaltungsreformen – ein "missing link" der Evaluationsforschung' [Transaction costs of administrative reforms – a 'missing link' of evaluation research], in W. Jann, M. Röber and H. Wollmann (eds), *Public*

Management. Grundlagen, Wirkungen, Kritik. Festschrift für Christoph Reichard zum 65. Geburtstag [Public Management. Basics, Effects, Critique. In Honour of Christoph Reichard's 65th Birthday], Berlin: Edition Sigma, pp. 371–90.

Kuhlmann, S. and H. Wollmann (2011), 'The evaluation of institutional reforms at sub-national government level. A still neglected research agenda', *Local Government Studies*, **37**(5), Special Issue on Evaluating Functional and Territorial Reforms in European Countries, 479–94.

Kuhlmann, S. and H. Wollmann (2013), *Verwaltung und Verwaltungsreformen in Europa* [Public Administration and Administrative Reforms in Europe], Wiesbaden: VS Verlag für Sozialwissenschaften.

Kuhlmann, S., J. Bogumil and S. Grohs (2008), 'Evaluating administrative modernization in German local governments: success or failure of the "New Steering Model"?' *Public Administration Review*, **68**(5), 851–63.

Kuhlmann, S., J. Bogumil, F. Ebinger, S. Grohs and R. Reiter (2011), *Dezentralisierung des Staates in Europa: Auswirkungen auf die kommunale Aufgabenerfüllung in Deutschland, Frankreich und Großbritannien* [Decentralization of the State in Europe: Impacts on on Local Level Task Performance in Germany, France and Great Britain], Wiesbaden: VS Verlag für Sozialwissenschaften.

Lachaume, J.-F. (1996), 'Les modes de gestion des services publics' [Modes of public service provision], *Les Notices de la Documentation Française*, No. 11, 63–9.

Lachaume, J.-F. (1997), *L'administration communale* [Municipal Administration], 2nd edition, Paris: LGDJ.

Lane, J.-E. (ed.) (1997), *Public Sector Reform – Rationale, Trends and Problems*, London: Sage.

La Porta, R., F. Lopez-de-Silanes, A. Shleifer and R. Vishny (1999), 'The quality of government', *Journal of Law, Economics and Organization*, **15**(1), 222–79.

Larsson, T. and J. Trondal (2005), 'After hierarchy? The differentiated impact of the European Commission and the Council of Ministers on domestic executive governance', ARENA Working Papers No. 22, Oslo: ARENA.

Laux, E. (1999), 'Erfahrungen und Perspektiven der kommunalen Gebiets- und Funktionalreformen' [Experiences and perspectives of local territorial and functional reforms], in H. Wollmann and R. Roth (eds), *Kommunalpolitik* [Local Politics], 2nd edition, Opladen: Leske + Budrich, pp. 168–85.

Leach, R. and J. Percy-Smith (2001), *Local Governance in Britain*, Basingstoke: Palgrave Macmillan.

Leemans, A.R. (1970), *Changing Patterns of Local Government*, The Hague: IULA.

Lehmbruch, G. (1993), 'Institutionentransfer. Zur politischen Logik der Verwaltungsintegration in Deutschland' [Institutional transfer. On the political logic of administrative integration in Germany], in W. Seibel, A. Benz and H. Mäding (eds), *Verwaltungsreform und Verwaltungspolitik im Prozess der deutschen Einigung* [Administrative Reform and Administration Policy in the Process of German Unification], Baden-Baden: Nomos, pp. 42–66.

Lehmbruch, G. (1996), 'Die ostdeutsche Transformation als Strategie des Institutionentransfers. Überprüfung und Antikritik' [East German transformation as a strategy of institution transfer. Review and anti-critique] in A. Eisen and H. Wollmann (eds), *Institutionenbildung in Ostdeutschland. Zwischen externer Steuerung und Eigendynamik* [Institution Building in East Germany. Between Promotion from Outside and Dynamics from Inside], Opladen: Leske + Budrich, pp. 55–72.

Leibfried, S. (1992), 'Towards a European welfare state? On integrating poverty regimes into the European Community', in Z. Ferge and J.E. Kolberg (eds), *Social Policy in a Changing Europe*, Frankfurt a.M.: Campus Verlag, pp. 245–79.

Lemmet, J.-F. and C. Creignou (2002), *La fonction publique locale* [Local Public Service], Paris: LDGJ.

Lenk, T., O. Rottmann and R. Albrecht (2011), 'Rekommunalisierung in der Energieversorgung' [Remunicipalization in energy supply], *Public Governance*, 7(1), 6–11.

Lepsius, M.R. (1995), 'Institutionenanalyse und Institutionenpolitik' [Institution analysis and institution policy], in B. Nedelmann (eds), *Politische Institutionen im Wandel* [Political Institutions in Transition], Opladen: Leske + Budrich, pp. 392–403.

Libbe, J., J.-H. Trapp and S. Tomerius (2004), 'Gemeinwohlsicherung als Herausforderung – umweltpolitisches Handeln in der Gewährleistungskommune' ['The challenge of ensuring the public interest – environmental policy action in the ensuring local authority in Germany], *DIfU Networkpapers*, **8**.

Libbe, J., S. Hanke and M. Verbücheln (2011), 'Rekommunalisierung– Eine Bestandsaufnahme' [Remunicipalization – an inventory], DIfU-Papers, Berlin: DIfU.

Lidström, A. (2010), 'The Swedish model under stress. The waning of the egalitarian, unitary state?', in H. Baldersheim and L.E. Rose (eds), *Territorial Choice*, Basingstoke: Palgrave Macmillan, pp. 61–79.

Liedtke, B.H. and A. Tepper (1989), *Sozialverträglicher Technikeinsatz in der Kommunalverwaltung. Erfahrungen mit einem kommunalen Bürgeramt* [Socially compatible Use of Technology in Local Government. Experience in a Local Service Centre], GMD Report No. 177, Munich and Vienna: Oldenbourg.

Lijphart, A. (1971), 'Comparative politics and the comparative method', *The American Political Science Review*, **65**(3), 682–93.

Lijphart, A. (1984), *Democracies. Patterns of Majoritarian and Consensus Government in Twenty-one Countries*, New Haven, CT and London: Yale University Press.

Lijphart, A. (1999), *Patterns of Democracy. Government Forms and Performance in Thirty-six Countries*, New Haven, CT: Yale University Press.

Linder, W. (2009), 'Das politische System der Schweiz' [The political system in Switzerland], in W. Ismayr (ed.), *Die politischen Systeme Westeuropas* [The Political Systems of Western Europe], 4th edition, Frankfurt a.M.: Springer, pp. 567–605.

Lippert, I. (2005), *Öffentliche Dienstleistungen unter EU-Einfluss. Liberalisierung – Privatisierung – Restrukturierung – Regulierung* The Provision of [Public Services Under EU Influence. Liberalization – Privatization – Restructuring – Regulatory] Berlin: Edition Sigma.

Lippi, A. (2003), 'As a voluntary choice or as a legal obligation? Assessing New Public Management policy in Italy', in H. Wollmann (ed.), *Evaluation in Public Sector Reform. Concepts and Practice in International Perspective*, Cheltenham, UK and Northampton, MA, USA: Edward Elgar Publishing, pp. 140–68.

Lippi, A., N. Giannelli, S. Profeti and G. Citroni (2008), 'Adapting public–private governance to the local context', *Public Management Review*, **10**(5), 619–40.

Local Government Pay Commission (2003), *Report of the Local Government Pay Commission*, October 2003.

Lodge, M. (2007), 'Next Steps und zwei Schritte zurück? Stereotypen, Executive Agencies und die Politik der Delegation in Großbritannien' [Next Steps and two steps back? Stereotypes, executive agencies and the politics of delegation in the UK], in W. Jann and M. Döhler (eds), *Agencies in Westeuropa* [Agencies in Western Europe], Wiesbaden: VS Verlag für Sozialwissenschaften, pp. 48–78.

Loewenstein, K. (1969), *Verfassungslehre* [Constitutional Theory], Tübingen: Mohr.

Löffler, E. and M. Vintar (eds) (2004), *Improving the Quality of East and West European Public Services*, Aldershot: Ashgate.

Longo, F. and H. Plamper (2004), 'Italiens Staats- und Managementreformen am Beispiel der Controllingsysteme und der Leistungsvergleiche' [State and management reforms in Italy exemplified by systems of control and benchmarking], in S. Kuhlmann, J. Bogumil and

H. Wollmann (eds), *Leistungsmessung und vergleich in Politik und Verwaltung* [Measurement and Benchmarking in Politics and Administration], Wiesbaden, VS Verlag für Sozialwissenschaften, pp. 323–40.

Lorrain, D. (1995), 'France. Le changement silencieux' [France. Silent change], in D. Lorrain and G. Stoker (eds), *La privatisation des services urbains en Europe* [Privatization of Urban Services in Europe], Paris: La Découverte, pp. 105–29.

Loughlin, J., F. Hendriks and A. Lidström (eds) (2010), *The Oxford Handbook on Local and Regional Democracy*, Oxford, UK: Oxford University Press.

Löwe, J. (2003), 'Ökonomisierung der öffentlichen Wirtschaft und die EU-Wettbewerbspolitik' [Commodification of public sector and EU competition policy], in J. Harms and C. Reichard (eds), *Die Ökonomisierung des öffentlichen Sektors. Instrumente und Trends* [The Marketization of the Public Sector Instruments and Trends], Baden-Baden: Nomos, pp. 183–201.

Lynn, Jr., L. (2006), *Public Management, Old and New*, London: Routledge.

Mabileau, A. (1996), *Kommunalpolitik und -verwaltung in Frankreich. Das 'lokale System' Frankreichs* [Local Politics and Administration in France. The 'Local System' of France], Basel: Birkhauser.

Mabileau, A. and C. Sorbets (eds) (1989), *Gouverner les villes moyennes* [Governing Medium-sized Municipalities], Paris: Pédone.

Magnier, A. (2003), 'Subsidiarity: fall or premise of local government reforms. The Italian case', in N. Kersting and A. Vetter (eds), *Reforming Local Government in Europe*, Opladen: Leske + Budrich, pp. 183–96.

Manow, P. (2002), 'Was erklärt politische Patronage in den Ländern Westeuropas? Defizite des politischen Wettbewerbs oder historisch-formative Phasen der Massendemokratisierung' [What explains political patronage in the countries of Western Europe? Deficits of political competition or historical formative stages of mass democratization], *Politische Vierteljahresschrift*, **43**(1), 20–45.

March, J.G. and J.P. Olsen (1984), 'The New Institutionalism: organizational factors in political life', *American Political Science Review*, **78**(3), 734–49.

March, J.G. and J.P Olsen (1989), *Rediscovering Institutions: The Organizational Basic of Politics*, New York: Free Press.

Marcou, G. (2000), 'La réforme de l'intercommunalité' [Reform of the inter-municipality], in G. Marcou (eds), *Annuaire 2000 des Collectivités Locales. La réforme de l'Intercommunalité* [2000 Local Government Yearbook. Inter-municipal Reform], Paris: CNRS, pp. 3–10.

Marcou, G. (2010) 'La réforme territoriale. Analyse du nouveau projet de réforme des collectivités territoriales' [Territorial reform. Analysis of the new project of local government reforms], in J.-C. Némery (ed), *Quelle nouvelle réforme pour les collectivités territoriales françaises?*, (Which new reform of the French local authorities ?) Paris: Editions Harmattan, pp. 21–80.

Marcou, G. (2012), 'Quel avenir pour la région en France: Décentralisation ou autonomies régionales' [What future for the region in France? Decentralization and regional autonomy], in A. Lucarelli and M. Verpeaux (eds), *Régionalisme italien et régionalisme français* [Italian and French Regionalism], Paris: Editions Harmattan, pp. 1–20.

Marcou, G. and H. Wollmann (2008), 'Europe', in *Decentralization and Local Democracy in the World. UCLG 2008 'GOLD-Report'*, Barcelona: UCLG, last accessed 14 March 2014 at http://www.cities-localgovernments.org/gold/Upload/gold_report/gold_report_en.pdf, 129–69.

Mark, K. and R. Nayyar-Stone (2002), 'Assessing the benefits of performance management in Eastern Europe. Experience in Hungary, Albania, and Georgia', unpublished paper (NISPAcee Annual Conference).

Maurer, A. (2003), 'Germany. Fragmented structures in a complex system', in W. Wessels, A. Maurer and J. Mittag (eds), *Fifteen into One? The European Union and its Member States*, Manchester: Manchester University Press, pp. 115–49.

Mayer, F. (2006), *Vom Niedergang des unternehmerisch tätigen Staates* [On the Decline of the Entrepreneurially Active State], Wiesbaden: VS Verlag für Sozialwissenschaften.

Mayntz, R. and H.-U. Derlien (1989), 'Party patronage and politicization of the West German administrative elite 1970–1987. Towards hybridization?', *Governance*, **2**(4), 384–404.

Mayntz, R. and F.W Scharpf (1975), *Policy-making in the German Federal Bureaucracy*, Amsterdam: Elsevier.

Mayntz, R. and F.W. Scharpf (eds) (1995), *Gesellschaftliche Selbstregelung und politische Steuerung* [Societal Self-regulation and Political Steering], Frankfurt a.M: Campus Verlag.

McCubbins, M.D. and T. Page (1987), 'A theory of congressional delegation', in M.D. McCubbins and T. Sullivan (eds), *Congress. Structure and Policy*, New York: Cambridge University Press, pp. 409–25.

Mehr Demokratie e.V. (2003), *1. Volksentscheid-Ranking – Die direktdemokratischen Verfahren der Länder und Gemeinden im Vergleich* [Referendums – Ranking – Direct Democratic Procedures in the *Länder* and Municipalities Compared], Berlin: Mehr Demokratie e.V.

Meininger, M.-C. (2000), 'The development and current features of the French civil service system', in H. Bekke and F.M. van der Meer (eds), *Civil Service Systems in Western Europe*, Cheltenham, UK and Northampton, MA, USA: Edward Elgar Publishing, pp. 188–211.

Meneguzzo, M. (1997), 'Ripensare la modernizzazione amministrativa e il NPM. L'esperienza italiana: innovazione dal basso e sviluppo della governance locale' [Rethinking administrative modernization and NPM. The Italian experience: low innovation and development of local governance], *Azienda Pubblica*, **10**(6), 587–606.

Mény, Y. (1988), 'France', in D.C. Rowat (ed.), *Public Administration in Developed Democracies*, New York and Basel: Marcel Dekker, pp. 273–93.

Mény, Y. (1992), *La corruption de la république* [The Corruption of the Republic], Paris: Fayard.

Mergel, T. (2005), *Großbritannien seit 1945* [Great Britain Since 1945], Göttingen: UTB.

Merton, R.K. (1957), *Social Theory and Social Structure*, Glencoe, IL: The Free Press.

Meyer-Gohde, P., S. Meinshausen, D. Schierek and P. von Flotow (2013), 'Entflechtung und Rekommunalisierung von netzgebundenen Infrastrukturen' [Unbundling and remunicipalization of of grid-based infrastructures], *Zeitschrift für öffentliche und gemeinwirtschaftliche Unternehmen*, **36**(1), 17–37.

Meyer-Sahling, J.-H. and T. Veen (2012), 'Governing the post-communist state. Government alternation and senior civil service politicisation in Central and Eastern Europe', *East European Politics*, **28**(1), 1–19.

Meyssonnier, F. (1993), 'Quelques enseignements de l'étude du contrôle de gestion dans les collectivités locales' [Some lessons from the study of management control in the local communities], *Revue Politiques et Management Public*, **11**(1), 129–45.

Mill, J.S. (1991 [1835]), 'Considerations on representative government', in J. Gray (ed.), *John Stuart Mill: On Liberty and Other Essays*, Oxford and New York, pp. 5–128.

Millward, R. (2005), *Public and Private Enterprise in Europe: Energy, Telecommunication and Transport 1830–1990*, Cambridge, UK: Cambridge University Press.

Montin, S. (1999), 'Central state government reforms. Country report on Sweden', unpublished manuscript.

Montin, S. (2011), 'Swedish local government in multi-level governance', in H. Reynaert, K. Steyvers and E. Van Bever (eds), *The Road to Europe. Main Road or Backward Alley for Local Government in Europe*, Brugge: Vanden Broele, pp. 71–92.

Montin, S. and E. Amnå (2000), 'The local government act and municipal renewal in Sweden', in E. Amnå and S. Montin (eds), *Towards a New Concept of Local Self-government*, Bergen: Fagbokforlaget, pp. 157–85.

Moran, M. and B. Wood (1993), *States, Regulation and the Medical Profession*, Buckingham: Open University Press.

Moravcsik, A. (1994), *Why the European Union Strengthens the State. Domestic Politics and International Cooperation*, Cambridge, MA: Harvard University Press.

Morstein-Marx, F. (1959), *Einführung in die Bürokratie. Eine vergleichende Untersuchung über das Beamtentum* [Introduction to Bureaucracy: A Comparative Study of the Civil Service], Berlin and Darmstadt: Neuwied.

Morstein-Marx, F. (1962), *Control and Responsibility in Administration. Comparative Aspects*, Ann Arbor, MI: University of Michigan.

Morstein-Marx, F. (1965), 'Verwaltung in ausländischer Sicht. Ein Querschnitt durch das Schrifttum' [Administration from a foreign perspective. A cross-section through the literature], *Verwaltungsarchiv*, **56**(2), 105–22.

Mouritzen, P.E. and J.H. Svara (2002), *Leadership at the Apex. Politicians and Administrators in Western Local Governments*, Pittsburgh, PA: University of Pittsburgh Press.

Mouritzen, P.E. (2010), 'The Danish revolution in local government. How and why?', in H. Baldersheim and L.E. Rose (eds), *Territorial Choice*, Basingstoke: Palgrave Macmillan, pp. 21–41.

Mühlenkamp, H. (2010), 'Was bewirkt die Karotte vor der Nase? – Ein kritischer Blick auf anreizorientierte Entgeltsysteme im öffentlichen Sektor' [What effects does the 'carrot before your nose' have? A critical view on the incentive-related payment systems in the public sector], in A. Gourmelon and M. Mroß (eds), *Führung im öffentlichen Sektor* [Leadership in the Public Sector], Baden-Baden: Nomos, pp. 131–46.

Müller, W.C. (2001), 'Patronage by national governments', in J. Blondel and M. Cotta (eds), *The Nature of Party Government*, Basingstoke: Macmillan, pp. 141–60.

Münter, M. (2005), *Verfassungsreform im Einheitsstaat. Die Politik der Dezentralisierung in Großbritannien* [Constitutional Reform in the Unitary State. The Policy of Decentralization in the UK], Wiesbaden: VS Verlag für Sozialwissenschaften.

Naschold, F. (1995), *Ergebnissteuerung, Wettbewerb, Qualitätspolitik* [Management by Results, Competition, Quality Policy], Berlin: Edition Sigma.

Naschold, F. and J. Bogumil (2000), *Modernisierung des Staates. New Public Management in deutscher und internationaler Perspektive* [Modernization of the State. New Public Management from a German and International Perspective], 2nd edition, Opladen: Springer.

Naschold, F., W. Jann and C. Reichard (1999), *Innovation, Effektivität, Nachhaltigkeit. Internationale Erfahrungen zentralstaatlicher Verwaltungsreform* [Innovation, Effectiveness, Sustainability. International Experience of Central State Administration Reform], Berlin: Edition Sigma.

Naulleau, G. (2003), 'La mise en œuvre du contrôle de gestion dans les organisations publiques: les facteurs de réussite' [The implementation of management control in public organizations: success factors], *Revue Politiques et Management Public*, **21**(3), 135–47.

Nemec, J. (2008a), 'Public management reforms in CEE. Lessons learned', in G. Bouckaert, J. Nemec, V. Nakrošis, G. Hajnal and K. Tönnison, *Public Management Reforms in Central and Eastern Europe*, Bratislava: NISPAcee, pp. 343–72.

Nemec, J.-C. (2008b), 'Public management reform. Slovakia', in G. Bouckaert, J. Nemec, V. Nakrošis, G. Hajnal and K. Tönnison, *Public Management Reforms in Central and Eastern Europe*, Bratislava: NISPAcee, pp. 287–316.

Némery, J.-C. (ed.) (2010), *Quelle nouvelle réforme pour les collectivités territoriales françaises?* [What Further Reforms for the French Local Authorities?], Paris: Editions Harmattan.

Niskanen, W.A. (1971), *Bureaucracy and Representative Government*, Chicago: Aldine Atherton.

Norton, A. (1994), *International Handbook of Local and Regional Government. A Comparative Analysis of Advanced Democracies*, Aldershot, UK and Brookfield, VT, USA: Edward Elgar Publishing.

Oates, W. (1972), *Fiscal Federalism*, New York: Harcourt Brace Jovanovich.

OECD (1995), *Governance in Transition. Public Management in OECD Countries*, Paris: OECD.

OECD (1998), *Economic Outlook, No. 64*, Paris: OECD.

OECD (2000), *Regulatory Reform in Hungary*, Paris: OECD.

OECD (2003), *Fiscal Relations Across Government Levels*, Paris: OECD.

OECD (2005), *Performance-related Pay Policies for Government Employees*, Paris: OECD.

OECD (2008), *Public–Private Partnerships. In Pursuit of Risk Sharing and Value for Money*, Paris: OECD.

OECD (2009), *Government at a Glance 2009*, Paris: OECD.

OECD (2011), *Economic Outlook, 2011* (1 and 2), Paris: OECD.

Offe, C. (1991), 'Die deutsche Vereinigung als "natürliches Experiment"' [The German Federation as a 'natural experiment'] in B. Giesen and C. Leggewie (eds), *Experiment Vereinigung. Ein sozialer Großversuch* [Experiment Association: A Large-Scale Social Experiment], Berlin: Rotbuch, pp. 77–86.

Offe, C. (1994), *Der Tunnel am Ende des Lichts. Erkundungen der politischen Transformation im Neuen Osten* [The Tunnel at the End of the Light. Explorations of the Political Transformation in the New East], Frankfurt a.M. and New York: Campus Verlag.

Olsen, J.P. and B.G. Peters (eds) (1996), *Lessons from Experience. Experimental Learning in Administrative Reform in Eight Countries*, Oslo: Scandinavian University Press.

Olsson, J. and J. Aström (2003), 'Why regionalism in Sweden?', *Regional & Federal Studies*, **13**(3), 66–89.

Olsson, J. and J. Aström (2004), 'Sweden', in S. Dosenrode and H. Halklev (eds), *The Nordic Regions and the European Union*, Aldershot: Ashgate, pp. 77–92.

Ongaro, E. (2009), *Public Management Reform and Modernization. Trajectories of Administrative Change in Italy, France, Greece, Portugal and Spain*, Cheltenham, UK and Northampton, MA, USA: Edward Elgar Publishing.

Ongaro, E. and G. Valotti (2008), 'Public management reform in Italy. Explaining the implementation gap', *International Journal of Public Sector Management*, **21**(2), 174–204.

Oppen, M. (1997), 'Der Bürger und Kunde als ProMotor im Modernisierungsprozess – Kundenorientierte Dienstleistungsgestaltung in internationaler Perspektive' [The citizen and customer as a promoter in the modernization process – customer-focused service design in an international perspective], in F. Naschold, M. Oppen and A. Wegener, *Innovative Kommunen. Internationale Trends und deutsche Erfahrungen* [Innovative Local Authorities. International Trends and German Experiences], Stuttgart: Kohlhammer, pp. 231–68.

Ostrom, V. and F.P. Bish (1977), *Comparing Urban Service Delivery Systems: Structure and Performance*, Beverly Hills, CA: Sage.

Ostrom, E., R. Gardner and J. Walker (1994), *Rules, Games, and Common-pool Resources*, Ann Arbor, MI: University of Michigan Press.

Page, E.C. (1992), *Political Autonomy and Bureaucratic Power. A Comparative Analysis*, 2nd edition, Brighton: Harvester.

Page, E.C. (2010), 'Has the Whitehall model survived?', *International Review of Administrative Sciences*, **76**(3), 407–23.

Page, E.C. and M.J. Goldsmith (eds) (1987), *Central and Local Government Relations. A Comparative Analysis of West European Unitary States*, London: Sage.

Page, E.C. and V. Wright (eds) (1999), *Bureaucratic Elites in Western European States*, Oxford, UK: Oxford University Press.

Painter, M. and B.G. Peters (2010), 'Administrative traditions in comparative perspective: families, groups and hybrids', in M. Painter and B.G. Peters (eds), *Tradition and Public Administration*, Basingstoke: Palgrave Macmillan, pp. 19–30.

Palermo, F. (2005), 'Italy's long devolutionary path towards federalism', in S. Ortino, M. Zagar and M. Vojtech (eds), *The Changing Faces of Federalism. Institutional Reconfiguration in Europe from East to West*, Manchester: Manchester University Press, pp. 182–201.

Peters, B.G. (1996), 'Theory and methodology', in H.A.G.M. Bekke, J.L. Perry and T.A.J. Toonen (eds), *Civil Service Systems in Comparative Perspective*, Bloomington, IN: Indiana University Press, pp. 13–41.

Peters, B.G. (1999), *Institutional Theory in Political Science. The 'New Institutionalism'*, London and New York: Continuum.

Peters, B.G. (2008), 'The Napoleonic tradition', *International Journal of Public Sector Management*, **21**(2), 118–32.

Peters, B.G. (2009), *The Politics of Bureaucracy. An Introduction to Comparative Public Administration*, 6th edition, London: Routledge.

Peters, B.G. and J. Pierre (2004), *Politicization of the Civil Service in Comparative Perspective. The Quest for Control*, London: Routledge.

Peters, B.G. and J. Pierre (eds) (2007), *Handbook of Public Administration*, London: Sage.

Peters, B.G. and D.J. Savoie (1998), *Taking Stock – Assessing Public Sector Reforms*, Montreal/Kingston, ON: Centre for Management Development and McGill-Queen's University Press.

Petersson, O. (1994), *Swedish Government and Politics*, Stockholm: Fritzes.

Petitt, P. (2004), 'Depoliticizing democracy', *Ratio Juris*, **17**(1), 52–65.

Pfeil, E. (2010), 'Hungarian public service reform. Multipurpose microregional associations', in P. Swianiewicz (ed.), *Territorial Consolidation Reforms in Europe*, Budapest: Open Society Institute, pp. 255–64.

Pierre, J. (1994), *Den lokala staten. Den kommunala självstyrelsens förutsättningar och restriktioner* [Local Government. Local Self-government Conditions and Restrictions], Stockholm: Almqvist & Wiksell.

Pierre, J. (1995a), 'Governing the welfare state. Public administration, the state and society in Sweden', in J. Pierre, (ed.), *Bureaucracy in the Modern State. An Introduction to Comparative Public Administration*, Aldershot, UK and Brookfield, VT, USA: Edward Elgar Publishing, pp. 140–60.

Pierre, J. (2010), 'Administrative reform in Sweden. The resilience of administrative tradition', in M. Painter and B.G. Peters (eds), *Tradition and Public Administration*, Basingstoke: Macmillan, pp. 191–202.

Pierson, P. (2004), *Politics in Time. History, Institutions, and Social Analysis*, Princeton, NJ and Oxford, UK: Princeton University Press.

Pleschberger, W. (2009), 'Die Modernisierung der kommunalen Verwaltung. Outsourcing kommunaler Aufgaben im Vormarsch' [The modernization of municipal administration. Advances in Outsourcing of municipal activities], Austrian community paper, No. 12-2009/01-2010, 33–5.

Pohl, H. (1991), 'Entwicklung des Verwaltungsrechts' [Development of administrative law], in K. König (ed.), *Verwaltungsstrukturen der DDR* [Administrative Structures of the GDR], Baden-Baden: Nomos, pp. 235–49.

Polanyi, L. (1944), *The Great Transformation. The Political and Economic Origins of Our Time*, New York: Farrar & Rinehart.

Pollack, M.A. (1997), 'Delegation, agency and agenda setting in the European Community', *International Organization*, **51**(1), 99–134.

Pollitt, C. (2001), 'Clarifying convergence. Striking similarities and durable differences in public management reform', *Public Management Review*, **4**(1), 471–92.

Pollitt, C. (2005), 'Decentralization. A central concept in contemporary public management', in E. Ferlie, L. Lynn and C. Pollitt (eds), *The Oxford Handbook of Public Administration*, Oxford, UK: Oxford University Press, pp. 371–97.

Pollitt, C. (2010), 'Riggs on comparative public administration. Looking back half a century', *International Review of Administrative Sciences*, **76**(4), 761–6.

Pollitt, C. (2011), 'Not odious but onerous. Comparative public administration', *Public Administration*, **89**(1), 114–27.

Pollitt, C. and G. Bouckaert (2004), *Public Management Reform. A Comparative Analysis*, Oxford, UK: Oxford University Press.

Pollitt, C. and G. Bouckaert, (2009), *Continuity and Change in Public Policy and Management*, Cheltenham, UK and Northampton, MA, USA: Edward Elgar Publishing.

Pollitt, C. and G. Bouckaert (2011), *Public Management Reform. A Comparative Analysis – New Public Management, Governance, and the Neo-Weberian State*, 3rd edition, Oxford, UK: Oxford University Press.

Pollitt, C., J. Birchall and K. Putman (1998), *Decentralising Public Service Management. The British Experience*, Basingstoke: Palgrave Macmillan.

Pollitt, C, C. Talbot, J. Caulfield and A. Smullen (2004), *Agencies. How Governments Do Things Through Semi-autonomous Organizations*, Basingstoke: Palgrave Macmillan.

Pollitt, C., K. Bathgate, J. Caulfield, A. Smullen and C. Talbot (2001), 'Agency fever? Analysis of an international policy fashion', *Journal of Comparative Policy Analysis*, **3**(3), 271–90.

Praetorius, B. and S. Bolay (2009), 'Implementing energy efficiency innovations: the strategic role of local utilities', last accessed 14 March 2014 at http://cleanenergysolutions.org/node/1445.

Premfors, R. (1998), 'Reshaping the democratic state. Swedish experiences in a comparative perspective', *Public Administration*, **76**(1), 141–59.

Proeller, I. and J.P. Siegel (2009), 'Performance management in der deutschen Verwaltung – eine explorative Einschätzung' [Performance management in German administration – an exploratory assessment], *der moderne staat* (dms), **2**(2), 455–74.

Promberger, K., J. Bernhart, G. Früh and R. Niederkofler (2000), *New Public Management in Italien* [New Public Management in Italy], Bozen: European Academy of Bozen/Bolzano (EURAC).

PricewaterhouseCoopers (PwC) (2008), *Leistungsorientierte Bezahlung in deutschen Kommunalverwaltungen. Lohn für Leistung statt Dienst nach Vorschrift* [Performance-related Pay in German Local Governments. Pay for Performance Instead of Working by Rule], Berlin: PwC.

Quack, S. (2005), 'Zum Werden und Vergehen von Institutionen – Vorschläge für eine dynamische Governanceanalyse' [Growth and decay of institutions – proposals for a dynamic analysis of governance], in G.F. Schuppert (ed.), *Governanceforschung. Vergewisserung über Stand und Entwicklungslinien* [Governance Research. Reassurance about the Status and Lines of Development], Baden-Baden: Nomos, pp. 346–70.

Raadschelders, J.C.N. (2011), 'Commentary – between "thick description" and large-n studies. The fragmentation of comparative research', *Public Administration Review*, **71**(6), 831–3.

Raadschelders, J.C.N. and M.R. Rutgers (1996), 'The evolution of civil service systems', in H.A.G.M. Bekke, J.L. Perry and T.A.J. Toonen (eds), *Civil Service Systems in Comparative Perspective*, Bloomington, IN: Indiana University Press, pp. 67–99.

Raadschelders, J.C.N., T.A.J. Toonen and F.M. van der Meer (eds) (2007), *Comparative Civil Service Systems in the 21st Century*, Basingstoke: Palgrave Macmillan.

Reichard, C. (1994), *Umdenken im Rathaus. Neue Steuerungsmodelle in der deutschen Kommunalverwaltung* [Rethinking in the Town Hall. New Steering Models in German Local Administration], Berlin: Edition Sigma.

Reichard, C. (2001), 'Strategisches Management in der Kernverwaltung' [Strategic management in the core administration], in P. Eichhorn and M. Wiechers (eds), *Strategisches Management für Kommunalverwaltungen* [Strategic Management for Local Administrations], Baden-Baden: Nomos, pp. 80–91.

Reichard, C. (2002), 'Institutionenökonomische Ansätze und New Public Management' [Institutional economics approach and NPM] in K. König (eds), *Deutsche Verwaltung an der Wende zum 21. Jahrhundert* [German Administration at the Turn of the 21st Century], Baden-Baden: Nomos, pp. 585–603.

Reichard, C. (2006), 'New institutional arrangements of public service delivery', in C. Reichard, R. Mussari and S. Kupke (eds), *The Governance of Services of General Interest Between State, Market and Society*, Berlin: Wissenschaftlicher Verlag, pp. 35–47.

Reichard, C. and M. Röber (2012), 'Remuncipalization in Germany – trends and interpretations', unpublished manuscript.

Reimer, S. (1999), '"Getting by" in time and space. Fragmented work in local authorities', *Economic Geography*, **75**(2), 157–77.

Rein, M. and D.A. Schön (1977), 'Problem setting in policy research', in C.H. Weiss (ed.), *Using Social Research in Public Policy Making*, Lexington, MA: Lexington Books, pp. 235–50.

Rein, M. and D.A. Schön (1993), 'Reframing policy discourse', in F. Fischer and J. Forester (eds), *The Argumentative Turn in Policy Analysis and Planning*, Durham, NC: Duke University Press, pp. 145–66.

Reiners, M. (2008), *Verwaltungsstrukturreformen in den deutschen Bundesländern. Radikale Reformen auf der Ebene der staatlichen Mittelinstanz* [Administrative Structural Reforms in German Länder. Radical Reforms on the Meso level], Wiesbaden: VS Verlag für Sozialwissenschaften.

Reiter, R. (2010), 'Zwei Schritte vor, einer zurück? – Dezentralisierung der Sozialhilfepolitik in Frankreich' [Two steps forward, one back? Decentralization of social welfare policy in France], in J. Bogumil and S. Kuhlmann (eds), *Kommunale Aufgabenwahrnehmung im Wandel. Kommunalisierung, Regionalisierung und Territorialreform in Deutschland und Europa* [Local Government Task Performance in Transition: Municipalization, Regionalization and Territorial Reform in Germany and Europe], Wiesbaden: VS Verlag für Sozialwissenschaften, pp. 255–78.

Reiter, R., S. Grohs, F. Ebinger, S. Kuhlmann and J. Bogumil (2010), 'Impacts of decentralization. The French experience in a comparative perspective', *French Politics*, **8**(2), 166–89.

Rhodes, R.A.W. and J. Wanna (2009), 'Bringing the politics back in. Public value in Westminster parliamentary government', *Public Administration*, **87**(2), 161–83.

Rhodes, R.A.W., J. Wanna and P. Weller (2010), *Comparing Westminster*, Oxford, UK: Oxford University Press.

Ricciardi, A. (2010), *Das deutsche und italienische Wohlfahrtsstaaten-Modell. Konservative Regime?* [The German and Italian Welfare State Models: Conservative Regimes?] Köln: Grin Verlag.

Richter, P. (2010), 'Kommunalisierung der Schulaufsicht – Erfahrungen aus der Baden-Württembergischen Verwaltungsstrukturreform' [Municipalization of school supervision – experiences from Baden-Württemberg's administrative structural reform], in J. Bogumil and S. Kuhlmann (eds), *Kommunale Aufgabenwahrnehmung im Wandel. Kommunalisierung, Regionalisierung und Territorialreform in Deutschland und Europa* [Local Government Task Performance in Transition: Municipalization, Regionalization and Territorial Reform in Germany and Europe], Wiesbaden: VS Verlag für Sozialwissenschaften, pp. 67–88.

Richter, R. and E.G. Furubotn (1996), *Neue Institutionenökonomik* [New Institutional Economics], Tübingen: Mohr.

Richter, P., T. Edeling and C. Reichard (2006), 'Kommunale Betriebe in größeren Städten. Ergebnisse einer empirischen Analyse der Beteiligungen deutscher Städte über 50 000 Einwohner' [Municipal enterprises in larger cities. Results of an empirical study of the involvement of German municipalities with more than 50 000 inhabitants], in W. Killian, P. Richter and J.-H. Trapp (eds), *Ausgliederung und Privatisierung in Kommunen. Empirische Befunde zur Struktur kommunaler Aufgabenwahrnehmung* [Outsourcing and Privatization in Municipalities.

Empirical Findings on the Structure of Municipal Task Performance], Berlin: Edition Sigma, pp. 56–84.

Ridley, F.F. (2000), 'The public service in Britain. From administrative to managerial culture', in H. Wollmann and E. Schröter (eds), *Comparing Public Sector Reform in Britain and Germany*, Aldershot: Ashgate, pp. 132–52.

Riegler, C. and F. Naschold (eds) (1997), *Reformen des öffentlichen Sektors in Skandinavien* [Public Sector Reforms in Scandinavia], Baden-Baden: Nomos.

Riggs, F.W. (1954), 'Notes on literature available for the study of comparative public administration', *The American Political Science Review*, **48**(2), 515–37.

Riggs, F.W. (1976), 'The group and the movement. Notes on comparative development administration', *Public Administration Review*, **36**(6), 648–54.

Riggs, F.W. (2010), 'Trends in the comparative study of public administration', *International Review of Administrative Sciences*, **76**(4), 750–60.

Ritz, A. (2003), *Die Evaluation von New Public Management* [The Evaluation of New Public Management], Bern: Haupt.

Röber, M. (2009), 'Privatisierung adé? Rekommunalisierung öffentlicher Dienstleistungen im Lichte des Public Managements' [Goodbye privatization? Remunicpalization of public services provision in the light of public management], *Verwaltung & Management*, **15**(5), 227–40.

Röber, M. and E. Schröter (2000), 'Local government services in Britain and Germany', in H. Wollmann and E. Schröter (eds), *Comparing Public Sector Reform in Britain and Germany*, Aldershot: Ashgate, pp. 171–97.

Röber, M. and E. Schröter (2004), 'Europäische Metropolen im Vergleich. Institutionenentwicklung zwischen Konvergenz und Divergenz' [European metropolitan cities compared. Institutional development between convergence and divergence], *Deutsche Zeitschrift für Kommunalwissenschaft*, **43**(2), 129–58.

Rodden, B. (2002), 'The dilemma of fiscal federalism. Grants and fiscal performance around the world', *American Journal of Political Science*, **46**(3), 670–87.

Rokkan, S. (1970), *Citizens, Elections, Parties. Approaches to the Comparative Study of the Processes of Development*, Oslo: Universitetsforlaget.

Rose, R. (1982), *Understanding the United Kingdom. The Territorial Dimension in Government*, New York: Chatham House Publishers.

Rose, R. (1993), *Lesson Drawing in Public Policy. A Guide to Learning Across Time and Space*, Chatham, NJ: Chatham House.

Roseveare, D., M. Jorgensen and L. Goranson (2004), 'Product market competition and economic performance in Sweden', Economic Department Working Paper No. 388, last accessed 10 March 2014 at http://www.oecd-ilibrary.org/content/workingpaper/735381855384.

Rouban, L. (1999), 'The senior civil service in France', in E.C. Page and V. Wright (eds), *Bureaucratic Elites in Western European States. A Comparative Analysis of Top Officials*, Oxford, UK: Oxford University Press, pp. 65–89.

Rudzio, W. (2003), *Das politische System der Bundesrepublik Deutschland* [The Political System of the Federal Republic of Germany], 6th edition, Opladen: Leske + Budrich.

Saatweber, V.-S. (2004), 'Das europäische Selbstbewertungsinstrument Common Assessment Framework (CAF)' [The European self-assessment tool Common Assessment Framework (CAF)], in S. Kuhlmann, J. Bogumil and H. Wollmann (eds), *Leistungsmessung und -vergleich in Politik und Verwaltung* [Performance Measurement and Benchmarking in Politics and Administration], Wiesbaden: VS Verlag für Sozialwissenschaften, pp. 227–49.

Sabatier, P.A. (1993), 'Advocacy-Koalitionen, Policy-Wandel und Policy-Lernen. Eine Alternative zur Phasenheuristik' [Advocacy coalitions, policy change and policy learning. An alternative to the heuristic phase model], in A. Héritier (ed.), *Policy-Analyse. Kritik und Neuorientierung.*

PVS-Sonderheft [Policy Analysis. Critique and Reorientation. PVS Special Issue], **24**, Opladen: Westdeutscher Verlag, 116–48.

Sack, D. (2006), 'Liberalisierung und Privatisierung in den Kommunen – Steuerungsanforderungen und Folgen für Entscheidungsprozesse' [Liberalization and privatization in the municipalities – controlling requirements and consequences for decision-making processes], *Deutsche Zeitschrift für Kommunalwissenschaften*, **45**(2), 25–38.

Sadran, P. (2006), 'The evolution of public personnel systems in France. Structure and reforms', in V. Hoffmann-Martinot and H. Wollmann (eds), *State and Local Government Reforms in France and Germany, Divergence and Convergence*, Wiesbaden: Springer, pp. 75–88.

Sahlin-Andersson, K. (2001), 'National, international and transnational constructions of New Public Management', in T. Christensen and P. Laegreid (eds), *New Public Management. The Transformation of Ideas and Practice*, Aldershot: Ashgate, pp. 43–72.

Santini, A. (1990), 'Préface', in J.-C. Michel, *Les sociétés d'économie mixte locales* [Public–Private Companies], Paris: Librairie.

Sausman, C. and R. Locke (2007), 'The changing role of the British senior civil service. Challenge and reform', in E.C. Page and V. Wright (eds), *From the Active to the Enabling State. The Changing Role of Top Officials in European Nations*, Basingstoke: Palgrave Macmillan, pp. 89–207.

Schäfer, R. (2007), 'Daseinsvorsorge kommunal oder privat? Erfolgreiche Kommunalisierung der Abfallentsorgung in Bergkamen', Unveröff Diskussionspapier im Rahmen der 16 Kölner Abfalltagung [Public service provision – Municipal or private? Successful municipalization of waste disposal in Bergkamen, unpublished discussion paper as part of the 16th Cologne Waste Conference].

Schalauske, J. and S. Streb (2008), 'Schweden. Wettbewerbsmodernisierung im Wohlfahrtsstaat' [Sweden. Modernization by competition in the welfare state], in H.-J. Bieling, C. Deckwirth and S. Schmalz (eds), *Liberalisierung und Privatisierung in Europa. Die Reorganisation der öffentlichen Infrastruktur in der Europäischen Union* [Liberalization and Privatization in Europe. The Reorganization of the Public Infrastructure in the EU], Münster: Westfälisches, pp. 215–44.

Scharpf, F.W. (1999), *Regieren in Europa. Effektiv und demokratisch?* [Governing in Europe. Effective and Democratic?], Frankfurt a.M. and New York: Campus Verlag.

Scharpf, F.W. (2000), *Interaktionsformen. Akteurzentrierter Institutionalismus in der Politikforschung* [Forms of Interaction. Actor-centred Institutionalism in Policy Research], Opladen: Leske + Budrich.

Scharpf, F.W., B. Reissert and F. Schnabel (1976), *Politikverflechtung. Theorie und Empirie des kooperativen Föderalismus in der Bundesrepublik* [Policy Interwovenness. Theory and Empirical Research of Cooperative Federalism in the Federal Republic], Kronberg: Scriptor Verlag.

Schedler, K. (2008), 'The study of public management in Switzerland', in W.J.M. Kickert (ed.), *The Study of Public Management in Europe and the US*, London: Routledge, pp. 144–66.

Schedler, K. and I. Proeller (2000), *New Public Management*, Bern: Haupt.

Scheele, U. and D. Sterzel (2000), *Öffentlicher Personennahverkehr zwischen Gemeinwohlinteressen und Markt* [Public Transport Between the Public Interest and the Market], Baden-Baden: Nomos.

Schefold, D. (2007), 'Verfassungs- und Verwaltungsrecht' [Constitutional and administrative law], in S. Grundmann and A. Zaccaria (eds), *Einführung in das italienische Recht* [Introduction to Italian Law], Frankfurt a.M.: Verlag Recht und Wirtschaft, pp. 22–118.

Schmid, J. and S. Frech (eds) (2004), *Der Sozialstaat. Reform, Umbau, Abbau?* [The Welfare State: Reform, Restructuring, Downsizing?], Schwalbach: Newsreel Verlag.

Schmidt, M.G. (2000), Demokratietheorien [Democratic Theories], 3rd edition, Wiesbaden: VS Verlag für Sozialwissenschaften.

Schmidt, S.K. (2004), 'Rechtsunsicherheit statt Regulierungswettbewerb. Die nationalen Folgen des europäischen Binnenmarktes für Dienstleistungen', Habilitationsschrift [Legal uncertainty rather than regulatory competition. The national impact of the European internal market on the provision of services. Habilitation thesis], Hagen: FernUniversität.

Schmidt, S.K. (2008), 'Beyond compliance. The Europeanization of member states through negative integration and legal uncertainty', *Journal of Comparative Policy Analysis*, **10**(3), 297–306.

Schmidt, V. (2008), 'Discursive institutionalism. The explanatory power of ideas and discourse', *Annual Review of Political Science*, **11**(1), 303–26.

Schmidt-Eichstaedt, G. (1999), 'Autonomie und Regelung von oben' [Autonomy and regulation from above], in H. Wollmann and R. Roth (eds), *Kommunalpolitik* [Local Politics], 2nd edition, Opladen: Leske + Budrich, pp. 323–37.

Schnapp, K.-U. (2004), *Ministerialbürokratien in westlichen Demokratien. Eine vergleichende Analyse* [Ministerial Bureaucracies in Western Democracies: A Comparative Analysis], Opladen: Leske + Budrich.

Schnapp, K.-U. (2006), 'Comparative public administration', in J. Bogumil, W. Jann and F. Nullmeier (eds), *Politik und Verwaltung. PVS-Sonderheft* [Politics and Administration: PVS Special Issue], 37, Wiesbaden: VS Verlag für Sozialwissenschaften, pp. 327–53.

Schröter, E. (2001), 'Staats- und Verwaltungsmodernisierung in Europa. Internationale Trends und nationale Profile' [State and administrative modernization in Europe. International trends and national profiles], in E. Schröter (ed.), *Empirische Policy- und Verwaltungsforschung. Lokale, nationale und internationale Perspektiven* [Empirical Policy and Administration Research. Local, National and International Perspectives], Opladen: Leske + Budrich, pp. 421–51.

Schröter, E. (2011), 'New public management', in B. Blanke, F. Nullmeier, C. Reichard and G. Wewer (eds), *Handbuch zur Verwaltungsreform* [Handbook of Administrative Reform], 4th edition, Wiesbaden: VS Verlag für Sozialwissenschaften, pp. 79–89.

Schultz, R. and S. Harrison (1986), 'Physician autonomy in the Federal Republic of Germany, Great Britain and the United States', *International Journal of Health Care Planning and Management*, **1**(5), 335–55.

Schuster, F. (2003), *Der interkommunale Leistungsvergleich als Wettbewerbssurrogat* [Inter-municipal Benchmarking as a Competitive Surrogate], Berlin: Verlag für Wirtschaftskommunikation.

Schwanke, K. and F. Ebinger (2006), 'Politisierung und Rollenverständnis der deutschen Administrativen Elite 1970 bis 2005 – Wandel trotz Kontinuität' [Politicization and role perception in the German administrative elite 1970–2005 – continuity in spite of change], in J. Bogumil, W. Jann and F. Nullmeier (eds), *Politik und Verwaltung. PVS-Sonderheft* [Politics and Administration: PVS Special Issue], **37**, Wiesbaden: VS Verlag für Sozialwissenschaften, pp. 228–49.

Segal, L. (1997), 'The pitfalls of decentralization and proposals for reforms', *Public Administration Review*, **57**(2), 141–9.

Selden, S.C. (2007), 'Innovations and global trends in human resource management practices', in B.G. Peters and J. Pierre (eds), *Handbook of Public Administration*, London: Sage, pp. 62–71.

Selznik, P. (1957), *Leadership in Administration*, New York: Harper and Row.

Sharpe, L.J. (1993), 'The United Kingdom: the disjointed meso', in L.J. Sharpe (ed.), *The Rise of Meso Government in Europe*, London: Sage, pp. 246–95.

Sharpe, L.J. (2000), 'Regionalism in the United Kingdom. The role of social federalism', in H. Wollmann and E. Schröter (eds), *Comparing Public Sector Reform in Britain and Germany*, Aldershot: Ashgate, pp. 67–84.

Shonfield, A. (1965) *Modern Capitalism*, Oxford, UK: Oxford University Press.

Singer, O. (1993), 'Policy communities und Diskurs-Koalitionen. Experten und Expertise in der Wirtschaftspolitik' [Policy communities and discourse coalitions. Experts and expertise in economic policy making], in A. Héritier (eds), *Policy-Analyse. Kritik und Neuorientierung.*

PVS-Sonderheft [Policy Analysis. Critique and Reorientation. PVS Special Issue], **24**, Opladen: Westdeutscher Verlag, pp. 149–74.

Skelcher, C. (1998), *The Appointed State. Quasi-governmental Organizations and Democracy*, Buckingham: Open University Press.

Skelcher, C. (2000), *Advance of the Quango State*, London: LGIU.

SKF/SCB (Svenska Kommunförbundet/Statistiska Centralbyrån) (2004), *Vad kostar verksamheten i Din kommun? (Was kosten die Tätigkeiten in Deiner Kommune?)* [How Much Do the Activities in Your Municipality Cost?], Fiscal Year (2003), Stockholm.

Smullen, A. (2010), *Translating Agency Reforms. Rhetoric and Culture in Comparative Perspective*, Basingstoke: Palgrave.

Sommermann, K.-P. (2002), 'Verwaltung und Governance im Mehrebenensystem der Europäischen Union – Resümee und Perspektiven' [Administration and governance in the multi-level system of the European Union – summary and perspectives], in S. Magiera and K.-P. Sommermann (eds), *Verwaltung und Governance im Mehrebenensystem der Europäischen Union* [Administration and Governance in the Multi-level System of the EU], Berlin: Duncker & Humblot, pp. 193–6.

Soós, G. (2003), 'Local government reforms and the capacity for local governance in Hungary', in N. Kersting and A. Vetter (eds), *Reforming Local Government in Europe*, Wiesbaden: VS Verlag für Sozialwissenschaften, pp. 241–60.

Sotiropoulos, D.A. (2009), 'Southern European bureaucracies in comparative perspective', *West European Politics*, **27**(3), 405–22.

SOU (2007a), *Hållbar samhällsorganisaton med utvecklingskraft. Anvarskommitténs slutbetänkande (Nachhaltige Sozialstaatsorganisation und Innovationskraft)*, Schlussbericht, Feb. 2007 [Sustainable welfare state organization and innovation capacity. Final report], last accessed 14 March 2014 at http://www.regeringskansliet.se/sb/d/8728/a/77520.

SOU (2007b), *Anvarskommitténs*, slutbetänkande [Responsibility Commission, final report], English language summary.

Spanou, C. (2001), *Permanent Challenges? Representing Greece in Brussels in the National Coordination of EU Policy*, Oxford, UK: Oxford University Press.

Special Eurobarometer 307 (2009), *Rolle und Einfluss lokaler und regionaler Gebietskörperschaften innerhalb der Europäischen Union* [Role and Influence of Local and Regional Authorities within the EU], last accessed 14 March 2014 at http://ec.europa.eu/public_opinion/archives/ebs/ebs_307_de.pdf.

Speer, B. (2002), 'Governance, good governance und öffentliche Verwaltung in den Transformationsländern Mittel- und Osteuropas' [Governance, good governance and public administration in the transition countries of Central and Eastern Europe], in K. König et al. (eds), *Governance als entwicklungs- und transformationspolitisches Konzept* [Governance as a Developmental and Transformational Political Concept], Berlin: Duncker & Humblot, pp. 207–75.

Statistisches Bundesamt (Federal Statistic Office) (2003c, 2005), 'Pflegestatistik' [Care services statistics], Bonn: Statistisches Bundesamt.

Steffani, W. (eds) (1995), *Demokratie in Europa. Zur Rolle der Parlamente* [Democracy in Europe. The Role of Parliaments], Opladen: Westdeutscher Verlag.

Stegmann McCallion, M. (2008), 'Tidying up? European regionalization and the Swedish "regional mess"', *Regional Studies*, **42**(4), 579–92.

Steinkämper, B. (1974), 'Klassische und politische Bürokraten in der Ministerialverwaltung der Bundesrepublik Deutschland. Eine Darstellung sozialstruktureller Merkmale unter dem Aspekt politischer Funktionen der Verwaltung' [Classical and political bureaucrats in the ministerial administration of the Federal Republic of Germay. An account of socio-structural characteristics from the aspect of the political functions of administration], dissertation, Universität Köln.

Steinmo, S. and K. Thelen et al. (eds) (1992), *Structuring Politics. Historical Institutionalism in Comparative Analysis*, New York: Cambridge University Press.

Stellermann, R., A. Jaitner, S. Kuhlmann and G. Schneider (2009), *Evaluation der Erfahrungen mit dem Leistungsentgelt nach TVöD im Bundesbereich* [Evaluation of the Experience with the Performance-related Pay as TVöD in the Federal area], Berlin: Bearing Point.

Stewart, J. (2000), *The Nature of British Local Government*, Basingstoke: Palgrave Macmillan.

Stewart, J. (2003), *Modernising British Local Government*, Basingstoke: Palgrave Macmillan.

Stoker, G. (1991), *The Politics of Local Government*, 2nd edition, London: Macmillan.

Stoker, G. (1998), 'British local government. Under new management', in D. Grunow and H. Wollmann (eds), *Lokale Verwaltungsmodernisierung in Aktion* [Local Government Modernization in Action], Basel: Birkhäuser, pp. 371–85.

Stoker, G. (1999), 'Quangos and local democracy', in M.V. Flinders and M.J. Smith (eds), *Quangos, Accountability and Reform. The Politics of Quasi-government*, Basingstoke: Palgrave Macmillan, pp. 40–54.

Strid, L. (2004), 'Comparative municipal quality networks in Sweden', in S. Kuhlmann, J. Bogumil and H. Wollmann (eds), *Leistungsmessung und -vergleich in Politik und Verwaltung* [Measurement and Benchmarking in Politics and Administration], Wiesbaden: VS Verlag für Sozialwissenschaften, pp. 267–76.

Strömberg, L. and T. Engen (1996), 'Sweden', in E. Albaek, L.E. Rose, L. Strömberg and K. Ståhlberg (eds), *Nordic Local Government. The Association of Finish Local Authorities*, Helsinki: Association of Finnish Local Authorities, pp. 235–70.

Struyk, R.J. (2003), *Contracting With NGOs For Social Services. Building Civil Society and Efficient Local Government in Russia*, The Urban Institute, last accessed 10 March 2014 at http://www.urban.org/publications/410871.html.

Sturm, R. (2002), 'Devolutions- und Verfassungsreformprozesse in Großbritannien' [Devolution and constitutional reform processes in the UK], in U. Margedant (ed.), *Föderalismusreform. Föderalismus in Europa II* [Federalism Reform. Federalism in Europe II], St. Augustin: KAS, pp. 48–63.

Sturm, R. (2003), 'Das politische System Großbritanniens' [The political system of Great Britain], in W. Ismayr (eds), *Die politischen Systeme Westeuropas* [The Political Systems of Western Europe], 2nd edition, Opladen: Leske + Budrich, pp. 225–62.

Sturm, R., (2006), 'Staatsaufbau und politische Institutionen' [State structure and political institutions], in H. Kastendiek and R. Sturm (eds), *Länderbericht Großbritannien* [Country Report: United Kingdom], 3rd edition, Bonn: Bundeszentrale für politische Bildung, pp. 135–63.

Suleiman, E.N. (1974), *Politics, Power, and Bureaucracy in France. The Administrative Elite*, Princeton, NJ: Princeton University Press.

Suleiman, E.N. (ed.) (1984), *Bureaucrats and Policy Making. A Comparative Overview*, New York: Holmes and Meier.

Sundström, G. (2004), 'Management by measurement. Its origin and development in the case of Sweden', Working Paper 2004, Stockholm: Stockholm Centre for Organizational Research.

Swianiewicz, P. (2003), *Public Perception of Local Government*, 2nd edition, Budapest: Open Society Institute.

Swianiewicz, P. (2010) (ed.), *Territorial Consolidation Reforms in Europe*, Budapest: Open Society Institute.

Talbot, C. (2004), *The Agency Idea. Sometimes Old, Sometimes New, Sometimes Borrowed, Sometimes Untrue. A Critical Analysis of the Global Trend to Agencies, Quangos and Contractualisation*, London: Routledge, pp. 3–21.

Teller, N. and E. Somogyi (2005), *Public Services in Hungary*, accessed 10 March 2014 at http://www.fes.hr/E-books/pdf/Reforms%20of%20Public%20Services/05.pdf.

Temesi, I. (2000), 'Local government in Hungary', in T. Horváth (ed.), *Decentralization. Experiments and Reforms*, Budapest: Open Society Institute, pp. 343–85.

Temesi, I. (2003), 'Transfer of municipal property in Hungary', in G. Péteri (ed.), *From Usage to Ownership Transfer of Public Property to Local Governments in Central Europe*, Budapest: Open Society Institute, pp. 27–44.

Thedieck, F. (1992), *Verwaltungskultur in Deutschland und Frankreich. Dargestellt am Beispiel von französischen und deutschen Gemeindeverwaltungen und unteren staatlichen Verwaltungsbehörden* [Administrative Culture in Germany and France. The example of the French and German Local Administration and Lower State Administration], Baden-Baden: Nomos.

Thoenig, J.-C. (2005), 'Territorial administration and political control: decentralization in France', *Public Administration*, **83**(3), 685–708.

Tiebout, C. (1956), 'A pure theory of local expenditures', *Journal of Political Economy*, **64**(5), 416–24.

Tiessen, J. (2007), 'Die Resultate im Blick. Kontraktsteuerung in Schweden' [The results in view. Management by contracts in Sweden], in W. Jann and M. Döhler (eds), *Agencies in Westeuropa* [Agencies in Western Europe], Wiesbaden: VS Verlag für Sozialwissenschaften, pp. 138–71.

Tittor, A. (2008), 'Privatisierung von Staatsbetrieben in Ungarn. Vom "Gradualismus" zur Europäisierung' [Privatization of state enterprises in Hungary. From 'gradualism' to Europeanization], in H.-J. Bieling, C. Deckwirth and S. Schmalz (eds) (2008), *Liberalisierung und Privatisierung in Europa. Die Reorganisation der öffentlichen Infrastruktur in der Europäischen Union* [Liberalization and Privatization in Europe. The Reorganization of the Public Infrastructure in the EU], Münster: Westfälisches, pp. 277–305.

Töller, A.E. (2010), 'Measuring and comparing the Europeanization of public policies', *Journal of Common Market Studies*, **48**(1), 413–40.

Tondorf, K. (2006), 'Diskriminierungsmechanismen beim Leistungsentgelt' [Discrimination mechanisms in performance pay], in S. Baer and D. Englert (eds), *Gender Mainstreaming in der Personalentwicklung* [Gender Mainstreaming in Staff Development], Bielefeld: Kleine, pp. 76–102.

Trapp, J.-H., S. Tomerius and J. Libbe (2002), 'Liberalisierung und Privatisierung kommunaler Aufgabenerfüllung – strategische Steuerung statt operatives Management?' [Liberalization and privatization of municipal services – strategic management rather than operational management?], in Dies (ed.), *Liberalisierung und Privatisierung kommunaler Aufgabenerfüllung. Soziale und umweltpolitische Perspektiven im Zeichen des Wettbewerbs. Reihe DIfU-Beiträge zur Stadtforschung* [Liberalization and Privatization of Municipal Services. Social and Environmental Perspectives under the Auspices of Competition. DIFU Series Contributions to Urban Research, **37**, Berlin, 241–52.

Treisman, D. (2007), *The Architecture of Government. Rethinking Political Decentralization*, Cambridge, UK: Cambridge University Press.

Trench, A. (2009), 'Das Vereinigte Königreich. Die zweite Stufe der Devolution' [The United Kingdom. The second stage of devolution], *Jahrbuch des Föderalismus. Föderalismus, Subsidiarität und Regionen in Europa* [Yearbook of Federalism 2009. Federalism, Subsidiarity and Regions in Europe], Baden-Baden: Nomos, pp. 138–52.

Tsebelis, G. (2002), *Veto Players. How Political Institutions Work*, Princeton, NJ: Princeton University Press.

Tullock, G. (1965), *The Politics of Bureaucracy*, Washington, DC: Public Affairs Press.

Ullrich, C.G. (2005), *Soziologie des Wohlfahrtsstaates. Eine Einführung* [Sociology of the Welfare State: An Introduction], Frankfurt a.M: Oxford University Press.

Universität Potsdam/KGSt (2003), *Kommunale Betriebe in Deutschland. Ergebnisse einer empirischen Analyse der Beteiligungen deutscher Städte der GK 1-4. Abschlussbericht* [Local businesses in Germany. Results of an Empirical Analysis of the Involvement of German Cities in the GK 1-4]. Final Report, Potsdam.

Valentiny, P. (2007), 'Les services locaux et nationaux de l'énergie en Hongrie' [Local and national energy services in Hungary], in G. Marcou and H. Wollmann (eds), *Annuaire 2007 des Collectivités Locales* [Local Government Yearbook 2007], Paris: CNRS Editions, pp. 173–92.

Vandenabeele, W. and S. van de Walle (2008), 'International differences in public service motivation. Comparing regions across the world', in J. Perry and A. Hondeghem (eds), *Motivation in Public Management. The Call of Public Service*, Oxford, UK: Oxford University Press, pp. 223–44.

Van der Meer, F.M. (ed.) (2011), *Civil Service Systems in Western Europe*, Cheltenham, UK and Northampton, MA, USA: Edward Elgar Publishing.

Van de Walle, S., S. Roosbroek and G. Bouckaert (2008), 'Trust in the public sector. Is there any evidence for a long-term decline?', *International Review of Administration*, **74**(1), 47–64.

Van Dooren, W. and S. van de Walle (eds) (2008), *Performance Information in the Public Sector: How It Is Used*, Basingstoke: Palgrave Macmillan.

Van Otter, C. (1999), 'Öffentlicher Sektor im Wohlfahrtsstaat' [Public sector in the welfare state], in C. Riegler and O. Schneider (eds), *Schweden im Wandel – Entwicklungen, Probleme, Perspektiven* [Sweden in Transition – Developments, Problems, Perspectives], Berlin: BWV.

Varga, Z. (2006), 'Die Verwaltungsmodernisierung in Ungarn' [Administrative modernization in Hungary], in H. Hill (ed.), *Verwaltungsmodernisierung in den Staaten Europas – Länderberichte II* [Administrative Modernization in the Countries of Europe – Country Reports II], Speyer, pp. 695–737.

Verband kommunaler Unternehmen (VKU) (2009), *VKU Kompakt*, Berlin.

Verbuecheln, M. (2009), 'Rückübertragung operativer Dienstleistungen durch Kommunen am Beispiel der Abfallwirtschaft' [Re-Insourcing of operational services by local authorities – the example of waste management], DIfU Papers, Berlin: DIfU.

Verschuere, B. and D. Barbieri (2009), 'Investigating the 'NPM-ness' of agencies in Italy and Flanders', *Public Management Review*, **11**(3), 345–73.

Vesselin, D., K.H. Goetz and H. Wollmann (2006), *Governing After Communism. Institutions and Policymaking*, Lanham, MD: Rowman & Littlefield.

Vrangbaek, K. (2010), 'Structural reform in Denmark 2007–09. Central reform processes in a decentralized environment', *Local Government Studies*, **36**(2), 205–22.

Wagener, F. (1969), *Neubau der Verwaltung* [Re-Construction of the Administration], Berlin: Duncker & Humblot.

Wagener, F. (1976), 'Typen der verselbständigten Erfüllung öffentlicher Aufgaben' [Types of the autonomous operation of public functions], in F. Wagener (ed.), *Verselbständigung von Verwaltungsträgern* ['Autonomization' of administrative actors], Bonn: Internationales Institut für Verwaltungswissenschaften, pp. 31–51.

Waiz, E. (2009), 'Daseinsvorsorge in der Europäischen Union – Etappen einer Debatte' [The Provision of Public servicesin the the EU – stages of a debate], in A. Krautscheid (ed.), *Die Daseinsfürsorge im Spannungsfeld von europäischem Wettbewerb und Gemeinwohl. Eine sektorspezifische Betrachtun* [The Provision of Public Services in the Tension between Between European Competition and Common Good], Wiesbaden: VS Verlag für Sozialwissenschaften, pp. 41–76.

Wallace, H. (2005), 'An institutional anatomy and five policy modes', in H. Wallace, W. Wallace and M.A. Pollack (eds), *Policy Making in the European Union*, 5th edition, Oxford, UK: Oxford University Press, pp. 49–60.

Weber, M. (1921), *Wirtschaft und Gesellschaft*, Tübingen: Mohr.

Wegener, A. (2004), 'Benchmarking-Strategien im öffentlichen Sektor. Deutschland und Großbritannien im Vergleich' [Benchmarking strategies in the public sector. Germany and Britain compared], in S. Kuhlmann, J. Bogumil and H. Wollmann (eds), *Leistungsmessung und -vergleich in Politik und Verwaltung* [Performance Measurement and Benchmarking in Politics and Administration], Wiesbaden: Springer, pp. 251–66.

Wegrich, K. (2009), *Better Regulation? Grundmerkmale moderner Regulierungspolitik im internationalen Vergleich. Zukunft Regieren. Beiträge für eine gestaltungsfähige Politik 2009, Nr. 1* [Better Regulation? Basic Features of Modern Regulatory Policy in International Comparison. Future Governance. Contributions to an Effective Policy, No. 1], Gütersloh: Bertelsmann Foundation.

Wehner, E. (2005), *Von der Bundespost zu den Global Players Post AG + Telekom AG. Profiteure und Verlierer der Privatisierung* [From the Federal Post to the global Players Post-AG and Telekom AG], München: ISW.

Weingast, B.R. (1995), 'The economic role of political institutions. Market-preserving federalism and economic development', *Journal of Law, Economics and Organization*, **11**(1), 1–31.

Wilcox, M. and M. Bugaj (2004), 'Evaluating performance in local government. A comparison of Polish and UK councils', EGPA working paper.

Williamson, O.E. (1985), *The Economic Institutions of Capitalism. Firms, Markets, Relational Contracting*, New York: Free Press.

Wilson, D. and C. Game (2006), *Local Government in the United Kingdom*, 4th edition, Basingstoke: Palgrave Macmillan.

Wilson, D. and C. Game (2011), *Local Government in the United Kingdom*, 5th edition, Basingstoke: Palgrave Macmillan.

Wilson, W. (1941), 'The study of administration', *Political Science Quarterly*, **56**(4), 481–506.

Winchester, D. and S. Bach (1999), 'Britain. The transformation of public service employment relations', in S. Bach, L. Bordogna, G. Della Rocca and D. Winchester (eds), *Public Service Employment Relations in Europe. Transformation, Modernization or Inertia?*, London and New York: Routledge, pp. 22–55.

Wittrock, B., P. Wagner and H. Wollmann (1991), 'Social science and the modern state. Policy knowledge and political institutions in Western Europe and the United States', in P. Wagner, C. Hirschon Weiss, B. Wittrock and H. Wollmann (eds), *Social Sciences and Modern States*, Cambridge, UK: Cambridge University Press, pp. 28–85.

Wollmann, H. (1995), 'Variationen institutioneller Transformation in sozialistischen Ländern' [Variations of institutional transformation in socialist countries], in H. Wollmann, H. Wiesenthal and F. Bönker (eds), *Transformation sozialistischer Gesellschaften. Am Ende des Anfangs* [Transformation of Socialist Societies. At the End of Beginning], Opladen: Westdeutscher Verlag, pp. 554–70.

Wollmann, H. (1996a), 'Institutionenbildung in Ostdeutschland. Neubau, Umbau und "schöpferische Zerstörung"' [Institution building in East Germany. New construction, reconstruction and 'creative destruction'], in M. Kaase, A. Eisen, O.W. Gabriel, O. Niedermayer and H. Wollmann, *Politisches System* [Political System], Opladen: Leske + Budrich, pp. 47–153.

Wollmann, H. (1996b), 'Ausgangsbedingungen und Diskurse der Verwaltungsmodernisierung' [Initial conditions and discourses in local government modernization], in C. Reichard and H. Wollmann (eds), *Kommunalverwaltung im Modernisierungsschub?* [Local Administration in the Modernization Push?], Opladen: Leske + Budrich, pp. 1–50.

Wollmann, H. (1997a), 'Transformation der ostdeutschen Kommunalstrukturen. Rezeption, Eigenentwicklung, Innovation' [Transformation of the East German municipal structures. Reception, self-development, innovation], in H. Wollmann, H.-U. Derlien, K. König, W. Renzsch and W. Seibel (eds), *Transformation der politisch-administrativen Strukturen in*

Ostdeutschland [Transformation of the Political-Administrative Structures in East Germany], Opladen: Leske & Budrich, pp. 259–329.

Wollmann, H. (1997b), '"Echte Kommunalisierung" und Parlamentarisierung. Überfällige Reformen der kommunalen Politik- und Verwaltungswelt' ['Genuine municipalization' and parliamentarization. Overdue reforms of the local political and administrative world], in H. Heinelt and M. Mayer (eds), *Modernisierung der Kommunalpolitik* [Modernizing Local Politics], Opladen: Leske + Budrich, pp. 235–45.

Wollmann, H. (1999a), 'Kommunalvertretungen. Verwaltungsorgane oder Parlamente?' [Local councils. Administrative bodies or parliaments?], in H. Wollmann and R. Roth (eds), *Kommunalpolitik. Politisches Handeln in den Gemeinden* [Local Politics. Political Action in Local Government], Opladen: Leske + Budrich, pp. 50–72.

Wollmann, H. (1999b), 'Entwicklungslinien lokaler Demokratie und kommunaler Selbstverwaltung im internationalen Vergleich' [Development trends in local democracy and local self-government in international comparison], in H. Wollmann and R. Roth (eds), *Kommunalpolitik. Politisches Handeln in den Gemeinden* [Local Politics. Political Action in Local Government], Opladen: Leske + Budrich, pp. 186–205.

Wollmann, H. (2000a), 'Evaluierung und Evaluierungsforschung von Verwaltungspolitik und -modernisierung – zwischen Analysepotenzial und defizit' [Evaluation and evaluation research of administrative policy and modernization – between analytical potential and deficit], in R. Stockmann (ed.), *Evaluationsforschung* [Evaluation Research], Opladen: Leske + Budrich, pp. 195–233.

Wollmann, H. (2000b), 'Comparing institutional development in Britain and Germany. (Persistent) divergence or (progressing) convergence?', in H. Wollmann and E. Schröter (eds), *Comparing Public Sector Reform in Britain and Germany*, Aldershot: Ashgate, pp. 1–26.

Wollmann, H. (2002a), 'Verwaltungspolitische Reformdiskurse und -verläufe im internationalen Vergleich' [Administrative reform discourses and trajectories in international comparison], in K. König (ed.), *Deutsche Verwaltung an der Wende zum 21. Jahrhundert* [German Administration at the Turn of the 21st Century], Baden-Baden: Nomos, pp. 489–524.

Wollmann, H. (2002b), 'Die traditionelle deutsche kommunale Selbstverwaltung – ein Auslaufmodell?' [Traditional German local self-government – a phase-out model?], *Deutsche Zeitschrift für Kommunalwissenschaften*, **41**(1), 24–51.

Wollmann, H. (2003a), 'Evaluation in public sector reform: towards a "third wave" of evaluation?', in H. Wollmann (ed.), *Evaluation in Public-sector Reform*, Cheltenham, UK and Northampton, MA, USA: Edward Elgar Publishing, pp. 1–11.

Wollmann, H. (2003b), 'Evaluation and public sector reform in Germany. Leaps and lags', in H. Wollmann (ed.), *Evaluation in Public-sector Reform*, Cheltenham, UK and Northampton, MA, USA: Edward Elgar Publishing, pp. 118–39.

Wollmann, H. (2003c), 'Evaluation in public sector reform. Trends, potentials and limits in international perspective', in H. Wollmann (ed.). *Evaluation in Public-sector Reform*, Cheltenham, UK and Northampton, MA, USA: Edward Elgar Publishing, pp. 231–58.

Wollmann, H. (2003d), *Evaluation in Public-sector Reform*, Cheltenham, UK and Northampton, MA, USA: Edward Elgar Publishing.

Wollmann, H. (2004), 'Local government reforms in Great Britain, Sweden, Germany and France. Between multi-function and single-purpose organisations', *Local Government Studies*, **30**(4), 639–65.

Wollmann, H. (2006), 'Staatsorganisation zwischen Territorial- und Funktionalprinzip im Ländervergleich. Varianten der Institutionalisierung auf der dezentral-lokalen Ebene' [State organization between territorial and functional principles across countries. Variants of institutionalization on the decentralized-local level], in J. Bogumil, W. Jann and F. Nullmeier (eds), *Politik und Verwaltung. PVS-Sonderheft* [Politics and Administration Special Issue], **37**, Wiesbaden: VS Verlag für Sozialwissenschaften, pp. 424–52.

Wollmann, H. (2008), *Reformen in Kommunalpolitik und -verwaltung. England, Schweden, Deutschland und Frankreich im Vergleich* [Reforms in Local Politics and Administration: England, Sweden, France and Germany Compared], Wiesbaden: VS Verlag für Sozialwissenschaften.

Wollmann, H. (2009), 'The ascent of the directly elected mayor in European local government in West and East', in H. Reynaert, P. Delwit, J.-B. Pilet and K. Steyvers (eds), *Local Political Leadership in Europe*, Brugge: Vanden Broele, pp. 115–48.

Wollmann, H. (2010a), 'Das deutsche Kommunalsystem im europäischen Vergleich – Zwischen kommunaler Autonomie und "Verstaatlichung"?' [The German local government system in European comparison – between local autonomy and 'nationalization'?] in J. Bogumil and S. Kuhlmann (eds), *Kommunale Aufgabenwahrnehmung im Wandel. Kommunalisierung, Regionalisierung und Territorialreform in Deutschland und Europa* [Local Government Task Performance in Transition: Municipalization, Regionalization and Territorial Reform in Germany and Europe], Wiesbaden: VS Verlag für Sozialwissenschaften, pp. 223–52.

Wollmann, H. (2010b), 'La réforme des collectivités locales. Vers un "big bang" ou une autre "mini" réforme?' [The local government reform. Towards a 'big bang' or another 'mini' reform?], in J.-C. Némery (eds), *Quelle nouvelle réforme pour les collectivités territoriales françaises?*, Paris: Editions Harmattan, pp. 349–59.

Wollmann, H. (2010c), 'Territorial local level reforms in the East German regional states (*Länder*): phases, patterns and dynamics', *Local Government Studies*, **36**(2), 251–70.

Wollmann, H. (2011), 'Provision of public services in European countries. From public/municipal to private and reverse?', *Croatian and Comparative Public Administration*, **11**(4), 880–910.

Wollmann, H. (2013), 'Elargissement des compétences législatives des Länder allemands. Quelles leçons pour les régions françaises ?' [Enlargement of the legislative powers of the *Länder*: what lessons for the French regions?], *Pouvoirs Locaux*, **98**(III), 101–10.

Wollmann, H. and G. Bouckaert (2006), 'State organisation in France and Germany between territoriality and functionality', in V. Hoffmann-Martinot and H. Wollmann (eds), *State and Local Government Reform in France and Germany*, Wiesbaden: Springer pp. 11–37.

Wollmann, H. and T. Lankina (2003), 'Local government in Poland and Hungary. From postcommunist reform towards EU accession', in H. Baldersheim, M. Illner and H. Wollmann (eds), *Local Democracy in Post-Communist Europe*, Opladen: Leviathan, pp. 91–122.

Wollmann, H. and G. Marcou (2010), 'From public sector-based to privatized service provision. Is the pendulum swinging back again? Comparative summary', in H. Wollmann and G. Marcou (eds), *The Provision of Public Services in Europe. Between State, Local Government and Market*, Cheltenham, UK and Northampton, MA, USA: Edward Elgar Publishing, pp. 240–60.

Wollmann, H. and E. Schröter (eds) (2000), *Comparing Public Sector Reform in Britain and Germany. Key Traditions and Trends of Modernisation*, Aldershot: Ashgate.

Wollmann, H., E. Balboni, J.-P. Gaudin and G. Marcou (2010a), 'The multi-level institutional setting in Germany, Italy, France and the U.K. A comparative overview', in H. Wollmann and G. Marcou (eds), *The Provision of Public Services in Europe. Between State, Local Government and Market*, Cheltenham, UK and Northampton, MA, USA: Edward Elgar Publishing, pp. 15–48.

Wollmann, H., H. Baldersheim, G. Citroni, G. Marcou and J. McEldowney (2010b), 'From public service to commodity: the de-municipalization of energy provision in Germany, Italy, France, the UK and Norway', in H. Wollmann and G. Marcou (eds), *The Provision of Public Services in Europe. Between State, Local Government and Market*, Cheltenham, UK and Northampton, MA, USA: Edward Elgar Publishing, pp. 168–90.

Wright, V. (1990), 'The administrative machine. Old problems and new dilemmas', in P.A. Hall, J. Hayward and H. Machin (eds), *Developments in French Politics*, Basingstoke: Palgrave Macmillan, pp. 114–32.

Ziekow, J. (ed.) (2003), *Verwaltungswissenschaften und Verwaltungswissenschaft. Forschungssymposium anlässlich der Emeritierung von Klaus König* [Administrative Sciences and Public Administration. Research Symposium on the Occasion of the Retirement of Klaus König], Publication Series of the University of Speyer, Berlin: Duncker & Humblot.

Zohlnhöfer, R. (2001), *Die Wirtschaftspolitik der Ära Kohl. Eine Analyse der Schlüsselentscheidungen in den Politikfeldern Finanzen, Arbeit und Entstaatlichung, 1982–1998* [The Economic Policies of the Kohl Era. An Analysis of the Key Decisions in the Areas of Public Finance, Labour and Denationalization, 1982–98], Opladen: Leske + Budrich.

Zürn, M. (1992), *Interessen und Institutionen in der internationalen Politik. Grundlagen und Anwendungen des situationsstrukturellen Ansatzes* [Interests and Institutions in International Politics. Basics and Applications of the Situation Structural Approach], Opladen: Leske + Budrich.

Zürn, M. (1998), *Regieren jenseits des Nationalstaates. Globalisierung und Denationalisierung als Chance* [Governing Beyond the Nation State. Globalization and Denationalization as an Opportunity], Frankfurt a.M: Suhrkamp.

Zürn, M. (2000), 'Democratic governance beyond the nation-state. The EU and other international institutions', *European Journal of International Relations*, **6**(2), 183–221.

Index